Rhino Tanks and Sticky Bombs

CAMPAIGNS & COMMANDERS

GREGORY J. W. URWIN, SERIES EDITOR

Rhino Tanks and Sticky Bombs

GI Ingenuity in World War II

Robert P. Wettemann Jr.

University of Oklahoma Press : Norman

This book is published with the generous assistance of the Kerr Foundation, Inc.

Library of Congress Cataloging-in-Publication Data

Names: Wettemann, Robert P., author.
Title: Rhino tanks and sticky bombs : GI ingenuity in World War II / Robert P. Wettemann Jr.
Other titles: GI ingenuity in World War II
Description: Norman : University of Oklahoma Press, [2025] | Series: Campaigns and commanders ; volume 79 | Includes bibliographical references and index. | Summary: "Hybrid study that examines the juncture between American cultural and military history to explain why American technological ingenuity and prowess in the Second World War proved so successful"—Provided by publisher.
Identifiers: LCCN 2024044674 | ISBN 9780806195391 (hardcover)
Subjects: LCSH: World War, 1939–1945—Technology. | Soldiers—United States—Intellectual life—20th century. | Technology—United States—History—20th century.
Classification: LCC D810.S2 W48 2025 | DDC 940.54/8373—dc23/eng/20250226
LC record available at https://lccn.loc.gov/2024044674

Rhino Tanks and Sticky Bombs: GI Ingenuity in World War II is Volume 79 in the Campaigns and Commanders series.

The paper in this book meets the guidelines for permanence and durability of the Committee on Production Guidelines for Book Longevity of the Council on Library Resources, Inc. ∞

Contents

Preface

> You take a standard issue GI sock, cram it with as much Comp B as it can hold, rig up a simple fuse, then you coat the whole thing with axle grease. That way when you throw it, it should stick. A bomb that sticks, a sticky bomb. Come up with a better way to knock the tracks off a tank, I'm all ears.
>
> —*Capt. John H. Miller, 2nd Ranger Battalion, Saving Private Ryan*

Although depicting World War II weapons, uniforms, and infantry combat with unprecedented accuracy, Paramount Pictures' 1998 production *Saving Private Ryan* is fiction and not a documentary. The film was inspired by Sgt. Frederick "Fritz" Niland of the 101st Airborne Division, sent home by a US Army chaplain after his brothers, Preston and Robert, were killed in Normandy and Edward was shot down and presumed dead over Burma. Robert Rodat and director/producer Steven Spielberg set their film during the Normandy invasion, though Gen. George C. Marshall did not order the rescue of a 101st Airborne Division paratrooper. Moreover, Capt. John H. Miller of the 2nd Ranger Battalion, the French village of Ramelle, and a bridge defended by GIs using "sticky bombs" never existed.

There is, however, some truth behind the "sticky bomb." *Field Service Regulations—Operations*, chapter 10, section V, paragraph 687, instructed that "improvised combustibles and explosives thrown by individuals against the most vulnerable portions of enemy armored vehicles are valuable means of supplementing close-in anti-mechanized defense."[1] Sticky munitions appeared in articles published by the *Infantry Journal*, *Popular Mechanics*, and the *Cavalry Journal*, thereby establishing that such devices were part of American popular culture during World War II, not the fabrications of a 1990s Hollywood film producer.[2]

In addition to the "sticky bomb," few field fabrications conceived during the war gained as much notoriety as the "rhino tank." General Eisenhower regarded the device, built by Sgt. Curtis Culin of the 102nd Cavalry Reconnaissance Squadron to breach the hedgerows of Normandy, crafted from repurposed German beach obstacles, as "a simple invention that restored the effectiveness of the tank," a point he reinforced later in a CBS interview with Walter Cronkite on D-Day's twentieth anniversary.[3] Benefiting greatly from hindsight, Eisenhower lauded Culin's invention as "a godsend" for the American invaders, for reasons that are explored in greater detail in chapter 5.[4]

Such devices only hint at larger questions regarding American ingenuity in World War II.[5] Juxtaposing the Jewish prophet Isaiah's "swords into plowshares," erstwhile citizens of the 1930s cast aside their oft-repaired automobiles and tractors for the abundant jeeps, tanks, and aircraft of modern warfare. In doing so, the same young men who, inspired by Tom Swift, the Hardy Boys, and *Popular Mechanics*, had kept their jalopies and tractors running throughout the Great Depression brought this improvisational thinking and technical creativity to the modern battlefield. They were the first American generation to grow up with access to the internal combustion engine, doing so in a society that emphasized this freethinking and problem solving as the "American Way."[6]

When the Japanese attack on Pearl Harbor brought the United States into World War II, American GIs, from the outset, fell back on their technical ingenuity cast in a climate of want, creatively engineering effective solutions to wartime problems.[7] When US servicemen enhanced the offensive or defensive capabilities of their military hardware, looked for ways to perform their jobs more effectively, or simply made conditions more livable, they employed a tinkerer's mentality honed during the Depression to improve on existing war machines. As a result, US soldiers enhanced the communications capabilities of the American combined arms team, developed armored landing craft to provide antiaircraft support for Pacific invasions, built stoves to heat airfield tents, or modified weapons to make them more effective. They did so by drawing on a unique sense of American ingenuity that was a product both of the Depression and of growing up in a society that had unprecedented access to machine technology.

This technical creativity must be considered not just a distinctively American trait, but a contributing factor to Allied victory. Unlike other Allied as well as Axis soldiers, Americans were born into a society that in 1939 possessed more motor vehicles per capita than all the remaining Allies and Axis combined. Consequently, Americans demonstrated an unprecedented technical aptitude and willingness to adapt during World War II. Although other nations fielded mechanized armies during the course of the conflict, they either lacked a population intimately familiar with machine technology or approached technology from a different perspective than did citizens of the United States.

Not all results of American ingenuity translated into immediate tactical or operational success, for not all of these ersatz solutions worked. The US military command structure, however, frequently demonstrated a willingness to evaluate, accept, and employ promising efforts to improve both the fighting power as well as the general comfort of US servicemen. Through American ingenuity bred during the Depression, GIs developed technical solutions from the bottom up, rather than having innovation forced on them from the top down. Although many improvements first developed by troops in the field were later employed by the military as a whole, American technical ingenuity at the tactical and operational levels must first of all be considered an important source of ultimate Allied victory.

A number of scholars have addressed American wartime innovation and fighting effectiveness, but they generally fail to connect American culture, the Great Depression, and the technological creativity of the GI in World War II.[8] Recent studies of the American GI often reference technical ingenuity but do so only in passing, recognizing that each nation's army was a distinct product of its own society and culture.[9] *Rhino Tanks and Sticky Bombs: American Ingenuity in World War II* intends to take a more holistic examination of the emergence of American technical creativity, based on the premise that before GIs were GIs, they were civilian products of the Depression, and consequently, the GI ingenuity witnessed during World War II must first and foremost be considered to be a reflection of American society and culture as it manifested itself in the 1920s and 1930s. Thus, there is a strain of American exceptionalism to my argument, though I would contend it is carefully proscribed, and limited to the unique historical moment that was World War II.

At least a passing word must be offered on what this book is not. It is not a comprehensive study of the evolution of individual tanks, aircraft, armored vehicles, weapons, and tools of war employed by American soldiers throughout World War II. An attempt to provide just a list of books of that ilk would dwarf this volume. Nor is it a combat history of American forces during the war. Those already exist. Finally, it is not an attempt to discuss every field-improvised device or modification made by GIs during World War II. To do so would take more than the twenty-three years I have already spent on this project. Instead, *Rhino Tanks and Sticky Bombs* is an attempt to tell a story of what freethinking and mechanically minded citizen soldiers could do, when serving in a highly mechanized and motorized army whose flexible leadership offered them the latitude to solve problems in the way they knew best—by using American ingenuity.

Twenty-three years is a long time to work on a project. During that time, I have received encouragement from a host of mentors, colleagues, students, friends, and family. Mark Grotelueschen and I first discussed the concept after watching *Saving Private Ryan*, and early on, we framed many of the questions about American ingenuity and technical modification that form the central themes of this book. Eddy Woodfin and Keith Volanto were in the office as well, and I remain thankful for their friendship. Thanks also to Kurt Hackemer, a friend and trusted colleague who took a green graduate student under his wing many years ago. I lack the words to properly thank Joseph G. Dawson III, who has always been there with kind words, wisdom, and tough love, first in graduate school and in the following years. I would not be where I am in my career without him as an example—as a scholar, advisor, and friend.

In 1999, I participated in the US Military Academy Summer Seminar in Military History. Since then, I have joined Galen Perras, Nick Sarantakes, Stan Adamiak, and Mike Creswell on conference panels to explore aspects of this project and am thankful for their feedback, as well as for encouraging comments offered by Alan Millett, Gregory J. W. Urwin, and Andy Weist.

Don Frazier, Robert Pace, and Gary Shanafelt trusted a scholar trained in nineteenth-century American civil-military relations with teaching on the twentieth century, and I am grateful they brought me to McMurry University in 2001. There I discovered the big shoes left behind by Robert Sledge. We have all gone our separate ways, but their friendship and support remain treasured gifts.

I came to the US Air Force Academy Department of History in 2007, first as a visiting professor, and am now blessed to call DFH home. Thanks to John Abbatiello, Chuck Steele, Doug Kennedy, John Prince, Ben Jones, Eric Frith, John Plating, Grant Weller, John Farquahar, Cameron McCoy, PJ Hussey, David Martin, Jonathan Couch, Chris Reith, Peter Euyler, and Brian Laslie for reading and commenting on early parts of this work. DFH's Distinguished Visiting Professors Jay Lockenour, Greg Hospodor, Kathryn Barbier, and Joe Glatthaar, along with visiting scholar Don Bishop also provided comments. DFH leadership has provided support at every step of the way. Col. Mark Wells brought me to DFH, and I am forever in his debt. I am also thankful for the guidance and friendship of Col. Margaret "Meg" Martin and more recently Col. Matt "Meta" Dietz, who ably assisted me in talking through some of the final aspects of this book.

I am appreciative of the support offered by Phil Kwong, Paul "PK" Carlton, Katharine Maguire, Steve "Scoobie" Kotlarchuk, Dan Smith, Bryon Greenwald, the Second World War Reading Group, and my oldest and dearest friend

Scott Trapp, who have all helped me write a better book. To my USAFA cadets who have heard about Doc's book for over a decade, *Rhino Tanks* is finished, and you promised to buy a copy . . .

Thanks are also due to Dr. Tim Nenninger and the staff at the National Archives in College Park, Maryland; Terry Young and the librarians at McMurry University; Dr. Joel Hebert and the USAFA Library and Special Collections staff; Kevin Bailey and Linda Smith at the Dwight D. Eisenhower Presidential Library in Abilene, Kansas; Kip and Christy Lindberg of the Branch History Office, US Army Chemical, Biological, Radiological, and Nuclear School, Fort Leonard Wood, Missouri; Dr. Denise Neil at the 45th Infantry Division Museum; the staff at Oklahoma State University Special Collections in Stillwater, Oklahoma; and the staff of the US Army History and Education Center in Carlisle, Pennsylvania. I am also greatly appreciative of the Ike Skelton Combined Arms Research Library at Fort Leavenworth, Kansas, whose digital archive made research for this book exponentially easier.

A number of World War II veterans graciously shared their time with me in the early phases of research for this project. Sadly, most of them have joined their comrades in arms who did not survive the war after having spent a portion of their youth ridding the world of tyranny. My eternal thanks go to Henry Bellmon, James Cupples, Anthony Daly, Forrest Guth, William Hahn, Seymour Lichtenfeld, George Mahoney, Dwight Orman, J. T. Rutherford, John Speed, Jack Terzian, John Truluck, E. J. Turman, and Richard Winters.

I am also appreciative of James "Kent" Calder, Joe Schiller, Andrew Berzanskis, anonymous readers, and the editorial staff at the University of Oklahoma Press for shepherding this project from draft to final published version. While happily publishing with "OU Press," however, my inner voice is forever screaming, "Go Pokes!"

I reserve my final words of thanks for my family, who have always supported me. In my first book, I thanked my parents for providing a shining example of how to live life in the academic world. I hope I have successfully continued their example. Sarah and Andrew, this book is older than both of you. I hope you appreciate it, as well as your father's love. For my wife, Kay, words are inadequate to express how much I appreciate your love, support, and encouragement. Those thanks are eternal.

CHAPTER 1

Tom Swift, Model Ts, and Growing Up "American"

Almost every boy in this country knows how to handle a motor vehicle, and many of them understand a great deal about the repair of motor equipment.

—*Chief of Staff George C. Marshall*

In November 1939, the recently appointed chief of staff of the US Army, Gen. George C. Marshall, appeared before a House Committee on Appropriations subcommittee, advocating for the Emergency Supplemental Appropriation Bill for 1940, and outlining future needs of the US Army. In light of recent German aggression in Poland, he requested $120 million to increase the regular army and the National Guard, equip reactivated units, provide reinforcements for the Panama Canal Zone and Puerto Rico, and improve the army's training program. After calling for manpower increases in anticipation of American participation in the war in Europe, Marshall soon pivoted to his most important point: seeking funding to mechanize the US Army, explaining the impact of motor vehicles and their absolute necessity in modern warfare.[1]

Outlining $16 million in basic motorization needs for five triangular divisions, Marshall argued these vehicles would be transformational. Though he did not directly connect motor vehicles and American ingenuity, he underscored Americans' familiarity with machines, specifically the internal combustion engine. In modernizing the US Army, Marshall explained, "motors take the place of animals." Prior to 1939, a marching soldier determined how fast an army could move, with top speed being governed by the speed of a horse. During the 1918 Meuse-Argonne offensive, 21,000 troops marched from

Saint-Mihiel to the front in a single night, but it took days to move horse-drawn artillery and machine guns the same distance. With vehicles, all units could "move as a division . . . together at motor speed," with the use of vehicles by the US Army greatly enhancing the effectiveness of future army operations.[2]

Perhaps more than any other American officer at the time, Marshall understood the importance of motorized vehicles to modern warfare. Vehicles, and the machine technology that produced them, coupled with the ability to maintain, modify, and adapt them to the changing character of war, were requisite for any nation that wanted to be successful at war in the twentieth century. Moreover, Marshall understood the lean years of the Great Depression, and how they had shaped the generation that would serve in the next great global conflict. In the years following the end of the Great War, the young Americans who grew to be the soldiers, sailors, and airmen of World War II reached maturity in a mechanized and technological society that extolled the virtues of modern machinery. As this generation endured the trials of the Depression, the challenges brought on by shortage, breakage, and want only enhanced their ability to embrace technically creative solutions to overcome the mechanical challenges of the day. Unlike the soldiers who served in the other Allied (and Axis) armies, these unique social and economic circumstances provided American servicemen an arena that allowed them to develop a tinkerer's mindset. When faced with a mechanical challenge, they were uniquely suited to creatively engineer a solution, a skill that would be immensely beneficial, both in peace and in war. As the boys of this emerging age of American machines became the GIs of World War II, they faced challenges that existing technology could not overcome. Encountering these exigencies of war, they simply fell back on necessity and invented a solution. When applying ingenuity to the challenges presented by war, Americans possessed a distinct advantage over the other Allied (and Axis) powers, an advantage that was a direct product of Tom Swift, Model Ts, and growing up "American."

In the aftermath of the Great War, American journalist Frank Parker Stockbridge wrote that Germany lost due to "Yankee ingenuity in the application of scientific knowledge and technical skill to military and naval ends." In *Yankee Ingenuity in the War*, Stockbridge reviewed the great American mechanical and technical inventions of the conflict, chronicling the "mobilization of science and industry" that brought victory to the Allied Powers. Thanks to the "organizing and directing genius of American manufacturers," once the United States entered the war, it "became a contest of machine power as much as of manpower."[3] Stockbridge was no stranger to the world of machines. Five years earlier, he billed the contraption-designing Rube Goldberg as America's "most popular cartoonist."[4] In the ensuing years, Stockbridge had not only served as managing editor of *Popular Mechanics*, but also contributed a series of articles to the older *Popular Science* (formerly *Popular Science Monthly*). Reflecting on the wartime record of American technical creativity, Stockbridge considered it undeniable proof that "necessity is the mother of invention." As former publicity adviser to then–presidential candidate Woodrow Wilson, he correctly predicted that when the United States faced its next great crisis, "no small share of the victory will be due to Yankee Ingenuity."[5]

Ten years after the guns of the western front fell silent, Stockbridge initiated a decade-long study to discover what America was reading. In 1931, he offered a comprehensive summary of his findings, observing that "probably seven-eighths of all the people of America above the age of ten know how to read." Thanks to advances in technology and economic developments that produced a new leisure class, popular reading rose to unprecedented levels, with more than 8,134 new titles published in the United States in 1930 alone. With books costing less than two dollars each, he suspected that the average adult American purchased and read an average of "more than four books a year."[6]

Stockbridge concluded that by 1930, the subject matter in popular American books and magazines was entirely different from what it had been ten years earlier. The age characterized by the "literature of disillusion" had given way to a "skeptical age," one that heralded Nobel Prize–winner Sinclair Lewis as the "most popular writer in America," with titles like *Babbit* and *Main Street* high on the list of bestsellers. By the end of the 1920s, Stockbridge sensed the emergence of "hard-boiled age, an age in which youth is not accepting dogma from its elders without checking up for itself." In this new decade, He saw a "new generation just now coming along which did not experience the war disillusionment" that had faced its forebears. The books being "read most eagerly, [and] accepted most heartily, have been the books which purported to interpret the world of today in terms of life as these disillusioned young people believed it to be, and not in terms of an antiquated code, which had failed them and the rest of mankind when it was most needed." Simply stated, Stockbridge saw the emergence of "more constructive literature" that served to "exalt new standards—standards and ideals compatible with what youth of today knows to be the truth about life, or believes to be the truth, which amounts, after all, to the same thing."[7]

Part of this "constructive literature" was an increasing volume of prose that exalted an emerging American machine culture, a genre to which Stockbridge himself had already contributed. In 1872, E. L. Youmans began publishing *Popular Science Monthly*, building the magazine's reputation by documenting the great inventions of the day: the telephone, the electric light, the airplane, and the automobile. By the early twentieth century, the magazine added articles by theorists and inventors to its continued discussion of inventions and new scientific developments. When the Great War began, the magazine subtly shifted its emphasis from pure science to popular technology, with Youmans seeking to capitalize on the ever-increasing popularity of the automobile and encouraging the American tinkerer. Beginning in April 1918, the magazine sponsored a contest for the best new labor-saving invention to improve automotive operation. The winners of the contest, announced each June, typified the emerging generation of inventive Americans, as both were "young men in whom invention seems to be a cradle-gift, for neither makes his living as an engineer."[8]

Subsequent issues stressed a growing American penchant for inventiveness and technical creativity, a trend that continued throughout the 1920s. In April 1923, the magazine reported how the Huntington School for Boys in Boston, Massachusetts, formed a "*Popular Science* Club," whose members read the magazine to stimulate discussion about the latest technological developments. By 1924, "kinks"—practical do-it-yourself suggestions to automobile owners—became a regular issue feature. In April 1926, the best reader-provided suggestion won ten dollars, a prize that remained advertised in the automobile "kinks" column well into the 1930s. By 1928, a readership of more than 350,000 subscribers benefited not only from a series of articles penned by contributing editor Frank Stockbridge, but also from a barrage of articles lauding technical creativity. In an effort to maintain readership during the Great Depression, the editors even reduced the cover price from twenty-five to fifteen cents per issue beginning in September 1932, in the process helping attract an additional 100,000 more subscribers before World War II began.[9]

Thirty years after the appearance of *Popular Science Monthly*, Henry Windsor began publishing a competing magazine, *Popular Mechanics*, dedicated to the wonders of science and technology that would be, as Windsor intended, "written so you can understand it." The weekly publication soon became a monthly, focusing on the wonders of the technological world and the possibilities offered by all things mechanical. The format of *Popular Mechanics* offered the latest scientific and technological news, with Stockbridge himself contributing a number of articles appearing between 1914 and 1915.[10] In 1915, the editors introduced a how-to section that, like similar columns in *Popular Science Monthly*, encouraged the American tinkerer. Although the Depression forced many publications into bankruptcy, the economic crash actually benefited *Popular Mechanics*. Readers struggling to endure the nation's worst economic crisis "wanted to save money by doing things themselves and fixing things that broke."[11] *Popular Mechanics* showed them how to do it, in the process encouraging, if not creating, a culture adept at solving its own mechanical problems, a trend that would pay great dividends during World War II.

Like the "*Popular Science* Club," the editors of *Popular Mechanics* attempted to develop a legion of new readers by appealing to the mechanical interests of young boys. In 1936, General Motors vice president for research Charles Kettering offered secrets to winning a soapbox derby, capitalizing on the success of the previous year's contest finals held in Akron, Ohio. Kettering was emphatic in the notion that while "blindly following" a set of blueprints and specifications may provide you with a car, it was "a far greater benefit" if a boy would just start building and let his "own initiative, inventiveness and ingenuity" rule the day.[12]

By targeting the rising generation, the editors of *Popular Mechanics* tried to capture the attention of the same adolescents turning toward what Stockbridge characterized as "constructive literature" to satisfy their cravings for news about the latest technological advancements. Although he never explicitly explained what he meant by "constructive literature," his support for periodicals that encouraged this new popular machine age suggest a close connection with the rising tide of popular machine consciousness. By the 1930s, not only had publications like *Popular Science Monthly* and *Popular Mechanics* captured the nation's attention, but young boys also had a growing host of adolescent heroes who used technological tinkering to great effect to solve their own problems.[13]

In 1906, publishing magnate Edward Stratemeyer published the first "Motor Boys" novel authored under the pseudonym Clarence Young. Recognizing that the motorcycle was "fast taking the place of the ordinary bicycle," and the auto was "taking the place of our horses," the series featured Bob Baker, whose father was a rich banker, Ned Slade, son of a successful department store-owning father, and Jerry Hopkins, the only son of a wealthy widow. Stretching to twenty-two volumes before the series concluded in 1922, the books featured the boys in a series of adventures in which motorized vehicles figured prominently. In the first book, the boys rode motorcycles, though by the book's conclusion, they were ready for automobiles. Subsequent adventures featured motorboats, airplanes, and submarines, as well as the opportunity to serve in the US Army.[14]

Only a few years after publication of the first Motor Boys novel, *Tom Swift and His Motor-Cycle* introduced Tom Swift, the boy inventor, whose ensuing adventures always included him tinkering with the latest technology. Over the course of the next three decades, Victor Appleton, the pseudonym for writers employed by Edward Stratemeyer, related Swift's exploits, with the Stratemeyer Syndicate publishing new novels at an astounding pace of better than one a year. Between 1910 and 1941, forty Tom Swift novels explicitly encouraged teenage boys to engage in America's growing technological society. Throughout the series, the authors never explored the actual origins of Swift's mechanical genius, usually describing it as a combination of the boy's innate talents and his penchant for mechanical creativity. In *Tom Swift and His Electric Runabout*, the fictional boy's father, "natural inventor" Barton Swift, discovered his son working on a new electric battery, to which he observed, "So that's what you've been tinkering with over the last few weeks, eh Tom? I suspected it was a new invention, but I didn't suppose it was that." A subsequent installment in the series found Tom making additions to his noisy aeroplane, in an effort to win the friendship of Mary Nestor. When she raised her concerns about the functionality of an instrument on the craft, Tom replied, "No, not broken. It's only a little auxiliary dingus I put on to make it easier to read the barograph, but I think I'll go back to the old system. Nothing to do with flying at all, except to tell how high up one is." In this way, each novel in the series cast Swift's technical creativity as a product of his environment, coupled with the fictional boy's famous inventor/father constantly exposing him to the tools of science and technology he used to improve his world. The result was that virtually every adventure found the "young inventor" using his mechanical wits to repair or modify automobiles, airplanes, motorcycles, and speedboats, or inventing useful new technologies and apply them to great effect in solving the mystery of the day.[15]

The series enjoyed wide popularity, particularly among American youth.[16] In 1926, the sixteenth year of the Swift series, a survey of 36,750 schoolchildren in thirty-four cities throughout the United States revealed that 98 percent of them read books published by the Stratemeyer Syndicate, and of those, Tom Swift was among their favorites. While the technically crafty Tom Swift helped make the genre popular, he was, however, far from being the only figure to make a significant impact on the technological fiction that captured the minds of the future World War II generation.

Virtually every young American boy who grew up in the late 1920s and 1930s knew the Hardy Boys. In 1927, Franklin W. Dixon, the nom de plume for Leslie McFarlane, introduced an audience of young, predominantly male readers to Joe and Frank Hardy. The opening pages of *The Tower Treasure*, the first installment in the series, found two "bright-eyed boys on motorcycles" riding along a cliffside road one bright spring morning. Recognizing the danger posed by the steep embankment and hundred-foot drop to the sea, the fictional brothers narrowly escaped injury when an unknown redheaded driver at the wheel of a "racing automobile" almost ran them off the road. Angered by the other motorist's recklessness, the boys completed their errands, eventually making their way to the home of their chum, the portly Chet Morton, whereupon they discovered that his yellow roadster, the same "gay-looking speed wagon" that made Chet one of the most popular boys in Bayport, had been stolen.[17] During the course of solving this and other mysteries, the Hardy Boys never strayed far from machines, for Edward Stratemeyer, the publisher of Tom Swift who hired McFarlane and others to write under the Dixon pseudonym, regarded the boys as quintessentially mobile, a trait reinforced throughout the series. Riding their motorcycles through the streets of Bayport in their first adventure, they soon expanded their mechanical horizons by acquiring a motorboat, the *Sleuth.* Solving the Shore Road mystery allowed the boys to enter into automobile ownership. From that point forward, readers frequently found the Hardys, along with pal Chet, in the boys' High Street garage, where they "kept their motorcycles and the decrepit auto they had bought with their savings." In the twenty novels published before 1941, the boys spent much of their spare time tinkering with the engine of one of many vehicles they acquired in their adventures.[18]

While the Hardy Boys did not encounter an airplane until *The Great Airport Mystery* published in 1930, Charles Lindbergh's 1927 transatlantic flight helped Americans' interest in air travel literally take off. Throughout the country, a sense of "air mindedness" fueled a growing American passion for aviation.[19] A year before Lindbergh's flight, Edward Stratemeyer sought to capitalize on the popularity of flying with *Tom Swift and His Airline Express; or, From Ocean to Ocean by Daylight.* Between 1900 and 1940, at least forty different popular series devoted to aviation appeared in print, telling of young boys who explored the skies in airships, built their own versions of the Wright Flyer, or fought in the skies over Europe during World War I. One author was none other than military aviation pioneer Henry Harley "Hap" Arnold, who, beginning in 1928, wrote six books for younger readers highlighting the career of US Army Air Service pilot Bill Bruce.[20] Arnold's and others' efforts notwithstanding, no work of juvenile fiction attracted the attention of future airmen as effectively as *G-8 and His Battle Aces.* Between 1933 and 1944, G-8, the flying spy created by former World War I Signal Corps air cadet Robert Hogan, appeared in 110 issues of the air war pulp magazine. In these, G-8 faced a wide variety of foes, from "batlike monsters, their eyes on fire, their breath a poison vapor," to "bombs piloted by living beast men," in the process capturing the fascination of the next generation of military pilots.[21]

Like Swift and the Hardy Boys, the G-8 series captured the technical fascination of young men throughout the United States, particularly as its stories related to flight, a trend perpetuated by the *American Boy* magazine between 1927 and 1934. During that time, the Airplane Model League of America (AMLA) took advantage of Lindbergh's transatlantic flight, publishing a series of articles inspiring boys to build "free flight" airplane models. In his first such article, AMLA secretary Merrill Hamburg professed that "many great leaders in aviation got their start by building models," citing, among others, Glenn

Curtis, as one who learned "the fundamental principles of aeronautics" in miniature form. Over the course of the next thirteen years, the magazine published a host of detailed blueprints designed to get boys to build airplane models, and the publisher hosted regional and national model railroad competitions.[22]

Paralleling the appearance of Tom Swift, the Hardy Boys, Bill Bruce, G-8, and the AMLA were several other types of "constructive literature" featuring boy inventors as their chief protagonists. Most notable were Gerald Breckenridge's "Radio Boys" series, which appeared between 1921 and 1932. In these books, radio tinkerers Frank Mennick, Bob Temple, and Jack Hampton made small improvements to their crystal wireless radio sets. Eventually the trio created entirely new radio products. In *The Radio Boys as Soldiers of Fortune* (1925), they created a "Synchronizer" capable of transmitting "a whole moving picture film . . . not by telegraph, but by radio." Although the boy radio inventor as a genre declined by the mid-1930s, the creative psyche developed in these series lived on, to be replicated by those World War II servicemen who realized new needs for communication during the course of the conflict.[23]

Almost universally, the youth fiction heroes who appeared before World War II extolled the merits of machines. These novels and serials, which featured a host of other fictional technologically minded heroes, collectively offered a carefully crafted subtext that American boys could invent almost anything. These ideas were not, however, limited to pulp novels, for popular magazines also capitalized on the American fascination with science and technology. Building on the tradition of tinkering, *Popular Science* and *Popular Mechanics* went to great lengths to further cultivate and foster the American desire to innovate. By 1941, subscribers to these popular publications and the young boys who had grown up reading the adventures of Tom Swift, the Hardy Boys, and others stood poised to provide the manpower for an American military uniquely positioned to fight a modern, mechanized war.[24]

American fascination with machinery was not limited to popular magazines and pulp novels, for it could also be found in John Steinbeck's *The Grapes of Wrath*, which won the 1940 Pulitzer Prize for literature. Steinbeck's epic tale of life in the Great Depression further epitomized the pervasive ingenuity present in the United States during those hard times. After Tom Joad and his family were "tractored" off their farm, they had no choice but to look west for salvation. Nursing their truck from Oklahoma to California, they came to depend on brother Al and his ability to "tinker an engine." Eventually, Steinbeck characterized Al as the "soul of the car." As the family made their cross-country journey, he was "one with his engine, every nerve listening for weaknesses, for the thumps or squeals, hums and chattering that indicate a change that may cause a breakdown." According to Tom Joad, this was a unique trait. This mechanical ability was something that had become part of the American psyche, for in Joad's distinctive vernacular, you "got to grow into. . . . It ain't just knowin'. It's more'n that. Kids now tear down a car 'thout even thinkin' about it."[25]

Collectively, stories like those penned by Steinbeck, as well as those offered by the Stratemeyer Syndicate and published in *Popular Science* and *Popular Mechanics*, could not have enjoyed the popularity they did had the population of the United States not had some familiarity with technology. In the two decades that followed the Great War, the growth of a new machine age as lauded on the printed page simply reflected the ever-increasing amount of technology that had come to dominate all facets of American society. Credit for much of this veritable technological explosion should fall at the feet of one man, Henry Ford, whose contributions to industry indelibly changed the popular landscape.[26]

Shortly after founding Ford Motor Company in 1903, the father of American mass production boldly proclaimed, "I am going to democratize the automobile. . . . When I am through everybody will be able to afford one, and about everybody will have one." Within a few short years, the automobile in the United States ceased to be a plaything of the rich. Thanks to the efforts of Charles Sorensen, who joined Ford as a patternmaker in 1905, the company pioneered use of the assembly line, thereby reducing costs and increasing output, such that a single car could be built in an hour and a half. By 1920, one out of every two cars on American roads was a Ford Model T.[27] The ever-increasing popularity of the Model T prompted humorist Will Rogers to opine that the automaker had singlehandedly changed the habits of more people than Caesar, Mussolini, Charlie Chaplin, Clara Bow, Xerxes, Amos 'n' Andy, and George Bernard Shaw.[28]

Henry Ford's impact was not limited to the Model T. During the interwar period, other American automobile companies began embracing "Fordism" to increase their own production numbers, with the net result being a significant increase in overall American automobile manufacturing.[29] Despite the onset of the Great Depression, the United States continued to cultivate this unique potential; as World War II began, no nation on the planet could claim an industrial might and mechanical talent to challenge that which could be found in America. Although consumer credit buying of new gadgets and machines become so widespread during the 1920s contributed to the overall severity of the Depression, yet installment purchasing made these same machines, especially the automobile, available to Americans at unprecedented levels.[30] Statistics maintained by the League of Nations in 1939 established American automobile production levels at more than 2,490,000 annually, well above that of all other nations that would align themselves as members of either the Allies or the Axis.[31] Not only did US factories produce more automobiles than any

World per Capita Automobile Ownership, 1939

Country	Cars per 1,000 People
United States	227
United Kingdom	54
France	51
Germany	25
Italy	11
USSR	5

Statistics on motor vehicle ownership per capita were extracted from Kroener, Müller, and Umbreit, *Organisation und Mobilisierung des Deutschen Machtbereichs*, 1:651. The author wishes to thank Gary Shanafelt for his assistance in translating from the German.

other country, but by 1939 the American population possessed as many cars per capita as the rest of the Allies and Axis nations *combined* (see table 1.1).[32]

While these statistics are compelling in their own right, superiority in automobile production and per capita vehicle ownership on the part of the United States can not alone prove that American servicemen in World War II understood technology better and were more effective tinkerers and innovators than soldiers in other armies. The sheer volume of automobiles made in the United States, however, ensured that virtually every future World War II GI had some familiarity with operating an automobile, something that could not be said about soldiers elsewhere in the world. The Model T, and other automobiles of the 1920s and 1930s, were not so dependable nor user-friendly as the turnkey vehicles that would later come into being, such as those introduced by Chrysler in 1949.[33] Even on the best of days, driving prewar automobiles required "personal mechanical involvement." Ford owners frequently "took it apart, made adjustments, added accessories, pampered it, tinkered with it almost daily, worried and brooded over it, cussed it when it failed, and bragged about it when it performed superbly." Simply stated, driving a Model T on a daily basis demanded "creative imaginations" to "cope with most of its idiosyncrasies."[34]

In *Only Yesterday: An Informal History of the 1920s*, author Frederick Lewis Allen explained the lengthy process required for the fictional Mr. Smith, living only a few months after the armistice, to simply start his Model T. Though Smith owned one of "less than seven million cars registered in the United States in 1919," Allen quickly pointed out that ten years later, there were "over twenty-three million cars" in the United States. After Mr. Smith set "the spark and throttle levers" so that they resembled the face of a clock at "ten minutes to three," the driver got out, turned the starter crank with his right hand, and "as the engine at last roars," jumped in his car and moved "the spark and throttle to twenty-five minutes of two." Allen lamented that Mrs. Smith was not available to "sit in the driver's seat and pull that spark lever down before the engine has time to die." Once Mr. Smith was at the wheel with the engine running, he released the hand break, shifted his foot from the low-gear to the high-gear pedal, and was on his way, becoming another American driver navigating a growing network of open roads that were beginning to link the United States together.[35]

If men like Mr. Smith, or future American GIs who used their automobiles to escape the "supervision of parents and chaperones," had not pampered, cussed at, and bragged about their Model Ts, chances are good they may have performed comparable processes on a farm tractor, for Henry Ford's influence extended from the nation's roads to its rural fields as well.[36] In 1883, Ford attempted to build a steam-powered field plow before inventing a practical automobile. He did not build the first farm tractor in the United States, however; some 200 companies had already produced 51,000 tractors before the first Fordson tractor rolled off the assembly line in 1917. Fordson produced 350 tractors daily by 1921, doubling that number by 1924. Within three years, overall production topped 650,000, leading company officials to boast in May 1927 that they had built half the tractors in use in the United States. Compact and simple like the Model T, the Fordson tractor was not as successful as its urban counterpart, though that did not mean that mechanization in the agricultural world lagged behind that of urban America, as numerous other companies competed against Ford. By the mid-1920s, International Harvester, J. I. Case, John Deere, Allis-Chalmers, and Minneapolis Steel and Machinery Company all offered their own tractors for the growing agricultural implement market.[37] Between 1930 and 1940, tractor use on American farms increased dramatically. As reported in the *Sixteenth Census of the United States*, the number of farms utilizing tractors in 1940 increased 165.5 percent from the previous census, with 851,457 farms having tractors in 1930, and 1,409,697 possessing them a decade later.[38]

The introduction of the farm machine indelibly changed the American agricultural landscape, as these metal behemoths tore open the plains and exposed the topsoil, in the process becoming one of the villains in Steinbeck's *Grapes of Wrath*. But even in the midst of the Dust Bowl, scientific farming practices plus the addition of a cheap tractor stood ready to challenge the horse's dominance on the American farm. While foreign countries still relied on horse-drawn implements, the affordable tractor mechanized the American farm, transforming the farmer of yesteryear from "a clod into an operator, from a dumb brute into a mechanic."[39]

This kind of technical knowledge was never far from the minds of future American servicemen who grew up during the Great Depression. Their fascination with machines made them willing consumers of a new genre of "constructive" and decidedly technological literature, both fiction and nonfiction. Thanks to Henry Ford's desire to "build a motor car" at a price low enough so that "no man making a good salary will be unable to own one," American youth growing up in the 1920s and 1930s stood ready to embrace this new mechanized age in earnest and to great effect. Even before World War II began, this unique American machine culture produced an army of young men that could readily blend technical familiarity with Depression-inspired creativity, solving mechanical problems with the ingenuity and desire to innovate that would be critical to ultimate Allied success.[40]

Before the Great War provided future chief of staff George C. Marshall with the opportunity to observe the challenges of moving troops and artillery with horses on the battlefields of the western front, the rising officer purchased his own Model T while commanding elements of the 13th Infantry in 1916. Taking advantage of his automobile as a means to break the monotony of army service while isolated in the Philippines, the officer who would advocate motorizing the US Army on the eve of World War II sought to familiarize himself with his new purchase. Although confessing he "was not all mechanical," Marshall nonetheless took his car's engine apart to see how it worked, saying, "I just had to do it."[41]

Comparable experiences followed Marshall when he was named commander of District 1 of the Civilian Conservation Corps in June 1933. When Congress created the organization in March 1933, it did so specifying that the US Army would assume near total control of the organization's direction and operation. During his tenure with the CCC, first in South Carolina and later supervising thirty-five CCC camps in Oregon and southern Washington, Marshall acquired a keen insight into the technical and mechanical capabilities of the American people. A member of his staff later commented that Marshall's time with the CCC gave him an unprecedented "feeling for civilians that few Army officers . . . have . . . had. . . . He didn't have to adjust to civilians—they were a natural part of his environment. . . . I think he regarded civilians and military as part of a whole."[42]

What particularly impressed Marshall was the initiative of CCC men, which he witnessed firsthand in the camps of the Pacific Northwest. Completing a district review in June 1937, he praised those young men "determinedly trying to make up [their] deficiencies in education, or to fit [themselves] practically for a position in civil life." He specifically noted the "ingenuity displayed in some temporary camps in arranging or fixing things in a convenient fashion." With this in mind, Marshall recognized that the CCC would be a valuable source of "wholly dependable men who have demonstrated unmistakably that they have both the character and the ability," and although it was impossible to know in 1937, many would become citizen-soldiers in the years that followed.[43]

Future airman Chuck Yeager cultivated similar skills while working with his father in the family fields of West Virginia. In his youth, Yeager developed familiarity with single-cylinder gas-powered water pumps required to keep his family's crops growing. The young Yeager's job was to keep feeding gasoline into the small stationary engines and manage their regulators and magnetos. By the time he enlisted in the US Army Air Corps in 1941, he could "take apart a car motor and put it back together again. . . . I just understood motors—a natural ability, like having exceptional eyes and the coordination to be a crack shot." As a test pilot after the war, Yeager later recalled that "when I encountered dome regulators flying the X-1, I knew more about them than the engineers, from working with Dad's regulators as a kid."[44]

Future Marine Corps tanker Henry Bellmon learned about machines in the wheatfields of north-central Oklahoma. After his father "decided tractors had come to stay," he traded several horses "as a down payment on an Allis-Chalmers tractor." During the Depression, Bellmon learned the intricacies of machines while keeping the family tractors operational on the farm near Mulhall. Not only did Bellmon's experience help him as a marine tanker, but when his captain began organizing their company, the future Silver Star winner encouraged his superior to seek out "those whose records indicated that they had been in the 4-H or FFA clubs." Bellmon believed that targeting these sorts of recruits "would bring in the farm boys who could probably maintain and operate machinery with a minimum of problems," as farm success demanded functional equipment. Such foresight reaped great dividends in the marine tank battles of the Pacific.[45]

Like their rural counterparts, small-town boys in interwar America enjoyed considerable freedom, hindered only by the financial constraints of the Depression, which bred the sense of mechanical self-sufficiency popularized in *Popular Science* and *Popular Mechanics*. Before he enlisted in the United States Marine Corps, Robert Haney not only had "driveaway" jobs delivering new cars from Detroit to owners throughout the country, but recovered and repaired electric motors and sold them for "whatever the traffic would bear."[46] As men like Haney matured, so did their interests. By their teen years, many were like future marine James W. Johnson, who "liked cars and motorcycles, pool halls and ball games." In 1936, Oklahoman Jack Scott, who eventually served in the 36th Division's 111th Combat Engineer Battalion, bought a barely functional 1927 Willys-Overland Whippet for twelve dollars from a local salvage yard. As Scott said, "The things we did [during the Great Depression] to entertain ourselves were unbelievable. . . . We even built our own cars"; he tinkered with the Whippet in a manner not unlike Frank and Joe Hardy until it eventually ran. Two years later, he received a used 1934 Ford for Christmas. To a high school senior like Scott, a car, even one he had to build himself, was like "wings to a bird."[47]

During the Depression, those fortunate enough to own cars did whatever they could to keep them running, which instilled an all-important sense of mechanical self-sufficiency in future GIs. Although he longed to fly, John F. Kinney accepted a commission as a second lieutenant in the US Army Reserve in July 1936. He eventually transferred to the Marine Corps, after both the army and the navy disqualified him from pilot training. His quest, however, was built on a background of technical mastery. While in high school, he learned to drive a neighbor's Caterpillar tractor, and he signed up for an automobile mechanics class while in college. After completely tearing down the engine in his father's Oldsmobile and reboring the block and installing bigger pistons and rings, he did the same to a four-cylinder Chevrolet truck the family also owned. Taking over all the mechanical maintenance for his father, he eventually found employment as an aircraft mechanic for Pan American Airlines, hoping that just being around airplanes would help him find a way into a cockpit.[48]

Others coupled their mechanical acumen with thrift, a trait required during hard economic times. While visiting friend Bob Kalb in Bradford, Pennsylvania, while on vacation from Ohio State University during the summer of 1927, young Curtis E. LeMay witnessed a structure fire at a garage. Finding in the rubble a partially damaged Model T with its wheels "burned off" that was "years younger than my own faithful 1918 type," the bold future flyer tested the starter, and it turned over. Recognizing the car's potential despite having its "top charred off and the upholstery scorched out," he made a deal with the insurance company and bought the vehicle as is. Over the course of the next twenty-four hours, LeMay and his companion visited a local junkyard, where he traded his own car, minus the wheels, for an old coupe body, wiring, lights, and a steering wheel. Returning to the burned-out car he had purchased the day before, LeMay replaced its wheels with those from his old car, then "dumped the body, put the coupe body on; we wired the thing, and put on the new steering gear." With everything "stirred up and mixed together and bolted up," LeMay drove his "new" car back to Columbus, Ohio.[49]

Such demonstrations of thrift and ingenuity were commonplace among Americans trying to make ends meet during the Depression. After his November 1937 wedding, Lt. Ross Greening, a pilot who eventually served as the armament officer on the 1942 Doolittle Raid, set off cross-country with his new bride in a thirdhand 1935 Plymouth. Leaving El Paso, Texas, for Barksdale Field,

Louisiana, their trip came to a halt with a "clatter and bang," as the right wheel spring of their car disintegrated. After salvaging springs from a 1936 Chevrolet, they made their way to Fort Worth in a "still wobbling" automobile. Departing the next day, mechanical disaster struck as "the right front axle snapped in half and the wheel slid underneath the front of the car," bringing their honeymoon to an abrupt stop. With only $17.50 to his name, Greening spent $16.50 at a nearby junkyard for the axle assembly from a 1936 Plymouth. Borrowing tools from a local mechanic, he installed the axle, then drove with his wife to his next duty station with a dollar in his pocket.[50]

Numerous GIs shared similar experiences with cantankerous Depression-era automobiles. Future pilot Robert Brulle, who immigrated to the United States from Belgium with his parents in 1929, pooled his resources with four fellow lieutenants at Richmond Army Air Base and bought a 1935 Plymouth. The car's starter often failed, requiring the five pilots to push-start the car, and they had to repeatedly rub soap over a small hole in the gas tank, but the quintet nonetheless enjoyed a roadworthy vehicle.[51] Elmer Bendiner, a B-17 navigator who flew in the Schweinfurt raid, recognized the "comradely feelings" his copilot had toward machines, a product of his experiences with recalcitrant vehicles. Bendiner's copilot was "wonderfully attuned to the hums, whirs, quirks and moods of an aircraft," having worked his way through school by hauling twenty-five-foot house trailers with "old and usually eccentric" cars that forced a driver to get to know his machine quickly.[52]

Many of these future servicemen recognized the importance of publications like *Popular Science* and *Popular Mechanics.* John Kinney, who later cobbled together aircraft as the engineering officer for the Marine Corps squadron defending Wake Island, considered partnering with a friend to purchase the "Penguin," a do-it-yourself airplane kit advertised in *Popular Science* in 1926. Shortly thereafter, Kinney, still fascinated with the prospect of flying, built a mock-up of an airplane cockpit, mounting a model of a Curtiss Hawk biplane built from a photo in *Popular Mechanics* on a broomstick and connecting it by a series of strings and pulleys to allow him to simulate actual flight.[53]

Other future pilots became fascinated by the exploits of *G-8 and His Battle Aces*, recalling the pulp's influence in sparking their love for the air. Tuskegee airman Charles Dryden remembered "reading anything and everything about flying, especially a pulp magazine, *G-8 and his Battle Aces*." He spent the time between G-8 issues painstakingly building rubber band–powered model planes and stringing them up from the ceiling of his room. As he wrote later, "Everyone on the block knew about the crazy Black kid who wanted to fly." Before Robin Olds became a football star at West Point, G-8 and his fictional compatriots were the "real men that moved through my daily life" inspiring the eventual P-38 and P-51 double ace. Joseph Rutter, who grew up on a Pennsylvania farm before flying A-20s with the 312th Bomb Group in the Pacific, remembers his fascination with early aviators, an interest fueled by *Battle Aces* magazine. By his adolescence, he could "quote line and verse" from the tales of fictional flyer Phineas Pinkham and devoured Beirne Lay Jr.'s *I Wanted Wings* and Charles Nordhoff and James Norman Hall's *Falcons of France*. The ultimate product of this fascination was a generation of boys who became "true believer[s] in the religion of flight," and they did so through a familiarity with machines. When the US Army sent future general of the air force Henry "Hap" Arnold to flight instruction with the Wright brothers in Dayton, Ohio, he and fellow aviator 2nd Lt. Thomas Milling spent their first few days at the Wright factory. There they mastered "the construction and maintenance features of the Wright Machine," recognizing that after they learned how to fly, they would also have to keep the plane operational, as "there were no crew chiefs nor aircraft mechanics in the Army in those days."[54] To Bruce Gamble, a marine flyer in VMF-214, the famed Black Sheep Squadron commanded by Gregory "Pappy" Boyington, nothing was better for maintaining aircraft than having "backyard mechanics who knew how to take things apart and put them back together again," essential for keeping them in the fight.[55]

But simply having the backyard mechanic's ability to keep machines running does not explain American ingenuity in World War II. An army had to be mechanized, something that General Marshall acted on when named chief of staff in 1939. This demand for a mechanized and motorized army produced what others claim he called "America's greatest contribution to modern warfare," and the effective replacement for the horse. Arguably the most identifiable vehicle of World War II, which finally bore the official designation US Army Truck, the quarter-ton, 4 × 4 Command Reconnaissance Car, popularly known as the "jeep," revolutionized modern mechanized warfare. Emerging as a jack-of-all-trades for the American military, the jeep was the product of a curious union between military engineers and the American automotive industry. Not only did it transform the American military, but its path to development was as emblematic of American mechanical ingenuity as was the vehicle itself.[56]

As early as 1933, the army had sought a fleet of standardized vehicles to replace the motorized hodgepodge of the interwar period, initially approving commercially available trucks including the Marmon-Herrington 4 × 4 half-ton, the Dodge 4 × 4 1.5-ton, the GMC 6 × 6 2.5-ton, and the Mack 6 × 6 six-ton.[57] The US Army, however, also recognized the need for a lightweight "gasoline-propelled conveyance not much higher than a man crawling (or is it creeping), that would be able to carry a one- or two-man crew, a gun, and plenty of ammunition, and scoot from one firing position to another at five to ten miles an hour." The call yielded a number of vehicles for testing, including one fabricated from the Fort Benning salvage pile at the request of Brig. Gen. Walter C. Short, assistant commandant of the Infantry School. Turning to Capt. Robert G. Howie, an instructor in the Tank Section, and aided by "long-time tanker and expert mechanic" Master Sergeant (M.Sgt.) M. S. Wiley, and Sgt. G. L. Rush, the trio assembled something best described as a Rube Goldberg contraption based on an Austin Bantam engine and radiator, a propeller shaft, universal joints, and rear axle assembly mounted on a frame welded together from steel channel, perched on four commercially available 6.00.9 tractor tires. The odd-looking, low-profile vehicle known interchangeably as the "Howie Machine-Gun Carrier" or "belly flopper" carried two men in a prone position, along with an 81 mm mortar, .50-caliber machine gun, or 37 mm antitank gun, and was capable of a top speed of twenty-eight miles per hour.[58]

When completed, the "Howie Machine-Gun Carrier" joined a light, Swiss-made "Benz" car, the "Bantam," produced by the American Bantam Car Company of Butler, Pennsylvania, and many others in a series of tests conducted by the Quartermaster Technical Committee on Transportation, which met at Holabird Quartermaster Depot, Maryland. The committee concluded that while the vehicles were small and lightweight, they lacked the power for modern battlefield conditions. Agreeing to the essentiality of such a vehicle, former navy commander Charles "Harry" Payne, a fast-talking, freewheeling Bantam Company "assistant to the president," approached Gen. George A. Lynch, chief of infantry. Determined to keep the small manufacturer from going bankrupt, Payne assured Lynch that despite the underwhelming performance of the initial Bantam car in the early tests, the company "could, and would" develop a new vehicle to meet army specifications. Detailing Lt. Col. William F. Lee, chief of arms, equipment, and finance in the Office of the Chief of Infantry to Butler, to inspect company facilities, Lee returned with a positive report, and Bantam quickly took the lead in developing a new vehicle.[59]

Releasing vehicle characteristics, Lt. Col. Lee, joined by Payne and Frank Fenn, Bantam's president, met with Lt. Col. Ingomar M. Oseth of the Office of the Chief of Infantry, Col. L. J. Atwood (Office of the Chief of Cavalry), and Quartermaster Department representatives to outline specifications for the new vehicle. Agreeing on general dimensions, the team drew a chalk outline on the floor of a vacant building and, upon reviewing the dimensions and performance characteristics of the underperforming Bantam car, began building an altogether new vehicle. By early July, the team completed their mock-up. After securing approval from the chief of infantry, they distributed these new specifications to other companies interested in the project.[60] The new vehicle would be no more than thirty-six inches high, weigh no more than 1,300 pounds, have cross-country ability and grade ability equal to other standard vehicles, carry at least two men, a machine gun, and 3,000 rounds of .30 ammunition (effectively a 600 lb payload), and have four-wheel-drive capability. Companies had forty-nine days to deliver their pilot model, with the remaining models due twenty-six days later.[61]

When the Ordnance Committee released vehicle specifications on 27 June 1940, 135 other companies joined Bantam in bidding on the project. Hoping to win the contract, Payne enlisted American freelance engineer Karl Probst to join Bantam's engineers racing to meet the deadline to deliver the prototype. The intrepid Payne began ordering off-the-shelf components from a host of manufacturers, putting his intimate understanding of the automotive industry to use, in order to provide the engineering team with the vital subassemblies they needed. The result was a vehicle improvised from the wheels up, cobbled together from parts sourced from a number of different automotive manufacturers, based on Probst's design drawings that he made along the way. Bantam fabricators started with wheels from the Kelsey-Hayes Wheel Company, mounted them on four-wheel-drive axles and differentials produced by the Spicer Engineering Company of Toledo, Ohio, braced them with Gabriel Company shock absorbers, engaged them to a Warner Gear transfer case, and anchored an engine from the Continental Motors Company and radiator from Marmon-Herrington to a frame made by the A. O. Smith manufacturing company. Combining parts from more than twenty vendors, the Bantam team completed their test model on 23 September 1940, delivering it to the Holabird Depot a scant thirty minutes before the submission deadline.[62]

The Bantam vehicle faced exhaustive tests designed to break it, though success in its trials did not mean the company would receive the contract.[63] Payne soon garnered a reputation as an "annoying pest" within the Quartermaster Department, though that did not prevent him from seeking endorsement for "his" jeep at the highest levels. Making his way to the office of Secretary of War Harry Woodring, he was redirected to Chief of Staff George Marshall's office. Encountering Maj. Walter Bedell Smith, assistant to the secretary of the General Staff, Payne made a pitch for his vehicle to Marshall's assistant. Convinced of the vehicle's utility, Smith proceeded to interrupt General Marshall in a staff meeting, delivering a three-minute condensed version of Payne's pitch for the new vehicle. Reflecting on Smith's argument, Marshall simply asked what he thought of the jeep, to which his secretary replied, "I think it's good." Marshall concurred with Smith's assessment and agreed to purchase seventy vehicles for testing by the "Infantry and other branches"; the tests led to "increasingly promising results."[64]

Although Payne mobilized the Bantam Company's collective ingenuity to produce the first jeep, other companies ultimately stole much of Bantam's thunder.[65] By 1 January 1941, the War Department contracted with Bantam, the Willys-Overland Company, and Ford Motor Company for 1,500 units from each manufacturer. Unfortunately for Bantam, Willys and Ford possessed more robust productive capacity, and the two competitors won the production contracts. Working from the original Bantam plans, the two established automakers produced more than 640,000 "Willys" jeeps, vehicles that, in the eyes of Ernie Pyle, "did everything, went everywhere, as faithful as a dog, as strong as a mule, and as agile as a goat."[66] Perhaps more than anything else, the jeep came to define the American GI, providing a unique platform for the application of American ingenuity in Europe, Asia, and beyond.

Only a few days before the War Department offered production contracts for the jeep, President Franklin D. Roosevelt delivered his sixteenth "fireside chat" to the people of the United States. With the war in Europe barely more than a year old, the president told his audience that this was "not a fireside chat on war, it is a talk on national security." The president described an imminent threat, as it was only a matter of time before members of the Tripartite Pact would begin directing their animus against the United States. In the meantime, Americans must "support those nations defending themselves against attack by the Axis" and provide them "the implements of war, the planes, the tanks, the guns, the freighters which will enable them to fight for their liberty and for our security." Recognizing the need to "keep war away from our country and our people," Roosevelt called for a practical military policy, one that harnessed "American industrial genius, unmatched throughout the world in the solution of production problems," to protect the defenders of liberty from the forces of fascism. It was at this point the president pledged that the United States must become a "great arsenal of democracy," capable not only of producing the necessary tools of security for the people of the United States, but also of offering the tools of war to those who stood in the face of the Axis powers, and "meet the threat to our democratic faith."[67]

To assist other democracies in fighting fascism, Roosevelt called for a "swift and driving increase in our armament production," recognizing that "to change a whole nation from a basis of wartime production of implements of peace to a basis of wartime production of implements of war is no small task.[68] The Lend-Lease Act of March 1941 opened the floodgates of American industry to any and all nations that chose to resist German, Italian, and Japanese militarism and oppression. For many nations, this support came in the form of jeeps, trucks, tanks, planes, and other motor vehicles produced by the same factories that allowed the United States to possess more automobiles per capita than all the

Axis and Allied nations combined prior to 1939. Not only was the United States able to supply its own military with the tools of modern warfare, but many of those machines found their way into Allied hands, who benefited greatly from American mass production.[69]

To coordinate the herculean production demands of Lend-Lease with American military needs, Roosevelt revived the World War I–era National Defense Advisory Commission (NDAC), naming General Motors head William Knudsen, president of the Amalgamated Clothing Workers Union Sidney Hillman, and chairman of the board of US Steel Edward Stettinus Jr. to lead the organization. While it was relatively easy for the commission to direct clothing manufacturers to switch from making civilian shirts and pants to military uniforms, and for automobile and motorcycle industries to retool existing assembly lines in order to mass-produce jeeps, half-tracks, and tanks, the mass manufacture of aircraft was a different matter entirely. This transition would provide yet another example of the link between American ingenuity and mass production.[70]

Prior to 1939, there was little demand for mass-produced aircraft, as planes were boutique products, manufactured by hand and often one at a time, "as a tailor would fit a suit of clothes."[71] President Roosevelt's dramatic 1940 call to produce 50,000 aircraft a year demanded a revolution in American aircraft production, as the number of planes he hoped to build represented nearly the total number of aircraft produced in the United States since the Wright brothers first flight. By 1940, the United States had already increased production from 6,000 to nearly 12,000 planes per year, but the president's new call stretched existing American aircraft production to its limits.[72]

To address aircraft production, The NDAC turned to its Office of Materiel Division, established in 1926 under the auspices of the Office of the Chief of the Air Corps.[73] By 1939, the division evolved to manage research, development, procurement, and the logistical requirements for the entire US Army Air Corps. Nonetheless, at the time of the invasion of Poland, American aircraft manufacturers produced only about fifty planes a week.[74] Once war broke out in Europe, France and Great Britain ordered more than 1,500 additional planes from the United States, further straining American production, though most foreign orders were for training or obsolete planes not in demand. Following Poland's defeat, the lifting of the arms embargo designed to preserve American neutrality, coupled with Roosevelt's "cash and carry" program, prompted France and Great Britain to order 1,000 planes from the Air Corps. In addition to making planes such as the B-18A, A-20, and P-40 available for foreign purchase, by March 1940, the Air Corps began releasing newer airframes, making the P-38, B-17, B-24, B-25, and B-26 available to Allied customers.[75] As

Ordnance Department Selected Motor Vehicle and Weapons Production, 1 July 1940–31 December 1945

Item	Quantity
Tanks (all types)	88,410
Other combat vehicles (armored cars, tracked cargo carriers, half-tracks, recovery vehicles)	46,706
Medium trucks	428,196
Heavy-heavy trucks	153,686
Other trailers	499,494
Cars, motorcycles, and other vehicles	224,272
Heavy field artillery weapons	7,803
Light field and antitank weapons	54,532
Tank guns and howitzers	116,097
Guns and howitzers for self-propelled weapons	27,080
Aircraft guns (all types)	156,587
Antiaircraft weapons	49,775
Rocket launchers (all types)	635,128
Mortars (all types)	105,054
Machine guns (all types)	2,679,819
Motor carriages for self-propelled weapons	46,706
Light trucks (all types)	988,167
Light-heavy trucks	812,262
Semi-trailers	59,731
Tractors	34,295
Vehicular machine-gun mounts	332,579
Rifle, Garand, .30-caliber	4,014,731
Rifle, Springfield, .30-caliber	1,318,951
Rifle, Lee Enfield, .303-caliber	1,030,228
Browning automatic rifle	188,380
Carbine, .30-caliber	6,117,827
Submachinegun, .45-caliber	2,008,267
Automatic pistol, .45-caliber	1,877,069
Revolver, .38-caliber	889,203
Shotgun, 12-gauge	429,074

Statistics extracted from Smith, *Army and Economic Mobilization*, 9–11.

foreign purchases absorbed most of the domestic aircraft production capability, American producers hoping to supply the nation's military would have to dramatically increase their production to translate President Roosevelt's lofty goal of 50,000 planes into an achievable reality.[76]

By the end of 1940, NDAC spokesman William Knudsen had already gone to Chrysler, Chevrolet, Wright, Pratt & Whitney, and Packard to secure production contracts for tanks, 75 mm high explosive shells, and Rolls-Royce Merlin liquid-cooled V-12 engines at their existing factories in and around Detroit. But Knudsen had saved the largest and most ambitious project for last. Having convinced a reluctant Henry Ford to build 4,000 Rolls-Royce aircraft engines, Maj. James "Jimmy" Doolittle returned to the father of the moving assembly line to ask if the company would be willing to lend its manufacturing talents to the construction of the four-engine Consolidated B-24 Liberator, to date the largest and most expensive plane in the American inventory, with a 110-foot wingspan and more than a million parts.[77]

Despite Henry Ford's opposition to entangling his company with Roosevelt and the "warmongers of Europe," the nation's largest auto producer soon capitalized on the opportunity to apply Fordism to aircraft manufacturing. In January 1941, he sent his son Edsel Ford, accompanied by his sons Henry II and Benson, along with Ford Motor Company vice president Charles Sorensen to San Diego, California, to tour the Consolidated Aircraft factory with company president Reuben Fleet. Throughout the day, Sorensen, a hard-driving Danish immigrant who joined Ford as a patternmaker in 1905 before innovating foundry practices for mass production and eventually rising to senior management, carefully documented the processes by which the small company hand-made each huge, four-engine, twin-tailed bomber.[78] Sorensen, whose stubbornness had earned him the sobriquet "Cast-Iron Charlie" from Henry Ford, quickly realized that Consolidated's manufacturing process limped along, in his own words, "on a wing and a prayer," utilizing outdoor facilities subject to fluctuating weather conditions. He characterized the Consolidated plant as a small-volume "job shop," composed of general-purpose equipment geared toward individual tasks, with intermittent production based on demand, a trend characteristic of most contemporary aircraft manufacturers. With each B-24 being built one at a time and subject to the weather, Sorensen projected it would take three years to produce 1,000 planes, far below the number desired by the NDAC. Discouraged by the plant's paltry output, Sorensen expressed this to Fleet, who challenged the Ford pioneer to explain how to increase production. The vice president of the world's largest automobile manufacturer simply replied, "I'll have something for you tomorrow morning."[79]

Returning to his room at the Hotel del Coronado, Sorensen labored through the night, translating Fordism to the mass production of the B-24. Recognizing that comparing construction of "a Ford V-8 with a four-engine Liberator was like matching a garage with a skyscraper," the proven industrial innovator applied mass assembly methods devised for automobiles to the massive bomber. Considering the plane's 1.2 million parts, Sorensen broke the B-24's design down into nine principal components further made up of "subunits and fractional units required for their assembly." Calculating each unit's manufacturing requirements, operation, timing, and necessary floor space, Sorensen tallied each subassembly's requirements on individual pieces of paper, then arranged the pages into piles as he would machines on a shop floor, translating thirty-five years of production experience into the production of "not only something I had never put together before, but the largest and most complicated of all air transport in numbers and at a rate never before thought possible." By 4:30 in the morning, Sorensen had designed a factory with a mile-long assembly line, to be housed in a construction plant large enough for fifty-four individual assembly stations, complete with overhead cranes to stand entire assemblies on end to facilitate speedy construction. Sorensen's plan reduced build time from 140,000 to 100,000 man-hours per plane.[80]

The plant Sorensen designed after a frenetic night of scribbling was eventually built at Willow Run, just west of Detroit. When completed, it was the largest factory building in the world, with over eighty acres of floor space. Within sixteen months, Ford translated mass-production methodology pioneered in the automotive industry to the production of aircraft, producing B-24s Liberators at the then mind-boggling rate of more than one plane per hour. After the attack on Pearl Harbor, the government began aggressively expanding aircraft

Selected Army Air Forces Procurement Deliveries of Aircraft, January 1940–December 1945

Item	Quantity
B-17 Flying Fortress	12,692
B-24 Liberator	18,190
B-25 Mitchell	9,816
B-26 Marauder	5,157
B-29 Superfortress	3,898
P-38 Lightning	9,536
P-40 Warhawk	13,738
P-47 Thunderbolt	14,683
P-51 Mustang	14,686
C-46 Commando	3,180
C-47 Dakota	10,368
C-78 Bobcat	3,206
A-20 Havoc	7,385
AT-6 Texan	15,094
BT-13 and BT-15 Valiant	11,537
PT-13, 17, 27 Kaydet	7,539
PT-19, 23, 26 Cornell	7,802
L-2, 3, 4, 14 Grasshopper	8,990

Smith, *Army and Economic Mobilization*, 27.

production facilities to meet wartime demand, building factories like the one at Willow Run throughout the country, including one outside Chicago that nearly doubled the size of the Ford plant with an enclosed shop floor of 147 acres.[81] Embracing mass-production techniques to produce a host of fighter aircraft, as well as B-17s, B-24s, and eventually B-29s, manufacturers limited aircraft design changes resulting in single plane patterns, allowing them to produce large numbers of standard airframes as quickly as possible. Producing single aircraft models, however, posed significant challenges, as the various theaters of operations possessed unique operational requirements that a single airframe could not always meet.[82]

More than 2.7 million American men would serve in the US Army's eighty-nine combat divisions engaged by war's end, with an additional 3 million men in military support services.[83] Another 2.4 million men and women would fill the ranks of the US Army Air Forces at its peak strength in 1943, with 3.4 million in the US Navy and 475,000 in the US Marine Corps.[84] Well before these soldiers, airmen, sailors, and marines entered combat, efforts were undertaken to transform the nation's citizens into soldiers. The passage of the Selective Service and Training Act in September 1940 led to the registration of more than 16 million eligible draftees between the ages of twenty-one and thirty-five, a generation of young men who had grown up with the American cult of the machine. They could operate internal combustion engines and other mechanical contrivances, knew what was needed to keep them running, and were often able to invent new gadgets to either make them more effective or keep them going under adverse conditions.

Just a few months before the Japanese attack on Pearl Harbor, former army officer and visionary Maj. Malcolm Wheeler-Nicholson extolled the virtues of technical creativity in an article published in *Mechanix Illustrated*, a magazine with the same focus as *Popular Science* and *Popular Mechanics*.[85] The former cavalryman observed that "Mr. Hitler's war plans have not taken account of one intangible in the complex which is America: Yankee Ingenuity!"[86] Chronicling "a race of traders and tinkerers with an inventive turn of mind—the same type of people who today make up the readers of *Mechanix Illustrated*," Wheeler-Nicholson noted that throughout American history men like Samuel Colt, Richard Gatling, and the Wright brothers personified Yankee ingenuity. Boasting that nearly every "major military mechanism existing could be traced directly or indirectly to American technical cleverness," Wheeler-Nicholson boldly professed that "when Herr Hitler puts on the heat, then America will produce!" The forward-thinking author extolled the virtues of mass production and American ingenuity, and although the strained conditions of the opening phases of the Pacific War were yet to come, he specifically noted that "imagination, adaptiveness and mental agility" coupled with the ability to improvise had come to typify what it meant to grow up American.[87] Such traits were a unique product of growing up in the United States as part of the first generation to have widespread access to the internal combustion engine, together with the formative influences of the Great Depression and American popular culture. This formative crucible would be the source of American ingenuity in World War II.

CHAPTER 2

Improvising a Defense in the Pacific

> Improvisation will be the watchword. Such changed conditions will require a modification in type of the officer, a type possessing all the cardinal military virtues as of yore, but possessing an intimate understanding of the mechanics of human feelings, a comprehensive grasp of world and national affairs, and a liberalization of conception which amounts to a change in his psychology of command.
>
> —*Brig. Gen. Douglas MacArthur*

In 1919, his first year superintending the United States Military Academy, Brig. Gen. Douglas MacArthur forecast a new way of thinking for the army's future leaders. Only a few years removed from a conflict where "personnel was of necessity improvised, both at the front and at the rear," the forward-looking reformer elevated innovation to a level just below principles of duty, honor, and country. Henceforth, a successful nation must not only be prepared to mobilize a mass army, but must do so in an adaptive organizational structure that allowed its military to react to the circumstances and technologies that defined conflict.[1]

During his three-year tenure as superintendent at West Point, MacArthur tried to inculcate this new way of thinking. Recognizing that future officers would be leading draftee armies of shopkeepers, farmers, and factory workers, the decorated World War I veteran looked to encourage personal flexibility and creativity among leaders of citizen-soldiers, while at the same time encouraging the study of history and emerging features of modern warfare like the internal combustion engine. Despite his best efforts, MacArthur ultimately lost out to institutional inertia. Upon finishing his tour at the Academy, he ranked thirty-eighth out of forty-six army brigadier generals and received orders to the Philippines, tasked with defending them in case of war with Japan.[2]

Having failed to encourage forward thinking at West Point, MacArthur spent most of the next two decades in the Philippines, first commanding a brigade in the Philippine Division, and eventually commanding US Army Forces Far East (USAFFE).[3] Defense of the Pacific figured prominently at every level in War Plan Orange, which was adopted by the Joint Army-Navy Board in 1924 and revised until its absorption into the Rainbow 1 plan in August 1939.[4] Although MacArthur, US Army generals, and Washington officials all recognized the threat Japan posed to American possessions in the Pacific, a variety of political, economic, and interservice concerns, and circumstances further exacerbated by Great Depression, made it impossible to amass the requisite material or manpower to prepare an effective defense of the Philippines.[5]

When the Japanese attacked Pearl Harbor and US holdings in the Pacific, American defenders quickly turned to MacArthur's mantra of innovation and technical creativity out of absolute necessity. Under circumstances markedly different from those their commander encountered at West Point in 1920, American ingenuity became the rule. Shocked defenders of Pearl Harbor, beleaguered guardians of Wake Island and the Philippines, army and navy aviators flying off carriers in the Pacific, and US Marines, sailors, and airmen operating elsewhere found themselves forced to make do. Facing overwhelming odds, often outclassed technologically, and lacking meaningful resupply or reinforcement, Americans defending the Pacific had no choice but to repurpose, repair, reuse, or adapt existing military hardware, forging solutions with whatever they had on hand. The result was an improvised defense in the first years of the Pacific War. Not always successful, these intrepid defenders bought valuable time in the war against Imperial Japan, giving the sleeping giant of American industry time to rise and begin production on a path to victory.

On 3 November 1941, Maj. Gen. Lewis H. Brereton reported to USAFFE headquarters in Manila, as requested by Gen. Douglas MacArthur, to command newly arrived air assets and existing forces comprising the Far East Air Force (FEAF). Having met with Generals Henry "Hap" Arnold and Carl "Tooey" Spaatz, Brereton recognized the gravity of the situation in the Southwest Pacific and brought MacArthur the latest revisions to the Rainbow plan. Although MacArthur did not expect war with Japan prior to April 1942, Brereton knew that US forces faced grave challenges, as "shameful neglect of military aviation during the past twenty years" left American forces in-theater "neither the equipment nor manpower organized and available for the 100 percent employment of the program required." Faced with shortcomings with respect to both trained aircrews and aircraft, Brereton forecast that any defense of the Pacific would be "a question of improvisation all along the line."[6] The devastating attack on the US Pacific Fleet on 7 December 1941, coupled with the destruction of US Army Air Forces in the Philippines, made Brereton's words, not to mention those offered by MacArthur two decades earlier, eerily prophetic. After these costly surprise attacks, one thing became painfully certain: until American industry could meet the demands of a two-front war, Americans responsible for defending the Pacific would be on their own. Without resupply or reinforcement from the United States, soldiers, marines, sailors, airmen, and, in some cases, civilians would be forced to rely on their ingenuity in the early phases of the war in the Pacific.

The "date which will live in infamy" marked the first demonstration of emerging wartime ingenuity. As attacking aircraft of the Imperial Japanese Navy rained destruction down on US naval and air forces at Pearl Harbor, Americans on the ground reacted with creative energy, mounting a makeshift defense with whatever weapons were available. Those sailors assigned to Ford Island Naval Air Station, Pearl Harbor, were perhaps the most effective in demonstrating American ingenuity while fighting back on that infamous day. Seaman 2nd Class Victor Kamont initially joined fellow sailors to fill bomb craters and secure aircraft stationed at Luke Field after the initial Japanese attack. In a lull between the two waves of Japanese aircraft, Kamont and his compatriots stripped AN/M2 Browning .30-caliber light machine guns (the lightweight aircraft version of the M1919 Browning .30-caliber) from damaged Consolidated PBY Catalina flying boats of VP-11 and VP-12 squadrons and mounted them on portable work benches dragged onto the tarmac from nearby maintenance shops. Clamping these guns into vises, they opened fire on subsequent Japanese aircraft, as the makeshift mounts "proved very effective after the wheels were chocked up."[7] Nearby, engineering chief of VP-11 George R. Jackson, Ensign Jack Coley, and others recovered AN/M2s from other PBYs. Coley soon recognized the challenge of employing these guns against the enemy, as PBY machine-gun mountings were "just a ring in a mount with a yoke that allowed the gun to pivot and elevate." Finding some pipes in a nearby public works compound, they pounded them into the ground with sledge hammers. Once in place, they dropped the pin of the machine-gun yoke into the ends of the upright pipes and opened fire. To further protect their position, they surrounded themselves with vehicles making "a circle like the old covered wagon trains used to do," though Jackson later observed that this crude arrangement "fell far short of a planned, well-fortified, anti-aircraft battery."[8]

Not far away, Chief Warrant Officer John W. Finn, the chief aviation ordnanceman at Naval Air Station Kaneohe Bay distinguished himself, in the process earning the war's first Medal of Honor. Spying his squadron's painter wildly manning a Browning .50-caliber machine gun, Finn took over, knowing that an ordnanceman would be more effective with the weapon. Seizing a mobile gunnery tripod typically used for training purposes, Finn moved to an open area and quickly mounted the heavy machine gun. He fired on the attacking Japanese for the next two hours, his own safety at risk. Shot in the right foot and left shoulder, he kept fighting, despite receiving nineteen additional wounds. After the attack, he was given medical assistance before returning to the hangars to arm those planes that had survived the attacks.[9]

The next day, President Franklin Roosevelt asked Congress for a declaration of war against Japan. In his defiant speech, he listed the additional US holdings attacked by the Japanese: Midway Island, Wake Island, Guam, and the Philippines. Cognizant of the Rainbow plans, American defenders throughout the Pacific knew the chance of meaningful reinforcement or resupply from the United States was slim. With much of the Pacific fleet sunk or burning at its moorings in Pearl Harbor and most American aircraft in the Philippines destroyed on the ground at Clark Field, not only would the remaining American assets in the Pacific have to fight with a decided disadvantage, but until American production could effectively ramp up, they would be forced to improvise.

After an 8 December bombing raid damaged or destroyed most of Wake Island's aircraft (eight out of twelve Grumman F4F Wildcat fighters that made up Marine Corps Fighter Squadron VMF-211), Japanese forces arrived to challenge the 1,742 Americans trapped on Wake. With little in the way of external material support, the mixed force of 524 Marine Corps and US Navy personnel, together with 1,218 civilian contractors employed by the Morrison-Knudsen Corporation, had no choice but to rely on the material in their possession when the Japanese invasion fleet arrived on 11 December. Embracing the Depression-era mantra of "Use it up, wear it out, make it do, or do without," they would have their hands full countering the invaders of the Rising Sun.[10]

Marine aviator 2nd Lt. John F. Kinney joined VMF-211 on Wake Island only a few days before the first Japanese air raid. The initial attack not only destroyed seven Wildcats and damaged another, it also killed the squadron's engineering officer, 1st Lt. George A. Graves. In the raid's aftermath, squadron commander Maj. Paul A. Putnam, aware of Kinney's background as an electrical engineer and former Pan American Airlines aircraft mechanic, informed the newcomer that lacking any other mechanics familiar with the Wildcat, "you are now the squadron engineering officer—we have four planes left. If you can keep them flying, I'll see that you get a medal as big as a pie." With Technical Sergeant (T.Sgt.) William Hamilton assisting, the pair quickly set about to maintain the two flyable aircraft and return any salvageable planes to service as soon as possible.[11]

Kinney had little to work with. Lacking repair manuals and spare parts, and with most of their tools destroyed in the first Japanese raid, Kinney begged and borrowed from the Pan Am contractors still on the island and salvaged whatever he could from wrecked planes, knowing that "my life and the lives of others on the island might very well depend on how well we kept our planes performing." With Hamilton's untiring assistance, they "patched up bullet holes with scraps of sheet metal and self-tapping screws, spliced in new radio wires, and made what other repairs we could" to damaged F4F Wildcat number 8. Despite an unrepairable auxiliary gas tank and missing pieces of the Plexiglass hood, they managed to get it airworthy. With Wildcat 8 flyable, they looked to F4F number 9, though the "lack of maintenance manuals and proper tools made this more of a job than it should have been." Replacing the propeller motor, one blade, and the relay with salvaged parts, the pair made a fourth plane combat capable. As word of their efforts filtered throughout the island, contractors from the construction camp appeared with a large roll of electric wire, and Kinney was grateful, for it allowed him to keep "wiring [the planes] together."[12]

For the next two weeks, Kinney balanced his time between flying sorties over the island and keeping the four remaining Wildcats operational, aided by US Navy Aircraft Machinist Mate 1st Class James F. Hesson and civilian contractors experienced with tractor repair. Maintaining the remaining aircraft was a constant struggle. When damage to Wildcat 9's engine reduced the squadron from four aircraft to three, Kinney decided that instead of trying to diagnose Wildcat 9's problem, he would replace the engine and return it to service. The only challenge was cobbling together a "new" engine from two old ones. Using "the nose section of number 5 and the main section of number 2," he hoped to fabricate a single complete engine to go into Wildcat 9. Before he could complete the operation, however, the Japanese scored a direct hit on the revetment protecting Wildcat 10, damaging its tail. Kinney quickly abandoned plans for assembling a new engine from parts, instead extracting the undamaged engine from Wildcat 10 and installing it in number 9, a nine-hour-long project.[13] Major Putnam characterized Kinney's efforts as "magical," praising him and his crew of volunteer military and civilian mechanics saying:

> With almost no tools and a complete lack of normal equipment, they performed all types of repair and replacement work. They changed engines and propellers from one airplane to another, and even completely built up new engines and propellers from scrap parts salvaged from wrecks . . . all this in spite of the fact that they were working with new types [of aircraft] with which they had no previous experience and were without instruction manuals of any kind. . . . Their performance was the outstanding event of the whole campaign.[14]

Kinney was not the only one on Wake resorting to expedience to keep things operational. The squadron's ordnance officer, Capt. Herbert Freuler, was Kinney's equal when it came to improvisation. He discovered that the Army Air Corps bombs available to the squadron were incompatible with marine aircraft. "Scrounging around and adapting metal bands from [their] water-filled practice bombs to [their] racks," Freuler built a workable solution, testing the "Wake Model Band" a few days later in a practice run in the ocean east of the island. As the Japanese siege progressed, the marines ran short of oxygen for their two-plane squadron. To support high-altitude operations, Freuler built a makeshift coupling that allowed the transfer of oxygen from large commercial oxygen welding tanks to the smaller aircraft oxygen tanks. Although the process was dangerous due to differing tank pressure, "it was better than nothing."[15]

By the time the Japanese invaded Wake, only two serviceable F4F Wildcats remained. Lacking starter shells, "like shotgun shells but without the pellets," to crank the engine, Kinney fabricated a giant slingshot, made of two bands tied by rope to a leather boot that fit over the end of a propeller blade, improvising an elastic with pieces cut from truck tire inner tubes. To turn the plane's engine, ground crewmen pulled on ropes attached to the other end of the tire tubes, a "very effective" homemade starter system. After starting the planes on 22 December 1941 for Captain Freuler and Lt. Carl Davidson, only Freuler returned from the last mission over Wake Island. Wounded after shooting down two Japanese planes, he nursed his damaged plane back to the island, landing just before losing consciousness. VMF-211 had lost its last plane. Major Putnam soon detailed the remaining squadron personnel to the marine battalion to defend against the Japanese invasion. When navy W. Scott Cunningham, naval commander of American forces on Wake Island, made the fateful decision to surrender on 23 December, Kinney and Freuler became prisoners of the Japanese, though that did not prevent them from future demonstrations of American ingenuity while serving as incarcerated guests of the Emperor.[16]

Like those on Wake Island, Americans soldiers defending the Philippines quickly realized that when the Japanese invasion came, "you threw the book away—and did what you could with what you had."[17] Before the attack on Pearl Harbor, Americans on the islands, MacArthur included, realized that to mount a meaningful defense, it would be necessary to overcome years of unrealistic planning and bureaucratic indifference on the part of the War Department. In addition to General Brereton, MacArthur benefited from contributions made by Gen. Hugh J. Casey. The former engineer assistant to the Office of the Military Advisor to the Commonwealth Government of the Philippines, Casey had returned to the United States to manage construction of the future Pentagon before assuming duties as the USAFFE chief engineer in September 1941.[18] As

Japan-US relations deteriorated, the Philippine Department began preparing, recognizing that expedience and ingenuity might become the order of the day. When Japanese planes struck Clark and Nichols airfields and destroyed the B-17 bombers comprising the primary striking arm of the FEAF as well as their P-40 fighter escorts, the expendable defenders of the Southwest Pacific realized that resourcefulness would be an absolute necessity.[19]

General Brereton ordered 17th Pursuit Squadron (Provisional), from Darwin, Australia, to mount an air defense of the island of Java in January 1942. The squadron's fifty-day existence as a fighting force was one of constant improvisation.[20] Commanded by Capt. Charles A. Sprague, squadron mechanics kept the planes in the air with "cotter pins and ingenuity," in the absence of meaningful resupply.[21] When navy A-24 dive-bombers arrived, squadron crew chiefs became blacksmiths, hammering out supports to fit army machine guns on navy aircraft, and modifying navy bomb catches to hold army bombs.[22] Outnumbered from the outset, the intrepid members of the 17th Pursuit Squadron fought bravely until "their wings burned off," boasted that the squadron traded seventeen American aircraft for more than fifty Japanese planes and pilots, deprived the Japanese of over two hundred trained airmen, and bought valuable time for the defense of the Southwest Pacific.[23]

In the interim, General Casey and others worked improvisational miracles defending the Philippine archipelago. Casey mobilized a corps of civilian demolition experts, asking for volunteers from the mining engineers and demolition experts employed by private companies in the islands. Offering them direct military commissions (a nonstandard practice subject to later confirmation and approval), his demolition experts became known as "Casey's Dynamiters." The general soon deployed them on specific missions to destroy key bridges and vital transportation choke points throughout the islands. Operating independently but directed by either W. L. McCandlish of the Hercules Powder Company or forward forces of the Philippine Army Divisions, these former civilians performed a valuable service in slowing the Japanese advance toward Bataan.[24]

Casey also requisitioned explosives from the Philippines Bureau of Public Works and mining companies on the islands to manufacture improvised munitions. His antipersonnel "Casey Cookie" and the antitank "Casey Coffin" represented the "making of something out of nothing, the lighthearted pitting of American ingenuity and humor against the grim reality of the enemy's endless material resources."[25] The "Casey Cookie" started with a three- by six-inch segment of bamboo, filled with one-half of a 40 percent dynamite cartridge. Encased in shrapnel consisting of metal slugs, nails, and scraps of wire, it used a nonelectric blasting cap and a three-inch fuse for detonation. Carrying it on a belt clip fashioned out of number ten wire, soldiers using the grenade would light the fuse, then knowing the fuse would burn for ten to eleven seconds, they held the grenade for up to five seconds before throwing it in the direction of the enemy (they were specifically instructed not to throw it immediately because the enemy might pick up the grenade and throw it back).[26] "Casey's Coffins" were a bit more complex. Securing 20,000 small wooden boxes from a Manila factory, ordnance engineers packed each with four to five pounds of dynamite, adding a trigger rigged from an electric blasting cap, small flashlight battery, and electrical contacts. When an object of sufficient weight (two or more men) passed over a buried "Coffin," the wooden cover would collapse, causing the electrical contacts to close the circuit and the blasting cap to set off the dynamite.[27] Both of Casey's innovations became valuable additions to the meager arsenals maintained by US and Filipino troops in their fight against the Japanese. Engineers on the islands also manufactured 1,000 bolos from leaf springs taken from wrecked cars and trucks and built ground mounts for machine guns scavenged from damaged aircraft.[28]

Airmen who could still fly struggled to resist in the air. Before the 8 December Japanese attack, MacArthur prepared an airfield at Del Monte, on the Philippine island of Mindanao, for the 7th Bombardment Group. On 5 December, Brereton ordered sixteen B-17s of the 14th and 93rd Bomb Squadrons to relocate, saving them from destruction at the hands of the Japanese. The emergency airstrip soon became a rough staging area for attempts to counter the Japanese attacks elsewhere on the island. Ground maintainers worked miracles to keep the remaining B-17s airworthy. Equipped with only one ordnance and one welding truck, they accomplished much, fabricating aircraft parts, improvising .30- and .50-caliber machine-gun mounts, and repairing their own vehicles. The airmen at Del Monte demonstrated their constructive prowess in building the "six and seven eights," a vehicle built from "a Diamond-T motor and steering wheel, a Dodge front end, a Ford rear end, a Chevrolet cab, and an ordnance bed."[29] Airman John Henry Poncio of the 19th Bomb Squadron faced similar circumstances, though ultimately had less to show for it. In defending Bataan, his 220 squadron mates extracted all the machine guns from the remaining planes in their squadron. They mounted thirty-two .50-caliber and sixteen .30-caliber machine guns in ground positions, manning them in anticipation of the reinforcements, planes, and supplies they hoped would arrive "any day now."[30]

Expecting reinforcements from the United States, the Philippine defenders did all they could to maintain their weapons. On 22 December 1941, Lester Tenney of the 192nd Tank Battalion climbed into his M3 Stuart light tank and roared off with his company into the first US tank battle of World War II. During the engagement, a Japanese shell hit one of his platoon's tanks, ripping "out the rear

[and] through the motor, taking with it many important parts." Fortunately for its crew, the Japanese round failed to detonate. The tank continued running, allowing it to proceed with the rest of the battalion back to their bivouac. Throughout the night, lead mechanic Nick Fryziuk worked tirelessly, "using makeshift parts, tubes, gaskets, and rods, anything to get the tank to run again." Limping back to the fight, they were infuriated when they reached Bataan in mid-January, for as they were forced to improvise, the rear-echelon ordnance group had hoarded spare tank and half-track engines, tracks, guns, and other useful parts at the warehouse, releasing them only to the defenders of Bataan.[31]

US Navy sailors patrolling Philippine waters also manifested technical creativity. For Lt. John Bulkeley and the seamen manning the six boats of Motor Torpedo Squadron Three, ingenuity meant keeping their plywood boats seaworthy with whatever they had, taking the fight to the Japanese even if their fragile craft were held together by "brace and wires."[32] Scrambling as defensive positions became more precarious, the navy left behind a barge loaded with fifty-gallon drums of aviation-grade, 100 octane gasoline used in the three Packard motors powering each boat. Unfortunately, saboteurs had dissolved wax into the fuel, thus clogging fuel filters. Regulations dictated that boat engines were to be changed after every hundred hours of operation, but with supply lines cut, routine maintenance became limited to a rudimentary engine overhaul. The result was a "terrible job," one that "any tank-town garage which overhauls a flivver" would regard as unspeakable, particularly when it came to replacing gaskets. Lacking replacement parts or sealing compound, the PT boat mechanics made do, carefully removing the old engine gaskets "as gently as though they were precious lace," gingerly returning them into the reassembled engine. Scavenging and rebuilding along the way, Bulkeley and his men fought on until the Japanese destroyed all six boats in the squadron, reducing the seventy-eight-man detachment down to four effectives. Their "expendable" label notwithstanding, the squadron played a significant role in helping stave off the Japanese invasion, eventually performing its most important task by evacuating General MacArthur from the Philippines to Australia on 11 March 1942.[33]

Less than one month later, the defenders of the Philippines capitulated. For Lester Tenney, John Poncio, and the others fortunate enough to survive the Bataan Death March, they employed their creativity while prisoners of the Japanese. For other Americans already present or destined to serve in the Pacific theater of operations, they drew inspiration from the woeful tale of the beleaguered American defenders of the Philippines.

Shortly after the Japanese invaded China, Capt. Claire Chennault began building a command in the Far East with a solid reputation for ingenuity. In

April 1937, the former fighter pilot instructor at the Air Corps Tactical School and author of *The Role of Defensive Pursuit* resigned his commission to become aviation adviser and trainer to the Chinese as they struggled to build their own air force. The fall of Nanking changed the strategic picture.[34] Following the near-total destruction of the Chinese air force, Gen. Chiang Kai-shek proposed forming an American squadron to fly for China, tasking Chennault with providing assistance in forming the First American Volunteer Group (AVG) for Chinese service.[35] To form his "Flying Tigers," Chennault advertised the generous terms offered by the Chinese to Army Air Corps, Naval Air Service, and Marine Aviation Wing servicemen.[36] More than one hundred American fliers resigned from American military service and in May, June, and July of 1941 signed on as "contractors," employed along with a number of mechanics by the recently formed Central Aircraft Manufacturing Company (CAMCO). This maneuver allowed these Americans to circumvent the US government's official position of neutrality in the Second Sino-Japanese War.[37]

Traveling to the Far East on passports identifying them as "tourists, businessmen, acrobats, artists, embalmers, vaudeville actors, and everything else but what they were," American airmen eventually made their way to Toungoo, Burma, to assume operational control over one hundred Chinese-purchased aircraft assembled by CAMCO "technicians." The Curtiss P-40B Warhawk fighters originally designated for Sweden through a Lend-Lease arrangement lacked radios, bombsights, bomb racks, and drop tanks to extend their range. To render them combat effective, AVG crews applied a mix of ingenuity and improvisation, fabricating gunsights, bomb racks, and the means to attach external fuel tanks out of whatever bits and pieces they could find. Before entering combat, Chennault recalled "much of our effort during training and combat was devoted to makeshift attempts to remedy these deficiencies."[38] With aircraft production a far cry from the "dizzy wartime totals" that would characterize American industrial capability during World War II, those men who flew with the AVG simply made do with what they had.

The AVG fliers first took to the air on 20 December 1941, interdicting a Japanese bombing raid directed toward Kunming, China. During the next eight months, the Flying Tigers flew to defend Rangoon, Burma, and the Burma Road that stretched from there into China. Maintenance became the AVG's greatest challenge. By April 1942, they were down to "thirty-six planes fit for combat, with another thirty-nine in various states of repair and forty-one lost in combat or operational crack-ups."[39] With only twenty P-40Es arriving as replacements, AVG pilot Robert Moody Smith lamented that, throughout their experience in Burma and China, "we had no spare parts. . . . We steal from the wrecks to keep the other planes flying."[40]

Smith and his compatriots relied on AVG crew chiefs who, like the defenders of Wake Island, kept the Flying Tigers operational "with practically no equipment." Charles R. Bond Jr., vice squadron leader of the First Pursuit Squadron who devised the distinctive, shark-mouthed markings that adorned all AVG P-40s, praised these mechanical wizards as the real "guts of this outfit," a point echoed when *Life* magazine featured the group in March 1942.[41] Praising the "handful of American pilots" who purportedly downed three hundred Japanese planes over three months, photographer George Rodger's photo essay showcased the primitive operating conditions of the AVG. Working "under mango trees in Burma," the outfit's crew chiefs and armorers repeatedly demonstrated American ingenuity, "patching up their battered planes with hand tools and old materials."[42] Initially, Robert Smith led a group of Flying Tigers into Toungoo to "scrounge for tools at the local shops, for we needed screwdrivers, pliers, and all sorts of odds and ends."[43] When pilots returned home with battle-damaged aircraft, or had "too hot a landing," crew chiefs like Frank S. Losonsky, a Chicago Aeronautical University graduate recruited to the AVG in May 1941, used his tools to great effect, working around the clock to repair planes. Pulling engines from planes using homemade wooden tripods or "a thick tree branch," they salvaged all available parts, relegating what was left to their "boneyard," for as Losonsky explained, "we kept everything that wasn't rusty, burned, or badly damaged."[44]

Not only did they patch bullet holes and strip damaged and strafed "P-40s of as much salvageable equipment as they could," crew chiefs also increased lethality against Japanese infantry.[45] Armorers Roy Hoffman and Charley Baisden experimented with a variety of homemade bomb racks on the P-40Bs, going so far as to employ "whiskey bottles filled with gasoline pushing lead pipe bombs through the flare chutes." Claire Chennault even reported spending "many hours in our Kunming machine shop trying to fashion an external bomb rack that would work on a P-40B." Eventually, the arrival of twenty P-40Es gave the group the ability to drop 570 lb Russian high explosive bombs on the Japanese, though these field-improvised fighter-bombers failed to keep the Japanese from seizing Burma, which forced an eventual retreat into China.[46]

On 4 July 1942, the men of the AVG completed their contracts and received the option of joining 23rd Fighter Group. Chennault, reinstated as a major in the US Army Air Corps, was promoted to colonel three days later, before pinning on a brigadier general's star twelve days after that. He assumed command over all US Army air assets in China. Only a handful of the Flying Tigers followed their former commander into the new organization.[47] In the meantime, other Americans, no less heroic than Chennault's Flying Tigers, continued to employ American ingenuity in conducting the first raids against Imperial Japan's holdings in the Pacific.

The day after the Japanese attack on Pearl Harbor, US Army reservist Maj. James "Jimmy" Doolittle, who as a boy had used plans found in *Popular Mechanics* magazine to build a glider and a monoplane before securing his pilot's license, wrote his old friend and chief of US Army Air Forces Gen. Henry "Hap" Arnold requesting assignment to a tactical unit. As soon as Arnold received the letter, he picked up a phone and called the MIT-educated aeronautical engineer–turned Shell Petroleum Corporation aviation director. Within a few hours, Doolittle was inbound to Washington, DC, to receive a promotion to lieutenant colonel and a posting on Arnold's staff as a troubleshooter. Almost immediately, Arnold tasked the recent volunteer with "Special Aviation Project No. 1," ordering Doolittle to plan an American air raid on Japan and giving him less than four months to execute it.[48]

Before training for the mission began, Doolittle had to prove it was possible. Selecting the North American B-25B Mitchell medium bomber as the best raiding platform, he worked with aeronautical engineers at Wright Field in Dayton, Ohio, to determine specifications. Once calculated, he sent eighteen planes to Mid-Continent Airlines in Minneapolis, Minnesota, for extensive modifications. At Doolittle's instruction, technicians removed extraneous metal, gun turrets, and other fittings, replacing them with extra fuel tanks that combined could carry the additional 440 gallons of fuel needed for a flight to Japan. After successfully launching an army bomber off a navy carrier, Doolittle received approval to begin assembling the pilots and aircrew for the mission.[49]

Doolittle selected men from the 17th Bombardment Group to crew his mission. They were a diverse lot but shared two things in common: a desire to strike back at the Japanese, and the ability to adapt and innovate to achieve mission success. Doolittle named Capt. Ross Greening, who had successfully replaced the axle on his 1935 Plymouth after his wedding, the mission's armament officer. Greening soon concluded that the B-25 bomber's Norden bombsight was unusable for conducting a low-altitude bombing mission against Japan before ditching in China. Not only was the expensive bombsight highly classified, something that American airpower advocates did not want falling into the hands of either the Japanese or the Chinese, but it was designed for high-altitude bombing. Quickly realizing that "we needed a substitute," Greening worked with Sgt. Edward Bain, his assistant technician, to improvise an alternative.[50]

Utilizing a standard Norden mount, the pair fabricated a crude bombsight from twenty cents' worth of scrap aluminum. Named the "Mark Twain" for its resemblance to a Mississippi River paddle-wheeled steamer, the new bombsight consisted of two parts. First was a vertical five-inch by seven-inch piece of Dural aluminum plate, rounded at the top and mounted perpendicular to the Norden mount, inscribed with markings ten degrees apart on the arc's upper quadrant. To this, the pair screwed a sighting bar, crafted not unlike a rifle sight, with two V notches, capable of being pivoted at the center of the circular arc to correspond with the inscribed markings. As Greening explained, "All the bombardier had to do was pivot the horizontal plane and tell his pilot to steer to line up the target." In addition to the bombsight, Greening removed the twin machine guns mounted in the plane's tail, replacing them with painted broomsticks that "appeared larger than the twin .50 caliber machine guns in the top turret." The reduction allowed each plane to carry an additional 120 pounds of fuel on the mission.[51]

Doolittle oversaw nonstandard adjustments to the individual B-25s, employing engine experts at Eglin Air Base to retune the planes' carburetors to achieve maximum range, even if the new tolerances lay outside regulations. After one well-meaning mechanic requested authority to restore all planes back to standard, Doolittle sought assistance from General Arnold. Without revealing the nature of the mission, the chief of the Army Air Forces prohibited anyone from changing or replacing what they perceived to be defective or damaged parts on any of Doolittle's planes without notifying the project officer or supervisor, even if that meant violating existing regulations.[52]

Launched from the deck of the carrier *Hornet* in April 1942, Doolittle's raid, though significant psychologically, did little real damage to the Japanese home islands. By the time of the raid, Japanese forces were threatening Allied lines of communication between Hawaii and Australia. To divert Japanese attention and keep these lines open, recently named CINCPAC Adm. Chester W. Nimitz ordered naval aviators from the carriers *Enterprise*, *Lexington*, and *Yorktown* to target Japanese airfields in the northern Marshall Islands in January, more than two months before the Doolittle raiders launched their mission.[53] The efforts of these intrepid Grumman F4F Wildcat pilots flying these missions provide yet another example of American ingenuity in the early months of the war. Flying prewar planes mounted with older technology, the Wildcat pilots had no choice but to improvise. By mechanically modifying their aircraft, as well as developing new combat tactics allowing the employment of sturdy, yet outclassed aircraft against the faster and more aerobatic and nimble Japanese Zero, they overcame significant material and tactical shortcomings, in the process innovating to assist future naval and marine aviators.

When men like naval aviators Lt. Cdrs. Wade McClusky and John S. "Jimmy" Thach, Lt. E. H. Butch O'Hare, and Lt. j.g. James S. Gray received their initial squadron assignments, their Grumman F4F-3 Wildcats were no match for the Zero. Despite their rugged construction, the Wildcats lacked armor, bulletproof windscreens, reflector gunsights, and self-sealing fuel tanks, despite the fact that air combat in Europe had proven such additions invaluable. Upon entering combat, Wildcat pilots and mechanics scrambled to fabricate these combat improvements. To assist the pilots and crews assigned to the *Yorktown* in Naval Squadron VF-42, Lt. j.g. William N. Leonard and his assistant, Ensign Walter Haas, spent their last days stateside scouring facilities throughout San Diego for N2AN illuminated gunsights. Once in hand, squadron armorers improvised mounts to replace older telescopic gunsights with more modern versions, at the same time rearranging dials on instrument panels to increase functionality, a practice soon adopted in other squadrons.[54]

For the pilots of VF-6 aboard the carrier *Enterprise*, they addressed the lack of aircraft armor to protect the pilot while sailing from Hawaii to raid Japanese airfields and facilities in the northern Marshalls. Under the direction of engineer officer Lt. j.g. Roger Mehle, squadron engineers "acquired" three-eighths-inch metal boiler plate from the *Enterprise* engine room, fabricating shields that they welded to the pilot's seats. While each plate added approximately 135 pounds of weight to the aircraft, it offered protection to Wildcat pilots. When the five planes of VF-6 launched a dawn attack on the Japanese airfield on Taroa Island on 1 February, flight leader Lt. James Gray downed two Japanese aircraft, but in dogfighting on his way back to the *Enterprise*, his plane received between thirty and forty holes, making it look like "the moths had been at it in the attic." Gray himself reported that the jury-rigged armor saved his life, a point echoed in the *Enterprise*'s official report of the raid, which noted that "the armor plate in Lieut. [Gray's] plane stopped several hits which might otherwise have been fatal." As it was, he successfully nursed his plane back to the *Enterprise*, which was no small task given its nearly severed rudder cable.[55]

By March, newer F4F-4s began making their way into not only VF-6, but other naval fighter squadrons as well. The new planes had foldable wings that allowed for a greater number to fit on each carrier and came with factory-installed armor to protect pilots and additional .50-caliber machine guns in each wing. These additions, however, did little to enhance an individual plane's performance, as the Japanese Zero, though lacking self-sealing fuel tanks and pilot armor, and armed with only a pair of 7.7 mm machine guns, still outperformed the Wildcat in the air.[56]

To solve this dilemma, veteran naval aviator Lt. Cdr. Jimmy Thach innovated, developing the tactics that enabled two Wildcats to outmaneuver a Zero in flight. Joining VF-3 in June 1939 and later commanding the *Lexington*'s fighter squadron, Thach initially taught Lt. Butch O'Hare, another crack pilot in the squadron, everything he knew about flying. Reviewing a 1941 intelligence report that confirmed the Zero outperformed the Wildcat in nearly every category, the pair devised flying tactics to turn the tables in the Americans' favor. Using kitchen matches on his Coronado, California, dining room table to simulate aircraft positions, Thach determined that a standard three-plane formation, containing a lead and two wingmen, was too unwieldy against Zeros. Instead, he proposed four planes in two sections, with the two left planes watching the tails of the two planes on the right, and vice versa. If an enemy plane targeted one section, the other section would wait until the enemy nearly had their partner pair in range before making a sharp turn in the direction of the attack. The quick turn served to alert the first pair of the impending attack. If the enemy aircraft broke to follow the turning section, this brought him into the guns of the other section; if it remained, it came under fire from the second. After developing the concept, Thach tested it with his own Wildcats, leading one combat section of four planes at half power, with O'Hare leading another four at full power, to simulate the superiority of the Zero. After sufficient practice with each group, it became clear that even with superior performance, the sudden turn by one section and subsequent pursuit by the attacker almost always brought the enemy under fire from the other section's guns. The sudden turn, coupled with the constant weaving back and forth, gave the underpowered American aircraft the advantage, a maneuver that worked in both theory and combat. Forwarding this new development on to Commander, Aircraft, Battle Force (ComAirBatFor), Thach initially recommended that all squadrons adopt the weave as a defensive tactic. ComAirBatFor was initially reticent, clinging to the prewar three-plane standard.[57]

Thach's recommendation notwithstanding, not all Wildcat pilots mastered the maneuver prior to the Battle of Midway. The men of the *Enterprise* VF-6 missed the Battle of the Coral Sea, as their carrier escorted the *Hornet* on the Doolittle raid. By the same token, some of the pilots from VF-42 who transitioned to VF-3 and the *Yorktown* prior to the showdown at Midway had not been briefed on the maneuver. John Lovelace, who had learned the maneuver as Jimmy Thach's XO in VF-3, was tragically killed when another plane from the *Yorktown* crashed into his on 30 May 1942 before he could pass the maneuver on to his new squadron.[58] The Battle of Midway, the climactic carrier battle of the Pacific, proved the value of the maneuver, and by October 1942 ComAirBatFor realized that a two-plane section represented a significant improvement over prewar carrier-based air doctrine and endorsed the "Thach Weave" as the "only way" for Wildcat pilots to engage the aeronautically superior Japanese Zero.[59]

While the "Thach Weave" represented a successful tactical addition to the arsenal of American Wildcat pilots, it did not prevent others from making further technological improvements to their aircraft. Considering that any extra minute in the air greatly enhanced the effectiveness of carrier-based air, Pearl Harbor–based technicians at the direction of Adm. William F. Halsey eventually developed a functional drop tank for the F4F. These engineers bypassed the cumbersome Bureau of Aeronautics, completing the development of an ersatz forty-two-gallon "tub-like" tank attachment and strapping it to an F4F-4 before testing. Jimmy Thach put the newly burdened F4F-4 through its paces, reporting that the tank added between three and five hours flight time, invaluable for future strike missions.[60] When Thach's VF-6 received eight new planes on 27 May, one came with the new drop tank, with instructions to convert the other seven planes once authorized by the Bureau of Aeronautics. Anticipating their use in the future, the squadron received fifty-four modified drop tanks.[61]

Naval engineers at the Pearl Harbor dockyard also had the opportunity to prove their worth as technical improvisers, working under altogether different circumstances. During the Battle of the Coral Sea, Japanese planes targeted the aircraft carrier USS *Yorktown*, scoring one direct hit and a number of near misses.[62] The sole direct hit penetrated the flight deck fifteen feet inboard of the carrier's command and control center "island," passing through three more decks before detonating in the fourth level, killing forty-four sailors and causing significant damage. The most significant near miss exploded off the port side, ripping hull plating and rivets apart. The near miss did more damage than the direct hit, as it significantly compromised the *Yorktown*'s seaworthiness.[63] In a herculean effort, the crew brought fires under control while damage control parties limited the flooding. After restoring flight operations, engineers managed to coax twenty-four knots from damaged boilers. Before turning and limping back toward Pearl Harbor, not only did the *Yorktown* recover its own aircraft, but it recovered many from the *Lexington*, which the Japanese sank in the battle.[64]

Before the crippled *Yorktown* returned to Pearl Harbor, Cdr. Joseph Rochefort and codebreakers at "Station Hypo" in Hawaii, convinced CINCPAC of Japanese designs on the Midway Islands. Realizing that time was of the essence, Nimitz knew that despite the damage suffered at Coral Sea, the *Yorktown* must be returned to service as quickly as possible, and in much less than the ninety days estimated by Adm. Aubrey Fitch, who commanded the *Lexington* and *Yorktown* in the battle. Admiral Nimitz's call for the *Yorktown* to return to service in less than three days demanded extensive technical ingenuity on the part of the Pearl Harbor engineers, as true repair work could not be done. For American naval engineers anticipating the return of the damaged *Yorktown* into Pearl, improvisation became their norm.[65]

In repairing the *Yorktown*, workers cut corners to speedily restore combat effectiveness, embracing expedients in place of long, costly, and regulation repairs. The need for a quick fix prevented riveting new plates over damaged portions of the hull, as riveting was laborious and time-consuming. The use of lap welds to secure new plates to compromised sections of the *Yorktown*'s hull allowed her return to service more quickly, but these were only a temporary fix, as another near miss could reopen the repaired section. Welding represented a significant compromise to integrity, as engineers secured the rivets by "ring welding" around the base of a rivet, rather than peening a hot rivet solidly into the (now) mechanically joined plate. Despite yielding a weaker joint, welding was much faster, as riveting required a four-man rivet repair team instead of a single welder. In addition to welded repairs to the hull, hundreds of men labored throughout the carrier, replacing damaged sections of internal framing at breakneck speed. Instead of carefully measuring damaged portions, drafting blueprints, and reconstructing damaged portions through the aid of plans and sketches, one team simply cut out damaged portions of the internal bulkheads. After fabricating wooden patterns, they hustled them to repair shops throughout Pearl Harbor where a second team of steel fabricators crafted replacements. Once completed, technicians manhandled the new steel aboard and welded it into place.[66] After a frenetic forty-eight hours of work involving hundreds of welders, hull technicians, and electricians, the *Yorktown* slid out of drydock and back into the waters of Pearl Harbor at 0900 on 31 May 1942, with the flight deck ready for aircraft, the hull watertight, and all systems functional—though not all were at 100 percent, as three of the ship's nine boilers remained inoperable. The "interim patch-up job," a product of American ingenuity bred out of necessity, rendered the *Yorktown* combat capable as American naval forces in the Pacific moved to counter the Japanese offensive against Midway.[67]

The Battle of Midway was barely over before the US Joint Chiefs of Staff began exploiting the victory. While the US Pacific Fleet had inflicted a serious blow, the Imperial Japanese Navy still threatened communication between Hawaii and Australia. To remedy this situation, CNO and commander in chief of the US fleet Adm. Ernest J. King, along with CINCPAC (Admiral Nimitz) and Vice Adm. Robert L. Ghormley, commander of the South Pacific Forces, directed an offensive into the Southwest Pacific. Their order, "Joint Directive for Offensive Operations in the Southwest Pacific Area Agreed upon by the United States Chief of Staff," issued on 2 July 1942, outlined a three-phase operation to both secure communication lines and mitigate any tension between the army and the navy. Admiral Nimitz received authority for Phase One, directed toward the islands of Santa Cruz, Tulagi, and the Lower Solomons (placing the latter into the admiral's area of authority in the South Pacific). General MacArthur maintained authority over the Southwest Pacific, to direct Phase Two, the retaking of the remainder of the Solomons and New Guinea, with the capture of Rabaul, New Britain, and New Ireland effectively grouped into Phase Three.[68]

Recognizing the need to protect the all-valuable line of communication between Australia and Hawaii, American leaders in the Pacific mounted an offensive toward Guadalcanal, carefully balancing the operational requirements of this Pacific offensive against the established primacy of the war in Europe. Code-named Operation Watchtower, the invasion of Guadalcanal by Gen. Alexander A. Vandegrift's 1st Marine Division quickly acquired the nickname "Operation Shoestring," owing to both the meager resources allocated to the invasion and the improvised nature of the campaign. With American success in the Southwest Pacific contingent on the ability to establish air superiority over islands in the Southwest Pacific, Watchtower planners targeted the Japanese airfield currently under construction on Guadalcanal. By capturing it, King, Ghormley, and Nimitz hoped that American land-based air assets could threaten Japanese holdings, particularly the air base on Rabaul.[69]

The American campaign to seize Guadalcanal was, at every step, one of improvisation. The marine invaders; the marine, army, and naval aviators of the "Cactus Air Force" flying out of newly enlarged Henderson Field and elsewhere; and the sailors who fought the Japanese in the Solomon Sea and down the New Georgia Sound (popularly known as the "Slot") simply had to make do with what they had in their efforts to achieve success. Strung out along a shoestring of an American supply line, the campaign gradually devolved into a battle of attrition, improvising, innovating, and making do with less, from which American forces emerged weary, but nevertheless victorious.

The first to face these challenges were the US Marines. Tasked with the first major amphibious operation of World War II, the beach landings on Guadalcanal provided the opportunity to test amphibious doctrine developed during the interwar period. Victor Croizat, a 1940 Syracuse University graduate commissioned into the Marine Corps via the Reserve Officer Training Corps, had received his assignment to the 1st Amphibious Tractor Battalion the day after the Japanese attacked Pearl Harbor. Anticipating that "knowing the book was the way to get ahead," he quickly discovered that the Landing Vehicle Tracked, or LVT, also known as the amphtrac, was "too new and untried to feature in any publications." Lieutenant Croizat worked to discover the LVT's capabilities and limitations, a process that "invited initiative and led to commands beyond what could normally have been expected." Testing amphibious operations with the planning and conduct of the Guadalcanal landings, he further honed his skills on Tarawa, Saipan, Tinian, and Iwo Jima, earning the rank of major by the end of the war.[70]

On the morning of 7 August 1942, Vandegrift's 11,000 marines stormed Beach Red, a 1,600-yard stretch of shoreline on the north side of Guadalcanal. Surprising 2,000 Japanese construction workers and a few soldiers, the Leathernecks secured the beach and consolidated their position. Moving inland the next day, they seized the unfinished airfield, renamed it Henderson Field, and began improvements, using abandoned Japanese equipment to complete and extend the airstrip. Advancing toward the Tenaru River, Col. Leroy P. Hunt of the 5th Marine Regiment saw the value of the river as a defensive position, but recognized that the river itself served as a barrier to effective inland resupply from the beach. Meeting with Croizat well before the landings, Hunt, a World War I veteran, asked about alternatives. In an ingenious stroke, Croizat ordered three amphtracs into the riverbed, decking them over with wooden planking, effectively transforming the vehicles into a serviceable bridge to facilitate both resupply and reinforcement from the beach.[71] Elsewhere on Guadalcanal, Capt. William Gray offered experiments his men had pioneered in the movement of field artillery in the absence of prime movers, first with a "snow-plow toboggan," and later with an improvised third wheel fabricated in the field.[72]

After the landings, seven Japanese cruisers and one destroyer sailed from New Britain and New Ireland down through the "Slot" to interdict American resupply efforts. The ensuing Battle of Savo Island, fought during the night of 9 August, represented one of the greatest defeats in US naval history, with one Australian and three American cruisers lost out of a total engaged force of five cruisers and seven destroyers.[73] In the battle's aftermath, Adm. Richard K. Turner withdrew the American ships supporting the invasion, leaving the marines ashore to their own devices. With the Japanese landing reinforcements at night, the marines on Guadalcanal anticipated a daily resupply, hoping that American craft could avoid Japanese aircraft attacking from Rabaul and elsewhere. These daytime resupply efforts, however, came to be greatly aided by the presence of the American aircraft stationed at Henderson Field.

Following the 20 August arrival of nineteen Grumman F4F Wildcats of VMF-223 and twelve Douglas SBD Dauntless torpedo bombers of VMSB-232 from the escort carrier *Long Island*, American air interdiction efforts, coupled with the requisite maintenance, logistical, and support functions of the Guadalcanal-based Cactus Air Force, were built on a foundation of creativity and innovation. With the initial contingent of marine aircraft bolstered by five US Army Bell P-400 Airacobras of the 67th Pursuit Squadron arriving on 22 August, and strengthened further by naval aircraft from the carriers *Saratoga* and *Enterprise* ordered to reinforce Guadalcanal (at one point landing at dusk aided by a makeshift lighting system of jeep headlights and flashlights), those aircraft became a joint force that eventually comprised sixty-four aircraft of various types. The constant defensive counterair operations mounted against attacking Japanese aircraft, coupled with interdiction and close air support sorties to aid marines on the ground, strained the aircraft maintainers at Henderson Field. In this battle of attrition, the pilots of the Cactus Air Force benefited greatly from the technical ingenuity of American mechanics on the ground. These wizards repaired damaged planes with whatever parts were available, and when they deemed a plane no longer airworthy, they relegated the damaged plane to the Henderson Field "boneyard," where it became a source of spare parts for other aircraft. In at least one case, Lt. DeWitt "Pete" Peterkin and navy mechanics of Torpedo Squadron Eight successfully "built" a TBF Avenger from parts scrounged from no fewer than five other aircraft, something the Japanese seemed incapable of doing, at least to Americans on the ground. As Fred Hitchcock, a ground crewman from the Fifth Air Force, later observed when inspecting Clark Field, the Philippines, after it had been retaken by US troops in 1945, "The Japanese didn't seem to have a coordinated salvage effort. I was on the detail that tried to reorganize the mess. One plane might be lacking a carburetor when another one, a hundred yards away, had a carburetor. But they never had the coordinated effort to pool the parts and get the maximum number of planes up."[74]

Even pilots not flying attack aircraft sought out-of-the-box solutions to keep operations on track. After Brig. Gen. Roy Geiger assumed command of the Cactus Air Force on 3 September, his aide and pilot, Maj. Jack Cram, utilized the general's private Consolidated PBY Catalina flying boat, the *Blue Goose*, to fly in "everything from toilet paper to beans" to resupply the island with essentials. Delivering a pair of torpedoes for use by the pilots of Torpedo Squadron Eight, he discovered that the squadron's TBF Avengers had been damaged in a Japanese raid. Cram soon theorized that if he could mount the torpedoes on the general's PBY and rig up a manual release, he could use the ungainly flying boat to attack Japanese troop transports reinforcing Guadalcanal. With General Geiger's approval, Cram mounted torpedoes on the *Blue Goose*, and on 14 October, the major had a group of Japanese transports putting troops ashore near Tassafarongo Point, on the north shore of the island thirteen miles from Henderson Field, in his sights. In a long glide from an altitude of 6,000 feet, Cram brought the unwieldly seaplane on an attack vector toward a pair of Japanese transports, then launched his two torpedoes. One missed, but the other struck its target, and it exploded and sank the craft. Under attack by enemy aircraft, Cram returned the *Blue Goose* to base, although in his escape, the Japanese hit the lumbering seaplane more than fifty times. Reporting to General Geiger, Cram's commander feigned anger upon hearing the report of his damaged plane but quickly heaped praise on Cram for his "damn fine job"; Geiger subsequently decorated his pilot with the Navy Cross.[75]

Cram's attack took place at a critical point in the Guadalcanal campaign, with marines trapped on the island and US forces unable to resupply them as a result of continued Japanese air attacks. These dire straits forced other craft to support the troops on Guadalcanal, with the destroyer and seaplane tender *McFarland* being tasked with transporting torpedoes, 37 mm ammunition, and 40,000 gallons of gasoline for use by the island's defenders—and in the course of her mission providing yet another example of American ingenuity. Anchoring off Lunga Point on 16 October, the crew, under the command of USN Lieutenant Commander John C. Alderman began discharging the *McFarland*'s volatile cargo while taking on 160 walking wounded when nine enemy dive-bombers dove on the stationary craft. Although the ship's gunners downed one Japanese plane and damaged another, one enemy dive-bomber managed to score a direct hit on the ship's fantail, destroying the depth charge racks and rudder. The *McFarland*'s crew suffered twenty-seven killed and twenty-eight wounded. As damage control parties extinguished fires and restored power to the engines, the ship's engineers could only coax five knots as they steamed toward Tulagi, and this was only possible by running the damaged port engine astern and the starboard engine ahead. The next day, Alderman steered the *McFarland* to an anchorage at the mouth of the Maliali River on Florida Island in the Solomons. The crew camouflaged the damaged vessel with branches and vines while others raided an abandoned Japanese seaplane base for materials to repair the rudder. Crewmen scrounged steel and telephone poles to use in their repairs. Three weeks later, they weighed anchor and steamed to Espiritu Santo, Vanuatu, confident that the naval base they had established on nearby Tulagi Island would remain operational for the remainder of the campaign.

By December, the Imperial Japanese Navy began withdrawing from Guadalcanal, though fierce fighting continued into early 1943. Nonetheless, the campaign's conclusion marked the beginning of the end of the war against Japan, as US forces in the Pacific never again faced trials and tribulations to the extent they had throughout the course of the six-month Guadalcanal campaign. Although many islands remained to be retaken, and the war against Japan would last another two and a half years, the fighting after Guadalcanal took on an altogether different character, largely as a result of increased resources available to US forces in the Pacific.

As the Guadalcanal campaign was drawing to a close, President Franklin Roosevelt and Prime Minister Winston Churchill met half a world away to discuss the future course of World War II. The Casablanca Conference defined future Allied strategy against both Germany and Japan. Although Soviet premier Joseph Stalin did not attend, the results of the conference were of direct interest to the Soviets, as the western Allies outlined future plans against Germany in hopes of forcing the Wehrmacht to withdraw forces from the eastern front. With Churchill winning out by advancing his "soft underbelly" strategy, calling for invasions of Sicily and Italy in advance of a cross-channel invasion of northern France, Roosevelt countered, calling for increased efforts to drive the Japanese from New Guinea, together with reopening the supply line between China and Burma.

With Roosevelt announcing "unconditional surrender" as the Allies' demand, logistical concerns dominated future diplomatic wrangling among them. By the time the two Anglo-American leaders met in Morocco, the United States was well on its way to becoming the "Arsenal of Democracy," though that did not mean that the United States had unlimited productive potential. True, the first two years of the war against Japan would be defined by want, and the constant need to improvise and make use of what was readily available, but by the end of the Guadalcanal campaign, the industrial power of the United States began producing enough to allow American ingenuity to take on a new form. This industrial capacity, coupled with conscious decisions made before the war had even begun, soon provided US servicemen with the opportunity to combine technical savvy with an indomitable spirit.

CHAPTER 3

Innovating around the Mediterranean

There will be shortages in equipment, for example. These are being made good as rapidly as possible, but so long as they exist, they are a challenge to your ingenuity and not an invitation to fall back on an overdose of close order drill and the other necessary but stultifying minutia which so irked the Army of 1917 that we still suffer from the repercussions. . . . Warfare today is a thing of swift movement. . . . It is not a game for the unimaginative plodder.

—Gen. George C. Marshall

On 11 December 1941, Adolf Hitler declared war on the United States, and the United States Congress responded in kind. The next month, President Franklin Roosevelt and British prime minister Winston Churchill met to outline Anglo-American war plans, which would be refined at Casablanca a year later. Establishing a "Germany First" strategy, the pair agreed to form a combined chiefs of staff in Washington, DC, embraced unity of command in all theaters of war, and settled command and supply decisions. Finally, they pledged an Anglo-American invasion of North Africa in 1942, followed by landings in Sicily and Italy.[1]

Early American operations in the Mediterranean were guarded, yet even in these hesitant first steps, American ingenuity manifested itself repeatedly. Advancing the Germany First strategy, the invasion of North Africa and the ensuing Mediterranean campaign showcased mass production in concert with the ingenuity and technical ability of the American GI.[2] Limited as they were by material shortcomings, when the US Army liberated Rome, it was difficult to find an American unit that had not demonstrated "Yankee ingenuity." Once the US military took prewar preparedness, training, and production into combat, it was only a matter of time before US forces blended their technical creativity with the overwhelming material production of the "arsenal of democracy" on the march toward victory in Europe.

Seven months before Operation Torch, the US War Department replaced General Headquarters Army (GHQ) with US Army Ground Forces (AGF), the Army Air Forces (AAF), and Services of Supply (later the Army Service Forces). US Army chief of staff Gen. George C. Marshall assigned Lt. Gen. Lesley J. McNair to command the AGF.[3] As a field artillery officer with more than thirty years' experience, McNair was the perfect choice to oversee the most dramatic expansion of the US Army in history. His talents regarding technical innovation, unit organization and training, and doctrinal development paid tremendous dividends to the US Army between the announcement of his posting as chief of staff, GHQ, and his ensuing role as commander of AGF prior to his fateful death during Operation Cobra in July 1944.

In one of his first moves as US Army chief of staff, General Marshall implemented a planned reorganization of the regular army divisional structure that had been more than a decade in the making. On 16 September 1939, Marshall announced the replacement of the older "square division" built for trench warfare, with 20,000 men organized into two brigades of two regiments each, by a more mobile and effectively manned "triangular division" of three regiments each, augmented by divisional artillery and reconnaissance units. Borrowing the tripartite structure from the Germans, each division (and the regiments therein, which also had been restructured into three battalions with regimental mortars and machine guns) possessed three maneuver elements plus an element of fire support. This not only allowed for greater mobility, control, and supply, but also permitted each echelon—be it at the divisional, regimental, or battalion level—simultaneously to establish a base of fire against the enemy, with the three maneuver elements either fixing the enemy in position, securing the flank, or being held in reserve.[4]

Marshall quickly looked to McNair, whose experience and administrative talents made him well suited in transitioning to the "triangular" division. Promoted to brigadier general in January 1937, McNair oversaw the training, equipment receipt, and consolidation of units that made up the initial "Proposed Infantry Division" (PID), organized at Fort Sam Houston, Texas, beginning later that March. As chief of staff of the new division, McNair directed organization, training, and tests of companies, battalions, and regiments, as well as divisional assembly and combat team tests, culminating in the evaluation of the entire division. In the process, McNair gave considerable attention to unit and motorization requirements and weapons needs, so that by the time the PID had completed its initial testing and Chief of Staff Marshall adopted the triangular division as the new standard for infantry divisions in the US Army, no one in the service was as familiar with the new structure as Brig. Gen. Lesley J. McNair.[5]

Marshall then tasked McNair with preparing the US Army for war, though in doing so, what he created was markedly different from the force outlined in the 1941 Victory Program, the initial plan for American involvement in World War II.[6] Anticipating support for a collapsing Soviet Union, Lt. Col. Alfred C. Wedemeyer's initial mobilization plan envisioned a massive American ground force of 215 divisions, though the Russian victory over the Germans at Stalingrad, coupled with concerns over potential American productive capability (even with material reductions made during McNair's evaluation of the PID), led to significant manpower cuts. By the time McNair assumed command of the AGF in March 1942, the force he directed consisted of the ten existing regular army infantry divisions, eighteen extant National Guard infantry divisions, and the single infantry division of the Hawaii-based Army of the United States, along with the regular army 1st and 2nd Cavalry Divisions, the 1st through 4th Armored Divisions, and 5th Armored Division of the Army of the United States.[7] Once at wartime strength and combat ready, these units became the core of US forces in the North African, Sicilian, and Italian campaigns.[8]

Before US landings in North Africa, McNair planned to raise thirty-five additional divisions, twenty-six of them infantry, though by the end of 1942, modification of the mobilization program resulted in the formation of thirty-eight divisions—nine armored, two airborne, and twenty-seven infantry. In the next year (1943), the US Army fielded another seventeen divisions, eleven of which were infantry. By the end of World War II, these units came together in the "Ninety Division Gamble," an army composed of ninety divisions built not around manpower, but around mechanization and mobility, which, when coupled with the ability to learn and innovate, proved sufficient for the United States to make a meaningful contribution to victory in World War II.[9]

The old infantry divisions of the regular army (constituted and activated before September 1940) as well as those of the National Guard (federalized between September 1940 and November 1941) transitioned to the new triangular divisional structure and trained in accordance with the peacetime standards built around the barracks life of the all-volunteer force.[10] The "invaluable leaven" of these "experienced officers and noncommissioned officers" stood "ready in technical knowledge" to effectively "unify the various elements of our professional and citizen soldiers into a great Army of the United States."[11] The 1940 Selective Service Act, which increased the US Army to 375,000 men, and President Roosevelt's 16 September federalization of the National Guard dramatically changed the manpower base of the peacetime army.[12] In short order, the prewar regulars and guardsmen were overwhelmed by volunteers and draftees as the United States eventually fielded the largest army in its history. On the way to a strength of 1,685,403 men by December 1941, the army continued to grow in size until reaching a peak strength of 8,266,373 in July 1945.[13]

This influx of citizens into uniform was accompanied by a purge of hundreds of officers who underperformed in the GHQ Maneuvers, prewar exercises held in September 1941 in East Texas and Louisiana for the purpose of evaluating the officers and men and effectiveness of new divisional structures. By the end of these exercises, General Marshall ordered the outright relief, reassignment, or retirement of thirty-one of forty-two corps or divisional commanders. The forced departure of National Guard officers represented a greater challenge, as their relief tended to be more contentious and, considering their political connections, much more public. In addition to the relief of the regular officers, Marshall ordered the retirement or discharge of 269 officers serving in the National Guard or Army Reserve, which together with those who were reassigned to noncombat roles totaled nearly 600 officers.[14]

In November 1941, noted newspaper columnist Walter Lippmann praised not only General Marshall and the War Department, but American society writ large in readying this "New Army" for an altogether different kind of war. Recognizing that this force represented "a complex organization of small teams of men each based on a tank, an armored car, a plane, or some other moving piece of apparatus," and that higher leadership involved "large-scale highly technical engineering," the nation's new soldiers were of an altogether different character. They were, "to an astonishing degree, dispersed and individualized and compelled to rely on their own initiative and resources." With respect to producing men who possessed such characteristics, Lippmann noted that the United States was without peer. In American society, "young men are used from childhood to motors and radios and traffic and to most of the equipment they handle and to the problems of supply and maintenance." Transitioning from peace to war, they were "already in their natural element, and the problem of making an army is the problem of developing sufficient officers who understand the military use of these civilian aptitudes."[15]

As seen previously, Pearl Harbor brought American traits of mechanical ingenuity and innovation into sharper focus. Once President Roosevelt and Prime Minister Churchill endorsed the Germany First strategy, GIs in the United States anticipated combat operations against the German armored juggernaut, often embracing expedient to complete their missions. Few entities embodied this knack for both technical and intellectual improvisation as much as the Tank Destroyer Center established at Camp Hood, Texas, on 21 August 1942. Upon Chief of Staff Marshall's decision to place all responsibility for antitank affairs under the War Department General Staff's G-3 division (instead of delegating it to one of the combat arms), General McNair began developing a tank destroyer force concentrated at the corps and army, rather than the divisional, level. Believing (albeit falsely) that the enemy would concentrate armor and utilize it like cavalry of old, McNair advocated a doctrine centered around "counterattack in the same general manner as against the older forms of attack"—that is, massing tank destroyers to counter tanks—as it was "poor economy to use a $35,000 medium tank to destroy another tank when the job can be done by a gun costing a fraction as much."[16]

To implement this vision, McNair turned to Lt. Col. Andrew D. Bruce, the first commander of the Tank Destroyer Center. Integrating lessons learned from the Louisiana Maneuvers, Bruce, formerly of the War Department's G-3 Planning Branch, took the lead in developing both doctrine and weapons systems to counter massed panzer forces. Adopting mass, mobility, firepower, and aggressiveness as the requisite characteristics for a successful tank destroyer corps, the first tank destroyers were best described as studies in expediency, combining a variety of readily available components into makeshift weapons systems. During the summer of 1941, the G-3 Planning Branch mounted a 75 mm gun on an M3 half-track, employing a handful of these so-designated M3 tank destroyers during the Louisiana Maneuvers. Similarly, technicians mounted a 37 mm antitank gun on the back of a three-quarter-ton Dodge truck with minimal armor or shielding, designating the result the M-6 tank destroyer until a light armored car could be developed. In crafting FM 18-5, *Organization and Tactics of Tank Destroyer Units*, Bruce highlighted such units' mobility and firepower, unwittingly setting the new tank destroyer units up for failure. In developing doctrine, he assumed that tank destroyers would execute their mission with benefit of effective intelligence, road priority, and favorable field conditions, while facing massed enemy armor that operated alone and not as part of a combined arms team. This offensive spirit featured prominently in the August 1943 *Popular Mechanics* article "Tank Busters." If operators of these fast, lightly armored tank destroyers lost their vehicles to enemy fire, these courageous and aggressive "stealthy hunters" used Molotov cocktails and "sticky bombs"—grenades stuffed in socks and slathered with axle grease or heavy oil—against enemy armor. With "accurate arms trained in America's sandlot baseball fields," these elite troops could "act more like Indians as they slither from cover to cover," stalking their armored prey.[17]

Troops emboldened by this sense of reckless bravado trained at the Tank Destroyer Center, the 1st and 3rd Infantry Divisions, the 1st and 2nd Armored

Divisions, the 1st Ranger Battalion, and elements of the 9th Infantry Division prepared for the assault on the North African coast. Living the virtues extolled by Walter Lippmann in describing the new American army, they girded for war, rejecting much of the old, prewar inertia as "normal channels of administration were abandoned."[18]

GIs demonstrated mechanical ingenuity and knack for innovation before leaving the United States. Readying for North Africa, the 2nd Armored Division organized landing teams of two light tank companies, an armored infantry company, an artillery battery, two engineer battalions, and a reconnaissance platoon. As training progressed, the armored infantry company struggled to keep their M3 half-tracks operational, as the vehicle's stationary rear idler spindle did not bend or give. While effective on roads and smooth surfaces, cross-country operational testing often resulted in thrown tracks or damaged suspension components. With these shortcomings, troops feared unarmored trucks would replace their half-tracks. Familiar with the M3's tracks and the design and function of a Caterpillar tractor, ordnance officer 1st Lt. Thomas Hauss and M.Sgt. Gerry Noble engineered a solution. Realizing that a commercially available eyebolt, nut, and coil spring would fix the problem, they took their solution to the 41st Armored Infantry Regiment's commander, Col. Sidney Hinds, who purchased parts and tested the modified M3. After a successful trial, Hinds took the solution to Lt. Col. Frederick Crab, the 2nd Armored Division's ordnance officer, who elevated the proposed solution to divisional commander Maj. Gen. Ernest N. Harmon. Instantly realizing the modification's value, Harmon approved the purchase of the parts, and in short order, all the M3s in the division (and future M3s and other variants manufactured for the army) could traverse rough terrain without fear of breakdown, greatly enhancing the mobility of American ground forces.[19]

Although the oft-maligned M3 half-track became the foundation for a host of variants (like the M3 tank destroyer), it was not the most significant mechanical platform used by US servicemen. According to famed war columnist Ernie Pyle, three vehicles "stood out above all others" in North Africa: the jeep, the 2.5-ton truck, and the Douglas DC-3. As uniquely American contrivances, all became test platforms for the American soldier, subject to modifications to either make them more effective or provide features that standard models lacked. All three vehicles appear in the opening pages of Gen. Omar N. Bradley's postwar memoir, *A Soldier's Story*. Their inclusion, along with specific modifications mentioned regarding each, provide insight into how American servicemen practiced mechanical ingenuity. Opening in Sicily in September 1943, Bradley's memoir begins with him sitting on a "foam rubber seat that had been scrounged from a German Mark IV tank in

Northern Tunisia," when he is buzzed by an observation plane that landed with a message to call Gen. George S. Patton in Palermo. Returning to the II Corps command post, Bradley went to his headquarters, a "caravan-truck ordnance had built me on the chassis of a 2½ ton truck." Within this custom vehicle, he had not only "cramped quarters but an office" outfitted "like a small ship's cabin with plumbing and fittings that had been ransacked from Oran and Algiers." Furthermore, he noted that "what scroungers had been unable to locate, ordnance had turned out in its mobile machine shops." Ringing Patton on the phone, he received a summons to meet with General Eisenhower at his command post, with Patton sending his C-47 to shuttle him to the meeting. When Bradley and Patton left to meet Eisenhower the next day, they boarded a "battle-weary bucket seater from Troop Carrier Command," for which the pilot had "scrounged two sway-backed, overstuffed chairs and wired them to the cargo rings on the floor." Their presence caused Patton to quip, "Real class . . . I wonder where in hell he swiped 'em."[20]

Bradley's mention of these vehicles indicates how far the US military had progressed in eleven months at war. When the first US troops stormed ashore on the North African coast in November 1942, improvising a softer jeep seat was the last thing on their minds. Instead, inexperienced GIs flopped down on cold, wet beaches and imagined the fight ahead of them. Scattered from Safi to Algiers, the troops of the Western, Center, and Eastern Task Forces and their British allies had clearly defined objectives. After establishing a defensible beachhead, they would secure control over French Morocco and Algeria, then move eastward, pinning Field Marshal Erwin Rommel's Afrika Korps against British Field Marshal Bernard Law Montgomery's Eighth Army driving west toward Tunisia from Egypt.[21]

The untested American troops came ashore with no combat experience, though as the campaign progressed "men and machines both passed their shakedown period in this war."[22] As US forces established their lodgment, American war machines differentiated them from both the French troops who broke with the Third Reich and their German adversaries. When GIs first began assembling jeeps in North Africa, it took ordnancemen twenty-five minutes to uncrate and assemble a single jeep. Eventually, they reduced assembly time to ten minutes. To foreign soldiers, the jeep became synonymous with the GI identity in North Africa. One French soldier, guarding a crossroads on a dark night, challenged a group of soldiers who approached his post on foot. Readying his submachine gun, the Frenchman asked them to identify themselves, and when they responded that they were Americans, the sentry "cut loose and blasted the group to ribbons." Inspecting the dead soldiers, it was discovered that they were, as suspected, Germans masquerading as Americans. When the

French sentry was asked how he knew the approaching party was the enemy, he responded simply, "That's easy—Americans, *they* come in Jeeps!"[23]

Despite American hopes for a "pell-mell race for Tunisia," determined German forces blocked the Allied First Army's advance eastward; by early December, General Eisenhower ordered a halt to refit "badly battered troops" and build up adequate resources for the spring campaign, informing the Combined Chiefs of Staff of his decision on 3 December. Subsequent Allied setbacks at Djebel el Guessa (6 December) and at Longstop Hill made it clear that Tunis would not fall in 1942. American armor and lightweight and underarmed tank destroyers were quickly overwhelmed, as their doctrine often left them to their own devices against coordinated German armor and infantry. Under cover of winter storms, US forces took two months to resupply, refit, and perform maintenance before resuming the offensive. Those troops not billeted in towns and villages throughout Algeria, Morocco, and Tunisia dug in, transforming foxholes into "homes away from home," and while the pup tent served as their basic shelter, the spaces they dug out underground at times became quite elaborate, "like sheik's palaces," incorporating electric lights, salvaged stoves, makeshift heaters, fireplaces with blackout hoods, and padded beds.[24]

The Allies abandoned the plan of pinning the Afrika Korps against the British Eighth Army and replaced it with a coordinated offensive by the two Allied armies, with American vehicular logistics and technical ingenuity soon converging to play a significant role. Eisenhower saw motor vehicles as critical to the Tunisian advance, noting the "profound effect" of an additional 5,400 trucks to the theater during the winter of 1942–43, plus the "Yankee energy and modern American methods" introduced to the Military Railway Service by Brig. Gen. Charles R. Gray Jr., deputy chief of transportation for the North African theater of operations. Gen. Brehon Burke Somervell left Casablanca to send a lengthy missive back to the War Department requesting more trucks and rolling stock which would significantly improve the logistical efforts in North Africa. After a single convoy delivered more than 4,500 crated vehicles to assembly centers, the Transportation Corps drafted drivers from existing in-theater units, and by mid-April, some 80,000 tons of truckborne material had reached GIs driving on Tunis, with an additional 240 tons arriving by train daily.[25]

The arrival of these vehicles from the emerging "arsenal of democracy," coupled with the technical creativity of the American GI, allowed for an ever-increasing demonstration of American ingenuity. GIs in the Mediterranean pursued a course comparable to that produced by Pacific necessity, as spare parts shortages forced rear-echelon support and ordnance workers to perform "miracles of maintenance" on material arriving from the United States. Recognizing that "a tank or vehicle in North Africa is worth ten times its value in the

United States and must not be abandoned until there is no hope of recovery," four ordnancemen at a depot in Libya built jeeps from junked vehicles with "begged, borrowed, or stolen parts" in their spare time. Dubbed the "Second-hand Jeep Corporation," they eventually built three vehicles and incorporated them into their unit's inventory, with the first one proudly bearing the name "Spare Parts."[26] Rejecting standard procedure, GIs, and ordnancemen in particular, learned "they could not operate by the book," a valuable lesson that would become even more apparent in Sicily and Italy.[27]

Salvaging parts and material quickly became the order of the day for units in North Africa. By the campaign's end, Capt. Joseph M. Montgomery of the 3488th Medium Maintenance Company reported that three-quarters of his company's work utilized parts reclaimed from wrecked or damaged vehicles. When no spare parts were available, ordnancemen made them in mobile shops.[28] To enable use of readily available machine guns, ordnancemen fabricated gun mounts from scrap, thereby permitting employment of a .50-caliber machine gun against both air and ground targets. In another case, they used aluminum landing gear stripped from a shot-down German Junkers JU-88 as a foundation for a pedestal mount. Ordnancemen built a trailer with the barrel of a 37 mm gun stripped from a downed P-39 serving as an axle, with wheels taken from a wrecked truck.[29] Artillerymen developed a variety of shell case straighteners and "undenters," allowing the employment of artillery rounds otherwise destined for condemnation.[30]

German land mines confronted GIs in North Africa, prompting improvised antimine countermeasures, though not all resulted in success. Witnessing a British Scorpion "Flail" tank in North Africa, men of the 89th Ordnance Battalion tried building their own out of an M1A1 Sherman Medium tank. Unfortunately, the material they used to re-create the boom, rotating drum, and heavy chains of the British version was too flimsy, dooming their efforts to failure.[31] Men from the 83rd Heavy Maintenance Company at Mostaganem, Algeria, attempted to "mineproof" a command car with quarter-inch armor plating scavenged locally. Building a wooden model of the car, they installed the armor plating for preliminary tests, tying a young goat in the driver's seat and detonating a Teller mine underneath the vehicle. Witnessing the demonstration, General Patton recorded the car's utter destruction, as the floor armor flew seventy feet in the air, with only "two small pieces of the goat" remaining.[32] Lieutenant Colonel William C. Westmoreland, of the 9th Infantry Division's 34th Field Artillery Battalion, lectured new divisions entering First Army stressing that his unit typically "sand-bagged the front and back of Jeeps, Command Cars and the cabs of trucks." His troops discovered that if you hit a German Teller mine with a sandbagged jeep, "you will probably get by with an injured or lost limb," and if you hit one in a sandbagged Command Car, "you have an excellent chance of not getting injured." He later hit a mine with his command car in Sicily, and due to the protective measures, only one of the car's four occupants was injured, and then only slightly.[33]

The Tank Destroyer Corps continued to improvise as their role changed significantly during the North African campaign. Encountering concentrated enemy armored formations in North Africa, US tank destroyer units found their doctrine "defective." In defending Tunisia, for example, the Afrika Korps used infantry, armor, and artillery together as a formidable combined arms team. US forces faced their first big setback at the Battle of Kasserine Pass (19–22 February), where veteran German troops forced the retreat of poorly led, green American troops fifty miles from their original positions.[34] German tanks mounting high-velocity 75 mm and 88 mm guns made quick work of American M3 tank destroyers mounting low-velocity 75 mm guns or M6 trucks with shielded 37 mm guns. American tank destroyers failed to perform effectively for one of three reasons: they lacked experience and proper training to use their expedient weapons in combat, as offensively minded doctrine clashed with tactical realities that pitted them against vastly superior weapons, or the high-profile M3 and M6 tank destroyers, unlike towed guns, were difficult to conceal in flat desert terrain. These failings "resulted in the loss of an undue proportion of our tank destroyers."[35]

Such shortcomings prompted changes to tank destroyer doctrine, with commanders in the field eventually employing their weapons in ways the designers had not intended. Lieutenant Colonel James Barney, of the 776th Tank Destroyer Battalion, commanded one of the handful of units fortunate enough to ride to battle on the recently developed M10 Gun Motor Carriage (GMC), which mounted a three-inch gun in an open-topped turret on a modified M4A2 Medium tank chassis. During the closing phases of the Tunisian campaign, Barney began using his M10s as indirect-fire artillery. Having trained elements of the 776th Tank Destroyer Battalion in these techniques, his efforts paid off when his dug-in tank destroyers successfully eliminated a battery of six German guns in March 1943. Days later, he employed his tank destroyers against Rommel's forces retreating along "Gumtree Road" east of El Guettar in Tunisia. Using a protractor and scale, compass, map, and a liberated German telescope, his troops successfully targeted German vehicles with the three-inch gun mounted on their M10s and, over three days, destroyed a "considerable" number of German vehicles.[36] Barney's success gave tank destroyers, both motorized and towed, new purpose, and the addition of these guns to the American artillery arsenal resulted in an increased demand for artillery forward observers.

Traditionally, artillery forward observers sought the highest elevation possible, using field of vision to both call in and adjust fire. During the course of prewar maneuvers in Louisiana, then-Col. Dwight Eisenhower, himself a licensed pilot, saw the potential for trained artillerymen in light aircraft functioning as forward observers. On 6 June 1942, the War Department formally adopted Organic Field Artillery Air Observation, employing the lightweight Piper Cub formally designated the L-4 and popularly known as the "Grasshopper." In the opening phases of the North African campaign, four pilots accompanied three assembled aircraft aboard the carrier *Ranger*, making an additional plane flyable after procuring tools (albeit with metric measurements), on the Casablancan black market. The handful of pilots and aircraft quickly proved their worth, not only as forward observers, but in providing aerial reconnaissance, resupply, medical evacuation, motor convoy location, camouflage inspection, as well as speedy transportation for senior officers and unit commanders. By February 1943, Fifth Army Headquarters demanded more trained pilots, adding nine officers and seven enlisted men to the ranks of the aerial artillerymen. Between 23 April and 8 May 1943, thirty-one planes conducted 715 missions, with aerial observation sections comprising two pilots with two planes, supported by a mechanic, a truck with trailer, a driver, and an additional ground crewman. Each section performed its own field maintenance, with trucks carrying their own spare parts; pilots and their crews often cannibalized wrecked aircraft to keep two planes airworthy, scrounging additional parts to keep the Grasshoppers flying.[37] *Little Lucy*, an L-4 piloted by Maj. Edward S. Gordon on more than one hundred missions in North Africa and Sicily, became "an international siren of parts." By the time *Lucy* retired, her ingenious maintainers had kept her flying by using landing gear adapted from a Messerschmitt Bf 109 and a French bomber, instrument panel parts from P-38s, P-39s, and P-40s and an armored half-track, glass from a P-40, tubing from a French fighter, and a tail assembly improvised from a cracked-up jeep.[38]

After Grasshoppers proved their mettle in North Africa, American commanders wanted these assets for the Sicily invasion. Colonel Don E. Carlton, Third Infantry Division chief of staff, sought L-4 observation aircraft to cover the invasion fleet, believing they could perform their valuable mission before US troops reached the shore. Initially identifying targets for naval shelling, the planes reverted to their artillery spotting roots once field artillery units had landed. Launching the planes, however, proved problematic. Three planes flew from the USS *Ranger* for the North African landings, but the carrier had returned to the United States. Moreover, the Grasshoppers could carry only two and a half hour's worth of fuel, rendering a flight from Sicily to the Tunisian coast impossible. Captain Brenton A. Devol Jr., Third Infantry Division

Artillery air officer, proposed building a flight deck on another vessel and launching L-4s from that. Although their recovery would be impossible, once Allied troops secured the Sicilian beaches, planes could land, refuel, and return to the air until formal landing strips could be seized or improvised. Identifying a Landing Ship, Tank (LST), as the most promising platform, US forces in Tunisia soon began converting LST 386, commanded by Lt. Harold Fleck, USNR, into an expedient aircraft carrier.[39]

Together with Devol, who had flown the first L-4 off the deck of the *Ranger*, dictating specifications, Lt. Col. Leonard Bingham, the 10th Engineer Battalion's commander, tasked intelligence officer Capt. Bertil V. Carlson to engineer the runway. Erecting a timber trestle system down the centerline of the ship, they built a flight deck 216 feet long and 10 feet wide, with 1-foot sideboards to keep a plane from running off the runway. With only a few days before the scheduled invasion, Devol approached Lt. Alfred "Dutch" Schultz and asked him if he wanted to volunteer to test the runway, to which he responded, "Fly off of an LST and direct Naval gunfire? No!"[40] When Schultz refused, Devol looked for other volunteers. Hoping to secure enough flyers to man two planes in case one either crashed on takeoff or got shot down, Lts. Oliver P. Board and Julian W. "Bill" Cummings eventually stepped forward to take on the mission.[41]

On 10 July 1943, D-Day for the invasion of Sicily, Lieutenant Board was the first intrepid airman to launch from the modified transport "carrier." Unfortunately, he failed to reach anyone ashore via radio and had to abort his mission. Taking off behind him, Lieutenant Cummings had better luck. Climbing into the sky from the deck of LST 386, Cummings spent the remainder of the day relaying the location of enemy guns firing on GIs on the beach, which helped naval gunners correct their fire to avoid inflicting friendly-fire casualties on US Army Rangers. Landing on the beach to refuel, he returned to the air to locate German gun nests, passing their positions on to American artillery and naval gun batteries. Even before the island was in Allied hands, Cummings received orders to report to 3rd Division Headquarters. Arriving on 28 July, he was met by Gen. Lucien K. Truscott, divisional commander. Cummings received a Distinguished Service Cross awarded for "extraordinary heroism" in taking off "from an improvised runway on the deck of an LST" and conducting essential forward air observation missions, in the process helping to save some 15,000 GIs.[42]

Before presenting Cummings with his Distinguished Service Cross, General Truscott observed American ingenuity in action on Sicily's northern coast. In the "race to Messina," General Patton's Seventh Army sprinted east to beat Field Marshal Montgomery's Eighth Army driving north from Mount Etna. To slow the Allied advance, German engineers blew 150 feet of the highway off the cliff face at Cape Calava, blocking the 30th Infantry regimental combat team from advancing from Brolo. When the 30th's Col. Arthur R. Rogers encountered the destroyed tunnel and road, he ordered the 10th Engineer Battalion to improvise a trestle and restore the road. Almost immediately, the men of the battalion, under the watchful eye of Ernie Pyle, "commandeered two little Sicilian fishing boats . . . lashed them together, nailed planking across them, and ran the bulldozer onto this improvised barge. They tied an amphibious jeep in front of it, and went chugging around Cape Calava at about one mile an hour." The engineers and their homemade navy set about drilling and blasting holes and employing timbers and winches to build "a bridge hung in the sky," anchored precariously on the edge of the cliff to reconnect the roadway the Germans had destroyed. Though "impatient," all General Truscott could do, while the engineers built the bridge out of thin air, was stay out of the way. Eighteen hours later, he drove his jeep over the creaking, makeshift bridge. Four hours after that, more bracing allowed passage of a three-quarter-ton truck. Eventually, a bulldozer brought the highway into full operation and US troops continued their march toward Messina.[43]

After capturing Messina, Allied leadership prepared to invade Italy, with the first British troops landing on 3 September. US troops followed on 9 September, with Gen. Mark Clark's Fifth Army facing heavy German resistance at Salerno. When the Italian government agreed to an armistice, Allied leadership anticipated minimal resistance. Hitler, however, ordered the defense of all Nazi-held territory outside Germany, and the Wehrmacht used the Apennines and a succession of rivers and mountain ridges to force a slow and costly slog up the Italian Peninsula, destroying any hopes of a speedy advance on Rome.

The Allied advance required fire support, and tank destroyer battalions soon resumed their improvised artillery role. By the start of the Italian campaign, Lt. Col. James Barney, building on techniques pioneered during the Tunisian campaign, reorganized the 776th Tank Destroyer Battalion. Barney divided his thirty-six-gun battalion into three companies of two six-gun batteries (instead of the three four-gun platoons prescribed in the table of organization). The larger groups provided the same practical coverage, but more importantly, the change released a platoon leader to assist in the company fire direction center or to serve as a liaison to accompanying infantry units. Establishing a fire direction center in each company, Barney assigned tasks based on capability, training notwithstanding, emphasizing efficiency and effectiveness above all else. As a result, one company's armorer was made a survey chief, and in another company, a cook became a plotter.[44]

Barney proved the efficacy of this reorganization in Italy, as his tank destroyers, along with the battalion commanded by Capt. P. C. Meachem, supported divisional artillery for "many months without relief." Employed alongside divisional artillery, the two units messed together, developing a strong sense of camaraderie that paid dividends. The result was an integrated communication system using more than ten miles of telephone wire stretched between the battalion command post, divisional artillery, tank destroyer liaison officer, and divisional headquarters. As these units worked together, their integration and cooperation increased. By the campaign's end, the improvised tank destroyer–artillery team could confidently "blast the enemy wherever we meet him within fourteen thousand yards."[45]

The Italian campaign produced many examples of American field ingenuity. As one officer observed, "Practically everything we do is improvised."[46] In some cases, it was as simple as mounting the battalion commander's artillery scope with pieces of scrap metal allowing him to observe a position while in a foxhole or prone behind cover.[47] Others fabricated rifle grenade sights from salvaged shell cases and parts from a wrecked German half-track.[48] Ordnance units mounted hoists on three-quarter-ton vehicles, or added folding drop benches to trucks and trailers to facilitate field maintenance.[49] By the campaign's conclusion, several tank destroyer battalions improvised covers for open-topped M10 and M18 Hellcats. Employing heavy timbers and sandbags, or light armored plates salvaged from half-tracks and hinged to the turret, tank destroyer troopers sought protection from shell fragments and errant rounds, though when evaluated, commanders stressed that covers must be easily removeable to allow hasty crew egress in the event of vehicle damage.[50] Following the arrival of the M7 Priest self-propelled howitzer, soldiers sought more effective communications in the new motorized artillery batteries.[51] Corporals Melvin E. Mason and Joe B. Windley, of Battery A, 47th Armored Field Artillery Battalion, mounted a wire spool to the back deck of an M7, using "spare parts at practically no cost." Distances between the self-propelled gun and the commander's vehicle of anywhere from fifty to two hundred yards, coupled with the noise generated from a nine-cylinder radial engine, made voice communication impossible. With the howitzer section continually hooked to the reel, a soldier could unwind enough wire to connect to the executive officer's field phone or switchboard using common electric plugs and sockets. Upon completion of a mission, the executive could disconnect the wire and the M7 crew could reel it up quickly before changing positions.[52] When terrain got more difficult, Lt. Col. Gordon J. Wolf began deploying telephone lines by air, calling on a ubiquitous L-4 observation plane. The pilot dropped one end of a wire cable to a gun battery, and flying at the slowest speed possible, played out the remainder of the wire from a reel bolted to the lift struts of the aircraft. Upon reaching the battery's observation post, he dropped the line, allowing troops at each end to connect to their switchboards.[53] Artillerymen spent considerable time adjusting the range of artillery shells by removing the projectile from its case, changing powder increments, and reassembling the round. Capt. Eugene W. DeMoore devised a "Separator for a Semi-Fixed Shell," submitting his design to the *Field Artillery Journal.* It sparked a host of responses from others who field-fabricated similar tools to perform the task.[54]

Ingenuity was often born out of desperate necessity. Sergeant Charles E. Kelly of L Company, 143rd Infantry Regiment, 36th Infantry Division, earned the nickname "Commando Kelly" for valor and ingenuity in combat at Altavilla, overlooking Salerno. Initially, Kelly joined Lt. John Morrissey and two fellow GIs to eliminate a German position threatening their battalion. Reducing that position, the quartet rejoined their company in a push toward the summit of Hill 424. In a raging battle for the rocky hill, Kelly's company found itself surrounded by Germans in a "real show" of a firefight. Isolated with his company in a three-story building, he fought from all three floors, burning out four automatic rifles as the enemy closed in. Kelly grabbed 60 mm mortar shells, and pulling their arming pins, lobbed them as expedient grenades. Covering L Company's retreat with a bazooka before firing a few rounds from an abandoned 37 mm antitank gun, he reportedly killed more than forty of the enemy, efforts that earned him the Congressional Medal of Honor.[55]

More often than not, ingenuity came from the soldier's increased familiarity with his equipment. Soldiers often recognized a need for "the simplest things," welding a water can rack or bedroll bracket to a tank's hull. Others welded an upright T-post to the front bumper of a jeep to protect against wires Germans stretched across roadways at neck level.[56] Other GIs built litter frames to mount on a jeep, which allowed multiple wounded GIs to be evacuated simultaneously.[57] GIs also adapted weapons to improve combat effectiveness. When US troops landed in North Africa, few had trained with the M1 rocket launcher and 2.36-inch rocket, popularly known as the "bazooka," as it resembled the musical instrument used by 1930s American comedian Bob Burns. In reports from North Africa, soldiers reported "little or no training in its use," and therefore "no confidence in its performance." Troops frequently abandoned the weapon as it failed to realize its potential. By the Italian campaign, however, GIs were clamoring for the bazooka and sought new ways to employ it effectively as an offensive weapon. In fighting near Nettunia along the Rapido River, a "thinking man" took four bazookas, mounted them to a frame built around a German shell casing, and fixed them to a machine-gun mount. The resulting "Nettunia Quad," as reported in a War Department official film, offered "four-way murder with a purpose" and represented a trial method of dramatically increased American infantry firepower.[58]

A capable commander who understood his equipment, recognized an unmet need or capability, and took the requisite steps to translate an idea into reality could often make a difference. By mid-December 1943, the first Republic P-47 Thunderbolts had arrived in Italy, with four going to the 65th Fighter Squadron, 57th Fighter Group. The addition of drop tanks under each wing or the fuselage greatly enhanced the Thunderbolt's range and effectiveness, extending its flying time. While its eighteen-cylinder Pratt & Whitney engine provided more than 2,000 horsepower, it could not outclimb the German Focke-Wulf Fw 190. It could, however, outdive just about anything, with wonderful diving characteristics that required little effort to keep the plane steady and level when racing toward the ground.[59]

While the 57th Fighter Group earned its reputation for scrounging, the ingenuity demonstrated by the group's 65th Fighter Squadron in modifying the Republic P-47 Thunderbolt transformed the Allied air campaign in Europe. In December 1943, the 57th Fighter Group, based in Foggia, Italy, received twelve new P-47 D15 aircraft. Adding four planes to each squadron of Curtiss P-40 Warhawks, the P-47 appeared to have limited utility for close air support (CAS).[60] After working out kinks associated with the new airframe, the liberal application of American field expediency transformed an otherwise oversized, sluggish, and underperforming high-altitude escort fighter into the war's premier CAS platform.

On 12 January 1944, Col. Gilbert O. Wymond confronted M.Sgt. William Hahn, informing his squadron's armament chief of the P-47's worthlessness in a CAS role. Early experiments with bomb sway braces mounted to each plane's external fuel tank drop wing pylons proved promising, though inconvenient placement of the tank release levers on the floor of the cockpit left of the pilot's seat required considerable leverage to engage.[61] Announcing the squadron's transfer to the Eighth Air Force in England to become bomber escorts, Wymond told his armament chief, "You are going to convert this crate into a dive-bomber." Dragging Hahn to the flight line, Wymond climbed into the cockpit of a P-47 and showed his armorer what he wanted. Wymond wanted the ability to put the plane into a dive, "take my left hand off the throttle and pull the releases as I keep my eye up to the gun-sight." And, Wymond exhorted, he needed the changes made immediately, as Generals Auby C. Strickland and Lewis Brereton would be attending a flight demonstration in two days.[62]

The pair spent the better part of the night under the wing of a P-47 brainstorming. Enlisting Sgt. Charles Appel as an assistant, Hahn scrounged wire cable and scrap aluminum parts for pulleys and handles (so as to not interfere with the plane's compass). Over the next twenty-four hours, they contrived a

Rube Goldberg–inspired solution, attaching a flat bar to the floor of the cockpit to serve as a fulcrum for the three cables controlling the drop mechanisms for the wing and belly tanks. Rerouting the cables up the firewall to the back of the instrument panel, they attached three toggles on a bar below the instrument panel. With this arrangement, a pilot could locate his target in the gunsight, drop his hand from the throttle, reach for the toggles, and pull them in a swift easy motion to drop bombs.[63]

Two days later, with Generals Strickland and Brereton as witnesses, Wymond climbed into the cockpit of the modified P-47, with 500 lb dummy bombs strapped to each wing. Climbing to an altitude of 6,000 feet before rolling over and diving on his target, Wymond dropped two bombs from an altitude of 1,000 feet, burying them into the ground exactly on target. Impressed by the demonstration, Strickland and Brereton told Wymond to modify the remaining P-47s in the squadron. Hahn and Appel adjusted both the bomb sway braces and the cable routing, further improving targeting by replacing the American gunsight with one "acquired" from a British Spitfire.[64] With these changes, the P-47 soon became the feared "Jabo" that rained terror on German ground forces for the remainder of the war.

This was the first step in enhancing the ground attack capabilities of the sturdy P-47. The 78th Fighter Group added 20 mm guns in the field, with other squadrons in both Italy and England mounting rockets under the wings, while ground crews in Sicily and Italy crafted a variety of cluster munitions packages.[65] Used extensively in Operation Strangle, the P-47 helped stop German movement on the Italian "Boot" in early 1944.[66]

While the transformational potential of the modified P-47s would not manifest itself until after the Normandy invasion, American troops stretched GI ingenuity to the limits on the Italian Peninsula. Maj. Robert Wilson, a regimental field artillery observer in Italy, encouraged drivers to "keep their eyes constantly peeled" for sandbags to reinforce the floorboards of their vehicles as protection against mines, reporting that "a regimental commander and his driver" were both saved from serious injury when their jeep ran over and detonated a mine.[67] One field artillery company ensured that each dugout in their company area had entertainment by building "Razor Blade" crystal radio sets, coiling copper wire around a grenade container, with carbon sticks for the crystal and a razor blade as the tickler. The homemade radio pulled in from two to four radio stations, and sometimes all four at once![68] Such expedients were not the exception but the rule, as familiarity with radios spawned by teen fascination and *The Radio Boys* produced field-expedient radios used throughout the Italian campaign.[69] A quartermaster in Italy built a collapsible shower, using a canvas water bucket, some pipe nipples, a C ration can, and a stopcock valve with other odds and ends to make a shower holding eighteen quarts of water that allowed several men to get wet, wash, and rinse all at once.[70]

Such expedients capitalized on the spare parts and material available to US troops after they secured the Anzio beachhead.[71] In employing field expedients, few solutions were off the table. Struggling toward Rome, German troops created elaborate mine defenses along each successive line of resistance. While advancing toward the south bank of the Rapido River, 36th Infantry Division engineers discovered a particularly challenging minefield, made up primarily of German Schü-mines, wooden antipersonnel weapons with a pressure-sensitive detonator holding 200 grams of TNT. With its limited metal content, a Schü-mine thwarted traditional mine detectors, as the detector coil had to pass extremely close to the mine for it to register, with ground shrapnel further masking its presence.[72] Furthermore, German machine guns covered the minefield, which made the 36th's traditional mine clearing virtually impossible. To solve the problem, an officer from the 111th Engineer Battalion requested three hundred sheep from the divisional quartermaster. Upon delivery, the unnamed engineer officer joined another officer and an enlisted man masquerading as Italian shepherds. Driving the flock into the minefield, the trio exacted a favorable result, literally driving lambs to the slaughter while coming under enemy fire. They did not withdraw until the "animated mine exploders" had completed their "task," thereby allowing the unit to continue its advance.[73]

Other soldiers looked not to livestock, but to hardware, to aid them in the advance toward Rome. Major Henry D. Tyson, assistant chemical officer for the 1st Armored Division, used existing materials to improve his unit's ability to clear a minefield. Familiar with the "Bangalore torpedo," Tyson took an inert 60 mm mortar round with its projection charges intact and welded a metal rod to its tip. He attached a Primacord "rope," made from twelve 100-foot sections of explosive cord to the end of the rod, coiling it carefully around a metal cage, securing 150 feet of twine to the end of the Primacord rope. To clear the minefield, Tyson fired the mortar into the field, straightened the rope using the twine, and detonated the explosive mine's "tail," thereby clearing a sixteen-inch wide path through the obstacles. Initial tests in front of three hundred British and American officers proved the new weapon's success, and by the end of the campaign, General Clark not only awarded Tyson a commendation, but the launcher earned an official designation as the M1 and M2 antipersonnel mine-clearing cable.[74] Other GIs built a collapsible artillery observation platform capable of being stowed in the back of a truck and fabricated remote-control "mangle buggies" out of Italian farm tractors that could pull a length of Primacord through a barbed wire entanglement prior to detonation. Ordnancemen at the arsenal in Capua modified tank grousers, extending the traditional grousers fixed to M4 Sherman tank treads by six inches to enhance the tank's ability to more effectively the navigate the Pontine Marshes.[75]

In the Italian campaign Gen. Mark Clark witnessed the development of a series of "ingenious devices," as GIs stuck at Anzio quickly "discovered the hard way that necessity is the mother of invention."[76] Improving on the "animated mine exploders" used by the 36th Infantry and Tyson's mine-clearing line charge, tanks began employing "snakes," long pieces of segmented metal tubing filled with TNT to clear minefields. After a tank pushed the "snake" into the minefield, tankers detonated the explosives, clearing mines buried as deep as five feet. Clark also recalled the efforts of 1st Armored Division tankers who "applied the experience of home-town garage men." Attaching a crane to the front of an M4 Medium tank, they fabricated a tool to drag damaged tanks from the battlefield, anticipating a vehicle later adopted as the M32 tank retriever.[77]

These devices fell short when compared to perhaps the most outrageous example of American ingenuity in World War II: the "Infantry Sled." Coordination of infantry and armor in Italy had emerged as a significant challenge, and 3rd Infantry Division GIs innovated to find the best means to advance in conjunction with armor. Aware that riding on a tank made infantry vulnerable, Brig. Gen. John W. "Iron Mike" O'Daniel devised a unique solution. Ordnancemen fabricated O'Daniel's brainchild from a conceptual sketch. Composed of half a torpedo shell fabricated from three-sixteenths metal plate, the sled accommodated a soldier lying prone. Infantry sledder John B. Shirley described how the device worked: "two parallel lines of six sleds joined together by steel rods in six locations along the lines of sleds would slide along the ground in tracks made by a tank pulling them." A platoon or squad leader riding in the right front sled could communicate with the tank commander by means of a headset and microphone tied into the tank's communication system. Building 360 sleds between 29 April and 14 May, troops of the 3rd Infantry Division assigned to the battle sled team then trained on the new conveyance. Many of these GIs were untried and untested, as experienced commanders did not want to sacrifice their experienced troops to an untested concept.

The 751st Tank Battalion dragged the sleds into action on 23 May, carrying hapless infantrymen behind them over rough ground at a speed of less than ten miles per hour. Shirley's sled got towed to the remnants of a pinned down infantry company, which negated any advantage provided by the new contraption. Several other sleds failed to get into action when enemy mines disabled their tanks. One sledborne infantry team joined in attacking a strongly fortified house, having been towed to within 150 feet before dismounting and joining the tank in routing the enemy. Success of the battle sled appeared to be the exception rather than the rule, however, as after-action reports noted the sled's performance as "not very satisfactory."[78] Despite the lack of success, ordnance troops salvaged sleds from Italy for use in the invasion of southern France.[79]

Although the tank sleds "contributed very little or nothing to the actual break-through" from the Anzio beachhead, Allied troops successfully overwhelmed the German defenses that had stymied them since the initial landings at Anzio in January.[80] In a move directed by Gen. Mark Clark, Gen. Lucian Truscott ordered his men northwest toward Rome, and the ancient city fell on 4 June 1944. The latter stages of the Italian campaign are often forgotten in popular memory in the rush to prepare for the Normandy invasion, but the soldiers who made that assault were cut from the same cloth as those who had served in North Africa, Sicily, and Italy. In some cases, those seasoned units formed the vanguard of those sent ashore on Omaha Beach or scattered from the night sky on the Cotentin Peninsula.

Regardless of their origins, those GIs shared similar attributes. American ingenuity was commonplace amid the martial structure that allowed the application of such talents in the field. Although there were material shortcomings as the war in Europe began, once American industry began producing, GIs serving throughout the Mediterranean embraced American ingenuity in earnest, and while, in the words of Gen. Dwight D. Eisenhower, "Yankee ingenuity and resourcefulness were tested to the limit," the efforts of American GIs certainly made General Marshall's comments on the subject made to the first graduates of the Officer Candidate School class seem prescient.[81]

After flying the second L-4 off LST 386, Lt. Bill Cummings returned to Fort Sill, Oklahoma, to train future Grasshopper pilots. During World War II, he gained considerable insight into the technical creativity of the American GI. In his memoirs, he recognized both the source and the value of such efforts, as he recalled, "Every GI had a good head. They were college graduates, they were bums from the street, they were men who had worked in the coal mines." But, he stressed, "they still had that good old Yankee ingenuity." Because of their abilities, Cummings knew that GIs could identify a problem and bring it to their superiors, who trusted them to come up with a functional solution. In doing so, however, he also knew that answers might come from unusual places, for "sometimes the lieutenants gave better solutions than the enlisted men, and sometimes the GIs gave better solutions than the officers."[82]

CHAPTER 4

Inventing the Air Wars

If we ourselves had chosen the kind of war to be fought, we could not have found one more suitable to our national genius. For this is a war of transport, of machines, of mass production, of flexibility, and of inventiveness, and in each of these fields we have been pioneers if not actual inventors.

—*John Steinbeck*

Three years after John Steinbeck gave life to the Joad family's truck in *The Grapes of Wrath*, Gen. Henry "Hap" Arnold invited the acclaimed author to observe the training of American bomber aircrews. In the summer of 1942, Steinbeck and photographer John Swope traveled 20,000 miles documenting how young American men became bomber crewmen. Writing the functional equivalent of a literary recruiting poster, *Bombs Away* tracked Joe the pilot, bombardier Bill, navigator Allan, and the "special kind of young men" who made up this skilled combat team.[1] In his book, Abner, aerial engineer and crew chief, embodied American ingenuity. Before the war, Abner was the "natural mechanic" inhabiting "every small town in America." A "wizard with an automobile," Abner spent his youth creating his own "fast, smooth-running automobile" from two abandoned Model Ts, uniting the frame of one with the engine block of the other, crafting his jalopy in the same way Curtis LeMay built his machine from a burned-out Model T and salvaged parts. From that point on, Abner's constant mechanical tinkering ensured his car "was never the same two days in a row." In his town, Abner had a reputation as a mechanical wizard who "talked to motors." When he left for war, his neighbors wondered who would keep their machines running, but for the members of his bomber crew, Abner assumed an essential role, able to man "any position in the ship in an emergency."[2]

The American airmen of World War II fought a new way of war. The notion of "slipping the surly bonds of earth" to fight among the clouds was less than two generations old.[3] In that short time, complex machines of aluminum and steel replaced the simple canvas-covered wooden craft of the Great War. The Abners of the airfield, along with the GIs of World War II, were the first generation to grow up with the full benefits of the internal combustion engine. In crafting tactical, operational, and strategic air doctrine during World War II, intrepid American airmen combined the machine with ingenuity to meet the unique needs of their respective theaters of operation. This new air war of machines and mass production was, in Steinbeck's words, uniquely suited to the "natural genius" of the US Army Air Force. By war's end, American airmen in all theaters had adapted both aircraft and emerging air doctrine to meet the needs thrust upon them by the exigencies of war, demonstrating American ingenuity while innovating air campaigns in both Europe and the Pacific.

Prior to World War II, few officers were as familiar with the intricacies of the manufacture and modification of military aircraft as Gen. George C. Kenney. A decorated World War I flier, Kenney graduated from the Massachusetts Institute of Technology in 1921 and soon applied his expertise in the Air Service's Engineering Division. After education at the Air Service Tactical School (ACTS) and Command and General Staff College, Kenney became an instructor at ACTS, teaching attack aviation and the employment of fast, agile, and well-armed bomb-dropping aircraft at low altitude. Sent to the Office of the Chief of the Air Corps in 1933, he became a problem solver in readying GHQ Air Force for combat. Testing his ideas at the Infantry School, he flew with an observation squadron at Mitchell Field, Long Island, before a posting to France as an assistant air attaché. Kenney escaped Paris before it fell to the Nazis, and his growing reputation with General Arnold earned him a new position in the Material Division at Wright Field, where Kenney assumed responsibility for aircraft design, procurement, and modification. Though absent from the U.S. Army Air Force's initial dealings with Ford Motor Company, Arnold sent Kenney to Detroit in February 1942 to ease the carmaker's transition from automobile to bomber manufacturing.[4]

On 12 July 1942, Arnold took Kenney to Chief of Staff Marshall, who tasked Kenney with resurrecting Gen. Douglas MacArthur's FEAF after the collapse in the Southwest Pacific Area (SWPA). Kenney received this posting to Australia at the nadir of American air strength in the Pacific. Down to only six hundred planes, General Marshall informed Kenney that he would have to make do with what was available. With the focus of offensive operations being Europe, Marshall made it clear to Kenney that his primary task was to assist MacArthur in maintaining a "strategic defensive" in the Pacific.[5] Kenney spent the next three days in Washington, DC, absorbing everything he could about the situation in the SWPA, at the same time scrounging "anything not nailed down" to augment his new command. With General Arnold displaying a casual indifference to the P-38 fighter, Kenney requested that fifty Fourth Air Force planes and pilots be transferred to his new command. Discovering 3,000 parachute fragmentation bombs, he ordered these "parafrags" shipped to Australia. Kenney then joined Maj. Gen. Millard "Miff" Harmon aboard an early-production B-24 modified into "a sort of passenger carrier," without "soundproofing, cushioned seats, heating system, or windows," but capable of making the journey from San Francisco to New Caledonia via Hawaii–Canton Island–Fiji, and from there to Australia.[6]

Meeting with Maj. Gen. Richard K. Sutherland, MacArthur's chief of staff, on 28 July 1942, Kenney heard of the terrible state of the SWPA's air force: the organization's shortcomings and general lack of faith in its "deadwood" officers. Meeting with MacArthur the next day, Kenney heard about the general antagonism between existing FEAF staff and MacArthur's headquarters, whereupon Kenney decided that "it was time for me to lay my cards on the table." The incoming air commander informed MacArthur that he would serve loyally, and that he "knew how to run an air force as well or better than anyone else." If anyone was doing anything wrong, Kenney "intended to correct them and do a real job." Impressed by his candor, MacArthur gave Kenney the right to run his own show, believing that the two were "going to get along together all right."[7]

Kenney soon earned MacArthur's accolades by applying the Depression-era adage "Use it up, wear it out, make it do, or do without," while fabricating an air interdiction campaign to defend against the Japanese in the Southwest Pacific. Taking off in "The Swoose," a B-17 command plane cobbled together in the field from two cracked-up bombers, Kenney inspected his new command with an eye toward reorganizing the SWPA air assets.[8] First, Kenney reflagged the Allied Air Forces as the Fifth Air Force, eliminating an otherwise dysfunctional joint Allied-Australian command structure, replacing it with parallel American and Australian organizations, but with Kenney initially functioning as his own chief of staff.[9] Creating a more flexible command, Kenney began readying it for combat. He discovered that the Fifth Air Force had only 517 planes available: 245 fighter-bombers, 53 light bombers, 70 medium bombers, 62 heavy bombers, 36 transports, and 51 miscellaneous aircraft. But this assessment was deceiving, for of the 245 fighters, 170 awaited salvage or overhaul, no light bombers were combat ready, only 37 medium bombers had guns and bomb racks, and 19 heavy bombers were slated for overhaul or rebuild. Those planes remaining were either commercial or training types wholly unsuitable for combat.[10]

In rendering these planes combat ready, Kenney soon recognized that the older, senior officers accustomed to the spit and polish of peacetime service were a "stumbling block" steadfastly clinging to "by the book" solutions. In contrast, junior officers and enlisted men fresh from the States quickly got things moving. Lacking replacement parts, aluminum sheet stock for repair work, and spare instruments to replace those damaged in combat, these products of the Great Depression willingly applied American ingenuity. Salvaging and repairing instruments from wrecks, they beat aluminum engine cowlings flat and fashioned crude ribs to replace those on damaged B-17s, even going so far as to use "scraps cut from tin cans" to patch aircraft bullet holes. As Kenney quickly discovered, "the salvage pile was their supply source for stock, instruments, spark plugs—anything that could be used by any stretch of the imagination," a skill developed during the lean years of their youth.[11] When Kenney realized that he only had about 150 American and 70 Australian combat-ready aircraft to counter the Japanese in the Southwest Pacific, the Fifth Air Force commander halted future salvage efforts. All would be rebuilt, "even if we had nothing but a tail wheel to start with."[12]

With the meager resources available, Kenney designed a new campaign to halt the Japanese in the Southwest Pacific. Experience soon proved prewar AAF strategic bombing doctrine futile, as heavy bombers simply could not hit cloud-covered airfields or Japanese shipping from high altitude. In the first month of Kenney's command, Fifth Air Force B-17s dropped 434 bombs, yet only achieved 19 hits, sinking only one transport and a second cargo ship. September 1942 was even worse, with 425 bombs yielding 9 hits with only one enemy ship sunk.[13] As high-altitude bombing proved wanting, the attack aviation specialist innovated both technologically and tactically to employ medium bombers based in Australia as low-altitude strike platforms. Kenney's improvised interdiction campaign, directed at both Japanese airfields and surface shipping, would prove crucial to halting the enemy advance on Port Moresby.

Kenney soon came to rely on Maj. Paul "Pappy" Gunn as his "super-experimental gadgeteer and all-around fixer" who could build, modify, or fly almost anything.[14] Growing up with dreams of flying in the Great War, Gunn enlisted in the navy in 1917, paying for his own pilot training while serving as an aviation machinist's mate. After the armistice ended his hopes of combat, he purchased and restored a condemned navy Curtiss SOC Seagull flying boat, scrounging and fabricating parts to make the plane airworthy. When the navy promised him a formal flight training course if he reenlisted, Gunn signed on for six more years, receiving his wings and chief airplane pilot rating a year later. Retiring in 1937, he got a job as maintenance superintendent for Philippine Air Lines. Gunn was living in Manila with his wife and children until the Japanese invasion, when he volunteered for service. The US Army commissioned him a captain, and he flew in an improvised squadron against the Japanese, ferrying the last American personnel from Manila to Australia.[15]

Arriving in Brisbane, Gunn organized a joint US-Australian crew to begin uncrating and assembling twenty Curtiss P-40 Warhawks sent to the theater in January 1942, scrounging, repairing, and making combat ready anything flyable in northern Australia. Kenney first encountered Gunn while visiting the 3rd Bomb Group in Charters Towers, Queensland. There the craft maintainer had been fabricating bomb racks for Col. "Big Jim" Davies of the 90th Bomb Squadron. Their Douglas A-20 Havoc medium bombers had been flown ahead from the United States to Australia, with the bomb racks sent by sea. Angered that "his" planes also lacked machine guns, Gunn found some .50-caliber machine guns and installed them in the nose of another A-20, adding two 450-gallon fuel tanks to extend the plane's range. After finishing these modifications, Gunn hopped into the cockpit to test his improvised raider along the northern coast of New Guinea. In a treetop-level pass over a Japanese airfield, he destroyed Japanese aircraft with his machine guns and set fire to a fuel dump, leaving a flaming path of destruction in his wake.[16]

Returning from his "experiment," Davies introduced Gunn to Kenney as "our engineer officer who invents new ways to make it hard for the Japanese every day." Reviewing Gunn's record, Kenney determined that "he wanted someone like Pappy to play with." Granting him two weeks to finish his improvised bomb racks, he ordered Gunn to Brisbane, naming him the Fifth Air Force's "Special Projects Officer." With Gunn under his command, Kenney now had the mechanical ability to translate his long-held ideas about low-altitude interdiction into reality. He immediately ordered the uninhibited mechanical genius to fabricate makeshift bomb racks to carry the parafrags Kenney had previously sent to the theater. Incorporating parafrags with nose-mounted machine-gun packages in medium bombers provided Kenney with powerful commerce raiders that, when directed against Japanese surface shipping, made a Southwest Pacific interdiction campaign possible.[17]

Third Bomb Group A-20s dropped their first parafrags on the Japanese airfield near the village of Buna on 12 September, following B-17s and B-26s in a raid that destroyed seventeen Japanese Zeros.[18] Success in this and subsequent low-altitude raids prompted Kenney to have Gunn install a cagelike metal rack that could hold two hundred parafrags into the bomb bay of a B-25.[19] The ensuing destruction led Kenney to request 125,000 more parafrags from Washington, in the meantime tasking Fifth Air Force ordnancemen in Brisbane to add parachutes to standard fragmentation bombs. Kenney's airmen also experimented with white phosphorus incendiary bombs, which had a dramatic impact on grass huts and Japanese fuel and ammunition dumps throughout New Britain and Rabaul. Kenney's men also improved the destructive power of 300 lb and 500 lb bombs by wrapping them with heavy steel wire and attaching instantaneous fuses to the end of a six-inch pipe extension affixed to the nose. When these "daisy cutters" detonated, the quarter-inch wire broke up in several-inch-long pieces, flung in whirring shards that not only "wailed and screamed like a whole tribe of disconsolate banshees," but cut two-inch diameter limbs off trees as far as a hundred feet away.[20]

Low-altitude bombing was only one aspect of American technical ingenuity in the emerging Pacific interdiction campaign. Embracing the merits of "flexible-minded, free-thinking leaders," Kenney put Gunn to work on a B-25 in Brisbane, ordering him to fill the plane's nose with as many .50-caliber machine guns with a standard ammunition load of five hundred rounds per gun as possible. Kenney left Gunn to his own devices but recommended four guns in the nose, two on either side of the fuselage, and three underneath, calculating the damage potential of eleven forward-firing machine guns. When Kenney checked on Gunn's progress a few days later, he discovered a "good looking package of four .50 caliber guns" mounted in the nose along with an additional pair on either side of the fuselage. Feeding ammunition to three machine guns underneath, however, posed a "tough problem," and Gunn scrapped the idea. When Kenney questioned Gunn about a potential weight imbalance caused by eight additional guns and 4,000 rounds of ammunition, Gunn retorted, "The C[enter of] G[ravity]? Hell, we threw that away to lighten the ship."[21] An initial flight test of the up-gunned B-25 left Gunn sweating profusely from exertion while trying to get the tail down on landing. He solved the imbalance by moving the fuselage-mounted guns three feet back with ammunition trays in the bomb bay, but this only generated new problems, as the vibration of the heavy machine guns popped rivets through the plane's aluminum skin. Gunn stiffened the sides of the plane with steel plates, but to no avail. Adding felt buffers between the steel plates and the skin solved the problem but only temporarily, as the vibration returned when the felt dried out. Finally, Gunn installed sponge rubber padding, and the result worked beautifully. Although Kenney had hoped for three additional guns in the nose, aiming the two top turret guns to the front ultimately gave Kenney a "commerce destroyer" with ten forward-firing .50-caliber machine guns. Kenney soon designated the 90th Bomb Squadron of the 3rd Bomb Group as his low-altitude attackers, with Gunn readying twelve more planes for use against the Japanese.[22]

In addition to Gunn's commerce raiders, Kenney revisited "skip bombing," a tactic he had theorized was possible while studying low-altitude attack aviation in the late 1920s.[23] Kenney had spent most of his flight to the Southwest Pacific discussing the concept with aide Maj. William Benn, whom he had brought from the Fourth Air Force. Kenney theorized that if he dropped a bomb with a five-second fuse from an altitude of fifty feet, it would skip like a flat stone across a calm body of water. After impacting a ship's hull, the bomb would sink until it detonated, with the resulting compressive explosion rupturing the hull and sinking the ship. Arriving in Australia, the pair borrowed a B-26 and targeted a coral formation offshore from Nandi, Queensland, with dummy bombs. The pair soon discovered that bombing from an altitude of one hundred feet, four hundred feet away from the target, at a speed of approximately two hundred miles per hour, yielded the best results.[24]

Tasking Benn with skip bombing trials, Kenney posted him to the 43rd Bombardment Group (Heavy), which was made up of the 63rd, 64th, 65th, and 403rd Bombardment Squadrons.[25] When Kenney arrived in Australia, the group barely existed, with planeless officers and men manning empty airfields, supply dumps, and weather stations throughout the continent. Kenney quickly ordered the "pieces picked up and assembled in the Townsville area," instructing them to make as many B-17s as possible flyable. By 24 August, the 63rd had eleven B-17s and twelve complete aircrews, with Benn as commander. As the remaining squadrons became operational, the group began testing low-altitude bombing, relying on night or dawn attacks at mast height to maximize surprise. The group soon built a reputation as effective low-altitude bomber pilots, with "Ken's Men" amassing a distinguished flying record in translating Kenney's theories on low-altitude bombing into an operational reality.[26]

By early 1943, Kenney had enough combat-effective aircraft to begin his interdiction campaign against an enemy that held nearly every advantage in the Southwest Pacific. From their base at Rabaul, the Japanese dominated the seas and were looking to threaten Allied forces at Port Moresby.[27] In response, Kenney began using Australian-based B-17s and B-24s in conjunction with PBY Catalina flying boats to track Japanese reinforcements destined for Lae and Salamaua. As aerial reconnaissance was continued throughout January, isolated air attacks suggested the Japanese were preparing a major convoy operation from Rabaul to strengthen these positions. The next month, reconnaissance efforts revealed a record number of ships in the bay, with intercepted Japanese radio transmissions suggesting a major Japanese convoy bound from Rabaul for Lae in early March 1943. With this intel in hand, Kenney prepared to strike, hoping to inflict maximum damage despite the meager number of aircraft he had available.[28]

Kenney readied heavy and medium bombers and fighters at Port Moresby, Milne Bay, and Dobodura and began planning how they would attack the Japanese convoy. By mid-February, six medium bomb squadrons were ready: B-25s from the 38th Bomb Group's 71st and 405th Bomb Squadrons, 3rd Bomb Group's 13th and 90th Bomb Squadrons, and A-20s from the 3rd Bomb Group's understrength 8th and 89th Squadrons functioning as a single unit. To this, Kenney added a squadron of Royal Australian Air Force Bristol Beaufighters, with four 20 mm nose cannons and six wing-mounted .303 machine guns, along with B-17s flown by "Ken's Men" of the 43rd Bombardment Group, escorted by P-40s from the 7th and 8th Squadrons of the 35th Fighter Group and P-38s from the 9th and 39th Squadrons of 49th Fighter Group. Kenney's strategy called for reconnaissance aircraft to located the enemy convoy, with heavy bombers attacking as it sailed north of New Britain. Once in range of the medium bombers, reloaded heavy bombers would drop a second bomb load from between 8,000 and 10,000 feet to scatter the remaining elements of the convoy in the Bismarck Sea. Shortly thereafter, B-25s would start their low altitude skip bombing runs, followed by up-gunned B-25s and Beaufighters to finish them off. If that was not sufficient, medium bombers could launch a second attack to defeat the convoy in detail.[29]

On the morning of 1 March 1943, eight destroyers and eight transports carrying 6,900 soldiers and supplies of the Japanese Eighteenth Army set sail from Rabaul to reinforce the 3,500-man garrison at Lae. Departing amid fierce storms, the Japanese used clouds and rain to shield their vessels from Allied reconnaissance. Once Fifth Air Force B-24s flying long-range reconnaissance missions spotted the convoy, crews manning the 268 planes in the mixed strike force prepared for action. The ensuing Battle of the Bismarck Sea, fought over 2–3 March, not only marked the effective end of the Japanese advance back to the Coral Sea but showcased the organizational, technical, and tactical ingenuity Kenney had promoted and encouraged since his arrival in Australia.[30]

Early the next morning, seven B-17s from the 63rd Bomb Squadron dropped the first bombs on the sixteen-ship convoy, engaging from 8,000 feet covered by P-38s from the 49th Fighter Group. A few hours later, B-17s from the 64th and 65th Bomb Squadrons hit the convoy, sinking a transport and damaging a second. While the B-17s returned to base, the Japanese convoy sailed through the night, fifty miles north of Cape Gloucester, New Britain, and past the island of Umboi before turning south through the Vitiaz Strait. At daybreak on 3 March, reconnaissance planes spotted the convoy, reporting to the remaining squadrons that the target had sailed into range about fifty miles southeast of Finschhafen, New Guinea. Those squadrons converged on the convoy with devastating results for the enemy. Following attacks by heavy and medium bombers from 7,000 feet, Australian Beaufighters strafed the ships, with B-25 skip bombers and commerce raiders following suit. The A-20s completed the attack, strafing and bombing the remaining undamaged Japanese vessels.[31]

In twenty minutes, the battle was over. At a cost of four fighters and two bombers, Kenney's Fifth Air Force attack destroyed all eight transports, sank or badly damaged four destroyers, downed twenty Japanese planes, and killed nearly 3,000 Japanese troops. After refueling and rearming, the American squadrons performed a coup de grâce on the remaining Japanese ships and survivors clinging to what remained of the convoy. Although General Kenney had no direct role in the Battle of the Bismarck Sea, his guidance and direction of the Fifth Air Force fostered the organizational, technical, and tactical innovation that produced the tremendous outcome in the waters off New Guinea. During the three-day-long battle, Kenney's flyers, using air assets greatly enhanced by American ingenuity, inflicted more damage on the enemy than during the entire New Guinea campaign. As Gen. Douglas MacArthur later argued, it was "the decisive aerial engagement" of the entire Pacific campaign.[32]

Soon after the Battle of the Bismarck Sea, General Kenney left for Washington, DC, to attend planning meetings with the Joint Chiefs of Staff. The result was Operation Cartwheel, a mutually supporting advance through the Solomon Islands and up the coast of New Guinea directed by Admiral Halsey and General MacArthur. Informal elements of this trip, however, positioned Kenney to further the application of American ingenuity to American aircraft in the future. Even before the battle, Kenney was looking to more effectively adapt new planes built in the United States to meet in-theater demands, recognizing the need to modify the basic production models to meet unique operational requirements.[33]

The first Consolidated B-24 Liberators arrived in the Pacific theater in the fall of 1942 to serve as long-range reconnaissance platforms, which made the Bismarck Sea victory possible. From the outset, the planes required in-theater modifications to make them both combat effective and functional. When the first squadron of B-24s arrived from the United States, General Arnold warned Kenney of potential cracks in the nose-wheel gear antishim collars that could ground all B-24s. Upon inspection, Kenney's maintainers found cracks, though an attempt at a quick fix of removing the collars and welding the cracks "just made more cracks." To bypass the issue, Kenney immediately ordered the fabrication of steel antishim collars in Brisbane. His solution delayed operational effectiveness but solved the problem. Other modifications stemmed from weather conditions in the South Pacific. New B-24s, and other new planes produced stateside, particularly the C-47 and B-25, came equipped with standard deicing and winterization equipment necessary for European service. Kenney created additional modification facilities to remove these features and accelerate the planes' readiness.[34]

Combat trials of recently arrived aircraft often revealed significant offensive or defensive weaknesses that crews brought to the immediate attention of command. In the B-24, for example, crews quickly discovered that the plane's forward armament was "unsatisfactory," for although the early model of the aircraft had four .50-caliber machine-gun mounts in the nose, their configuration in individual "eyeball" sockets meant that only one gun could be fired at a time. Colonel Arthur H. Rogers of the 90th Bomb Group recognized the potential of installing a twin gun tail mount in the nose of the aircraft, having undertaken comparable efforts while with the Air Depot in Hawaii. When Rogers brought this idea to Brig. Gen. Charles Connell, commander of the Fifth Air Force Service Command, Connell immediately brought Rogers to Kenney. Receiving the authorization for the modification almost immediately, Rogers removed a tail mount from a wrecked B-24 and reinstalled it in the nose of a B-24, which was subsequently christened "Connell's Special." When the B-24 was proven airworthy and combat effective, Kenney ordered all incoming B-24s from Hawaii to have their nose turrets retrofitted. To accelerate the operational capabilities of the planes already operating from Australia, the Fifth Air Force commander ordered seventy-one tail mounts shipped to Australia for field installation.[35]

Such field modifications prompted design changes in subsequent aircraft models, something that captured General Arnold's attention. Prior to leaving Australia, Kenney informed Arnold how Pappy Gunn transformed the B-25 into "a skip-bombing, strafing commerce-destroyer." During the Cartwheel meetings, Arnold called Kenney to his office, where engineering experts from Wright Field attacked Kenney's changes as "impracticable" and claimed that Gunn's additions to the medium bomber made it unflyable. Calling their bluff, Kenney calmly explained the role of the modified B-25s in the Battle of the Bismarck Sea, noting the retrofitting of sixty additional planes in the Townsville depots. Hearing this, General Arnold "glared at his engineering experts and practically threw them out of the office."[36] In his next breath, Arnold told Kenney he wanted "that man Gunn transferred to Dayton to teach my engineers something." Kenney, loath to lose Gunn's creative talents, reluctantly consented to send Pappy stateside for a month or two. Arriving in the United States, Gunn discovered air force paperwork the greatest obstacle to innovation. As he said, "Back in New Guinea we don't care if you can read or write if you can make a bomb rack work or get a gun to shoot." These challenges notwithstanding, Kenney realized that it was "much better" to make the modifications designed by Pappy Gunn in the United States rather "than under some palm tree in New

Guinea."[37] With all his creativity, Gunn might appear to be an exceptional case, but as many pilots and crewmen were quick to note, most aircraft maintainers were "just backyard mechanics who knew how to take things apart and put them back together again," as a member of Pappy Boyington's famed VMF-214 squadron described them.[38] With technical skills developed in the midst of Depression-era hardships, these men adapted quickly and improvised to face the exigencies of mechanized war.

Planning for Operation Cartwheel had significant consequences for future air operations in the Pacific. These efforts, however, were secondary to the primary Allied goal of defeating Nazi Germany.[39] While Kenney and Gunn had improvised an interdiction campaign to halt the Japanese advance into the Southwest Pacific, Allied soldiers and airmen in the European theater had begun their own air campaign. After invading North Africa in November 1942, American airmen in the Mediterranean theater demonstrated ingenuity and innovation comparable to the scroungers and tinkerers of the South Pacific. When the first airmen of the US Army Middle East Air Force (USAMEAF) landed to support Operation Torch, these winged crusaders showed the same talent and grit to increase their operational effectiveness, improve their living conditions, and make something of nothing.

Early American efforts in the North African air campaign were limited to the twenty-four B-24Es of the Halvorson Provisional Group, the 57th Fighter Group, and 12th Bomb Group. Eventually, the USAMEAF expanded to include one heavy and two medium bomb groups, and six pursuit (fighter) groups supporting Allied in-theater ground efforts.[40] The situation in North Africa represented a "difficult arrangement" at best. Prewar American air doctrine emphasized strategic bombing, employing heavy bombers against German sea communications, harbors, and the Italian fleet. American pilots soon found themselves in tactical, rather than strategic, operations, tasked with destroying enemy aircraft, tanks, motor transport, and landing fields.[41] Although such actions drew resources away from Eighth Air Force's emerging strategic bombing campaign mounted from England, they provided critical assistance to Allied troops pushing the Nazis out of North Africa, Sicily, and eventually Italy.

The 12th Bomb Group, ordered to North Africa in September 1942, derived success from men like 1st Lt. A. J. Maidel, of McAllen, Texas, who demonstrated "ingenuity, perseverance, and skill" in solving "daily the staggering man-made damage and havoc on things mechanical played by the natural elements of the African desert." He repaired the fuselage of a flak-torn American plane with parts cannibalized from wrecked French and German aircraft. With "little equipment to work with and supplies [that] were slow in arriving," mechanics and men like Maidel showed such inventiveness on a daily basis. When a plane went down, they "swarmed over it like a flock of vultures, stripping parts from one plane to enable another to fly," just like their frugal Pacific counterparts.[42]

In addition to stripping damaged aircraft, many airmen resorted to the same means by which General Kenney acquired parafrags for his command—that is, scrounging, a practice characterized by some as "a polite word for steal."[43] The German retreat across North Africa "presented the most fertile scrounging ground in history," and airmen quickly exploited this opportunity. Americans William "Benny" Benedict and Charles "Charley" Leaf, who had joined the Royal Canadian Air Force in 1941, were transferred to the Ninth Air Force after the United States entered the war, and both were coincidentally ordered to the 66th Squadron, 57th Fighter Group. Arriving in North Africa, the pair took scrounging to a new level. By Christmas 1942, Benny had a personal motor pool made up of a staff car, two motor cycles, and two trucks, one of which sported a small bungalow with bunks, furniture, radio, and electric lights. The pair eventually acquired an Italian Savoia-Marchetti trimotor bomber they christened the *Green Goose*, appropriated an abandoned Italian medium tank and drove it until it caught fire, stole a German Me-109 from a British airfield, and employed a German staff car in their desert adventures. The two continued their escapades when the 57th moved to Sicily, stealing six Messerschmitt Me-109s and repairing a German Fieseler Storch liaison aircraft claimed by a competing unit's salvage officers before taking off and leaving their rivals behind on a dusty runway.[44] Benedict and Leaf were only the tip of the 57th Fighter Group's unauthorized acquisition arm. The unit moved across the desert as a "rag-tag convoy of Army vehicles supplemented with captured German and Italian jeeps, staff cars, and trucks," filled with both authorized and "acquired" equipment, tents, trailers, baggage, and supplies. As noted by then-Lt. Michael McCarthy, "The 57th Fighter Group's reputation for scrounging and midnight requisitioning was notorious."[45]

Other scroungers looked to meet the omnipresent demands of thirsty airmen. Returning to the United States after the Doolittle Raid, Ross Greening rejoined the 17th Bombardment Group. After training on the B-26 Marauder, Greening and his group found themselves flying from austere Algerian airfields during the winter of 1943–44.[46] At Telergma, Greening supervised the efforts of Kentucky-born "Lieutenant Cornelius," who scrounged copper tubing from a wrecked B-26 to build a still. Claiming he could only run a still barefoot, the hillbilly distiller blended Arab wine with orange drink concentrate from Red Cross parcels to create "liquid lightning," quickly christened "Cornelius's Corn." The group generated more than $2,500 from selling the concoction before an unfortunate still explosion ended their moonshining. Continuing efforts to slake his group's thirst, Greening procured sugar and other ingredients from a local French brewery in exchange for poor quality, yet warm, French beer. Continuing to innovate, Greening addressed the refrigeration challenge by fabricating a sling that held a full keg of beer in the bomb bay of a B-26. After flying for "about three hours" in the "cold, rarified air," the pilot would call the control tower "advising all ground crews and personnel from the bomb groups to be on hand with canteens," as cold beer was on the way.[47]

In the spartan bases in North Africa, Sicily, and eventually Italy, American aircrews paired scrounging with technical creativity to improve their homes. Regardless of where they were, airmen attempted to "improvise an American community." Around fields that were dusty when it was dry and impassable with mud when it rained, the crews crafted dispersal areas, protective plane revetments, briefing rooms, mess facilities, and repair and supply depots from tents, sandbags, and whatever else they could find. In otherwise "deplorable" living conditions, officers shared tents with other officers, enlisted men bunked together, and both went to great lengths to make "jerry-built shanties created from God knows how many odds and ends," with some building "architectural works of art."[48] Accommodations varied greatly, leading one airman based at Foggia, Italy, to opine that "one could have visited fifty different quarters . . . and found fifty different kinds."[49] In Italy, Staff Sergeant (S.Sgt.) Ely Crinzman of Cranford, New Jersey, scavenged luggage racks from a wrecked B-24 and stretched a GI shelter half over the top, fabricating a door hasp complete with lock to secure his hut.[50] Others found "lumber, doors, glass, and nails and had erected some very comfortable homes."[51] Aerial engineers Sgt. Boyd Clark of Hastings, Michigan, Cpl. George Dryden of Washington, Pennsylvania, and Cpl. Milas Sabrowsky of Tigertown, Wisconsin, used native Italian stone and mud for the walls of their quarters using GI shelter halves as a roof.[52] Corporal Herbert Miller and S.Sgt. Edward Krigbaum scavenged lumber from aircraft belly tank crates, furnishing their "home" with a stove, sink, closet, and writing table, a practice followed by many others throughout the theater.[53]

Almost every airfield tent or shelter had a stove, rigged from oil drums and piping scavenged from any plane in the airfield "boneyard" by some "inventive genius."[54] These stoves generally followed a similar pattern: a fifty-five-gallon drum set over a small hole in the ground filled with stones, with a hole cut in the side and some rudimentary piping to channel smoke up through the roof of the tent. Outside the tent or hut, a glycol tank salvaged from a plane's deicing system held a supply of high octane aviation fuel, with hosing taken from a downed plane's oxygen system and a valve providing a controlled means to introduce the fuel into a combustion chamber.[55] To "light" the "stove," a small amount of fuel was poured onto the stones and ignited. Once the flames died down, the valve was adjusted to release a slow but steady drip of one drop of fuel at a time. When the fuel hit the superheated stones, it vaporized, generating adequate heat.[56]

Second Lt. George Mahoney, who flew B-24s with the 766th Squadron, 461st Bomb Group, out of Cerignola, Italy, built a similar stove, but instead of a stone heat chamber, he used a 75 or 88 mm shell casing, perforated for air intake, brazed to the bottom of the fuel drum. After priming the stove by running a little gas into the casing and igniting it, subsequent gas droplets vaporized, thereby generating heat.[57] Master Sergeant Bill Hahn, of the 65th Fighter Squadron, 57th Fighter Group, described a stove made from half of a fifty-five-gallon fuel drum, using a four-inch-diameter metal lid cut from a bomb detonator can as the heating element, connected by copper tubing to a fifty-five-gallon drum reservoir "laid horizontally on an elevated stand" outside the tent. Hahn was "very cautious at first, thinking of the one hundred octane fuel that might burst into flame from a flash back," but he "never had a bad fire, nor did we destroy a tent." Technical Sergeant R. E. Wilson remembered his "home-made combination coal and oil burner that worked quite well when regulated just right, so it was a pretty good deal."[58]

Sometimes makeshift stoves became disastrous, either by operator error, poor construction, or system failure after corrosive aviation fuel degraded the pilfered rubber oxygen tubing connecting the stove to the reservoir. John Muirhead of the 301st Bomb Group labeled his stove-making squadron mate a "madman," due to the fact that his "piping was a disgrace; his joints weren't sealed." He had blown up three tents, and lived in another with leaking "octane all over the bloody floor." Nonetheless, Muirhead noted that there "was a passion in his ineptness, and his pyrotechnics were the talk of the group."[59] Corporal Harold "Red" Kempffer of the 830th Bomb Squadron, 485th Bomb Group, recalled that while lighting his stove, built in a manner similar to Mahoney's, the entire contraption was "lifted off the ground with one big bang" when a pool of fuel suddenly ignited.[60]

Inventive airmen also built water heaters and cleaning facilities for personal and squadron use. Master Sergeant Roy Moyer used a pair of empty fifty-gallon oil drums, native Italian stone, and some piping to create a hot water heater that he shared with his three hutmates.[61] Using gasoline drums and forty feet of three-quarter-inch piping scavenged from planes, Cpl. John Wharton built a heated water station used to clean his mess kit after each use.[62] Other squadrons used the ubiquitous fifty five-gallon fuel drum along with "junkpiles of equipage abandoned by the enemy" to fabricate single tank wash troughs heated by individual stoves, or individually heated washbasins, like those developed by the 515th Bomb Squadron, 376th Bomb Group, in San Pancrazio.[63] When the opportunity presented itself, airmen scrounged parts to build outdoor shower facilities. These often incorporated many of the same elements—scavenged drop tanks, fifty-five-gallon drums, and piping—as smaller heaters, but were especially prized as they gave airmen the luxury of a regular shower.[64] The "Earthquakers" of the 12th Bomb Group built a shower in a small greenhouse in Italy. Acquiring pipe, a few faucets, and two pipe wrenches, they purchased pipe unions on the local market, which allowed them to link shower heads to a homemade hot water heater; the result "worked better than we had expected," with the airmen quickly lining up to get a shower "anywhere along the pipeline."[65]

Airmen throughout the Mediterranean also fabricated washing machines to take the "tattle-tale gray" out of their clothes. William Dach and Howard Anderson of the Twelfth Air Force Service Command in Sicily built theirs from scrounged parts from a captured German antiaircraft searchlight, wooden paddles mounted on a core made from a German 88 mm shell casing, a tub from a French fifty-five-gallon oil drum, and a driving gear mechanism salvaged from an Italian truck, powered by a gasoline-driven generator connected to an American one-half horsepower electric motor.[66] Propeller specialist Sgt. John Dowell, serving with the Fifteenth Air Force in Italy, adapted his top-loading washer from a repurposed trash can with power from a small engine via a serpentine belt. Corporal Elbert R. Spears mounted half a fifty-five-gallon fuel drum on three legs for his washer, with power provided by a fuel transfer pump motor.[67] In the documentary *Thunderbolt*, the men of the 57th Fighter Group demonstrated their laundry station, with homemade pump, fuel can heating unit, and improvised washing drum on legs, with an agitator powered by a small motor.[68]

Airmen furnished their bases "as if they would be there forever," creating rest and relaxation facilities to offer a much needed break from combat. Sergeant Theodore Hills from a B-24 group in Italy salvaged Lockheed P-38 auxiliary drop tanks and added a "put-put" engine scrounged from a wrecked Italian bomber to create a pontoon boat, a common fabrication among aircrews stationed near water.[69] The 57th Fighter Group's 66th Fighter Squadron dammed a stream in Italy to create their own swimming hole and beach club, before relocating to the Mediterranean coast. These "yachtsmen" created watercraft very similar to Sergeant Hills's, recognizing "that an old wing tank and a few odds and ends" made quite a boat. Their crew chief "scrounged parts from wrecked Jerry planes and banged up Italian cars" and added "old parachutes for sails," and the squadron was soon in possession of a small powered sailboat assembled from "the best quality junk.[70]

The Mediterranean air campaign has often been regarded as a distraction from the Combined Bomber Offensive (CBO) authorized at the Casablanca

Conference in January 1943. Like Kenney's campaign in the Southwest Pacific, the emerging CBO was, like most of the air war, a product of experimentation and ingenuity. When Lt. Gen. Frank M. Andrews joined Maj. Gen. Ira C. Eaker to direct the Eighth Air Force in February 1943, the paucity of resources in England shocked him. To prosecute the CBO, the "Mighty Eighth" needed more planes and men to fly them. With fewer than twenty new aircraft arriving in England each week, Eaker and Andrews struggled to achieve operational goals, especially considering the heavy casualties suffered on early missions.[71] While Lt. Cols. Harold George and Kenneth N. Walker, along with Majs. Haywood S. Hansell Jr. and Laurence S. Kuter, studied strategic bombing extensively in preparing Air War Plans Division plan number 1 (AWPD-1), making the plan operational proved difficult. AWPD-1, developed after Germany's invasion of the Soviet Union in June 1941, projected directing 6,800 medium and heavy bombers operating from bases in Great Britain against key industrial targets in Germany to knock the Germans out of the war.[72] It did not, however, consider tactical and operational deficiencies discovered in combat against a determined enemy. These shortcomings required a process of trial and error, with solutions provided by the ingenuity of American airmen as they mastered whatever resources they had available.

When Col. Curtis LeMay took command of the 305th Bomb Group in May 1942, the organization was little more than "a series of typewritten sheets." With only three planes and a handful of men at his disposal, LeMay embraced "temporary expediency" to assemble his group and make it combat ready.[73] Creating a relentless training regimen that earned him the sobriquet "Iron Ass," LeMay led a group that eventually received orders to deploy to England to join the Eighth Air Force. At a stopover in Scotland, he ran into Col. Frank Armstrong, an old friend commanding the 97th Bomb Group, the first American B-17 unit to bomb Germany. In a brief interrogation, Armstrong told LeMay two things: flak was "really terrific," and if B-17s flew straight and level for any length of time, losses would be catastrophic. Armstrong's answers shocked LeMay, for it gave him no insight into how he could successfully lead untested pilots into combat without getting most of them killed.[74]

Given considerable latitude to dictate flying formations, LeMay's first four-squadron mission was a debacle. Inexperienced pilots were unable to fly in a tight formation, and flak evasion maneuvering resulted in bombs slung "every which way." LeMay began considering a "master formation" to maximize his planes' .50-caliber machine guns and produce an accurate bomb drop. On the next mission, LeMay posted himself in the lead plane's top turret and directed every plane into its proper position by radio. The result was the "Lead-High-Low, the wedge-shaped combat box." LeMay made further refinements on subsequent missions, with the Eighth Air Force eventually adopting his combat box. In the process, LeMay built his bomb group the same way he rebuilt his Model T, from "assorted materials"—some from the "junkyard," others "designated as tired veteran or retread material," and a lot "reclaimed," ultimately achieving "sound performance" from his group.[75]

Having created an effective high-altitude strategic bombing formation, LeMay turned to the flak challenge. Evasive action to avoid flak scattered planes, resulting in bombs landing "clear out of the picture." Armstrong's admonition against flying straight and level notwithstanding, LeMay used an old ROTC artillery manual to calculate a theoretical threat potential based on the accuracy rate of French 75 mm artillery. Adopting a level and straight approach at 25,000 feet, he determined that a German 88 mm flak gun would score one hit for every 372 rounds fired. Based on these calculations, LeMay theorized that Armstrong was wrong. The calculating commander determined that bombers could fly in formation for longer than ten seconds en route to the aiming point. Taking commands from the lead, the resulting bomb drop would be much more accurate than before.[76] LeMay tested the new formation on 23 November 1942, joining four other groups on a seven-minute bomb run against Saint-Nazaire.[77] On that mission, the 305th only "lost two Forts [Flying Fortresses], both to enemy fighters."[78] While the group suffered losses, its bombs fell accurately on the targeted German submarine base.[79] Embracing "straight and level dedication," LeMay's group proved the efficacy of formation flying on a long approach to the target, a practice subsequently adopted by the entire Eighth Air Force.[80]

The combat box allowed a B-17 group to bomb accurately and employ interlocking fields of fire to defend against enemy fighters. It was not, however, perfect. The same day LeMay led his group over Saint-Nazaire, Nazi fighter pilot Oberleutnant Egon Mayer broke with established German fighter tactics and mounted a head-on attack against an American bomber formation.[81] With early B-17s and B-24s possessing little in the way of forward-facing armament, Mayer realized the vulnerability of bombers if fighters attacked from "12 o'clock high" (pilot's parlance for straight ahead and above).[82] In the ensuing months, losses from head-on enemy fighter attacks more than doubled. LeMay, not to mention General Eaker, quickly recognized that both B-17s and B-24s needed better nose armament, though when Eaker requested these additions to replacements arriving from the United States, he received word that newer models with those features were months away.[83] Subsequent models of the B-17 featured a remotely operated Bendix chin turret, with the B-24 employing the nose turret engineered in the Pacific by the 90th Bomb Group. In the interim, pilots and aircrews offered complaints, critiques, and suggestions to ground crewmen, engineers, and factories back in the United States, and American ingenuity eventually solved the problem.

Three American B-17 bomb groups—the 91st, 303rd, and 306th—all claim to be the first to place forward-firing .50-caliber machine guns in a B-17. The 306th flew its first mission over Lille, France, on 9 October 1942, with the 91st mounting its first mission against Brest on 7 November. The 303rd followed on 17 November, joining both other bomb groups in attacking submarine pens at Saint-Nazaire.[84] After these early missions, aircrews from all three groups, based at Bassingbourn (91st), Molesworth (303rd), and Thurleigh (306th), requested more firepower in their planes' nose. Their maintainers and ground crewmen, despite being isolated from each other by around thirty miles of English countryside, arrived at similar solutions to the same problem nearly simultaneously.

The 306th Bomb Group, the "first over Germany," appears to have the best claim as first, for by the end of 1942, the group considered themselves veterans, having devised "standard operating procedures" adopted by the entire Eighth Air Force.[85] Having discussed the B-17s head-on vulnerability in the waning weeks of 1942, armorer Sgt. James C. Green and welder Benjamin Marcilonis of the group's 367th Bomb Squadron fabricated a solution. Enlarging an existing .30-caliber gunport to fit the heavier .50-caliber machine gun, the two built a suspension system inside the nose. While the new addition could cover only part of the plane's nose because of its proximity to the Norden bombsight, it nonetheless represented a significant step forward. Bringing their solution to the group, and later to the B-17 modification center at Langford Lodge, their improvement met rave reviews, and the pair received the Legion of Merit on 3 April 1943.[86]

Lieutenant George "Buzz" Birdsong of the 91st Bomb Group, followed the lead of the 306th in advocating for a .50-caliber nose gun in his B-17F, the *Delta Rebel*. Seeking out sheet metal crew chief Sgt. Whit W. Hill from the 323rd Bomb Squadron, Birdsong inquired as to the addition's potential practicality. Aided by welders Eddie Boisvert and Jimmy Hufmann, Hill worked in a small room off a hangar at their base in Bassingbourn. Despite opposition from the squadron engineering officer, they rigged up a tripod to support the gun from some steel tubing and armor plate. With help from the 441st Sub Depot Plexiglass shop, they cut a hole in the nose, strengthened the area, and installed the gun. When tested in the *Delta Rebel*, the gun worked, leading to similar additions in the *Eagle's Wrath* and other planes in the squadron and group. Some bombers even received a two-gun package built from mounts extracted from the tails of other planes.[87]

Lieutenant Harry Gobrecht claimed that the 359th Bomb Squadron of the 303rd Bomb Group first installed guns in a B-17, prompted by Capt. Ross C.

Bales, pilot of the *Idaho Potato Peeler*, after a "close call with German tactics started him thinking." Aided by S.Sgts. Ed Russell and Anthony Sequion of the 328th Service Squadron, they stripped a nose cone from a damaged B-17 that had been forced to make a belly landing at Bovingdon. They added guns from a salvaged tailgun to a gun mount, then mounted the entire assembly into the nose of the B-17F *Joe Btfsplk* of the 360th squadron, a plane named after a character in the popular "L'il Abner" comic strip.[88]

Other pilots increased forward firepower through other means. Lieutenant Robert T. Krout of the 452nd Bomb Group devised a "crude wire contraption" to fire a nose gun by remote control, which he successfully employed against an Fw 190.[89] Captain Nathan Mazer, a "gung ho" armament officer in the 384th Bomb Squadron, removed the chin turret from a B-17 and replaced it with six .50-caliber machine guns capable of being fired remotely by the pilot, though the plane went down on a mission before it could be tested.[90] Wanting even more firepower, the 385th Bomb Group scrounged a British 20 mm cannon and mounted it in the nose of the B-17F *Roundtrip Jack*. When first tested in August 1943, the recoil vibrated cockpit instruments and the muzzle blast cracked the glass panel over the gun barrel. It was used operationally on 15 August in a mission to Vitry-en-Artois before higher authority condemned the modification as unsafe, as the blowback overstressed the nose components.[91] Collectively, these efforts prompted Wright Field engineers to mount a pair of .50-caliber guns in a swiveling nose mount, a common feature on many B-17s arriving in England by September 1943.[92] These efforts reached their culmination with the development of the Bendix remotely operated chin turret, which was added to the final production models of the B-17F and made standard in the B-17G, bringing the overall defensive armament of the B-17 up to thirteen .50-caliber machine guns.[93]

Some pilots asked for supplemental armor in their aircraft. In November 1942, an engineer officer in one squadron flying B-24Ds (possibly the 93rd Group) requested the installation of armor plate to the nose compartment floor to protect the pilot, navigator, and bombardier. The addition helped the plane's overall balance, with the armor becoming a standard feature in later models of the plane.[94] Lieutenant Hal Turell, a bombardier and navigator from the 445th Bomb Group, recalled an armor plate kit installed in front of the instrument panel that was subsequently removed because of an unfavorable weight addition. He noted, however, that crews subsequently had the welding shop cut plates to fit crew seat bottoms, as "they knew what needed to be protected."[95] Colonel Dale O. Smith, commanding the 384th Bomber Group, installed plates beneath the pilot and copilot seats to protect "his most valuable parts," while also wearing his flak vest.[96]

Eventually, just about every plane used by the Eighth Air Force in World War II received some sort of modification, either at centrally located modification depots or in the field.[97] Captain John H. Truluck, who flew seventy-one missions with the 63rd Fighter Squadron, 56th Fighter Group, made a host of changes to his P-47 while flying out of his home base at Halesworth, England—some authorized, some not. Upon receipt of his plane, christened the *Lady Jane*, the Clemson ROTC product visited a Rolls-Royce dealership on his first trip to London, where he purchased a smoked glass sun visor and a side mirror. Aided by the squadron machine shop, he affixed both to the top of the plane's canopy to allow him to check his "six," a practice quickly adopted by other pilots in the squadron. Assisted by his crew chief, Sgt. James Walker, he installed additional ducting inside his plane's cockpit to directly channel warm air toward his hands and feet, a necessity when flying at escort altitudes.[98]

One modification, however, earned Truluck a rebuke from Fighter Command. During a 31 May 1943 mission, a P-47 piloted by one of the "most likeable" pilots in Truluck's squadron unexpectedly did a wingover and plunged into the sea off the Dutch coast, killing its pilot. On a subsequent mission, Truluck noticed his own oxygen consumption was above normal. After his crew chief checked his oxygen system, Truluck concluded that on a previous mission his fallen companion must have bumped his oxygen regulator lever (located near his elbow) when he entered the cockpit, switching it to full rich, a setting "normally used only in emergency." To address the problem, he told his crew chief to move the control a foot forward in the cockpit and forwarded the recommendation up his chain of command.[99]

That December, Truluck's squadron sent their planes to a rear-echelon repair depot for installation of paddle wheel propellers that increased the P-47's climb rate. When the *Lady Jane* returned, the oxygen regulator lever was in its original position, with Fighter Command citing Truluck for the lever's "improper location." Truluck promptly ignored the report, telling his crew chief to restore the lever to the modified position. In March 1944, Truluck's P-47 was recalled for the installation of water injection kits, and the plane received a second citation from Fighter Command. As before, Truluck ignored it and ordered his crew chief to return the lever to its modified forward position.[100]

The issue came to a head when an air inspector from Fighter Command arrived to Truluck's base and singled out his plane for a special inspection. In the chow line later that day, the air inspector, accompanied by representatives from Fighter Command, disciplined Truluck in front of the entire squadron for having his oxygen regulator lever in an unauthorized location. The pilot stood his ground and proclaimed, "Major, when you are flying, you can have the regulator any place that you like, but as long as my ass is up there being shot at, the regulator will be where I want it, and I don't give a damn what Wright Field and the Tech Manual say." A few days later, squadron commander Col. David Schilling summoned Truluck to report on the altercation with the inspector. After hearing his pilot's version of what happened, Schilling said, "Why the hell didn't you tell me? I'm having mine moved today." Truluck noted that several months later when a newer model of the P-47 recently arrived from the United States, the plane's oxygen regulator lever was in the location he had specified.[101]

Truluck relied on his crew chief, Sergeant Walker, to make the various modifications to the *Lady Jane*. Similarly, Curtis LeMay singled out engineer officer Lt. Benjamin Fulkrod as responsible for transforming the 305th Bomb Group into what it ultimately became. LeMay described Fulkrod, a former tech sergeant and line chief who was commissioned lieutenant shortly after the war began, as "a practical engineer officer to the point of genius." Recognizing that "good supply people and good engineering people naturally scrounged whenever and wherever they could," Fulkrod distinguished himself as the individual responsible not only for material the 305th was supposed to have, but also for "stuff [they] weren't supposed to have." Crafting tools, reamers, and other "logistical gadgets" and scrounging "raw parts to make new parts out of," Fulkrod used his technical skill and ingenuity to get the group's planes airborne, increasing his value to the group, which sought suitable replacements by enlisting "ex–filling station employees, or farmers who had been cutting sileage the year before."[102]

There is hardly a pilot or member of an aircrew who did not consider engineers like Fulkrod and aircraft maintainers like the 100th Bomb Group's Kenneth Lemmons the "unsung heroes of the air war."[103] These men worked tirelessly in unenviable conditions—rain, snow, dust, heat, or cold—to ensure that each plane had its full complement of bombs and ammunition and was ready to fly prior to each mission.[104] Employing "techniques of inventive maintenance," they "fought with ingenuity, intelligence, and interminable hours of hard work," in an often overlooked "war against the attrition of battle, against the wear of time and exposure, against shortage of material, and most of all, against the ruthless demands . . . pilots had to make on these machines." Without their efforts, pilots devolved into "impotent warriors who could do no more than shake [their] fists at heaven."[105]

Ground crewmen stalked the flight line long before the aircrews awoke, draining condensation from fuel lines and checking radios, oxygen lines, bomb loads, and safety pins to ensure that when the bombs dropped out, they would be armed and would explode on impact. Climbing into their planes for their mission, the crews greeted each other with heartfelt messages of "Good Luck" and waited for the "all clear" from the pilots before firing up the engines. After takeoff, ground crewmen ate a late breakfast at the mess or grabbed a few hours' sleep, ever-anxious for the return of "their" planes—and their flight crews. At the expected hour, they gathered, anticipating the "loud and definite" engine roar of an easy "milk run," meaning the return of most or all of the planes in a tight flying formation. Otherwise, they craned their necks and awaited the unfortunate—loose formations that were harbingers of a costly mission producing battle-damaged aircraft, injured aircrews, or even worse, planes lost to flak or enemy fighters.[106] Damaged airplanes meant work for the maintainers and ground crew. Lacking any set schedule other than "now," mechanics, electricians, prop specialists, sheet metal specialists, and service squadron maintainers swarmed the plane identifying what was damaged and what needed repair. When a damaged plane did not make it all the way to its home field, mobile repair units ventured out to patch up the plane and return it as quickly as possible.[107] The results from ground crewmen, both in repairing aircraft and in keeping them flying meant constant invention and improvisation—and liberal applications of American ingenuity.

Even at established air bases, scrounging for "supplies and parts" was commonplace.[108] Whit Hill, who helped engineer additional guns in the nose of the 91st's *Delta Rebel*, became resourceful to ensure that he had the requisite supplies to repair his squadron's aircraft. Arriving in England, their "equipment was limited by a table of authorization, which was inadequate to say the least." Borrowing sheet aluminum and using the machine shop of a nearby Royal Air Force maintenance unit, Hill either acquired or made enough "hand-rivet sets and other repair equipment" to perform his job. Ordered to attend an airframe school at the Eighth Air Force's Burtonwood supply depot, he and his engineering officer, a Captain Larson, took advantage of an opportunity to slyly make an illicit requisition. While distracting the depot guide, Hill loaded his supervisor's staff car with "much needed but unauthorized equipment such as straight and offsight electrical drills, rivet guns, rivet sets, bucking bars, etc.," so that on their return to base, they were "ready to meet the action."[109]

Working smarter, not harder, maintainers learned it was easier to bring the tools to the airplane, than the other way around. In Italy, Cpl. Eugene Comeau built a toolbox on wheels that carried "every tool needed for a complete engine change." With it in tow, he saved valuable repair time by eliminating the need to run "around the field or into 'Tech. Supply' for needed tools."[110] Others assembled a mobile metal shop complete with "air compressor for pneumatic riveting and a generator for electric drill motors" and two air storage tanks, mounting all on a tricycle powered by a one-cylinder gas engine.[111] A group of ground crewmen from the 401st Bomb Squadron, 91st Bomb Group, built the "Creep," a miniature, motorized tool truck. In addition to carrying tools, the Creep's crew used the "salvage masterpiece" to check booster coils; heat soldering guns; troubleshoot ignition harnesses, high-altitude heating suits, and instrument panels; or even start a plane's engine.[112] The sheet metal crews in Whit Hill's group repurposed surplus bomb-loading carts, "modifying them into portable sheet metal work benches that included electrical and air compressors, a floodlight, workbench with vise, storage for sheet metal and parts and room for eight tool boxes," that could be towed behind a jeep.[113] Such creations were similar to mobile battery chargers made by 1st Lt. Lawrence Trost and T.Sgt. Hugh Jones; a jeep-mounted field-testing unit that checked manifold pressure, tachometer, fuel, and oil pressure and navigation instruments designed by Sgt. Roland Brouillette and Cpl. Ernest Earn; a spray cart built from salvaged parts by S.Sgt. Edward La Pinsky; or the all-purpose mobile maintenance shop with eight special attachments that ranged from derrick, to battery charger, to radio equipment, built on an M-2 Cletrac High Speed Tractor by Sgt. Leo Alton, an effort that earned him the Legion of Merit.[114]

Other ground crewmen devised new tools, gadgets, or machines to maximize efficiency while servicing their aircraft, "resurrecting spare parts from the scrap heap, substituting when possible, and making equipment when necessary."[115] In addition to his rolling tool cart, Corporal Comeau fabricated a mechanical finger to twist safety wire in tight spots. He rolled this tool, along with wrenches and sockets of his own design, throughout Italy on an aircraft servicing cart of his own design.[116] Sergeant Jack C. Freeman fabricated a sump plug wrench from used scrap iron to facilitate the plug's quick and easy removal in the Pratt & Whitney R-1830-Twin Wasp engine (used in the Consolidated B-24 Liberator and Douglas C-47).[117] The Pratt & Whitney R-1830-model engine inspired numerous tools, for Sgt. Virgil Smith designed a wrench to tighten push rod housing gland nuts on both the R-1830-43 and -65 engines. In Italy, T.Sgt. John Greed used scrap metal to build a mock-up test outfit for fast-feathering systems, as well as a device to pre-oil engines.[118] Staff Sergeant James J. Voukon salvaged materials to build a special propeller wrench to secure the four-bladed props to the propeller shafts of P-51s while maintaining the planes in England, while airmen in Algeria transformed a fifty-five-gallon drum mounted on a metal frame into a reclamation drum facilitating salvage and reclamation of small nuts, bolts, and washers.[119]

For the men of the US Signal Service Group, theirs was anything but an individual effort, for many unwittingly discovered they had been communicating in the United States as peacetime "ham" radio enthusiasts. Master

Sergeant Francis J. Chotkowski, who had operated amateur station W1KZV out of his home in Chelsea, Massachusetts, discovered that T.Sgt. Russell L. Lewis answered to the call letters W4CSZ from Atlanta. After training at several Signal Corps schools in the United States, in England they became comrades in arms, repairing radio units used in Flying Fortress bombers. Their efforts resulted in the construction of a complicated tuning machine to test all seven different pieces of radio equipment carried in a B-17. Recognizing that the issued, truck-mounted test platform was grossly impractical for rapid airfield tests, they cannibalized parts to create a man-portable version weighing two pounds. They also built work tables and code oscillators, repaired broken radios for their own use, and fixed and repaired all sorts of Signal Corps gear at their airfield in England. According to their commander, Capt. Jack Millard, every man in the outfit was a "triple threat man," capable of refurbishing, repairing, or fabricating additional parts to keep radios operational. After attending numerous training schools, they applied their ingenuity to all sorts of work, earning Signal Corps accolades along the way.[120]

Airmen also solved supply problems by creating many desperately needed parts and fittings from scrap. In the 93rd Bomb Group, T.Sgt. Angelo Lauri earned "Man of the Month" accolades in *Ordnance Sergeant* magazine for his improvised bomb safety clips; he invented a machine that produced a sufficient supply of pinlike clips to ensure that bombs being carried in aircraft did not prematurely detonate. "Using scrap materials ranging from bicycle parts to automobile springs," Lauri's machine produced nearly 1,500 clips in an hour, whereas a "laborious manual method" produced only a fraction in the same period.[121] Master Sergeant Maynard Gibbs of the 509th Bomb Squadron, 351st Bomb Group, used parts from a damaged top turret ammunition motor to build an electric screwdriver.[122] Master Sergeant Frank Kuret modified a discarded brake shoe grinder to grind milling machine cutters.[123] Technical Sergeant James W. Turner's field coil pole shoe expander allowed him to install new field coils in repaired airplane starter motors eight times as fast as he could before, saving valuable time and effort when crews needed to quickly return planes to flight status.[124]

Some base-made devices were elaborate constructions that employed mechanical power to accomplish larger tasks. Staff Sergeant Joseph Flitter salvaged a bomb hoist from a wrecked Flying Fortress and combined it with a landing gear retraction unit from a B-24 Liberator, mounting the combined hoist and boom on a small tractor to create a unit capable of removing a 500 lb propeller from an engine nacelle with relative ease.[125] Master Sergeant Charles D. Groff devised a similar tool for use by the First Tactical Air Force Air Depot from a carry-jack left behind when the Luftwaffe made a hasty retreat from northern France.[126] In Italy, S.Sgt. Granville Fannion scrounged parts from a downed Spitfire, a P-40, and several Italian vehicles to build a hydraulically operated rolling drop tank remover, capable of either installing or removing full drop tanks with ease.[127] Sergeant Joseph Ortolani made a wing hoist from scrap that could lift "a complete wing section of any plane, even a bomber."[128] Technical Sergeant George L. Mercer and M.Sgt. John Anthal built a water distillation unit used to replace the distilled water in aircraft batteries among Fifteenth Air Force planes in Italy. S.Sgt. George E. Rupp and M.Sgt. Woodrow Wingo fabricated a test chest incorporating "salvaged plane parts, a heating unit for controls, pressure pump, circulating hand pump, temperature indicator, and oxygen bottle" into a device capable of checking "coolant shutter control valves and the hydraulic systems" on the Lockheed P-38 Lightning. Master Sergeant Walter M. Bakula and Sgt. Everett R. VanCleave built a metalworking "duplicating machine" utilizing an acetylene torch to cut duplicate engine plates from sheet steel.[129]

Because they shared a common background and upbringing in the United States, the fact that airmen otherwise isolated from each other frequently improvised similar solutions to the same problem should come as no surprise. In the same way that airmen of three different bomb squadrons looked to solve the problems associated with weak forward armament of the B-17, airmen who struggled to change tires on B-17s and B-24s built similar machines to make their work easier. Major Joseph L. Myers's hydraulic wheel puller separated the 639 lb bomber wheel from its hub in less than two minutes.[130] Master Sergeant Dillard Centers, a "52-year-old Liberator crew chief" and the "oldest man in his group," built a similar device in Italy.[131] Men of the 535th Bomb Squadron, 381st Bomb Group, in England built an almost identical device to change the tires on their B-17s.[132] Their device was similar to that made in India by S.Sgt. Emil Martinelli and Cpl. Virgil Peoples, in China by S.Sgt. Louis Haslip and T.Sgt. A. R. Tye, and in Italy by the ever-creative M.Sgt. Walter Bakula.[133]

By the end of the war, airmen had saved time and effort and contributed to a strategic bombing campaign in Europe that ultimately involved 2.4 million men, 80,000 aircraft, and 243 aircraft combat groups, the vast majority of which arrived *after* April 1944. Despite the best intentions of AWPD-1, the strategic bomber campaign did not defeat Germany on its own, as many planes limped back to their bases "on a wing and a prayer," only to be repaired by intrepid aircrewmen on the ground. Even when augmented by the arrival of newer aircraft from the United States, Allied bombers took heavy casualties. Nonetheless, the almost constant presence of bombers over Nazi Germany ensured that while Allied forces learned how to defeat the Wehrmacht in France, the Netherlands, Luxembourg, Belgium, and eventually Germany itself, as many Nazi guns were pointed into the air as were directed toward Allied troops fighting on the ground.[134]

Having invented the combat box and made strategic bombing practicable by arguing for the effectiveness of a straight-and-level approach, Brig. Gen. Curtis E. LeMay departed Europe in the summer of 1944, bound for the Pacific theater to assume command over a second strategic bombing campaign, this time over Imperial Japan. Building on the foundation created by General Kenney at the Battle of the Bismarck Sea, and working through technical challenges with the B-29 similar to those encountered with the bombers and fighters conducting the air war in Europe, LeMay continued innovating. When the tactics used in Europe proved ineffective against the Japanese home islands, LeMay developed new ways to employ the B-29 Superfortress, resulting in a firebombing campaign that would lead to the destruction of Tokyo and the eventual decision to drop atomic bombs on Hiroshima and Nagasaki.[135]

In Japan, as had been the case in the Mediterranean and across northern Europe, success in American air campaigns came as a result of innovation, if not outright invention. This was the way it had to be, as Americans in the new US Army Air Forces had little in the way of established doctrinal experience to draw on. As Steinbeck had recognized in *Bombs Away*, "the Air Force has no centuries of trial and error to study; it must feel its way"—and "make its way in a new field where there are no precedents." And it was only the United States, where "speed, mechanics, and motors are almost born," that improvised air campaigns of this magnitude.[136]

In his 1944 report to Secretary of War Henry Stimson, General Hap Arnold recognized the uniqueness of the United States with respect to prosecuting this new kind of air war. First came the "staggering job of conversion," the necessity of transforming the nation's existing factories to the production of aircraft. This conversion, he argued, could take place "only in America," where a "tire manufacturer built fuselages and tail surfaces. A former pickle plant turned out skis and floats, and a manufacturer of girdles and corsets began making parachutes." However, as Charles Sorensen proved with the construction of the B-24, the link between the automobile and the aircraft was paramount, not only with respect to the means of production, but in terms of the familiarity and experience that young Americans had with the automobile before the war even began.[137]

As a result of the emerging American fascination with the automobile, the mechanical abilities of the typical American aircrew were well beyond those of the nation's adversaries, not to mention its allies. Recognizing that the nation's young men were "accustomed to teamwork, competition and mechanical processes," General Arnold noted that "the mechanical knowledge and experience gained from rebuilding a $10 used car has doubtless saved the life of many an American by enabling him to 'nurse' a damaged plane home."[138] This was a fact that was not lost on George Kenney, Curtis LeMay, nor the Abners of the airfields who spent their spare time devising Rube Goldberg–type contraptions to improve their ability to repair aircraft, enhance the world they lived in, and ensure the success of the American air wars in World War II.

During the lull between the two waves of Japanese attacks on 7 December 1941, ground crew at Naval Air Station Kaneohe Bay, Oahu, Hawaii, improvised machine-gun mounts, using shop workbenches and vises to hold the scavenged machine guns in place. Photo courtesy of National Naval Aviation Museum, 1987.096.001.037.

After observing the up-gunned Douglas A-20 Havoc flown out of Charters Towers, Australia, by the 3rd Attack Group, Gen. George Kenney ordered Maj. Paul "Pappy" Gunn to see how many .50-caliber machine guns he could fit into the nose of a North American B-25 Mitchell bomber. The addition of four side-mounted guns (two on each side of the fuselage), fired in conjunction with two in the top turret, along with eight that Gunn ingeniously mounted in the nose, created a highly effectively "commerce raider" that, employed along with skip-bombing tactics, wrought considerable havoc on the Japanese fleet at the Battle of the Bismarck Sea. Photo courtesy of NARA, 342-FH-3A44539-71467AC.

Capt. Brenton Devol Jr. engineered a 4 × 70 yard runway atop LST-906 in the Mediterranean during advance preparations for Operation Husky. Incapable of flying from North Africa to Sicily, L-4 observation aircraft instead took off from these makeshift carriers at multiple points during the landings, which greatly facilitated artillery support of troops on the ground. Photo courtesy of Naval History and Heritage Command, NH-94904.

Lt. Col. Gilbert Weymond and M.Sgt. Bill Hahn field-modified a P-47 Thunderbolt to make it into the premier close air support platform of World War II. The ingenious pair mechanically rerouted the aircraft drop tank release cables from a position behind the pilot's seat to toggles mounted below the instrument panel, making accurate bomb drops possible. Photo from the author's collection.

"Fire two more fer effect, Joe. I'm makin' a stovepipe."

Cartoonist Bill Mauldin, who served with the 45th Infantry Division, captured American ingenuity in his depiction of "Willie" and "Joe" while the division wintered in Italy. Copyright by Bill Mauldin (1944); used courtesy of Bill Mauldin Estate LLC.

When German minefields stalled the Allied advance from the Anzio beachhead, Maj. Harry Tyson created the 60 mm mortar, mine-clearing projector. Using an inert mortar round, a section of one-inch iron pipe, and twelve 100-foot strands of Primacord, the 1st Armored Division's chemical officer successfully created a device capable of clearing a path thirty yards long and eighteen inches wide. The 105th Engineer Combat Battalion, 30th Infantry Division, later adapted bazooka rounds for a similar purpose, eventually passing along their findings as part of "Combat Lessons" compiled by HQETOUSA. Photo courtesy of Branch History Office, US Army CBRN School, Ft. Leonard Wood, MO.

Brig. Gen. John O'Daniel invented the "Infantry Sled," hoping to successfully break out from the Anzio beachhead. Resembling a torpedo shell cut in half, the 529th Ordnance Heavy Auto Maintenance Company built 360 sled units prior to the offensive, each of which could tow twelve infantrymen behind a tank. Though initial results were unimpressive, O'Daniel salvaged those that remained and ordered them reused in the invasion of southern France. Photo courtesy of NARA, NAID 1540302.

Early models of both the Boeing B-17 Flying Fortress and Consolidated B-24 Liberator lacked adequate forward-mounted armament, requiring crews to modify the aircraft in the field to counter enemy aircraft coming in at "twelve o'clock high." Three different B-17 squadrons in England all claimed to have been the first to mount .50-caliber machine guns in the nose of a bomber, utilizing an arrangement similar to this one used by the 322nd Bomb Squadron, 91st Bomb Group, based out of Bassingbourn. Photo courtesy of NARA, 342-FH-3A6366-69348AC.

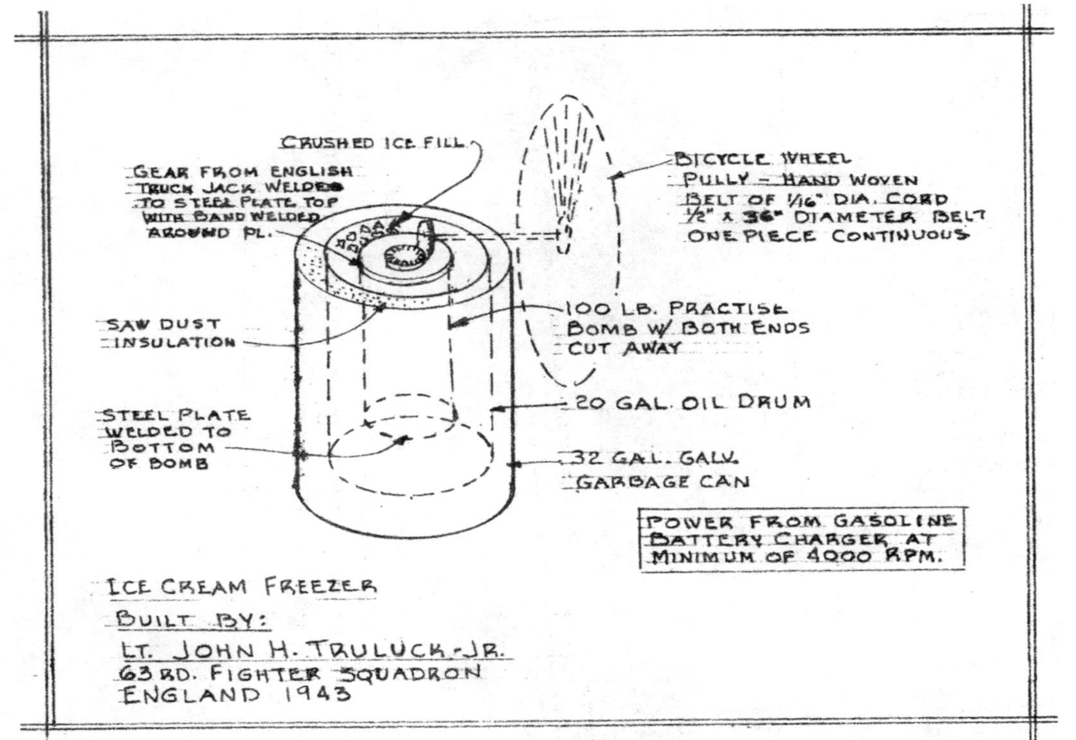

To satisfy his desire for good old American-style ice cream, clever P-47 pilot Capt. John Truluck fabricated an ice cream freezer from spare parts, which he subsequently wore out in meeting his squadron's demands. Here is his recollection of the materials he scrounged to build his freezer. Diagram from the author's collection.

Using parts scavenged from a wrecked British Spitfire, a Curtiss P-40, and other bits from around his base in Italy, S.Sgt. Granville Fannion of Paintsville, Kentucky, fabricated a hydraulic drop tank remover for use at his 15th Air Force airstrip. Fannion's device permitted the safe removal of full drop tanks for their subsequent reuse. Photo courtesy of NARA, 342-FH-3A23622-59455AC.

In advance of the Normandy invasion, Pfc. Forrest Guth of E Company, 506th PIR, modified his M1942 jump jacket by removing pockets from a spare jacket and sewing them to the upper sleeves and skirt of the jacket he would wear when he jumped into Normandy, filling them with extra "goodies" he wanted when he landed. His original uniform is on display at the D-Day Experience/ Dead Man's Corner Museum, in Saint-Côme-du-Mont, France. As company armorer, Guth also modified the M-1 carbine, converting it to a fully automatic weapon. Photo by author.

In efforts to defeat the challenges posed by the hedgerows of Normandy, the 747th Tank Battalion used "salad forks" to punch holes in the ancient field dividers. Once made, spent 75 mm artillery shells packed with explosives were thrust into the holes and detonated, blasting a path for tanks and infantry. Photo from the author's collection.

While based in Normandy, maintainers of the 354th Fighter Squadron field-modified a P-51B1 Mustang "Razorback" by removing a gas tank from behind the pilot's seat and installing a back seat, seen here as used by Maj. Gen. Pete Quesada and Gen. Dwight Eisenhower to scout over Normandy in advance of Operation Cobra. Photo copyright by the Imperial War Museums, FRE 401.

Engineers of the 94th Infantry Division welded two wheel hubs together in fabricating "Short Cut," a jeep adapted for rail use. This arrangement allowed Signals Officer Lt. Col. Albert Turner to patrol Saint-Nazaire following the unit's arrival in France in September 1944. Photo courtesy of NARA, 111-SC-232290.

Chief of Staff Gen. George Marshall's decision to motorize the US Army prompted the design and construction of the Bantam jeep, the prototype itself a product of American ingenuity. Assembled from parts and subassemblies taken from a variety of domestic auto manufacturers, more than 640,000 were produced during the war. Photo courtesy of Smithsonian Institution, National Museum of American History, TR.312822, US War Department photo.

In May 1944, a Consolidated B-24 Liberator fabricated on Charles Sorenson's assembly line managed to land safely as a result of American ingenuity. When enemy fire took out the plane's hydraulic system over Germany, the crew of Lt. James Dobson of the 446th Bomb Group took their parachutes, fastened them to the interior of the plane, and threw them out the waist gunner's windows just before they landed in England. Photo courtesy of NARA, 342-FH-3A05941-51638AC.

TO KEEP THE BATTLE MACHINES SLUGGING

Harvester Men Form Maintenance Battalion to Serve the Battle Line

FIGHTING MACHINES, like soldiers, suffer battle casualties. Tanks, trucks, tractors and guns immobilized in combat are useless until repaired.

The men who repair the wounded machines in swiftly-moving armored warfare may tip the scale to victory. Maintenance in the wake of battle calls for soldiers who can grind a valve or handle a tough welding job—men with whom mechanics is second nature.

Army Ordnance, in its quest for men to operate its mobile front-line machine shops, came to International Harvester and suggested the formation of a battalion of mechanical specialists from among Harvester's employes and dealers. Harvester tackled the recruiting job and assumed the expense. Within two weeks the enlistment quota was passed. Now this new maintenance battalion is part of another armored division.

From Harvester factories and service stations, and dealers' shops all over the United States, came mechanics skilled in the building and servicing of machines. They volunteered eagerly to go to the front lines to keep the combat equipment on the field of action.

They will serve with the first such battalion formed from the manpower of a single company. Harvester takes the greatest pride in the speed and enthusiasm with which these hundreds of men volunteered; and in the aptitude of the men now in field training, reported to us by the regular Army officers in command. They are worthy comrades of the 5000 Harvester men who preceded them into military service.

American mechanics are the world's best. They come from the factories, shops and service stations of America—free men—builders of a free land. The Army needs 100,000 more of these men, to be enlisted in many similar maintenance units. Their skills are among our greatest assets in keeping the battle machines slugging for Victory.

INTERNATIONAL HARVESTER COMPANY
180 North Michigan Avenue Chicago, Illinois

INTERNATIONAL HARVESTER

When the US Army needed additional ordnance units to support armored divisions raised for the war, recruiters turned to corporate America to supply experienced manpower capable of performing the required tasks. In 1942, the War Department called on the International Harvester Corporation to supply 859 men for the 134th Ordnance and Maintenance Battalion. The Harvester Men arrived in France in November 1944, served with distinction, and eventually earned a Meritorious Unit Citation. This advertisement lauding the Harvester Battalion appeared in *Life* in October 1942. Photo from the author's collection.

While imprisoned in German stalags, many American "kriegies" fabricated stoves from bits of scrap wood and metal. These blowers greatly enhanced the heating capacity of the meager fuel rations available to imprisoned Americans. Photo courtesy of Clark Special Collections, McDermott Library, USAF Academy.

Lt. Col. Charles Carpenter mounted multiple bazookas on the wings of his L-4 Grasshopper light observation aircraft. By the end of the war, he was credited with the destruction of several German armored cars and tanks while flying his field-engineered flying light "tank." Photo courtesy of NARA, 342-FH-3A16503-54496AC.

In efforts to counter the dreaded German 88 mm antitank gun and panzerfaust antitank weapon, American tankers added a variety of items, including bogey wheels, logs, sandbags, and concrete to up-armor their M4 Sherman tanks. Here, an M4 of the 2nd Armored Division sports concrete armor that was added to the front glacis plate to deter antitank fire. Photo courtesy of NARA, 111-SC-203168.

In early December 1944, the commanding officer of the 48th Tank Battalion, 14th Armored Division, ordered his battalion to up-armor their M4 Shermans with elaborate metal frames filled with sandbags. Toward the war's end, such efforts were deemed superfluous by Gen. George Patton, seen here ordering the sandbags removed from a 14th AD tank. Photo courtesy of NARA, 111-SC-436540.

As early as May 1944, some US tank destroyer battalions equipped with the M10 tank destroyer had begun fabricating armored tops to protect crews in the open-turreted vehicles. Here is one such effort devised by the 536th Ordnance Heavy Maintenance Company for Seventh Army in early 1945. Photo courtesy of NARA, 111-SC-206966.

GIs made a host of modifications to the ubiquitous jeep. During the winter of 1944, T.Sgt. Luther May of the 981st Engineer Maintenance Battalion fabricated "mudshoes" to enhance the traction of his jeep, adding a wire-cutting bar to the front bumper to protect against wires used by the Germans in efforts to decapitate unwary Americans. This jeep also sports a field-fabricated equipment rack mounted on the back of the vehicle. Photo courtesy of NARA, 111-SC-199098.

GIs from all theaters of operation used their ingenuity to help stay clean, fabricating a variety of laundry machines that ranged from simple propellers hooked to a cam shaft to drive a plunger, to elaborate powered devices cobbled together from a variety of parts. Propeller specialist Sgt. John Dowell built this washer from spare parts collected from his B-24 Liberator base in Italy. With his invention, he could do a week's worth of laundry in a few minutes. Photo courtesy of NARA, 342-FH-3A24136-53513AC.

Lt. Henry Bellmon of the 4th Marine Tank Battalion rests on his M4 Medium on Iwo Jima. Throughout operations in the Pacific, the battalion, filled at the war's outset with "4-H and FFA boys," made a practice of adding plank armor, a water tank, and a phone mounted in a satchel on the rear sponson of their tanks. Photo courtesy of NARA, 127-GW-347.

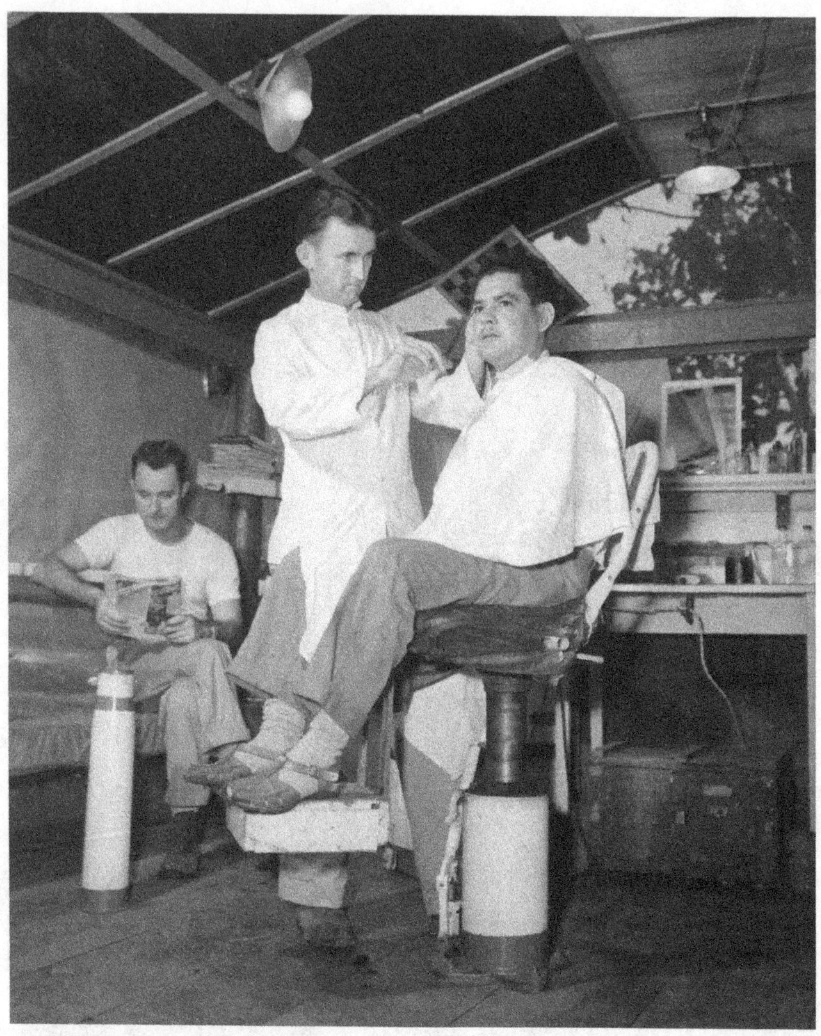

In a rear area in the South Pacific, Sgt. James Tankersly built a hydraulic barber chair, shown here as he gives Pfc. Jose D'Acosta a haircut. Fabricated from a discarded jack used to remove engines from B-24s, Tankersly's contrivance also used piping from a cracked up airplane, a few cushions, and nuts and bolts from the machine shop; he added an ashtray made from the decorated casing of a 90 mm antiaircraft shell. Photo courtesy of NARA, 342-FH-3A45164-67829AC.

In addition to building "General Heavey's Battleship," a decked-over LCM sporting two 20 mm antiaircraft guns, one 37 mm antiaircraft gun, four Martin B-26 top turrets with two .50-caliber machine guns each, and forty-eight rocket tubes, the men of Gen. William Heavey's 2nd Engineer Special Brigade supported landings in the Philippines with armored amphtracs. They gave their craft "teeth" by adding a 37 mm antiaircraft gun as well as .50-caliber machine guns and rockets. Photo from Second Engineer Special Brigade, *History*, 64.

The Abners of the airfield frequently fell back on their mechanical expertise to fabricate a variety of powered vehicles to help them get around their air bases. Sgt. Johnnie Thornburg built this scooter, which he used on Iwo Jima, from parts donated from a number of wrecked airplanes. Photo courtesy of NARA, 342-FH-3A42504-65023AC.

Airmen in both the European and Pacific theaters made use of abandoned drop tanks for a variety of projects. Here, aircrewmen from the Seventh Air Force in the Palau islands prepare to race their homemade boats. Fabricated from salvaged wing tanks, with oxygen tank outriggers attached to steel braces, their catamarans sported sails salvaged from old parachutes. Photo courtesy of NARA, 342-FH-3A38243-64424AC.

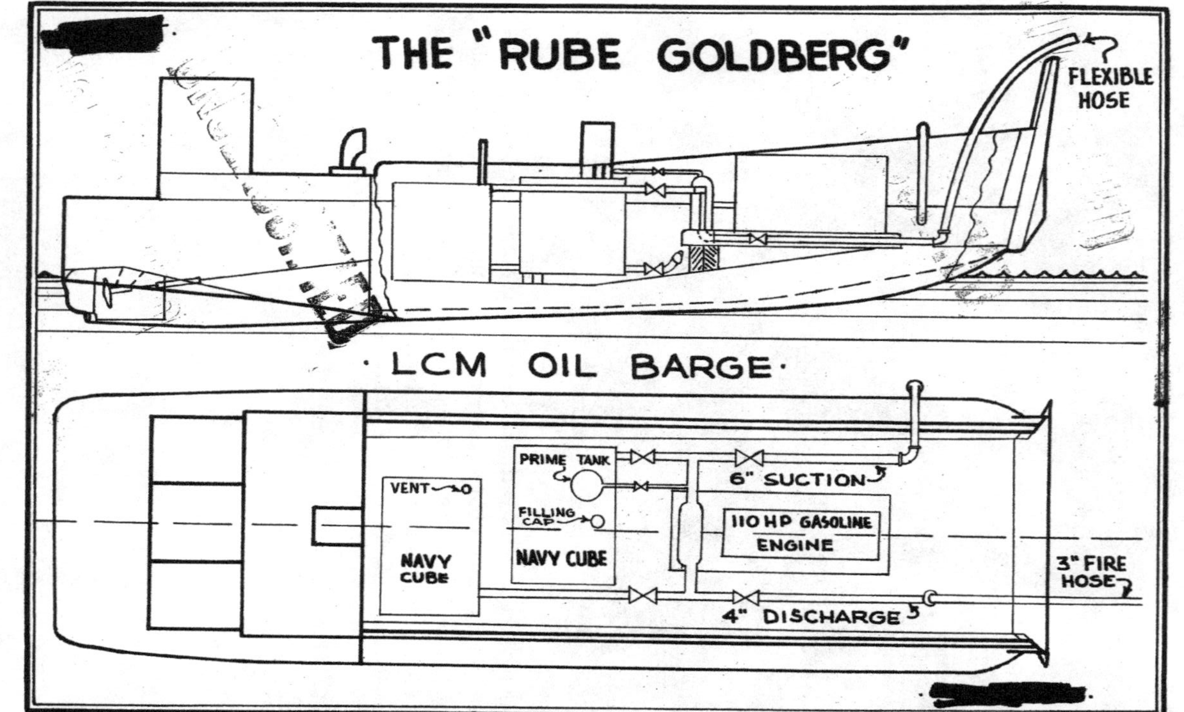

In clearing the fortified positions that blocked the entrance to Manila Bay, GIs of the 38th Infantry Division cobbled together an LCM pumper that they christened the *Rube Goldberg*, in honor of the American artist who made complicated machines to perform simple tasks. The contraption helped enable the recapture of the Philippines. Photo from "Report on the M-7 Operation, 38th Infantry Division, the Avengers of Bataan," WWII-Skelton.

CHAPTER 5

Cobbling Together a Crusade

There is, among the mass of individuals who carry rifles in war, a great amount of ingenuity and initiative. If men can naturally and without restraint talk to their officers, the products of their resourcefulness will be available to all. Moreover, out of the habit grows mutual confidence, a feeling of partnership that is the essence of *esprit de corps.*

—*Gen. Dwight D. Eisenhower*

The moment the first airborne pathfinders jumped from their C-47s into Normandy, the chief tools in their fight against the Germans were "ingenuity and initiative." Those paratroopers, as well as men of the 1st, 4th, 29th Infantry Divisions and 2nd Ranger Battalion who stormed Utah Beach and Omaha Beach knew their missions and had trained for them well before 6 June 1944. As Capt. Robert Miller of the 175th Regiment, 29th Infantry Division, recalled, however, everything changed upon contact with the enemy. During his regiment's preinvasion planning, Miller's commanding officer, Col. Paul "Pop" Good, picked up their operation plan and tried to tear "the biggest telephone book you've ever seen" in half. Unsuccessful in his attempt, Good threw the book over his shoulder and said, "Forget this goddamned thing. You get your ass on the beach. I'll be there waiting for you and I'll tell you what to do. There ain't anything in this plan that is going to go right."[1] Other commanders came to the same conclusion. The official history of the 743rd Tank Battalion recognized that in the Normandy invasion "Battle Plans don't stay the way they are drawn on paper."[2]

As American troops began the effort to liberate western Europe, ingenuity and initiative became their watchwords. The vast majority of the American everymen who invaded France on 6 June 1944, draftees into what Eisenhower called the "Great Crusade," possessed little if any combat experience. As chaos reigned supreme on D-Day, groups of officers and noncommissioned officers pried victory from the brink of defeat, leading American citizen-soldiers into Fortress Europe.[3] As GIs fought their way across the European continent, these men, and those that followed, evolved into "most formidable soldier[s]."[4] In defeating the Germans, these men embraced a steep learning curve, recognizing problems, improvising to achieve success, and passing this information up the chain of command.[5]

The cobbled-together nature of this campaign lasted well beyond the beaches of Normandy. It represented a curious amalgam of these Americans' youthful upbringing during the Great Depression and their exposure to machine technology, blended with their organization and training as they transitioned from citizens to citizen-soldiers. Beginning in the hedgerows of Normandy and continuing throughout the drive across France, American GIs learned and adapted, taking advantage of the vast array of technological support that accompanied the US Army in Europe. The result was the application of American ingenuity, as clever GIs tinkered and improvised with the war machines that were a part of the largest and most mechanized army ever assembled.

The American vanguard for Operation Overlord had arrived in Great Britain by the time General Eisenhower became supreme commander of the Allied Expeditionary Forces in January 1944.[6] Having recently witnessed "Yankee ingenuity and resourcefulness . . . tested to the limit" in North Africa, Eisenhower understood that the campaign in western Europe would further challenge the grit and mettle of the American soldier.[7] On 25 February 1944, Eisenhower, with the concurrence of the Combined Chiefs of Staff of the Allied Expeditionary Forces, issued Neptune, the US First Army operational plan for Overlord. According to the plan, the 4th Infantry Division would land on Utah Beach, supported by elements of the 82nd and 101st Airborne Divisions dropped behind the beaches to prevent the enemy from attacking the invaders on the Cotentin Peninsula. The 1st and 29th Divisions would target Omaha Beach, supported by elements of the 2nd and 5th Ranger Battalions.[8] Of the infantry divisions designated for the initial invasion, only the 1st had combat experience, having already "swallowed a bellyful of heroics" in both North Africa and Sicily.[9] While the 4th and 29th conducted extensive training exercises at the Assault Training Center after their arrival in Britain, neither unit had seen combat.[10] Of the airborne divisions, only part of the 82nd had combat experience. The 504th Parachute Infantry Regiment (PIR) remained in Italy, while the 505th PIR, which had jumped in Operation Husky in Sicily and Operation Avalanche at Salerno, transferred to England. They were joined by the 507th and 508th before jumping into Normandy as the 82nd Airborne.[11] The 101st Airborne was untested as a division, though it, like all the others, had conducted extensive training in the United States before deploying. After V and VII Corps established the American beachhead, Gen. Lesley J. McNair's mobilization plan made sixty-eight divisions available, thirty-five of which were designated for northern France, with thirty-three slated for Operation Dragoon, the proposed landings in southern France.[12] The Neptune plan stipulated that these follow-on units would arrive at a rate of roughly 29,000 troops per day, so that by D+14, nearly 500,000 troops total would be in France.[13]

American citizen-soldiers received comprehensive preinvasion training. For elements of the 507th PIR that had arrived in Northern Ireland in early December 1943, their regimen included rapid assembly and initiation of combat, securing and retaining the initiative, recognition of isolation as a normal battlefield condition, the need to attack or defend from any direction, and perhaps most importantly, the "improvisation of weapons and equipment."[14] This creativity manifested itself in a number of ways among members of the two airborne divisions. For some, this meant taking regularly issued equipment and enhancing its capabilities. Captain Chester B. McCoid, who jumped in as the company commander of B Company, 507th PIR, benefited from the regiment's "skilled armorers," who "devised a modification of the airborne M-1, A-1 folding-stock .30 caliber carbine," a weapon typically carried by company commanders. Spending about six dollars on a piece of metal rod, an inventive trooper installed it in the carbine's trigger housing. Pulling the trigger depressed weapon's sear spring, and instead of firing a single round, it continued firing until the trigger was released, offering "extra firepower" that "delighted" McCoid.[15] Lynn "Buck" Compton of Easy Company, 506th Parachute Infantry, carried a similar "deadly capable weapon," produced by company armorer Forrest Guth, but Compton lost his enhanced carbine when his "leg bag," a reinforced gear bag issued to many paratroopers before the invasion, was ripped away while jumping at an excessive airspeed.[16]

In preparing for the invasion, Brig. Gen. James M. Gavin, assistant divisional commander of the 82nd Airborne, recalled that most troopers were "all heavily overloaded." On average, a single trooper carried "an M-1 rifle loaded and ready to use, 156 rounds of rifle ammunition, a pistol with three clips of ammunition, an entrenching tool, a knife, a water canteen, a first aid packet, usually four grenades, reserve rations, some maps, and a raincoat," along with whatever personal gear they felt necessary.[17] Machine gunners and mortarmen carried even more, cramming additional items into spare pockets, bags, or pouches, adding between seventy and ninety pounds to their load.[18] To accommodate this additional gear, troopers modified their M1942 uniform jump jacket and trousers, already designed "with a number of large pockets." Regimental parachute riggers sewed patches of sturdy olive-colored fabric to stress points, or reinforced the elbows and knees of their uniforms. Others reinforced the pockets of their jacket and trousers.[19] Private 1st Class Forrest Guth of E Company, 506th PIR, did more than just reinforce his pockets. "Making something out of another," Guth removed three large pockets from unissued M1942 jump jackets and stitched two to his jacket's rear skirt, adding the third to the jacket's upper right sleeve. Initially adding half an ammo bandoleer to his other sleeve for his cigarette and pipe, which failed to meet expectations, he added a fourth pocket. Seeing his additions, other members of the 506th modified their jackets as well. It was a time, Guth recalled, that you could "make alterations to your equipment if it helped you perform your job."[20]

In readying First Army ordnance units, chief of ordnance Col. John B. Medaris not only oversaw special training to prepare his men for their mission; he also encouraged them to think outside established channels and modify their vehicles. Using M2 or M3 half-tracks as a donor platform, ordnancemen added quad .50 machine guns (heavy M2 .50-caliber machine guns in the typically trailer-mounted M45 Maxson turret) to 321 half-tracks, which were subsequently proven effective against aircraft and infantry.[21] North African, Sicilian, and Italian experience proved the value of added sandbags on the floorboards of trucks, jeeps, and other vehicles, leading to the practice's frequent adoption as a mine deterrent. At the same time, Medaris's ordnancemen welded supplemental armor to the floors of 510 armored cars.[22] For Lt. Belton Cooper of the 18th Armored Ordnance Battalion, 3rd Armored Division, British ordnancemen at Warminster modified "inadequately protected M4 and M4A1 Sherman tanks" by welding one-inch-thick armor plates over the tank's ammunition boxes, with additional armor on the sponsons and turrets. They also placed armor on the glacis plate over the driver's and assistant driver's compartments.[23] In advance of their scheduled 11 July landing, men of the 644th Tank Destroyer Battalion modified M10 tank destroyers. Despite being untested in combat, they recognized the need for protection from shellbursts and small arms fire in their open-topped turrets. To this end, they fabricated covers from one-quarter-inch armor plate and added hinged hatches to permit rapid egress, endorsing the improvisation of comparable covers on all M10 tank destroyers.[24] GIs of the 41st Armored Infantry Regiment, 2nd Armored Division, added 37 mm guns stripped from retired M6 motor carriages to their M2 half-tracks and changed the orientation of the 81 mm mortar mounted in their M4 half-tracks, pointing the mortar toward the front, rather than the rear of the vehicle, as it allowed the troops to bring the weapon into action more quickly.[25]

Not all modifications made by American troops yielded positive results. Brig. Gen. Donald Pratt, the 101st's assistant divisional commander, flew to Normandy in a fabric-covered CG-4 Waco glider, which could carry up to thirteen men, a jeep, a 75 mm howitzer, or a loaded jeep trailer. Lt. Col. Mike Murphy, reportedly one of the Army Air Force's best glider pilots, was Pratt's pilot, and he anticipated no problems delivering the general and his jeep. Unbeknownst to Murphy, well-intentioned but somewhat ignorant ground crewmen had modified Pratt's glider, installing sheet armor on the floor of the cargo compartment to protect its valuable cargo. When Murphy took off on the morning of 6 June, the only indication that his glider was different was that it took much longer to get airborne than normal. Flying from Aldermaston air base to France, Murphy sought "every bit of speed from the tow to gain as much altitude as possible" to keep the glider from stalling. Piloting the overloaded glider after separating from the tow plane was "like trying to fly a freight train," Murphy recalled. Coming in on wet grass at over sixty miles an hour, Murphy's up-armored and overweight glider skidded across the landing field and crashed into a hedgerow. The impact threw Murphy through the window with such force that he broke both his legs. The crash took the life of both Murphy's copilot and General Pratt. The sudden stop snapped the assistant divisional commander's neck as he sat upright in his jeep, making him, inauspiciously, the highest-ranking American officer killed in the invasion, an unfortunate victim of ingenuity gone horribly wrong.[26]

The men of Dog Company, 2nd Ranger Battalion, modified equipment to enhance their mission capabilities as they prepared to scale Pointe du Hoc and eliminate German artillery believed to be emplaced there. The British Department of Miscellaneous Development of the Admiralty provided them with rocket-propelled grapnel hooks to assist in ascending the rocky cliffs, S.Sgt. Jack Kuhn made significant additions to their four "DUKWs," the General Motors–produced amphibious six-wheeled 2.5-ton trucks. Visiting Merryweathers Ltd., a London firefighting equipment manufacturer established in 1692, he secured four extending ladders, mounted them on four DUKWs, adding a pair of Vickers K machine guns to the top of each. He hoped that each DUKW could "swim" to the cliff base and extend its ladder, with a Ranger atop each providing suppressing fire while the remainder of the company made their ascent and reduced the enemy battery.[27] Unfortunately for the Rangers, little went according to plan. Lt. Col. James Earl Rudder's best efforts notwithstanding, Dog Company not only arrived on the east, rather than the west, side of Pointe du Hoc, but they hit the beaches at 7:08 a.m., nearly forty minutes after their planned arrival time. Enemy fire sank one DUKW, and the others failed to reach the beach. In the chaos, the Rangers only extended one ladder, and

Sgt. William Stivinson clambered to the top, engaging the German positions with the twin Vickers machine guns before retreating from his lofty perch and ascending the cliffs by rope.[28]

The Rangers were not the only GIs who failed to reach their assigned objectives on 6 June 1944. In the 506th PIR of the 101st Airborne Division, only ten out of eighty-one planeloads, or "sticks," landed on their drop zones, with estimates suggesting that only about one in six paratroopers landed near assigned objectives.[29] Brig. Gen. Theodore Roosevelt Jr., the son of the former president, arrived on Utah Beach only to realize that lead elements of the 4th Division had landed a mile south of their intended landing spot. Faced with the decision of where to direct 30,000 men and 3,500 vehicles following them ashore, he famously stated, "We'll start the war from right here."[30] Elsewhere on Omaha Beach, the situation was even worse, as a strong current propelled one of the guide boats marking the "Dog" sector of the invasion beach eastward on the rising tide. With a guide boat out of position, and smoke and dust from naval gunfire obscuring visual references, some landing craft came ashore as far as a thousand yards from their assigned destination. With the men of each Higgins boat tasked with attacking key positions or seizing particular draws off the beaches, a missed location meant failed mission objectives.[31] As the carefully prepared invasion plan floundered on Omaha Beach, small groups of men, led by a junior officer or NCO, had no choice but to improvise, falling back on their training, ingenuity, and whatever materials were at hand to accomplish their assigned tasks. Initially stymied by strong German resistance, they improvised new plans on the fly, bypassed or overwhelmed German strongpoints that blocked their paths off the beach, and secured a lodgment that would allow reinforcements to land. Brig. Gen. Norman "Dutch" Cota came ashore just below the German defensive position, or *Widerstandsnest* (Wn) 68, and helped motivate troops on the beach that were paralyzed by German fire, famously calling on elements of the 5th Ranger Battalion to "lead the way." Second Lt. John Spalding and Capt. Joseph Dawson scaled the bluffs between Wns 62 and 64, leading a group of men from the 16th Infantry Regiment against those positions and making further movement off Omaha Beach possible. Lt. James "Jimmie" Monteith landed with elements of the 16th Infantry Regiment below Wn 60 and organized troops from his regiment, along with tanks of the 741st Tank Battalion, inspiring them to make their way off the beach. He took out multiple German positions before he was killed, actions for which he received the Congressional Medal of Honor.[32]

Like the invasion, resupply efforts quickly went awry. While First Army succeeded in landing nearly eight and one-third divisions on the first day, those troops lacked much of their transportation, armor support, artillery, and supplies. The supply situation was worst on Omaha Beach, where only 100 tons of a planned 2,400 tons of supplies arrived the first day.[33] The next day was not much better, with only 24 percent of a projected 14,500 tons of supplies, 87,000 of 107,000 troops, and about half of an estimated 14,000 vehicles making it ashore.[34] Until a port could be taken, resupply was limited to the beaches, with the planners recognizing that just storming ashore required more combat divisions than the beaches themselves could support.[35] Despite continued German opposition near Omaha Beach, army engineers quickly established V Corps supply dumps, with the first supplies arriving later on 7 June. Concurrent with these beach supply dumps, work began on artificial harbors in the British and American sectors to facilitate the landing of men, vehicles, and supplies until Cherbourg could be taken.[36]

After securing the beaches, the British War Office planned on building two artificial harbors, code-named Mulberry. When they expanded Neptune from three to five landing beaches, planners proposed fabricating a protected anchorage for each. They proposed sending obsolete merchant ships across the English Channel under their own power, scuttling them in place to form a crescent-shaped breakwater a few hundred yards off each coast. These sunken ships, called Gooseberries, offered a protected anchorage where shallow draft vessels could dock and offload cargo to DUKWs or smaller landing craft.[37] On the western end of Omaha Beach at Vierville-sur-Mer and in the British Gold Beach sector opposite Arromanches-les-Bains, engineers incorporated Gooseberries into two artificial harbors, comprising a number of special components to facilitate the docking and unloading of Liberty ships and other transports. Beginning in December 1943, engineers established construction sites throughout southern England, with some 45,000 men constructing, assembling, and transporting components of Mulberry A and B to Normandy.[38]

Both American Mulberry A and British Mulberry B contained similar components. First, American Naval Construction Battalions (Seabees) anchored bombardons, floating steel tanks two hundred feet long and twenty-five feet high, with a beam (width) of twenty-five feet, to the seafloor three miles offshore, creating a floating breakwater.[39] Halfway between the bombardons and the coast, they sunk huge concrete caissons known as Phoenixes in a line, forming additional breakwaters strengthened by Gooseberries, or in the case of the American sector, providing a protected anchoring point where Liberty ships could sail in and unload. In addition to the Phoenixes, Seabees anchored a series of floating pierheads connected to the coast by "Whales," eighty-foot sections of prefabricated floating road on pontoons between the pierhead and the shore.[40] Construction of the Gooseberries began on D+1, with Seabees installing the first bombardon off Omaha Beach the same day. The British sunk their first Phoenix off Arromanches on 8 June. By 12 June, Seabees completed placement of their Gooseberries on Omaha Beach, allowing for the rapid offloading of 27,000 men, 2,000 vehicles, and 8,000 tons of supplies.[41] The American Seabees, however, took shortcuts to get Mulberry A operational as quickly as possible. Possessing "less respect for the weather than the British, reinforced by an allegedly greater familiarity in operating the equipment in all weathers," the Americans did not anchor every Whale to the ocean floor, believing that alternate moorings provided a more stable roadway.[42] Assembling their Mulberry more rapidly than the overly cautious British, the Americans finished their construction by 16 June. At 4:43 p.m. that afternoon, LST 342 anchored at one of the floating piers and put seventy-eight vehicles onto the roadway; they made it ashore in thirty-eight minutes, a sight witnessing soldiers and sailors celebrated with great enthusiasm.[43]

The shortcuts taken by the seemingly more technically savvy Americans were not without consequence. Beginning on 19 June, the Channel storm that haunted D-Day planners finally materialized, and it relentlessly pounded both artificial harbors for three days. Mulberry A faced the brunt of the storm and, in Eisenhower's estimation, was damaged "beyond repair."[44] Once the storm blew through, Eisenhower ordered its undamaged components salvaged to restore Mulberry B to operational status. Dismayed by the destruction of Mulberry A, Eisenhower was nonetheless "impressed by the industrial might of America," as resupply efforts continued unabated despite witnessing the "wreckage on the landing beaches" that remained after the storm. For any other nation, "the disaster would have been almost decisive; but so great was America's productive capability that the great storm occasioned little more than a ripple in the development of our build-up."[45]

Before the storm, the American innovation of "drying out" LSTs—running them ashore and unloading their contents before refloating them on the subsequent tide (a practice pioneered in earlier landings in the Mediterranean and Pacific)—accelerated the landing of men, vehicles, and supplies.[46] By D+6, ordnancemen established inland supply dumps, with the capture of smaller ports at Grandcamp-les-Bains, Isigny-sur-Mer, and Port-en-Bessin allowing smaller vessels to unload. By D+12, 314,514 troops, 41,000 vehicles, and 116,000 tons of supplies reached the American sector, slightly below planning estimates, but given lower material consumption and favorable casualty figures, operational capabilities were unhindered.[47] As VII Corps advanced toward Cherbourg, the beaches remained the only means to bring men, vehicles, and supplies ashore. Cobbling this campaign together demanded innovation and improvisation. American logistical efforts soon exceeded original planning estimates, with 13,000 tons of goods arriving ashore on Omaha Beach in the week after the storm, more than the 10,000 tons anticipated, with 7,200 tons of supplies coming ashore on Utah Beach, well beyond its original projection of 5,700 tons.[48]

In its advance, US First Army benefited from the presence of divisional maintenance and repair units that began repair, recovery, and salvage efforts almost immediately. Beyond first- and second-echelon maintenance work performed by vehicle and machine operators, designated maintenance and ordnance units supporting combat units operated at the third echelon, or medium maintenance level, working from mobile shops located near troops in the field. Beyond that, mechanics performed heavy maintenance in fixed and semifixed shops, rebuilding major components and vehicles with replacement parts and subassemblies or by cannibalization at the fourth echelon. And finally, fifth-echelon maintenance reconditioned or rebuilt entire vehicles at established facilities at the base level.[49] As soon as First Army secured the areas beyond the beaches, normal maintenance units arrived with "full strength in mechanics and repair equipment" to initiate operations "as early as possible," using preprepared "beach packs" of supplies and necessary subassemblies that allowed them to work without resupply until D+15.[50]

These ordnance and maintenance companies quickly set up shop, "cleaning up equipment from the beaches" and moving items to assembly points where repair crews could go to work.[51] In the week after D-Day, journalist Ernie Pyle toured the "highly specialized repair companies . . . made up largely of men who were craftsmen in the same line in civil life." Pyle discovered Sgt. Edward Welch of Watts, Oklahoma, in one of the mobile maintenance companies. The former oil field worker had attached a cylindrical wire brush to the end of a swivel shaft and chucked it into an electric drill. Welch's new gadget "cleaned rust out of a rifle barrel in a few seconds" allowing him to return a discarded rifle to service in minutes rather than hours. In a nearby ordnance evacuation company, Pyle discovered a "freakish" tank job where teams welded a metal plug with slanted sides into an impact point on a disabled tank, filling the hole "the same as you'd plug a watermelon." Elsewhere, he met the "Diesel Boys," a group of knowledgeable mechanics who "knew the foreign tanks as well as their own."[52] Lt. Belton Cooper praised the work of his own 18th Armored Ordnance Battalion, who would "scrap the regulations" to get tanks and vehicles back into service as quickly as possible. Only a few weeks into the campaign, Belton's tankers faced a spark plug shortage, as the constant idling of the R975 Wright nine-cylinder air-cooled radial engines produced significant fouling. Exhausting their supply of spares, his ordnancemen cannibalized spark plugs from tanks "damaged beyond repair," and sandblasted them clean so that they could be installed elsewhere. Sandblasting "around the clock" exhausted their sand supply until an enterprising soldier's "individual initiative . . . saved the day." They gathered more sand from the beach, and after sifting and drying it, this in-the-field solution allowed the unit to recondition spark plugs and restore tanks to combat service.[53]

Some ordnancemen unwittingly found their way into combat. In converting the M3 Lee tank into the T-2, later known as the M31 armored recovery vehicle, the Ordnance Department sought to repurpose an otherwise obsolete tank. Rejecting the M3, with its light 37 mm turret gun and right-sponson-mounted 75 mm main gun with limited traverse, the renamed M31 received a more than effective A-frame block and tackle and winch assembly. In eliminating the 75 mm main gun, some units, seeking to maintain the tank's "ferocious appearance," replaced the sponson mount with a door and piece of pipe that resembled the original main gun. Three days after coming ashore on Omaha Beach, members of Able Company, 743rd Tank Battalion, with their M31 in support, advanced on the road between Maisy and Isigny supporting elements of 3rd Battalion, 116th Infantry Division. When GI tank maintainers in their M31 "bulging with extra bogie wheels and strung like some strange Christmas tree with a variety of chains, tools, [and] special maintenance equipment" surprised forty German soldiers, the startled Germans surrendered to a tank with a faux barrel, in reality "armed with nothing bigger than a machine gun."[54]

First Army maintenance men soon found themselves addressing other "tactical exigencies" that required "the design and manufacture of field modifications and special items of equipment."[55] Many of these cobbled-together expedients facilitated cooperation between tanks and infantrymen, as these units had not trained, much less fought, together until only a few weeks prior to D-Day. While the "principles of tank employment . . . continued to be sound," the nature of the terrain demanded tank-infantry cooperation at a higher level of effectiveness than in previous campaigns. This not only required additional training, but prompted improvised solutions to counter the German troops defending the Normandy hedgerows.[56]

Hedgerows, used by Norman farmers for centuries to define the limits of their fields, represented a challenge that few American intelligence officers anticipated before the Normandy invasion. Made of compacted earth between two and five feet wide and as many feet tall, "hedges were planted on top, and their roots prevented erosion," creating a "baffling maze" of fields shaped like "triangles, squares, rectangles, and odd geometric shapes left by generations of land division" separated by trails, paths, and sunken roads "ideal for covered supply routes and lines of defense."[57] Making use of these features, German troops had dug "good firing positions in the hedgerows parallel and perpendicular to the front," which permitted "very few troops with a large number of automatic weapons" to move among several points of defense, while "firing successive bursts in order to simulate a large number of men."[58] Employing "small arms, machine guns, mortars, bazookas, anti-tank grenades, bombs, mines, obstacles, and a few anti-tank guns," Germans used heavy firepower to mount a stalwart defense with "artillery and tanks in small numbers only."[59] The "blatant oversight" by Allied planners in failing to recognize these terrain features demanded that "new assault tactics had to be developed and practiced under fire," in order to achieve a breakout from the unique Normandy terrain.[60]

Initial American efforts paired a company of tanks with an infantry battalion, though neither had much familiarity with each other. To communicate, they improvised radio communications using an SCR-609 radio mounted on an infantry packboard. This expedient enabled coordination between the tank company and the infantry battalion commander, though maintaining contact was a challenge. Tanks often advanced beyond their attached infantry, then had to disengage and return to mop up resistance that was holding up their accompanying GIs.[61] Eventually, troops of the 2nd Infantry Division wired an EE8 field telephone handset directly into the tank's intercom system, allowing an infantry commander to direct his armor support personally. This practice was crafted by the tankers of the 743rd Tank Battalion, with T.Sgt. Ronald Heyland, "who had early in life been bitten by the radio bug," mounting an empty ammunition can on the rear of a tank to protect the phone handset.[62] The 743rd, along with men of the 744th and 747th Tank Battalions, were "unanimously enthusiastic" about these additions, though "to make the idea completely effective," all tanks needed radios, something that had not, as yet, happened. Consequently, "opportunities to obtain tank fire support" had not reached maximum effectiveness, because not all infantry recognized the potential for field-added tank-infantry communications. To address this, suggestions were published in "Battle Experiences No. 13, 1 August 1944" noting the "success" encountered by linking "a microphone or telephone on the outside of certain tanks connected with the intercommunication system of the tank" and reiterated in "Battle Experiences No. 17, 11 August 1944."[63]

Working in conjunction with the handful of dozer tanks capable of breaching the hedgerows, the infantry wanted more firepower, calling on ordnance units for assistance. The effort to establish an effective base of fire with automatic rifles or light machine guns before clambering over a hedgerow and into a field prompted requests for additional Browning automatic rifles (BARs) beyond the one typically allocated to an infantry squad, resulting in more effective means to use both heavy and light machine guns. Infantrymen recognized that, due to its weight, the Browning M2 .50-caliber machine gun "was not much help," as even using it in conjunction with a light machine-gun tripod yielded less than favorable results.[64] Second Infantry Division infantry looked to improve the employment of the M1919A4 .30-caliber machine gun, typically crewed by a gunner, assistant gunner, and two ammunition bearers. Lt. Col. A. J. Stuart, the division's ordnance officer, requested a bipod and shoulder mount to replace the M1919A6 .30-caliber machine gun's normal tripod, but upon discovering these were unavailable, he turned to First Army ordnancemen. These battlefield tinkerers crafted spike or sled mounts, or used BAR bipods in conjunction with an "improvised stock, similar in shape to that of a German MG-42, made from sheet metal, reinforced with wood" and "attached by four screws to the pistol grip," to create man-portable assault weapons. Lacking these additions, other infantrymen laid the light machine gun directly "on a hedgerow or convenient object," and fired in short bursts.[65]

Even with improvised tank-infantry communications and scrounged firepower, the shortage of dozer tanks beyond the four already present in each tank battalion made hedgerow combat extremely challenging. Confined to roads, M4 Mediums were vulnerable to presighted German mortar and antitank fire, which greatly limited their avenues of advance. Tanks could drive at the hedgerows, but driving up and over them exposed the M4's lightly armored underbelly to antitank, or *Panzerfaust*, fire. While US troops awaited additional dozer blades, they initiated in-field combined arms training to address the terrain challenges.[66] Two weeks after the initial landings, the 709th Tank Battalion established its headquarters one mile west of Cerisy-la-Forêt in Normandy, attaching B, C, and D Companies to elements of the 9th, 23rd, and 38th Infantry Regiments of the 2nd Infantry Division (with A Company in reserve). Beginning on 20 June, they began a vigorous training regimen that included coordinating tanks, infantry, and engineers against German defenders occupying the Normandy hedgerows. These efforts countered the opinions of some tankers that infantry officers were "on the whole, unfamiliar with tank tactics, capabilities, and tank terrain."[67] This training brought together infantry, engineers, and the four to six Medium tanks equipped with bulldozer blades assigned to a typical tank battalion.[68] A week later, the First Army's "Battle Experiences" circular stressed the use of dozer tanks, but when GIs discovered that they were "not always able to effect breaches," they improvised other means.[69]

This development had explosive consequences, with GIs looking to engineer units for help in solving these emerging field problems. By 22 June, the 29th Division began employing engineers to blast gaps in the hedgerows, allowing tanks to traverse the battlefield. With tanks offering suppressing fire to keep the enemy down, infantry moved into a field and seized the next hedgerow "perpendicular to the line of advance." After engineers blew holes in the hedgerows, tanks could "advance to the succeeding hedgerow line of the leading infantry elements" and repeat the process.[70] To facilitate these tactics, engineers preprepared charges, cramming twenty-nine half-pound blocks of TNT into sandbags, improvising an ignition system made up of a five-foot length of Primacord, a No. 8 nonelectric cap, a two-foot length of fuse and a fuse lighter. With this method, engineers dug two holes about six feet apart and one-third of the way through the hedgerows before inserting the charges into the prepared holes and tamping them down. Detonation produced a gap wide enough for a tank to plow through.[71] Other units adapted the M1A1 Bangalore torpedo, pushing several of these explosive-filled pipes through a hedgerow with a tank before detonating them.[72]

Units gradually realized the limitations of using explosives, as large roots and vines inhibited digging, and engineer personnel faced casualties as it took considerable time to dig holes and prepare charges in the field. On 11 July 1944, enemy fire prematurely detonated the preprepared satchel charges used by the 741st Tank Battalion, damaging tanks and forcing a suspension of their advance on Hill 192, northeast of Saint-Lô.[73] Of greater concern was the sheer volume of explosives needed to support the concerted movement of ten tanks, as elements of the 747th Tank Battalion and 115th Infantry team discovered on 24 June. The hole method required at least seventeen tons of explosives to make a mile-and-a-half advance through multiple hedgerows with multiple tanks. This was a prohibitive amount, considering that most supplies were still making their way from the beachheads. Regarding a 100 lb charge per hedgerow as "exorbitant," Lt. Col. Stuart G. Fries's 747th Tank Battalion, attached to the 29th Division, installed two four- to six-inch-long sharpened spikes made from 6.25-inch diameter steel pipe to the front of a tank. Driving into the hedgerow with these "salad forks" left behind two holes that could be filled with a smaller amount of explosives and detonated to blast a gap in the hedgerow that a tank could then proceed through.[74] While effective, this method had a significant shortcoming, for once the tank impacted the hedgerows, German troops quickly targeted that location with artillery and machine-gun fire, knowing that once the breach had been blown, that was where American tanks or infantry would follow.[75]

Using this method, these tankers made an "accidental discovery," realizing that if the tank hit high enough up on a hedgerow with adequate force, it "lift[ed] the top of the bank, including the large trees," effectively making a breach without demolitions.[76] Other tankers were not far behind in this discovery. By early July, crafty tankers fabricated a variety of similar hedge-busting devices, with the 747th moving from the "salad prongs" to a "greendozer," built from salvaged railroad rails; the 126th Armored Ordnance Battalion constructing their hedgerooter; and the 735th, 741st, and 746th Tank Battalions welding "hedge cutters," "hedge-busting attachments," and "hedgeclippers," respectively.[77]

Many of these devices were undoubtedly inspired by, if not copied from, the efforts of Sgt. Curtis G. Culin Jr. of the 102nd Cavalry Reconnaissance Squadron, who, working with Lt. Steve Litton of the squadron's maintenance detachment, invented the "rhino tank." Taking the "Czech hedgehogs" fabricated from steel I-beams that the Germans used on the Normandy beaches to rip the bottoms from approaching landing craft, American ordnancemen cut huge metal teeth from the obstacles with acetylene torches, welding them to a horizontal bar, creating a steel fork with five sharpened steel tines that resembled rhinoceros tusks. On 14 July, Gen. Omar Bradley, Gen. Courtney Hodges, First Army ordnance chief Col. John B. Medaris, and their aides witnessed a demonstration of the new field-expedient contrivance, fabricated by ingenious GIs who had struggled with the problem of the hedgerows since arriving in France. Attached to the front of a tank, the rhino device "cut through the growth as though slicing bread," at the same time keeping the tank nose down, so that it would not expose the thinly armored underbelly to an antitank round. Following this successful demonstration, the generals ordered the device to be kept secret while building as many as possible to give First Army's tanks an advantage. Over the course of forty-eight hours, First Army ordnancemen worked round the clock in workshops in and around Saint-Jean-de-Daye, with work accelerated through the efforts of Colonel Medaris, who mobilized welders and mechanics from maintenance companies and used tank transporters to haul the tetrahedrons from the beaches, further calling on the First Army G-4 to scour England for additional welding rods and oxygen and acetylene bottles.[78] In two days, the mass-production facility outside Pont-Hébert manufactured and installed 184 rhinos on medium tanks and 110 on light tanks, so that by 24 July, 60 percent of tanks employed in Operation Cobra mounted some variation of the bocage-busting device, though General Bradley prohibited their use before the breakout to maximize impact.[79] The tanks of the 3rd Armored Division benefited from the efforts of a Warrant Officer Douglas, a prewar welder who sketched out a design for a similar device to guide the efforts of ordnancemen servicing the 32nd and 33rd Armored Regiments. The "Douglas device" had "plow-type plates on the edges of the outboard cutters," though starting construction on 22 July, they were only able to equip fifty-seven tanks with the device.[80]

Operation Cobra began at 11:00 a.m. on 25 July 1944. The day before, heavy cloud cover between Periérs in the east and Saint-Lô in the west delayed a carpet-bombing mission flown by elements of the Eighth Air Force. Even with overcast skies, 317 heavy bombers of the 1st Bomb Division dropped 10,124 high explosive bombs and 1,822 fragmentation bombs. With planes flying perpendicular, as opposed to parallel to the American lines, a number of bombs unfortunately fell short, killing 25 and wounding 131 men of the 30th Infantry

Division. Despite previous assurances to General Bradley that the planes would fly parallel to American lines, the Eighth Air Force bombers repeated the mistake on 25 July when Cobra finally began. On that morning, nearly 1,500 B-17s and B-24s, joined by 380 medium bombers and 550 fighters dropped nearly 4,700 tons of bombs on an area south of the Saint-Lô–Periérs road. Designed to disrupt German defenses, the bombing mission's intended outcome was to open a path that would allow VII Corps, composed of the 1st, 4th, 9th, and 30th Infantry Divisions, accompanied by elements of the 2nd and 3rd Armored Divisions, to penetrate the German lines along a narrow front adjacent to the Vire River. The idea was to envelop German forces near Coutances, thereby isolating the Cotentin Peninsula. Unfortunately, the aerial bombardment went worse than it had the day before, with target misidentification, bombsight challenges, and decision-making errors resulting in thirty-five heavy bombers dropping their bombs prematurely again. The bombs fell on American troops, killing 111 men of VII Corps, including Gen. Lesley McNair, former AGF commander, who had been with frontline troops observing the men whose training he had so profoundly influenced.[81]

Misdropped bombs and the tragic death of General McNair notwithstanding, Operation Cobra must be considered a success. The 2nd Armored Division opened the door to France, exceeding the expectations of General Bradley and those associated with planning the operation.[82] By the end of July, VII Corps had penetrated the German lines, making advances measured in miles, rather than the yards that had characterized the advance in the immediate aftermath of the D-Day landings. Despite the gains made by VII and VIII Corps that resulted in the capture of Coutances, the question remains: how critical were the field-improvised "rhino" hedgecutters to Cobra's success?

In the immediate aftermath of World War II, the assessment of the "rhino tank" hedgerow-busting device was favorable. The European Theater General Board, convened in accordance with General Order 128 in June 1945, included an evaluation of the "rhino," calling it "simple, reliable, and effective." The board's only criticism was that "it's need was not anticipated, the most effective design conceived and standardized, and tanks equipped accordingly prior to landing" in Normandy.[83] General Bradley regarded Sergeant Culin's device as an invaluable invention that "came on the eve of its greatest need," providing the essential tool that gave American tanks "an upper hand in the bocage."[84] American historian Russell Weigley echoed this sentiment, praising the rhino as the tool that helped "cut through the hedgerows" and allow "the most mobile army in the world" to "capitalize on its mobility," a position also advanced by Richard Overy, who characterized the rhino cutter as the tool that allowed Americans to restore movement through the terrain.[85] Other scholars have been more critical of the rhino tank's effectiveness. Michael Doubler dismissed the innovation as "only one of many such methods invented and employed throughout First Army" to "bust the bocage."[86] Peter Mansoor noted that the prongs were "successful in combat," but tank-infantry communications and effective close air support were as important to overall American success.[87] James Jay Carafano is perhaps the most critical, in his attempt to expose the "myth" of the "hedgerow-busting rhino tank." "Never used" before the fighting in Normandy, Carafano argued that the "hedgerow cutters did not enable the armor to cut down even hastily prepared defenses" and thus was not responsible for the breakthrough.[88] "More myth than miracle," the rhinos were "no help because of the nature of the terrain."[89]

In reality, however, the answer lies somewhere in between. Far from being a panacea for the hedgerows of Normandy, the rhino hedgerow cutter played too significant a role prior to the Cobra breakout to be relegated to mythical status. The rhino tank represents perhaps the most well known example of American technical ingenuity during World War II. Presented with a problem, American GIs improvised and tried a variety of ideas until they came up with one that maximized effectiveness given the circumstances.[90] Blowing gaps in hedgerows with explosives required significant logistical support, which necessitated new methods. Physically digging holes evolved into the salad prongs, followed by greendozers, which matured into the rhino tank. Once these innovative ideas came to the attention of American leadership, Generals Bradley and Hodges and others had the foresight and operational flexibility to recognize the potential utility of the device, adopt the idea, and ensure its widespread dissemination. Unfortunately for the Allies, according to Eisenhower, "we were still without this contrivance when the First Army began its tedious southward advance to achieve a reasonable jump-off line for the big attack," but that assessment does not necessarily mean it was a useless endeavor, as the rhino gave "a tremendous boost to the morale throughout the Army."[91]

The First Army *Report of Operations* for October 1943–August 1944 cited the five hundred rhino tanks fabricated for First Army as critical to "restore freedom of action and cross country mobility," with after-action reports from the 741st, 746th, 747th, and 759th Tank Battalions specifically mentioning the utility of the device. The observations offered by tankers of the 759th Tank Battalion were the most compelling, for they noted that a full week after the Cobra breakout, their light tanks, "having previously been equipped with 'hedgerow busters,' of 'Rhinos,' fought on in close support of the advancing infantry." Moreover, "each tank had a hand mike or telephone fastened on the outside and connected to the interphone system for communication with friendly Infantry on the ground."[92] But beyond the rhino tank's value as a "morale factor to the troops" exhausted by the hedgerow fighting, it was difficult, if not impossible, for First Army to know that the French terrain would open up into more rolling terrain south of Saint-Lô; GIs poised to advance on 26 July were undoubtedly encouraged to know that with steel teeth welded to the front of their tanks, they had a way to navigate the terrain regardless.[93] Moreover, these inventions continued to be used well after Operation Cobra. First Lieutenant John D. Allbright, commanding B Company, 709th Tank Battalion, reported that while attached to 1st Battalion, 121st Infantry Regiment, in the Crozon campaign "on or about 14 September," moving his company through "poor terrain" resulted in one tank losing a track and "another tank broke off its hedge cutter, therefore when we jumped off in the attack I had three tanks but only one hedge cutter on my own tank."[94]

In addition to the development and employment of field-expedient hedgerow cutters by American citizen-soldiers, other commanders looked to improvised solutions to facilitate the rapid advance of American combined arms, leading to a robust air campaign that would provide a tremendous morale boost to American GIs on the ground as they eventually looked skyward over France and saw friendly fighters circling overhead. Drawn into the planning cell for Overlord in late 1943, Brig. Gen. Elwood R. "Pete" Quesada, fresh from battle experience in North Africa, soon found himself "a young kid commanding a very large tactical force," when named to direct IX Fighter Command in November 1943.[95] By February, the Allied Expeditionary Air Force established a combined fighter control center at Uxbridge, west of London, to direct Quesada's fighter command and Brig. Gen. Otto P. Weyland's XIX Air Support Command. Over the next few months, Eighth and Ninth Air Forces competed for arriving assets, with P-51s detailed to the Eighth Air Force as escorts for strategic bombers engaged against German targets during Operation Argument. In addition, P-47s that arrived in England assigned to Quesada had been upgraded with the innovations made to the Republic P-47 Thunderbolt by the 57th Fighter Group in Italy. Once in-theater, IX Fighter Command maintainers made further modifications by installing the B-7 bomb shackle and K-2 electrical bomb release on the P-47, an arrangement that the Army Air Forces Evaluation Board characterized as "outstandingly successful for close-in air operations."[96]

Equipped with these modified P-47s, Quesada's IX Tactical Air Command (IX TAC) initially targeted airfields, marshalling yards, railway centers, railroad rolling stock, and bridges over the Seine River to prevent German forces from moving into the coastal regions of northern France. While IX TAC performed a valuable interdiction role, initial cooperation between the air and ground elements was limited, as the air command and First Army operated independently. As the invasion neared, a limited number of army personnel assumed new roles as ground liaison officers, working within IX Bomber Command units headquartered at Marks Hall, Essex. Other ground liaison officers were integrated with air force S-2 and S-3 officers at headquarters, wings and groups of the IX and XIX TAC, directed from their headquarters at Middle Wallop (with advance headquarters at Uxbridge) and Aldermaston Court, Berkshire (with advance headquarters at Biggin Hill, Kent), respectively.[97] This, however, only marked the beginning of American air-ground cooperation in Europe, fashioned out of necessity from existing assets to meet the challenges of modern mechanized warfare.

Both before and during the invasion, Headquarters Ninth Air Force at Uxbridge directed all air efforts against the Wehrmacht in France. On 10 June 1944, Quesada advanced IX TAC to Normandy, establishing a spartan headquarters just a hedgerow away from Gen. Omar N. Bradley's US First Army headquarters. Three days later, the 70th Fighter Wing established an airfield at Cricqueville-en-Bessin and began operations from the Continent, with all Ninth Air Force fighter-bomber activity subsumed under IX TAC.[98] This force included elements of the 354th Fighter Group, were the first American flyers to use the P-51B-1 Mustang "Razorback" in combat, and due to the ingenuity of the men commanded by Capt. Richard E. Turner of the 356th Fighter Squadron, they were among the first Americans to have operational shower facilities "complete with hot and cold running water," on the Normandy beachhead.[99] Hot showers, however, were only one example of the squadron's mechanical ingenuity, as a pair of creative NCOs had taken a "war weary" P-51B and transformed it into a makeshift trainer. Removing the eighty-five-gallon fuel tank, armor, and elements of the communication system normally situated behind the pilot's seat, they installed a plywood seat, accessible by a removeable glass panel that allowed a passenger to cram himself in behind the pilot, though space restrictions prohibited an additional parachute.[100] This addition allowed the squadron to "demonstrate tactics to new pilots, and to give rides to our crew chiefs."[101] This, however, was not the most notable use of this specially modified plane during the Normandy campaign.

On 4 July, as Allied ground forces experimented with methods to blow paths through the Normandy hedgerows, General Eisenhower flew over from England to attend a First Army planning conference with an eye toward Operation Cobra, joining Generals Bradley and Hodges and all the principal American commanders, including General Quesada. As the meeting wrapped up, Quesada, avoiding "idle chit-chat," was starting for the door when General Eisenhower stopped him and requested a tour of the IX TAC airfields in France. While en route, Quesada explained his intent to fly a mission toward

Paris and asked the supreme commander if he wanted to go along, to which Ike concurred with "boyish enthusiasm."[102] Arriving at Cricqueville, Quesada and Eisenhower clambered into the P-51B-1 modified by the 356th Fighter Squadron, who flew out of a rough airstrip constructed a few miles south of Pointe du Hoc. Once in the back seat, the pair took what Eisenhower subsequently called a trip "in a fighter plane along the battle front in an effort to gain a clear impression of what were up against."[103] Joined by three escorting P-51s, Quesada later confessed he planned to fly to Paris and spark a dogfight. Conscious of the modified P-51's limitations, particularly with respect to challenging egress methods for his passenger, Quesada instead gave his superior an aerial tour of the Cherbourg peninsula and the rest of the Normandy battlefield, the first time in history a ground commander "personally reconnoitered the terrain of a planned battle operation from a fighter aircraft in the presence of the enemy."[104] After touching down, General Bradley and members of the press accosted Quesada and the supreme allied commander, as he watched the pair emerge from the P-51B-1 grinning "like sheepish schoolboys caught in a watermelon patch." Smoking and joking on the rough tarmac, even Eisenhower recognized that if he pulled a stunt like that again, General Marshall "would give me hell."[105]

The modified P-51B-1, however, was not the only mechanical field expedient used by Pete Quesada to enhance the operational effectiveness of IX TAC in Normandy. As an airman, Quesada quickly recognized that pilots and tankers saw the same terrain features differently. A tank officer might identify a tank hidden behind a tree a hundred yards in front of him, but for a fighter pilot racing overhead at four hundred miles per hour, it was difficult to differentiate a single tree from the hundreds in view. In Quesada's eyes, successful air support required placing someone who understood an airman's perspective in a tank, providing him with the means to relate what a ground commander saw in terms that an airman would understand. The challenge, however, came with the radio networks, as ground frequencies were incompatible with those used by Allied aircraft. Meeting with General Bradley, Quesada suggested placing a IX TAC SCB-522 VHF radio in the lead of an armored column, manned by a pilot. The pilot could take information from ground forces and relate those unique conditions in terms his fellow pilots could understand, imagining what "a flight of P-47s over every column from dawn to dusk" could accomplish.[106] Bradley ordered two tanks sent to the IX TAC immediately, but a confused soldier, wondering why Bradley would send tanks to the air force, redirected the tanks to Gen. Manton S. Eddy's 9th Infantry Division. When the two tanks arrived at Eddy's headquarters, an officer there "shooed them off," as they needed no replacements. Inquiring about the tanks later in the day, Bradley discovered their misdirection, again ordering two tanks to General

Quesada's command post in the next field. When they arrived, an air force officer unfamiliar with Quesada's intentions turned them away. These hiccups notwithstanding, by the end of the day, the tanks eventually made their way to IX TAC. With shade-tree mechanics installing SCB-522 VHF radios in his new tanks, Quesada's IX TAC soon possessed an "armored force" and stood ready to employ a field-engineered ground-to-air communications coordination capability.[107]

On 26 July, the day after Operation Cobra launched, Quesada began experimenting with SCB-522 VHF–equipped Sherman tanks manned by a divisional air support party officer providing "armored column cover." As three armored columns advanced on Coutances, Granville, and Villedieu-les-Poêles, relays of four P-47s flew half-hour shifts over each column, employing bombs or rockets against German troops on the ground. After flying seventy missions on 26 July, IX TAC aircraft flew one hundred missions the next day and continued on a comparable pace thereafter.[108] Air support party officer Lt. Col. James L. Zimmerman accompanied Combat Command A of the 2nd Armored Division from 22 July to 6 August as the division pushed south from Saint-Lô and toward Tessy-sur-Vire. Mounted in an M4 Medium tank, Zimmerman reported that only "a Lt. Reisling" was from the armored force, with the remaining four men in the tank being air force personnel. Typically riding in the column's fourth tank, marked with a yellow identification panel, Zimmerman initially sat in the loader's position, but he moved to the assistant driver's position as that gave him better vision overhead and greater ability to communicate with circling IX TAC P-47s. He directed as many as twelve planes at once, using the makeshift radio network to direct multiple P-47s against German tanks in positions around Villebaudon, south of Saint-Lô.[109] Flying P-47s loaded with bombs and retrofitted with rockets, the feared "Jabos" proved to be the bane of German troops' existence as Allied forces solidified their position on the Continent.[110] Such circumstances even led tanker Sgt. Harold E. Fulton to observe that the P-47, a plane that had "saved us so many times," was the "best tank weapon" in the American arsenal.[111] Following activation of Gen. George S. Patton's US Third Army, Gen. Otto Weyland's XIX TAC provided armored column cover, with planes conducting more than 12,000 sorties as Third Army spent much of August advancing toward the coastal town of Brest, before turning turned eastward and driving across France.[112] In the midst of this advance, one P-47 supporting Third Army encountered a column of German troops retreating eastward. As a plane swooped down to strafe the column, the Germans began waving white flags to surrender to the aircraft that threatened them. Aborting his strafing run, the Thunderbolt maintained overwatch until US armored personnel arrived to take them prisoner.[113]

By the end of August, the Allies put more than 2 million men and nearly 500,000 vehicles (the vast majority being American-made) ashore over the Normandy beaches.[114] After struggling ashore on 6 June, the US Army gradually achieved greater combat effectiveness, improvising and innovating as it began the crusade of liberation. Once tanks and infantry developed the mechanical means to coordinate their movement in the field, soldiers began to overcome German opposition in the stubbornly contested Normandy hedgerows. As planners envisioned the need for combat capabilities in three dimensions, airmen were increasingly embedded with armored units on the ground to communicate with pilots circling above, who then roared down in field-modified P-47 Thunderbolts, providing armored column cover that made the breakout from the Cotentin Peninsula and the subsequent drive across France possible. These developments were the work of ingenious American GIs in the field who realized technological shortcomings and modified existing bits of available military hardware to meet a tactical need.

As August waned, the Allied advance slowly ground to a halt. After winning the Battle of the Falaise Pocket on 21 August and liberating Paris four days later, the final act of the Overlord drama closed with the destruction or capture of nearly all German forces west of the Seine. Although the retreating Germans mounted occasional attempts at resistance, the Allied advance slowed as a result of logistical considerations rather than enemy opposition, with between 90 and 95 percent of Allied fuel, ammunition, and rations on the Continent stuck in depots that remained in close proximity to the invasion beaches.[115] After vacating Paris, the Germans continued retreating eastward, abandoning further opportunities to slow Patton's Third Army opposite water barriers posed by the Marne, Vesle, Meuse, and the Moselle Rivers. By the time the Allies captured Antwerp on 4 September, sixteen divisions were across the Seine, four more than originally planned, and some had already pushed more than 150 miles eastward in pursuit of the Wehrmacht before shortages of fuel and ammunition forced a halt. The Allies, however, had failed to secure an undamaged port closer to the front; consequently, the vast majority of supplies for the advance across France continued to come across the invasion beaches in Normandy.[116]

As Hitler ordered his generals to reconstitute and build up the Westwall (known to the Allies as the Siegfried Line) as the last line of defense before the Rhine, the nature of warfare in the European theater of operations began to evolve. On 2 September, General Eisenhower met with Generals Bradley, Hodges, and Patton to rearticulate his desire for an assault against Germany along a broad front. Such an approach allowed for a slow buildup of logistical support, so as not to deprive any single commander of the resources necessary for the advance. With American forces from southern France effecting a linkup with Patton's Third Army on 11 September, the German army truly had its back against its border, thereby allowing US forces to adopt a slower, more methodical advance against the Third Reich.[117]

The broad-front strategy also meant an evolution in the application of American ingenuity to the war in Europe. Transformational changes with respect to armor-infantry and air-armor communications in June and July 1944 had allowed American troops to outblitzkreig the Germans as they raced across France. As Allied forces neared the Franco-German frontier, US troops continued to practice American ingenuity, as the development of the American combined arms team, something fabricated largely from scratch in the fields of Normandy, eventually allowed Patton's Third Army to advance across much of France with its flanks exposed. With ever-increasing logistical support, GI efforts to enhance the technical capabilities of their existing tools persisted. Their new creations and ingenious adaptation of machines and weapons already at their disposal provided them with the requisite tools needed to achieve ultimate victory in Europe.

CHAPTER 6

Kriegies and Quan

Resourcefulness in Captivity

The first few weeks in prison were particularly difficult for all of us. . . . We knew it was up to us, both individually and collectively, to try and improve our situation, but we didn't know where to start. . . . Like many others, I withdrew into myself and began to spend most of my time alone. It was in this self-imposed solitude that I began to recall some of my earlier attempts at improvisation.

—*John F. Kinney*

Being captured by the Germans was like being stranded in an incredibly weird and inadequate world. [American prisoners] were always hungry. They had no tools, and scarcely any material except tin cans. Yet they re-equipped themselves with nearly as many things as a novelty store sells—and they pulled through.

—*Popular Science, July 1945*

During the course of World War II, approximately 130,000 American soldiers fell into the hands of the enemy and served time as prisoners of war. In the Pacific, the vast majority of the 27,000-odd Americans imprisoned by the Japanese lost their freedom early in the conflict between the fall of Guam three days after Pearl Harbor and the surrender of the Philippines in May 1942. These Americans spent the remainder of the war subject to isolation, abuse, starvation, forced labor, and otherwise unspeakable conditions, such that by August 1945 only slightly more than 60 percent still survived. In the European theater, of the approximately 93,000 Americans who spent a portion of the conflict as prisoners in German POW camps, over 99 percent survived.

Enduring an average of thirty-eight months behind barbed wire, American POWs imprisoned by the Germans lost more than sixty pounds each, though German adherence to the Geneva Convention spared these men from the harsh treatment that faced those who suffered in Japanese camps.[1]

Regardless of where they were imprisoned and who imprisoned them, American POWs shared one common trait: they practiced the same brand of technical ingenuity and improvisation behind barbed wire that they and other Americans demonstrated in combat. Lacking freedom and possessing limited resources, American POWs drew on their technical ability and the tinkerer's mindset to enhance their chances of survival. Using available materials, they worked tirelessly to break the monotony of prison camp life, building stoves, cooking utensils, and other day-to-day comforts to make captivity bearable. Ameliorating the often onerous conditions they faced, they embraced a familiarity with radios, machines, engines, and the technical tools of war sharpened at home during the Great Depression to relieve their experiences as prisoners. In those opportunities where they challenged their captors and attempted escape, Americans' technical creativity and mechanical ingenuity enabled them to engineer the tools and requisite equipment necessary to effect escape. Where escape was an impossibility, American POWs employed their technical prowess to otherwise frustrate and confound their captors while doing the utmost to resist.

On 22 July 1929, fifty-three nations came together in Geneva, Switzerland, and agreed to terms to govern the treatment of prisoners of war. The 1929 Geneva Convention contained ninety-seven articles that applied to all signatories regardless of whether or not their opponent had signed the convention. The treaty terms required the humane treatment of prisoners, including the provision of rations and accommodations equal in quality to those received by the base troops of the detaining power. The convention also explicitly prohibited prisoners from being forced to perform war-related labor functions. Prisoners could not assist in the transport of any material to units in combat, nor could they conduct dangerous or degrading work. While the United States and Germany signed the treaty, Japan did not, setting the stage for dramatically different treatment for American POWs in Europe versus in the Pacific.[2]

Responsibility for enforcing the Geneva Convention fell to the International Committee of the Red Cross (ICRC) based in Geneva. Throughout the war, the ICRC's agents, when permitted, conducted inspections to ensure that prisoner of war camps were "healthy places," and that prisoners received letters and care packages from home, as well as additional food, medical, and relief parcels prepared by the ICRC. The Red Cross did its best to enforce these provisions, though conditions between camps varied greatly, particularly comparing camps in the European and Pacific theaters.[3]

Officially, each American *kriegie* (prisoner) received one 11 lb Red Cross food parcel per week, although the challenges of getting these parcels from Red Cross headquarters in Switzerland to the various camps made their delivery anything but regular.[4] While the ICRC successfully delivered packages to Americans in German POW camps on a consistent basis, Americans held by the Japanese were much less fortunate, as camp administrators in the Pacific refused to distribute the parcels, hoarded them, opened them and damaged or stole their contents, or otherwise kept them from prisoners, the best efforts of the ICRC notwithstanding.[5] Prisoners relied on the Red Cross parcels (which were accompanied by medicines, tobacco and cigarettes, clothing, and a wide variety of comforts and toiletries) as a valuable supplement to their otherwise meager rations. Moreover, the perishable items (meat, powdered milk, coffee, margarine) arrived in tin containers that became the raw materials for much of the ingenuity practiced by American soldiers being detained.[6] Thus, it was no surprise when one American interned in Stalag VII-II reported that in his camp compound with "everyone squatting over little fires with pots and pans made from old tins," it looked like "a cross between a hobo jungle and a sanitorium."[7]

For clever Americans in German stalags, Red Cross parcels provided one of the most important items in their arsenal of inventiveness: the Klim can. "Klim" (*milk* spelled backward) was a dehydrated whole milk powder developed by a New York company for use in the tropics, where regular milk spoiled quickly. The US Army initially adopted Klim as part of the wartime Jungle ration, and the tin cans of dehydrated milk eventually found their way into Red Cross parcels. Approximately four inches in diameter and three inches deep, the cans were "as valuable as their contents," as they provided the basis for "tin can carpentry." In the words of Jerry Sage, an American Office of Strategic Services operative wounded and captured in 1943 who masqueraded as a shot-down pilot lest the Germans discover his true identity, Klim cans provided prisoners with "practically everything we needed."[8]

Eugene E. Halmos Jr., a B-24 navigator from the 489th Bomb Group shot down over the Netherlands on 29 June 1944, described the process by which these cans became the source material for kriegie innovation. Cutting off the "bead," where the sides of the can met the top and bottom, produced "a roll of quite presentable metal." Once flattened out with "kitchen knives, handles, whatever," kriegies transformed the round cans into sheets of tin, each one approximately three inches wide and a foot long. These sheets provided raw material for a wide variety of camp tools and survival items. Folding a single edge of one tin sheet upward an eighth of an inch and inserting the edge of a second sheet folded similarly downward and hammering along the seam to flatten it made a larger sheet. Repeating the process, prisoners could create a sheet of metal of almost any desired size. Using simple tools present in every barracks hut, and precious nails carefully guarded by every prisoner fortunate enough to find one, kriegies could bend, cut, and punch tin to transform flattened cans into a wide variety of useful camp products.[9]

For most kriegies, it was a simple affair to fashion rudimentary dishes, pans, and plates from flattened Klim tins; in some cases, they even salvaged solder from the can lids for sealing the seams of miscellaneous projects to make them watertight. Maj. William Orris of the 450th Bomb Group, who bailed out of his B-24 over Toulon five weeks before D-Day and spent the next eleven months in captivity, witnessed more elaborate products of kriegie ingenuity. He described how the more fastidious prisoners in his camp made flat irons from tin sheets, filling them with hot coals to press their clothes. Others built elaborate bake ovens they attached to the stoves found in every barracks building, or painstakingly used a nail to punch hundreds of holes in a sheet of tin to transform it into a percolator for the ground coffee that came in Red Cross parcels. The same technique could be used to create a rough grinding surface, which allowed kriegies to deconstruct crackers into flour suitable for baking. Of all the cooking utensils Orris related, the most elaborate was an ice cream freezer, made up of two different sized cans, with the smaller of the two containing a tin-can paddle. After packing the larger can with ice, prisoners made ice cream by rotating the paddle in the inner can with a bow pushed back and forth.[10]

These ingenious devices allowed American POWs to use their Red Cross packages and augment the otherwise meager rations they received from the Germans. Under such conditions, Ross Greening, who had flown in the Doolittle Raid and then procured alcohol in North Africa until his B-26 went down and he was captured, found life in prison camps "reduced to its barest essentials," with food being one of the most important things on a prisoner's mind. Thus, "no wonder that food and cooking occupied such an important place in prison camp life." Sergeant Angelo M. Spinelli, a photographer assigned to the Army Air Corps captured in North Africa when he unwittingly drove a truck full of German prisoners into the middle of a firefight, recalled the ranking American prison camp officer demanding that his fellow prisoners talk about something other than food. Immediately, one of his fellow prisoners remained true to his mechanically minded American upbringing by imagining a "shiny new auto—covered in mashed potatoes and gravy."[11]

Clever POWs applied the same sort of technical creativity to slake their thirst with something stronger than the powdered milk contained in their Red Cross parcels. In some cases, the production of alcohol had a practical function. In

Spinelli's camp, kriegies made liquor by collecting the dried fruits and raisins in the food parcels and transforming them in a still fabricated from bent up brass instruments sent by the YMCA, as the tubing lent itself to the construction of still condensers.[12] In other situations, alcohol production broke up otherwise monotonous camp life. Jerry Sage celebrated the Fourth of July with illicit alcohol in the summer of 1943. Relying on Al Hake, an Australian Spitfire pilot with a knack for metalworking, Sage managed to secure some tubing fabricated from soldered strips of Klim can rolled around a pencil. Augmenting this with copper tubing stolen from trombone slides, they managed to build a still that they kept filled with "devil's brew," cooking it at night with "shutters closed and blankets hung to shield out peeping German eyes." Donning a blue British RAF shirt and a pair of red-and-white-striped pajamas in a make-do imitation of Uncle Sam, Sage was joined by Harold "Shorty" Spire dressed as Paul Revere complete with tricorn hat, alongside three other kriegies with drum, flag, and fife in an inventive interpretation of the "Spirit of '76." The American-engineered day of fun, frivolity, and inebriation effectively reminded their fellow British prisoners what the day meant back in the United States.[13]

The preparation and consumption of liquor to celebrate special days like the Fourth of July provided only a temporary respite from the daily drudgery of the camps. With little to do, prisoners spent time between meals thinking of their next meal, and of more efficient ways to overcome the paucity of wood and coal issued to prisoners for heating and cooking purposes. To stretch meager fuel sources as far as they could, American kriegies built small stoves that could "burn almost anything short of rocks," as described by United Press correspondent Edward Beattie, who had been captured in 1944 and spent the remainder of the war in a stalag. He frequently cooked over a "smokey," a simple stove made from two quart-sized cans crimped together around a rough grate. Fueled by shredded Red Cross parcels, bits of wood, twigs, grass, and occasionally, coal, these stoves produced heat but coated everyone and everything in the vicinity with soot.[14] Jerry Sage, with tongue firmly in cheek, called their miniature stoves "smokeless cookers." The device, consisting of a "small can punched full of holes wired into the top half of a larger can, also punched," which had a door cut in the side and burned scraps of paper, cardboard, and kindling in the lower half of the can while consuming the "residue of combustible gases left in the smoke from the bottom." The result could "heat a cup of water or barley soup in a matter of minutes," perfect for making a hot drink on a winter's night.[15] More inventive prisoners transformed their "smokeys" into "smokeless heaters" by inserting a 1 lb margarine can and crafting a set of air intakes that reduced fuel consumption but increased heat output. The most ingenious kriegies "fashioned clever high compression blowers to get the last bit of heat from the meager supply of ersatz coal provided by the Germans." Starting with a "smokey" or "smokeless heater," these crafty prisoners rigged a fan wheel that operated inside a Klim can, powered by a hand crank mounted on a board. Straddling the invention, the cook cranked up his fire, which produced white-hot heat. When used, the output from these "ingenious little blast furnaces" left a cloud of smoke that "hung over the camp all day long."[16]

While kriegie camp stoves and blowers represented feats of engineering achievement, other POWs directed energy toward more secretive projects. America's prewar passion for radio communication enabled kriegies to build, use, and conceal simple radios capable of hearing news of the war from beyond the barbed wire. On the Italian front, a pair of American GIs made a foxhole radio out of a razor blade, a safety pin, a set of earphones, and a coil of wire. Imprisoned American troops were every bit as technically savvy. POWs embraced this technology that was part of the everyday fabric of American life throughout the 1930s.[17] In Stalag Luft III, Jerry Sage recalled that Dale Bowman was a "wizard at building and repairing tiny radios," a skill shared by Hal Decker of Auburn, Indiana. Between the two, they got the "best possible reception" from London, taking shorthand notes at night to share the next day.[18] Toward the end of the war, radios became more prevalent. In March 1945, in Stalag 3B at Fürstenberg on the Oder River, Pfc. Seymour Lichtenfeld of the 422nd Infantry Regiment, who was captured during the opening phases of the Battle of the Bulge, recalled German guards going "crazy" in efforts to find "more and more crystal sets" that kept materializing throughout his camp.[19]

Through fabrication of camp tools and cooking utensils from the ubiquitous Klim cans, craft projects that ranged from musical instruments to fully functional steamboats, "screwball contrivances," elaborate theatrical and musical productions, and Red Cross–facilitated recreation and sports activities, most American POWs did what they could to survive imprisonment.[20] After the invasion of Normandy, they followed illicit radio news in hopes that a rapid Allied advance would lead to their liberation. In the meantime, however, many tried to escape or otherwise confound their captors, digging tunnels, masquerading as German soldiers in homemade uniforms, or even disguising themselves as German female war workers and slipping through the stalag gates.[21]

Few camps saw as many escape attempts as the combined camps that made up Stalag Luft III near Sagan, Silesia (now Żagań, Poland). Over the course of the war, the Allied prisoners in the East, North, and South Camps engaged in a myriad of escape attempts, efforts that culminated in "the Great Escape" immortalized in the Australian POW Paul Brickhill's book (and the eventual 1963 United Artists film) of the same name. On the night of 24 March 1944, two hundred British POWs housed in the North Camp of Stalag Luft III attempted to escape out of a three-hundred-foot-long tunnel named "Harry."[22] Their efforts required a wide variety of clever contraptions, many of which were a product of years of experimentation and failed escape attempts: a bellows system that moved fresh air into the tunnel through Klim-can ducting, a trolley that moved dirt and men through the tunnel, improvised electric lighting, and a dirt disposal system. In support of the escape attempt, other prisoners forged identity papers and other requisite documents, fabricated clothing for the escapees, and produced maps and compasses that would help guide an escapee's way to freedom.[23]

Lieutenant Colonel Albert P. Clark was the second-highest-ranking US officer in the South Camp of Stalag Luft III when the British prisoners made their escape attempt. A member of the 31st Pursuit Squadron, Eighth Air Force, he had been among the first Americans shot down and imprisoned during World War II. Sent to Stalag Luft III in August 1942, he joined the British prisoners there as "Big S," tasked with providing secure hiding places for all requisite escape materials. Clark also oversaw the activities of a constantly growing number of American POWs who joined him in what came to be called "Little America."[24]

British or Australian prisoners provided much of the initial impetus for devices and escape practices and were the driving force behind the March 1944 escape attempt. An ever-increasing number of American POWs sent to "Little America" in the North Camp, however, joined the escape committee and improved on the efforts of Commonwealth POWs, a visible testament to American mechanical and technical creativity.[25] Second Lieutenant Charles "Hupe" Huppert improved the air bellows created by Norwegian Jens Muller. A mechanical engineer from Evansville, Indiana, Huppert "seemed to be able to design machinery in his head." Once he had his design in mind, he broke the bellows down into component parts and farmed them out for construction throughout the camp, eventually bringing them back together to complete the final assembly himself. Not only did Huppert "the Manufacturer" improve on the air bellows that kept the air in the tunnels fresh, but he designed a new device to more effectively develop intelligence photos.[26] Australian Al Hake, who provided Jerry Sage with the Klim-can tubing used in a still, ran the compass-making factory that provided potential escapees with all-important compasses. With cases manufactured from old phonograph records, the key component of the compass was a needle made from a sliver of magnetized razor blade. Upon arriving, Clark tasked his fellow American Captain John Bennett, a "skilled craftsman," to assist Hake in compass construction.[27] Bennett saw the "slow process" by which Hake "stroked the razor blade, always in the same direction, for hours at a time," but quickly realized there was a better way; "being American, I was soon into the mass-production, Ford-assembly-line-philosophy," he remembered. Taking a flat board, he made glue out of powdered skim milk and secured twenty blades to it. Then, by rubbing the magnet over the group of stationary blades, he "increased production overnight."[28]

Other Americans played similar roles, building on the efforts of other prisoners, yet at the same time demonstrating a uniquely American strain of technical ingenuity that often outstripped that of their Commonwealth counterparts. In addition to compasses, tinkerers fabricated wire cutters and other escape tools from everyday items found throughout Stalag Luft III. Second Lieutenant Robert Spurgin III of Indiana built a forge to make wire cutters, hardening the metal with sugar, the same process he used in making a series of saw blades.[29] Others crafted snips from blades off a stolen pair of ice skates or climbed a telegraph pole to pilfer the metal braces that supported the cross arms. When Wehrmacht and Luftwaffe guards at the camps confiscated wire cutters prisoners had fabricated from stove handles, the guards reported that the kriegie variety were often superior to the ones issued from German stores. Regardless, the cutters were an essential item to get through the often multiple barbed wire fences that ringed every camp.[30]

In virtually every stalag, "the ingenuity of American youth, married to 'mother necessity,'" provided POWs detained in Europe with all they needed to solve whatever challenge befell them while incarcerated by their Nazi captors.[31] Captured after their planes were shot down or seized during the Battle of the Bulge when the surprise and ferocity of the German counterattack caught American troops unawares, these indefatigable Americans spent the rest of the war behind barbed wire. For those Americans captured by the Japanese, however, their tenure in captivity was not only much longer, but since representatives of the Japanese Empire had never signed the 1929 Geneva Convention, these prisoners had only limited access to the ICRC support and other comforts afforded to their comrades in Europe. The vast majority of Pacific POWs, captured when the Philippines, Guam, Wake Island, and other US Far East possessions fell to the Japanese, endured harsh conditions with a bare minimum of food, clothing, and material support. Nonetheless, these Americans remained true to their mechanically minded upbringing and applied American ingenuity in efforts to live, survive, and frustrate their Japanese captors while serving as unwilling guests of the Emperor.

Within six months after the attack on Pearl Harbor, Americans defending Pacific outposts who survived the opening months of the war became prisoners of the Imperial Japanese Army. For soldiers of the Rising Sun, whose military code frowned on surrender, anything short of a sacrificial death for the Emperor was a disgrace, not only to oneself but to one's family and ancestors.

Consequently, Americans and Allies who surrendered rather than fighting to the death were regarded as less than human. They had sacrificed their honor, a fate worse than death itself.[32]

Japan claimed to abide by the 1929 Geneva Convention, though in practice, the Japanese rarely adhered to any of the treaty's articles and prohibited the ICRC from inspecting most camps. Consequently, most American prisoners faced a constant struggle for survival, forced to make do with scant rations, usually some combination of rice and watery soup of varying quality. In those circumstances where Red Cross parcels did reach their camps, Japanese soldiers frequently stole the parcels, as prisoners often recalled seeing their captors making off with cocoa, sugar, milk, and other parcel components.[33] In other cases, Red Cross parcels arrived on a less than consistent basis, as Japanese officers apparently "held out for their own use at least as many Red Cross packages as those they allowed to get to the prisoners."[34]

Most prisoners of the Japanese complained of both the lack, and generally poor quality, of the food they received and took whatever steps they could to supplement the meager rations they received, eventually embracing the Tagalog word *quan* (or *cuan*), loosely translated as "whatchamacallit" or "thingamajig"—over time adopting it as a noun, verb, and adjective. In the POW camp at Cabanatuan, it was not uncommon for prisoners to use the words *quan*, *quanning*, *quan* kitchen, to *quan*, and *quanning* hours to describe their various activities, particularly as they related to cooking.[35] Marine pilot John F. Kinney, whom the Japanese moved to Kiangwan Prison, in the suburbs of Shanghai, China, after a year in Woosung Prison, recalled the "ingenious device," contrived by Capt. Herb Freuler, a fellow officer in VMF-211, to improve the quality of the rice they received. Recognizing that "the rice we got was apparently the sweepings from the floor of some Chinese warehouse or had been threshed on the ground," Freuler built a wooden sluice box, "very much like those used by the gold miners of the nineteenth century," that separated the rocks from the day's rice ration, a machine that not only impressed the Japanese but removed the risk of damaging one's teeth by biting down on rocks, instead of rice.[36]

After "*quanning* up" whatever they could, Americans in the Pacific often built stoves of the same name to cook their meager rations. Most of those in the Philippines who used a "*quan* stove," built a fire in a gallon can, over the top of which they placed a grate "to serve as a cooking surface." Using bellows made out of canvas left over from a shelter half, they pumped oxygen to increase the intensity of the hot embers or charcoal, at the same time providing a nearly flame- and smoke-free fire, perfect for "cooking on the sly." Sergeant Carl S. Nordin, who enlisted in the army in September 1940, was a member of the Detached 2nd Quartermaster Supply (Aviation), attached to the 5th Air Base

Group on the Philippines and was captured on 10 May 1942. He fondly remembered the morale boost provided by smuggled coffee cooked up by fellow prisoner Dan Stoudt on his quan stove.[37] Others built "little hibachis," nesting two different-sized cans together, filling the space between with mud, and cutting a hole in the bottom for air intake. Using nails or scraps of wire over the top for a grate, the result was a stove that could "warm up a bowl of rice or toast a piece of bread."[38] Corporal Louis B. Read of the 31st Infantry remembered the use of quan stoves, "made out of the cans that the food in the Red Cross Parcels came in" in use at Cabanatuan. "Everybody had their own," he recalled, and "there must have been a million designs. You'd look out there, and they were all squatting around . . . a little fire going, his *quan* stove going with a little pot on it, a homemade pot made of these cans."[39]

Other prisoners had even more creative results. When small Red Cross stoves arrived at Kiangwan Prison in late 1943, not only did the Japanese limit their use to two hours a day, but the quality of the coal available was such that it took a "considerable amount of air" to get the fire started each day. Despite lacking the "required tools and materials," John Kinney fabricated a mechanical blower of a design not unlike those made by the kriegies in the German stalags. After stealing or making tools and cutting the tops and bottoms off eight Red Cross food packet tin cans and folding them into ductwork, he used plywood, scraps from the electric fence around the compound, and "a leather shoelace that served quite well as a drive belt," to make, on a "trial and error basis," a blower that started "about twenty stoves per day during the fall and winter" of 1943.[40]

Other American POWs fabricated creature comforts to make camp conditions more humane. While imprisoned in Camp O'Donnell in the summer of 1942, William C. Braly, a US Army colonel who had served in the defense of the Philippines, had to repair his violin, which he carried with him through the early phase of his captivity. After securing some "fish glue" from a Corporal Nishiyama, he used a shelter-tent rope in place of a clamp and fashioned a double boiler out of a small can inserted into a larger one. He was able to make his violin serviceable until the next rainy season, when he had to repeat the process.[41] When the Japanese subsequently moved Braly and other American prisoners to Taiwan, they confiscated a number of personal articles from the Americans. Fortunately for Braly, his captors allowed him to retain his violin, and on numerous occasions, members of the Japanese prison staff sought him out to play for them, as, he concluded, "the novelty intrigued them."[42]

By February 1945, Braly discovered a number of excellent musicians in a new camp in Mukden, Manchuria. Organizing them into an orchestra, Braly soon found himself named the leader, and he led practices twice a week for the benefit of men otherwise "starved for music." Directing a mixed symphony made up of violins, mandolins, guitars, piano accordion, trumpet, and string bass, Braly recalled that the last instrument "remarkably demonstrated that necessity is the mother of invention." Captain Neville L. Grow of the 92nd Coast Artillery had crafted the bass viol in one of the camp utilities shops in 1943. He salvaged wooden parts from scrap in the camp shop and an aluminum mess kit that "provided metal for pegs which meshed with fiber gears." Extracting fiberboard from extra POW name tags, he stole potassium permanganate, iodine, and alcohol from the hospital, a mixture that provided an "excellent mahogany stain," sealed with shellac smuggled in from a nearby factory. Still lacking strings, Grow solved the problem when the Japanese slaughtered a hog in camp. He secured some of the guts, cured them with a solution of styptic pencil and salt, and twisted them into strings. His success inspired Sgt. Slick Johnson, 59th Coast Artillery, to use the same techniques to build a guitar. Both resulting instruments had "every appearance of a professional job."[43]

Americans also applied unique technical skills to endure the challenging conditions of their captivity. John Kinney recalled an enlisted marine who tapped into his camp's electrical system and built a hot water heater. Other prisoners made or smuggled in commercial hot plates, or, in Kinney's case, built an electric bed warmer from an extra light socket, a light bulb, a switch, an empty tin can, and a couple pieces of wire. By rigging up the light socket inside a tin can punched with nail holes, the ensuing hot can could be passed over the blanket to warm it up. Such devices became very popular in Kinney's camp, so popular that at one point in his captivity, he claimed that the prison camp consumed as much electric power as the entire city of Shanghai. When the camp commander ordered a shakedown to confiscate as many of the illicit electrical appliances as could be found, the Americans fought back. Within a few weeks, some of the civilian electricians captured along with Kinney on Wake Island began monitoring further electric consumption, and even managed to manipulate the camp's electric meter so that it ran backward, effectively masking consumption from the Japanese as prisoners quickly resumed their preraid practices, crafting new water heaters, hot plates, and bed warmers.[44]

Most American soldiers possessed a modicum of technical ability and mastery of technology. This represented a stark contrast to their Japanese captors, the vast majority of whom lacked any appreciable mechanical aptitude, even something as simple as operating an automobile. In terms of technological understanding, soldiers of the Imperial Japanese Army, particularly those with lesser degrees of training and experience that were left behind to guard POWs, possessed considerably less technical understanding than GIs. Corporal

Martin Boyle, a marine who was captured when Guam fell, believed that if "Japan made an all-out industrial effort, they might catch up to where the U.S. was in 1920."[45] When the war began, Japanese men possessing mechanical skills were pressed into military service, leaving behind a work pool of elderly men and women. Products of a predominantly peasant society, their lack of education and general technical ignorance forced Japan's industrialists to seek others with mechanical aptitude. Consequently, the Japanese used Americans as a labor force, capitalizing on their expertise to serve as mechanics and drivers or as a skilled labor force in Japanese factories.[46] According to Boyle, the Japanese "weren't nearly advanced" as Americans were "in the use of machines and other labor-saving devices," requiring the use of American labor just to maintain the operability of much of their machine technology.[47]

After his capture on Bataan in April 1942, John Henry Poncio of the 91st Bombardment Squadron found himself forced into service as a driver for the Imperial Japanese Army, as the "average [Japanese] man or woman didn't even know how to drive." Tasked with driving five-ton Dodge trucks captured by the Japanese on Bataan, he impressed "Girocho," his Japanese guard, by his expert ability. Taking the wheel of a sluggish truck, he realized that "it was a power wagon with four-wheel drive." Put into the proper gear, "she smoothed out, running like a top," and this move, Poncio recalled, "made me an instant hit with my Japanese companion," who did not understand how such a truck should run. Poncio's abilities earned him a hard-boiled duck egg, though when he took his hands off the wheel to peel the egg and drove with his knee, "Girocho" snatched the egg from his hands, returning it only after he finished peeling the egg.[48]

Early on in his captivity, Sgt. Lester I. Tenney, a member of Company B, 192nd Tank Battalion, captured on Bataan in 1942, capitalized on his mechanical prowess (or the fact that he possessed more than most Japanese soldiers) to get out of Camp O'Donnell, where he was sent after he surrendered. When the Japanese asked for "truck drivers, welders and loaders," he stepped forward. Tenney and ninety other prisoners performed "simple, yet demanding" work, cutting up vehicles so that the Japanese could make use of the scrap metal. Most of his compatriots knew how to drive a truck, and their duties cutting up abandoned American vehicles for scrap served as a source of considerable frustration, because the prisoners soon realized that the Japanese never had any intention, much less ability, to use the vehicles that the Americans had sabotaged before they surrendered. On numerous occasions during Tenney's tenure as a prisoner, the Japanese sought out Americans with mechanical skills, abilities nonexistent among their Japanese captors. Moreover, when Americans "volunteered," the mechanically ignorant Japanese could not comprehend the wide range of technical skills, "so many a truck driver turned engineer overnight."[49] In October 1944, William Braly and other prisoners on Taiwan received orders from their captors to leave camp. Exempt from this order, Braly recalled, were "eight officers who were below the grade of colonel and three enlisted men whom the Nips were using as mechanics," a testament to the need for drivers and other mechanically minded men to help sustain the Japanese army.[50]

In stark contrast to their Japanese captors, who were raised within the confines of a society structured around honor, duty, and obedience to the Emperor, imprisoned Americans possessed a certain sneakiness about them that was also anathema to the Japanese. Anthony Iannarelli Sr., one of a group of Americans captured after Guam fell, discovered this difference firsthand when the intrepid sailor tried to trade a US Navy canvas hammock with a Japanese civilian employed as a carpenter. When the Japanese man could not figure out how to sneak the hammock past the guardhouse, Iannarelli simply unloaded the carpenter's cart, placed the hammock on the bottom, and then covered it back up with the odd pieces of lumber that the man used in performing his duties. After Iannarelli ensured that the act of subterfuge would be successful, the Japanese man looked at him and said, with absolute sincerity, "You Americans are really very smart," leading Iannarelli to realize that it was not simply his being smart, but that "being sly was not a part of the Japanese's culture."[51]

Blending American guile with forced duty as laborers provided Americans opportunities to take advantage of their captors' mechanical ineptitude and confound them. The result was that while laboring for the Japanese, Americans did everything they could to ensure that the work they performed aided the enemy as little as possible. Forced to work in Yokkaichi, Japan, Carl Nordin recalled not only trying to hold back as much as he could, but resorting to sabotage whenever possible.[52] After gaining the trust of their guards through diligent performance while laboring on a railroad repair detail, Nordin and his comrades subsequently earned the confidence of a "harried foreman" who entrusted them with "some of the technical work." Rebuilding a rail line damaged by an American bomb raid, they "purposely gauged one track a little too wide," where the track ran through a stretch of disturbed and uneven ground. When they arrived to work the next morning, "there was a locomotive lying on its side," something the Japanese attributed to unstable ground and poorly tamped railroad ties, not deliberate sabotage on the part of the Americans.[53]

When it came to damaging machines, Americans could easily outwit their less technically savvy captors, leading to repeated acts of sabotage. Lester

Tenney eventually found himself imprisoned in Camp 17 in Omuta on the island of Kyushu, about thirty-five miles east of Nagasaki. As part of a ten-man American coal-mining team, he eventually realized that on their daily trudge down into the mine, they passed the engine that powered the main conveyor belt for the entire complex. Knowing that if they could stop the motor, mine operations would grind to a halt, they hatched a simple, yet effective sabotage plan capitalizing on their captors' lack of mechanical know-how. When marched by the motor the next day, the first man stopped briefly to loosen the wing nut on the engine's oil reservoir. The next man in line removed the cover, with the next six men in line dropping rocks, hard coal, and anything else available into the open reservoir before the last two replaced the cover and tightened the nut. Making their way to their assigned work area, they labored for about an hour before "all hell broke loose." Their plan for sabotage was a resounding success, as the motor broke down, earning them a three-hour respite in the mine.[54]

Corporal Alton C. Halbrook was a member of the 4th Marine Regiment captured on Corregidor. After spending time in Cabanatuan, Camp O'Donnell, and Batangas, he realized that the "Japs didn't know anything about driving, and they didn't know anything about mechanic work." If you "acted natural, you could just tear the hell out of anything." Working in the Clark Field welding shops, he and his compatriots figured out a way to not only commit acts of sabotage, but to take a personal toll on their captors. As a wise, mechanically minded American providing lessons on the cutting torch, he told his Japanese captors to wear greasy leather gloves and cover the threads of the oxygen bottle with grease while screwing it down. After following his instructions, when the Japanese technician turned on the oxygen bottle, the entire assembly exploded, killing the technician instantly. Blaming faulty equipment, the Japanese not only never knew what hit them, but they failed to find fault with Halbrook or any other American for the incident.[55]

Private William A. Visage served with E Battery, 2nd Battalion, 131st Field Artillery, 36th Infantry Division, before he was captured in Madura, Dutch East Indies. While working in the shipyard in Nagasaki, he put metal drill shavings in a number of the dynamos that provided all the electricity to the factory, which would "flash out the whole facility." They also managed to cause a fire in the boiler shop by "running the boiler way past the danger point and then backing it down." Repeating this process without alerting the Japanese eventually caused the boiler to explode, causing considerable damage.[56]

Unlike American POWs in Europe, who after escaping could attempt to blend in with the local population and return to Allied lines, very few Americans successfully escaped from Japanese POW camps. Not only were prison camps in the Philippines, China, and Japan too isolated, but the physical differences between American POWs and the neighboring population made blending in impossible. Thus, all American POWs could do was endure and hope that the war would eventually end. As time went on, prisoners nonetheless gained better knowledge of the course of the Pacific War as American ingenuity provided them with the tools to not only glean information from outside their camps, but to preserve some record of their experiences so that appropriate punitive action could be taken once the war was over.

For a few months in late 1942, Japanese prison guards loaned American prisoners imprisoned on Mindanao a low-powered radio that could only receive the Japanese English-language station broadcast out of Manila. In short order, an American prisoner who had previously served as a radio engineer fabricated a new coil that allowed the set to reach San Francisco, but the Japanese confiscated the radio before the prisoners were able to obtain any real information on the course of the war. A few months later, using "materials of all kinds . . . [that] could be used by the person who had the necessary imagination and skill," Lt. Homer T. Hutchison, an engineer officer and electrical engineer by profession, built a radio. Trading for a tube smuggled into camp, he used salvaged materials for his receiver, hiding the assembly in the bottom half of a canteen, concealing it with the canteen cup. After he built the radio, the Japanese moved him into a barracks building that lacked electricity, forcing him to fashion a battery out of copper and zinc scraps, acid "stolen from the battery of a Nip truck," and zinc trouser buttons.[57]

After acquiring the right parts, it was easy to build a radio, for as John Kinney recalled, "it was not unusual for [American] boys of the 1930s to build their own primitive radios." Kinney attempted to make a crystal radio in the summer of 1943, having illicitly obtained a speedometer magnet and an ignition coil in the truck repair shop and fabricating his own earphone from a variety of parts he was able to beg, borrow, or steal. Using a Red Cross Nescafe powdered coffee can as a housing, he built a radio, but it initially failed to produce a signal. Checking his schematics with a few fellow prisoners, he made some changes, and finally got his radio working in time to hear of Italy's surrender in September 1943. Kinney concealed his radio throughout the remainder of the war, sharing news of the Normandy landings, the Allied victory in the Battle of Leyte Gulf, and the Japanese losses at Iwo Jima and Okinawa, events that greatly boosted prisoner morale.[58]

While the acquisition and successful concealment of a radio helped make living out the war more endurable for some POWs, others used their ingenuity to document their treatment, hoping to hold the Japanese accountable at war's end. Marine corporal Terence S. Kirk was captured in China shortly after

Pearl Harbor and spent the rest of the war in captivity. After time in a number of camps, he was moved to POW camp number three, near Fukuoka, Japan, where he joined nineteen other Americans as part of the *Yoheen* (scrap iron) gang. Kirk managed to scavenge enough materials in the camp to build a simple pinhole camera, obtaining photographic plates from Nishi, an American-born Japanese interpreter he had befriended in the camp. After cutting down 8 × 10 photographic plates to fit in a 4 × 5 camera, Kirk took five photos, illicitly developing the plates in a dark space made by hiding in a bathtub under a piece of plywood. Capturing conditions in the camp, along with three photos of malnourished prisoners suffering from beriberi, he delivered multiple copies of each of the five photographs he had taken. When he provided them to the US government when the war ended, Kirk was forced to sign a government-issued gag order prohibiting him from discussing his time as a Japanese POW.[59]

When the war was over and all prisoners were repatriated back to the United States, former POW Ross Greening organized an exposition highlighting the experiences of POWs held by the Germans during World War II, creating a display that contained a full-size replica of a sixteen-man barracks room from a German stalag. To open the exhibition in New York, Mayor Fiorello La Guardia planned to cut a string of barbed wire using a pair of wire cutters manufactured in a POW camp during the war. Arriving forty-five minutes late, he quickly clipped the wire, then made his way to the exit without so much as walking through the exhibit. Greening chased after him, then explained to the mayor that the event was more than "a simple public affairs appearance," as it was his "obligation to see an exhibit of extreme importance to the American public." Over the course of the next one and half hours, La Guardia dutifully made his way through the exhibit, glancing at a POW violin made from bed slats and swinging his legs while sitting on a camp bunk in a solitary confinement cell. When he arrived at the section of the exhibition emphasizing the materials manufactured by American POWs in preparation for the various escape attempts, he stopped and gave it more attention than he had given to any other aspect of the exhibit. He then proclaimed that it was "one of the best exhibitions of American ingenuity that he had ever seen."[60]

La Guardia, in recognizing POWs' ingenuity, saw the same thing that Terence Kirk's American-raised Japanese interpreter, Nishi, had seen when he told Kirk why he was willing to help him obtain photographic plates and develop them. Nishi said, "We think a lot differently in America than people elsewhere on Earth." While Nishi was not speaking specifically in terms of mechanical ingenuity and technical intuition, he might as well have been, for Americans were different. Based on the POW experience, both of Americans behind the wire in German stalags as well as of those who became prisoners of the

Japanese, it is clear that Americans possessed a view of technology that was a product of their upbringing. Once captured, those Americans unfortunate enough to become prisoners of war fell back on what they knew and understood and used that knowledge to survive. Conditions in the United States in the 1930s were rarely as severe as camp conditions in prison camps either in Europe or Japan. But that era of improvisation, ingenuity, and forced tinkering unwittingly provided American soldiers with the very training that was required for them to survive their time as prisoners of war in World War II.

CHAPTER 7

GI Jury-Rigging on the Road to Berlin

> The Americans, as a race, are the foremost mechanics in the world. America, as a nation, has the greatest ability for mass production of machines. It therefore behooves us to devise methods of war which exploit our inherent superiority.
>
> —*Gen. George S. Patton*

As GIs liberated Europe, American ingenuity assumed broader dimensions. Benefiting from an ever-expanding logistical base, American GIs demonstrated mechanical creativity from Normandy to Berlin. With ports eventually opened at Cherbourg, Le Havre, and Antwerp, the greater availability of Allied armor, jeeps, weapons, and other technology supported the Allies' slow advance across a broad front, providing GIs the opportunity to improvise and adapt their tools of war to the new conditions they encountered in the drive across western Europe. Theater-wide improvisation provided valuable resources as GIs neared and breached the Siegfried Line, struggled through the Lorraine and Vosges, countered the Wehrmacht in the Bulge, crossed the Rhine, and continued on the American drive toward Berlin. The result was a plethora of new devices and gadgets, as well as enhanced weapons and improved vehicles as GIs tinkered and addressed the challenges they encountered in the field.

American ingenuity employed by a fully mechanized US Army paid considerable dividends throughout the remainder of the war in Europe. Blending tactical and operational vision with logistical support and practical mechanical abilities, motor-savvy GIs adapted technology, perpetuating the "Use it up, wear it out, make it do, or do without" mentality embraced during the Great Depression. The contraptions and mechanical improvements made by these citizen-soldiers provided the balance of victory in the fight against Hitler's Germany. Such efforts were not lost on US Army leadership. While GIs in the field fabricated and modified technology, making improvements largely on their own volition, US commanders developed the means to review, inspect, and evaluate these jury-rigged solutions, carefully gauging the "validity of the indicated battle lessons."[1] Demonstrating institutional flexibility and offering considerable bureaucratic support, US Army leadership facilitated the rapid dissemination of these creative solutions across entire armies and army groups. Only within the American army were such notions possible.

Throughout the war, Headquarters, European Theater of Operations, US Army (HQETOUSA) collected "Combat Observations," sending officers into the field to discover the best tactics, techniques, and procedures practiced by active GIs. Distributed periodically between July 1944 and the end of the war, the findings opened with a lengthy endorsement from Gen. Omar N. Bradley noting that "Battle Experiences will be published regularly by this headquarters to enable units in training to profit from the latest combat experiences of our troops now fighting the Germans in France." Collected by the Combat Lessons Branch, G-3 Division, ETO, these reports are rife with examples of GI ingenuity. Besides the publication and dissemination of "Battle Experiences," however, there was little to facilitate a systematic passage of information between units, and consequently any exchange was largely on an ad hoc basis. By August 1944, however, Twelfth Army Group adjutant general Brig. Gen. H. B. Lewis distributed copies of the Combat Observers Immediate Reports, sending fifteen copies to the ETO's commanding general, nine copies to Supreme Headquarters Allied Expeditionary Force, six copies to 21st Army Group, and fifty copies to First, Third, and Ninth Armies.[2]

G-3 observers collected and evaluated this information while the Allies pursued a retreating German army across France, though by the end of the summer of 1944, the advances of both Gen. Courtney Hodges's First Army and Gen. George S. Patton's Third Army had outrun their supply lines. With most supplies still coming across the beaches due to sabotaged port facilities at Cherbourg and Le Havre, advancing American troops faced significant logistical shortcomings with respect to rations, ammunition, and fuel. Even with the unexpected capture of Antwerp by Field Marshal Bernard Law Montgomery's Twenty-First Army Group on 4 September, the Allies failed to capitalize on this new logistical hub, and both American armies, as well as their British counterpart, soldiered on with 3,500 tons of supplies daily, about half of what each army required.[3] With American engineers struggling to repair rail bridges destroyed by the ongoing Allied air interdiction campaign, the Services of Supply improvised to sustain the advance.

The result was a uniquely American blend of mechanical improvisation and logistical support. In August 1944, Col. Loren Ayers, chief of the Communication Zone Motor Transport Service, organized the Red Ball Express. Mobilizing forty provisional truck companies augmented by 1,500 vehicles taken from other units, the Express ran twenty-four hours a day for eighty-two days straight, ultimately moving more than 400,000 tons of supplies by 16 November.[4] A seat of the pants operation, the Red Ball Express developed significant problems, most of which stemmed from the operation's improvised nature. Of the 250,000 drivers pressed into duty from service companies, approximately 75 percent were African American, with nearly half of those coming from poor and rural areas throughout the South. Taking additional trucks from idle infantry divisions, the convoys exacted a tremendous toll on both drivers and vehicles. Many drivers learned about vehicles on the job, mastering the art of double clutching a 2.5-ton "Jimmy" or 1.5-ton Dodge truck while racing at breakneck speeds.[5] The hasty organization of these mechanical novices into derisively labeled "truck-destroyer battalions" resulted in wear and tear on overloaded and underserviced vehicles. Driving a one-way circuitous route, the constant operations led to the abandonment of 9,000 derelict vehicles along French roads between Saint-Lô and Soissons. Maintenance companies recovered many disabled vehicles, cannibalizing from various interchangeable vehicle models to return functional vehicles to service.[6] Not only did maintainers get trucks back on the road, but mechanically minded GIs possessing the "make do" attitude improvised, inventing tools to straighten bent axles, adapting British axles to fit on American trucks, or fabricating replacement parts in liberated French factories.[7] These makeshift repair facilities could not maintain every vehicle on the road, and despite their efforts, the Red Ball Express rolled along on bald or poorly retreaded and rebuilt tires, or made use of replacement tires scavenged from 37 mm gun carriages and even German vehicles as the Twelfth Army Group's supply convoy reached its operational peak.[8]

Even before the Red Ball Express, supply shortages fostered improvisation, with varying levels of success. The *Infantry Journal* described a "gasoline filter" fabricated from a fifty-five-gallon drum packed with alternating layers of fine screen, cotton, pulverized charcoal, and activated carbon. Pouring leaded gasoline through the layers produced "unleaded" fuel for field ranges, Coleman lanterns, and battery chargers.[9] "Experts" gave the filter a "thumbs down," an assessment thereafter advanced in HQETOUSA, "Battle Experiences."[10] Elements of the 9th Infantry Division fabricated replacement antennae from French transmission wire for the AN-130A antenna used on the SCR-300 radio.[11] When the supply of BA-40 batteries for the 600 series radios ran short, 12th Infantry Regiment communications officers substituted BA-2 batteries stacked in series with BA-23s placed parallel, connecting them with a base from a used BA-40 battery.[12] Other divisions replaced bazooka launcher batteries with a modified TL-122 flashlight wiring to the bazooka stock.[13]

Vehicle modifications contributed to greater combat effectiveness. The 315th Engineer Battalion, in concert with the service company of the 712th Tank Battalion, added a bracket to the front of an M32 tank recovery vehicle, allowing it to carry a forty-five-foot span of treadway bridge. Driving the vehicle into a moat or other obstacle requiring bridging, tankers could deploy the bridge from the inside of the vehicle, with one section accommodating infantry and two sections sturdy enough to support a tank.[14] The 628th Tank Destroyer Battalion proposed a ring mount for the existing turret-mounted .50-caliber machine gun to render it more effective against both enemy infantry and aircraft.[15] One tank destroyer unit relocated its .50-caliber machine gun to the turret's right front, an arrangement "used very effectively" against enemy infantry and bazooka fire.[16] Others replaced the .50-caliber machine gun with a single .30-caliber machine gun, carrying more ammunition in the same space.[17] The 66th Armored Regiment welded V-shaped shields of half-inch steel around the tank commander's position to protect him without having to "button up."[18] The 709th Tank Battalion removed the back of seats in their Mediums to facilitate easy access to the tank's escape hatch and replaced awkward hatch handles with wire loops for emergency opening.[19] Paratroopers of the 82nd Airborne Division armored their jeep, which they nicknamed "Little Ironsides," by adding armored screens around their open vehicle, and used it during the Market Garden and Bulge campaigns.[20]

Other GIs tinkered with their weapons. Lt. Col. J. D. Childs, the 9th Infantry Division's ordnance officer, made the M6A1 2.36-inch bazooka rockets "super sensitive," ensuring their detonation on softer targets (as opposed to only exploding on contact with a tank hull or other solid target). Transmitting this information to the War Department Observers Board, along with approbation from Maj. Gen. Clarence R. Huebner of 1st Infantry Division, prompted the recommendation that further modifications to the M6A1 rocket be made at army level to ease the workload of individual units.[21] GIs also discovered that with six inches of wire, a grenade launcher adaptor, and pair of pliers, they could modify a 60 mm mortar shell and use an M-1 Garand rifle to fire it through windows and into other structures with considerable accuracy.[22] Others taped three magazines for their M-3 submachine gun together, giving them ninety rounds of instantly available ammunition.[23] Troops from the 39th Infantry Division fabricated grenade booby traps, removing the pin from a white phosphorous or fragmentation grenade, attaching a wire from the grenade to a fixed point, and then carefully placing the grenade in its can so that when an enemy hit the wire, the live grenade popped out and detonated.[24] Technical Sergeant Dale Curtis of the 379th Infantry Regiment, 95th Infantry Division, made a two-wheeled trailer for a .50-caliber machine gun that he employed to great effect in street fighting in Saarlautern.[25] Others built even heavier weapons, as troops of the 9th Air Force Service Command's ordnance section assembled a four-ton machine-gun mounting tank from German, French, and American parts.[26]

The drive across France exposed weaknesses in American armor. General Bradley first recognized the shortcomings of American tanks while serving under General Patton in North Africa. While the M4 Medium outclassed the Germans with respect to dependability, possessing a "powerful engine" that could be "counted on to run without a breakdown," and with American mass production providing a "U.S. superiority in numbers," the German high-velocity 88 mm gun nevertheless gave German tanks a significant qualitative advantage, even against newer M4 Mediums mounting heavier 76 mm guns using hypervelocity armor-piercing (HVAP) ammunition.[27] Major William H. Burton, commander of the 46th Armored Infantry Battalion, reported in August 1944 that "no weapon in our task force" was "capable of dealing with the Mark VI tank under normal combat conditions." Even when taking on lesser German tanks, "it remains that our mediums must out maneuver the enemy when fighting against the Mark V's so as to provide for any shot except one against the front slopes." In short, Burton stated, "there is a definite need in our armored force for heavier and better armed tanks."[28]

Throughout the fall of 1944, Twelfth Army tankers rarely faced the *Panzerkampfwagen* VI Ausf. E, the feared Tiger tank. While a dozen of these fifty-seven-ton behemoths wrought havoc on US forces at Kasserine Pass, Hitler prioritized the eastern front over Normandy, dispatching the vast majority of Tiger tanks to Russia. In June at Villers-Bocage, 501st SS Heavy Tank Battalion Tigers commanded by Obersturmführer Michael Wittmann confounded the British, but after their destruction, Hitler continued ordering German Tigers to the eastern front, and when he discovered the errors of his thinking, it was too late.[29] Although the Wehrmacht had between 2,000 and 2,400 tanks in France on D-Day, German tank losses to the Allies were high. By 27 September, Gen. Walter Model reported only 239 tanks and assault guns remained in German Army Group B.[30]

In defending France, the Wehrmacht deployed both the dreaded German 88 mm *Flugabwehrkanone* and the Panzerfaust infantry antitank weapon, though in these encounters, the American "will to survive increased the innovative spirit." Shortly after arriving in Normandy, GIs mounted "sandbags and spare track blocks and wooden timbers to the faceplate of the tank for added protection against the murderous German antitank guns."[31] Crews of US tank destroyers, M5 light tanks, and eventually M4 Mediums employed sandbags "as an acceptable substitute for additional or spaced armor." One unit reported that sandbags stopped "a direct hit by an 88 mm projectile with no damage," while another claimed them "effective . . . against hostile rocket grenade projectiles."[32] Twelfth Army Group HQ Armored Section reported that "opinions as to the effectiveness of sand bags on tanks are divided," as "some feel that it assists the projectile in penetrating by preventing richochet [*sic*], whereas others have considerable confidence in its protection."[33] The 749th Tank Battalion concluded that "sandbags are worthwhile even at the expense of the added weight," citing damage to an A Company tank when a large-caliber antitank round struck the front of the M4 between the driver's and the assistant driver's positions. Twelfth Army Battle Experiences reported that "the armor plate was cracked and a sizeable 'well' was made but only minor injuries were sustained." This was the second time the same tank had been hit, though in the first case a "projectile glanced off causing no injuries because of sandbags." The same day, a German antitank round penetrated the turret of an M4 manned by B Company of the 749th, killing the gunner and loader and injuring the tank commander because the tank "was not sandbagged."[34] The unit's 20 September after-action report surmised that one of the tanks destroyed could have been "saved by use of sand bags on the outside of the hull."[35]

GIs up-armored their M4s on an ad hoc basis, though over time, some units standardized the practice. Stacking sandbags on glacis plates gradually gave way to more elaborate affairs utilizing chicken or communications wire to hold sandbags in place, while others fabricated metal sandbag racks.[36] The 48th Tank Battalion, 14th Armored Division, spent five days in early December 1944 sandbagging tanks.[37] These efforts to "counteract" German antitank weapons "impressed" cavalry observer Col. George W. Coolidge, who reported seeing sandbag shelves and brackets "welded to the front plate, sponsons and turret to hold the bags in place." Commanders of both the 25th and 48th Tank Battalions professed that despite the additional weight, sandbags saved at least eight tanks from enemy bazooka fire, providing "no marked decrease in performance of the tank" and adding "a morale factor as the crews were thoroughly impressed by them."[38] The 2nd Armored Division also added sandbags to their tanks, with Lt. Col. Wilson M. Hawkins, commander of 3rd Battalion, 67th Armored Regiment, and veteran of North Africa, Normandy, Belgium, the Netherlands, and eventually Germany noting that each of his battalion's tanks sported over one hundred sandbags "to make up for the tank's lack of armor and the penetrating ability of German guns."[39] Other 2nd Armored tankers shared Hawkins's assessment. Technical Sergeant William Schaning noted, "The armor plate on our tank is not nearly heavy enough, being hit from any angle it will mostly always be penetrated."[40] Sergeant Joseph O. Posecoi argued that "every outfit that has ever been up against a German Mark V tank" used 100 to 150 sandbags for added protection, although he recognized their addition did not always work.[41]

As General Patton's Third Army crossed the Moselle River on the road to Nancy, 4th Armored Division tankers relied on one of the more colorful practitioners of American ingenuity, draftee Charles Carpenter. A Centre College (Kentucky) graduate and history teacher at Moline High School (Illinois), Carpenter had been commissioned and assigned to fly the L-4 Grasshopper, eventually commanding all the 4th Armored Division's observation aircraft. Distinguishing himself by scouting for advanced landing fields outside Avranches, Carpenter employed his "Maytag Messerschmitt" to great effect.[42] Stymied by stubborn German defenses, he dismounted from his L-4 Grasshopper and, employing a nearby tank's .50-caliber machine gun, led elements of the division in liberating Avranches. Carpenter returned to his L-4 but wanted to do more than fly his commanding general around or spot targets for divisional artillery. Returning to the divisional depot, the intrepid Carpenter secured a pair of bazookas, attaching one to each wing, rewiring the trigger mechanism to the cockpit. After a successful test flight, Carpenter adopted the sobriquet "Bazooka Charlie" and expanded the offensive repertoire of his plane "Rosie the Rocketer" by adding two more command-detonated bazookas to each wing. In fighting near Arracourt on 19 September, Carpenter destroyed two German tanks from the air. During the day, he fired sixteen shells, challenging those who questioned his sanity proclaiming, "If we're going to fight a war we have to go on with it sixty minutes an hour and twenty-four hours a day."[43]

As GIs neared Metz, Hitler ordered its defenders to hold the pre–World War I fortifications that ringed the city. Despite having most of its guns and fire control apparatus removed for emplacement on the Atlantic Wall, Fort Driant retained operational turreted casemates connected by an extensive network of machine guns, pillboxes, and minefields that gave the Germans a commanding view of the Moselle Valley and Metz.[44] When defenders stopped elements of the 5th Infantry Division from crossing the Moselle on 7–10 September, XX Corps and Third Army planners ordered the 11th Infantry Regiment to attack Fort Driant on 27 September. Facing extensive barbed wire entanglements and dug-in positions, GIs failed to breach the lines despite liberal use of Bangalore torpedoes and satchel charges.[45] Following the failed attack, elements of the 7th Engineer Battalion improvised new weapons to arm newly formed assault teams, joining the 11th Infantry and 735th Tank Battalion. In the confused withdrawal of 27 September, GIs had abandoned pole and satchel charges and Bangalore torpedoes, which necessitated the wholesale fabrication of new equipment. Recovering the aforementioned weapons, the engineers crafted antiobstacle "snakes," reminiscent of those employed in Italy. They filled two hundred feet of eight-inch-diameter French-made iron pipe with explosives, attached metal antirotation fins and a wooden head to the leading end, and added fittings that permitted each snake to be either pushed or pulled by a tank. The improvised tank-infantry-engineer teams trained with the devices for two days, coordinating operations with EE-8 radios attached to each tank's exterior.[46] On 3 October, three combined arms teams attacked Fort Driant. One team concentrated on the fort's northwest corner, with a second attacking its southern walls, holding a third in reserve to exploit either team's success. Unfortunately for the attackers, the challenging nature of the terrain coupled with the finicky nature of the "snake" devices precluded success. A steep incline made it impossible to push the first snake through the barbed wire, while the second snake broke in two when its towing tank made a sharp right turn. Consequently, the long fight for Fort Driant continued. While GIs captured Metz by 22 November, Fort Driant remained in German hands until 8 December, with the battle earning a reputation as one of the "most grueling infantry small unit actions" of the war.[47]

The drive across forested France prompted calls for better camouflage.[48] Securing materials from a German camouflage dump at Gennevilliers, engineers of the 602nd Engineer Camouflage Battalion repurposed captured nets, twine, paint, and burlap into more effective camouflage for Twelfth Army Group tanks. Beginning on 30 October, the battalion welded sections of Sommerfeld airplane landing mat to M4 Mediums. Using the "light metal carpet made of wire netting strips, reinforced with steel bars" patented by German Kurt Joachim Sommerfeld of Uxbridge, England, in 1940, they also added a disruptive pattern of lusterless black and green paint. Lightweight and manufactured in twenty-five-foot by ten-foot rolls, Sommerfeld tracking formed the base for temporary airfields in Normandy, before the ingenious 602nd reconceived the material as a base for tank camouflage.[49] In October, the 602nd applied matting to tanks, half-tracks, recovery vehicles, and armored cars from the 19th Tank Battalion, 9th Armored Division, before moving on in November to tanks of the 2nd Tank Battalion, 89th Reconnaissance Battalion, 14th Tank Battalion, 811th Tank Destroyer Battalion, and 27th Infantry Regiment. The work of the 602nd continued through the remainder of the winter and into the spring as GIs added camouflage to vehicles of the 2nd, 17th, 19th, 31st, 746th, 786th, and 777th Tank Battalions, 489th Field Artillery Battalion, and 630th and 661st Tank Destroyer Battalions.[50]

Throughout the fall of 1944, heavy rains and muddy roads slowed the Allied advance to the Roer River, increased the chaos of fighting in the Hürtgen Forest, and delayed the crossing of the Belgian-German border. "Dismal rain" fell throughout October 1944, with the ensuing soggy conditions making a continued advance "well nigh impossible." With narrow tracks, M4 Mediums bogged down in sodden soil, as a tank exerted between 13.7 and 15.1 pounds of ground pressure per square inch, a problem not encountered in the sandier soils of North Africa, Sicily, and Italy.[51] Col. Creighton Abrams's 37th Tank Battalion developed "extended end connectors" that widened the tanks' track to increase effectiveness. Resembling upside-down scoops extending five inches wider than a tank track, the connector only contacted the road surface when engaged in soft ground. On 14 October 1944, Abrams's battalion fabricated end connectors for twenty-five tanks, about 75 percent of the unit. On 21 October, Generals Patton and Carl "Tooey" Spaatz enjoyed a "very interesting demonstration by tanks with and without ducks' feet" executed by A Company.[52] When the 2nd Armored Division advanced to the Roer, three-quarters of its tanks had French-manufactured extended end connectors, with other units receiving them throughout the winter.[53]

The extended end connectors solved part of the Twelfth Army Group's mobility issues, while other units sought to increase firepower. The 743rd Tank Battalion came ashore on D-Day and fought its way across France with the 30th Infantry Division, reaching the German border by mid-September. Anticipating crossing the Roer River in early December, the battalion not only began sandbagging its tanks, but received the secret T-34 Calliope rocket system. In early December, Sgt. Winston B. Eastes reported that seventeen B Company M4 Mediums, along with three captured German Sd.Kfz. 251 half-tracks, received the Calliope system, with the entire 743rd witnessing a demonstration on 9 December. Training with the rockets continued until 17 December, when the unit moved from its comfortable quarters with improvised electric lights and modified German stoves toward Malmedy, Belgium, to thwart the Ardennes counteroffensive.[54] In addition to rockets, the gunners of the 48th Tank Battalion experimented with a flamethrower mounted on one of their tanks, continuing tests conducted by XII Corps the previous November that built on efforts of the 70th Tank Battalion, which mounted flamethrowers on tanks to reduce bunkers along the Siegfried Line.[55]

In September, Hitler ordered a German offensive on the western front, conceiving a double envelopment along the Liège-Aachen axis, formalized by 21 October as *Wacht am Rhein* (Watch on the Rhine), with the retaking of Antwerp as the ultimate goal.[56] Throughout October and November, the Wehrmacht marshalled armor and vehicles for use by the Fifth and Sixth

Panzer Armies. At the same time, U-boats in the North Atlantic began tracking regional weather patterns, to identify low pressure systems over the ocean, intending to use fog and low visibility over Belgium and Luxembourg to conceal the advance and negate Allied air superiority. By early December, the German high command had completed its preparations, and Hitler directed the Ardennes counteroffensive to begin on 16 December.[57] Low clouds and fog were forecast from 16 through 23 December, with visibility limited to less than one hundred yards. By 20 December, some units began reporting snow, as competing weather systems from Russia and the Atlantic combined, producing snow, blizzards, and fog throughout the region.[58]

Unaware of Hitler's plans, American units took advantage of the lull in fighting to improvise winter gear and prepare for colder weather. The 602nd Engineer Camouflage Battalion designed snow camouflage capes in November, with First Army G-3 authorizing the manufacture of 2,000 capes with an option for 5,500 more.[59] The commander of the 331st Infantry facilitated foxhole construction in frozen ground, issuing each officer and GI a half-stick of TNT with fuse and detonator. Detonating the TNT in the frozen ground, a soldier could prepare a protective hole in ten minutes, with a full stick producing a hole that, within fifteen minutes, could shelter a single soldier from a tank.[60] Colonel B. R. Purdue of the 120th Infantry Regiment attempted to prevent frostbite and trench foot among his soldiers with woolen booties sewn from blankets worn with galoshes or while sleeping.[61] The 99th Infantry achieved similar ends by alternating thin socks with cellophane paper bags from 155 mm ammunition, at the same time placing rubber prophylactics over radio and telephone mouthpieces to prevent water condensation from freezing.[62] The 120th Infantry also "prepared and tested" toboggans for winter use, contracting with a civilian firm in Verviers, Belgium, to fabricate them for subsequent use by the 82nd Airborne during the Battle of the Bulge.[63] When infantry had to occupy the same positions for an extended period, they improvised for warmth. In addition to prefabricating rear area shelters that could be brought close to the front, dug in, and made habitable with the addition of straw and small stoves, other GIs built heaters from discarded ration cans or 81 mm shells, using gas-soaked mud or issued heat tablets as the heat source.[64] The first snowfall prompted a speedy painting of tank hulls, with First Army whipping up a whitewash of lime, salt, and water, with the tactical results reported as being "extremely effective" among units utilizing similar methods.[65]

When the Germans launched Wacht am Rhein on December 16, the Fifth and Sixth Panzer Armies caught GIs in the Ardennes sector totally unawares. As Tiger and Panther tanks smashed through thinly held American lines toward La Gleize and Bastogne, follow-on units clogged roads with the mule wagons and horse-drawn artillery that composed so much of the vehicle-starved Wehrmacht's logistical tail.[66] Capitalizing on bad weather that grounded American aircraft, the Germans made initial gains in the Battle of the Bulge, though when the weather cleared, Americans fought back, reducing the salient by the end of January.

As the snow fell, icy roads hindered American armor's mobility. End connectors or grousers provided traction in muddy terrain but were frequently knocked off or lost, and if they remained, they offered minimal utility on steep and winding hard-surfaced roads slickened by frozen precipitation.[67] Tanks with T41 or T51 flat rubber block tracks slipped on ice, and although the chevron-shaped metal grousers on the T48 rubber block track offered some traction, not all tanks had this track type, although some alternated individual rubber track with the metal chevron type or added metal cleats to alternating tracks with some success.[68] The 7th Armored Division replaced existing tank end connectors with a "traction wedge," fabricated from stainless steel or armored plate welded to every fourth extended end connector, which offered some improved traction. Others solved the problem by welding metal cleats to track surfaces in a variety of patterns. Ordnance maintenance companies of the 52nd Ordnance Group made "T"-shaped cleats to prevent bending caused by the side thrust of the track.[69] The 4th Armored cut off a portion of the T48 chevron and welded it to the track, with the 607th Tank Battalion welding similar pieces to the chevrons themselves.[70] Some XII Corps GIs manning the M4 or M5 artillery tractor welded a series of metal caulks to every other track shoe to provide increased traction.[71] While by no means a comprehensive list, these field-expedient track additions were "of great value" to GIs fighting in the Bulge, and their use continued on into early 1945.[72] While in Luxembourg in February 1945, T.Sgt. Luther May applied similar ingenuity to his jeep, fabricating what he called a "mud shoe" for use in either soggy ground or deep snow, extending the wheel hub of a normal jeep with pipe equal in diameter to the jeep hub, affixing angled cleats to the wider metal "wheel" to facilitate greater traction.[73]

American columns nearing Berlin faced stiffer Nazi resistance, and ingenious GIs looked beyond sandbags as a way to protect against heavier German antitank weapons they encountered. Lt. Belton Cooper noted GIs taking "every means available to reinforce the front glacis plate," adding spare track blocks, bogey wheels, sandbags, and a "combination of logs and sandbags laced together with chicken wire" to reinforce the front of the M4 Mediums.[74] By March 1945, tanks of the 740th Tank Battalion in Burg Bergerhausen, on the road to Cologne, sported a variety of logs, planking, spare track, and varied armor additions to their front glacis plates, hulls, and turrets.[75] Tankers of the Ninth Army, 14th Armored Division and 2nd Armored Division, mixed concrete to up-armor their tanks, with Lieutenant Cooper noting that when he arrived in Stolberg, tankers from his division obtained "sacks of cement from an abandoned cement factory."[76] Using "chicken wire and angle iron," they added three- to four-inch-thick patches to their tank, although he suspected that any advantage was probably "offset by the added weight, which crunched the forward bogey wheels and slowed the tank considerably."[77] Tankers of the 753rd Tank Battalion, however, found such additions worthwhile, with the company narrative for March 1945 noting the addition of sandbags to many tanks and at least one tank reinforced with supplemental armor made of concrete. On 23 March, near Neupotz, a tank from 3rd Platoon, C Company, took enemy fire that wounded its crew, though the "lack of fatalities was probably due to the fact that the tank had been heavily reinforced with concrete and the projectile spent itself before it broke the hull of the tank."[78]

As elements of the 10th Armored Division approached the Saar-Moselle Triangle, selected tanks "received five to six inches of armor plate on particularly vulnerable spots," allowing them to move directly against 88 mm guns with near impunity.[79] Such practices soon became commonplace with M5 light tanks, with additional armor welded to "the floor of light tanks underneath the driver and bow gunner," in efforts to reduce casualties.[80] When the M24 light tank began arriving in 1945 to replace the older M5, GI problem-solvers acted on recommendations from Col. George W. Coolidge, who in reviewing cavalry squadrons in February 1945 recommended "increased belly armor" in the M5; Coolidge noted that "the M24 light tank could well be investigated to determine if a similar weakness exists in this vehicle."[81] The 744th Tank Battalion acted accordingly, adding boiler or armor plate to "cover the driver and assistant driver's positions" and making the addition of sandbags on their tanks' front slope a "standard practice" by the time they reached the Roer.[82] Subsequent reports recommended additional armor plate to protect against mines in a manner similar to the M5A1, attaching a water can and baggage racks, along with other additions made to satisfy individual crews' preferences.[83] Like their Medium tank brethren, tank destroyer crews added field-improvised armor to their relatively thin-skinned vehicles. Maj. George McCutchen's troopers in the 813th Tank Destroyer Battalion were "strong believers in the use of sand bags as reinforcement," having witnessed "enough incidents to convince us that sand bags will deflect direct hits by anti-tank guns." Using scrap iron, they welded sandbag racks to destroyer front decks.[84] Like many Medium tank crews, many M10 tankers affixed logs to their vehicle sides as defense against the Panzerfaust, also utilizing them for road mats in muddy terrain and when crossing trenches.[85] The 702nd Tank Destroyer Battalion cut additional armor plate from

2nd Armored Mediums, bolting it in place using bolts already installed on their M10s for that purpose.[86] As the war in Europe neared a successful conclusion, some Allied commanders rejected supplemental armor, believing it caused unnecessary wear on vehicles. On 1 May 1945, General Patton encountered sandbagged tanks of the 14th Armored Division while driving between Freising and Moosberg, Germany. He ordered them removed, characterizing sandbags as "very stupid," for it "made the soldiers think the tanks could be hurt . . . overloaded the machinery . . . [and] provided no additional protection."[87]

The open-topped M10, M10A1, M18, and later M36 tank destroyers were particularly vulnerable to small arms fire, shell bursts, and tree fragments, as their turrets offered "no protection to crews from high burst artillery fire."[88] Some units, like Lt. Col. Henry Davisson's 634th Tank Destroyer Battalion, suspected that upon hearing an M10's engine, the enemy intentionally fired air bursts as opposed to traditional armor-piercing shells.[89] Even before arriving in France, Lt. Col. Ephraim F. Graham Jr.'s 644th Tank Destroyer Battalion fabricated turret covers from quarter-inch armored plate. As other tank destroyer units found themselves employed alongside infantry, they "improvised their own," with turret covers ranging from "a canvas spread, to deflect grenades, to metallic sheeting."[90] During the battle for the Hürtgen Forest, the 628th Tank Destroyer Battalion reported high casualties from mortar fire, air bursts, tree bursts, and white phosphorous from enemy artillery. The unit reported intense artillery blasts capable of destroying sandbag and log turret tops improvised by some crews.[91] After the fighting, the battalion's motor maintenance section fabricated covers made from captured German armored plate in early December.[92] The Ardennes counteroffensive halted all turret cover fabrications, though work resumed after the German advance was halted; upon reaching the Rhine River, all 628th battalion tank destroyers had armored covers.[93] In October, the 813th Tank Destroyer Battalion installed folding armored tops on their tank destroyers, allowing the vehicle commander "all around observation."[94] By February 1945, the unit's full and half turret covers, fabricated from plate "secured from various sources," had "saved many lives from overhead shrapnel bursts and small arms fire." Providing a "very fine morale factor with the crews," they recommended "enclosed turrets" for all self-propelled tank destroyers.[95] Several other enterprising units added armored covers to their M10s or M36s.[96] The 703rd Tank Destroyer Battalion covered half the turret with armor plate, supporting it with four-inch by six-inch metal blocks spaced six inches apart, with the arrangement affording head protection but not limiting visibility.[97] The 644th improvised turret covers with six sections of armor plate, each weighing approximately 150 pounds, with other commanders recommending similar adaptations.[98]

As the fight across Europe continued, ingenious GIs continued making changes and adjustments to weapons and equipment. In addition to using "sticky bombs" in antitank defense, Maj. E. J. Edgerton of the 38th Cavalry Squadron experimented with flamethrower fuel, which added to the existing charge of a rifle grenade transformed it into an incendiary round. Others fabricated antipersonnel mines from ordinary bean cans, using three pounds of dynamite or C-2 explosive compound, nails, and a No. 8 blasting cap.[99] Troops of the 14th Armored Division improvised "flash hiders" for the M-3 submachine gun, carbine, and M-1 rifle from a .50-caliber shell casing, while others increased the effectiveness of the M-3 by inserting parts of an M-1 rifle spring into the M-3's driving rods, increasing the submachine gun's accuracy and cyclic rate. Other ordnancemen modified the M1919A4 machine gun, fabricating bipod mounts and shoulder stocks for the division's infantry. Beyond converting the .30-caliber M-1 carbine to full automatic, others brazed magazines together in a staggered pattern, to allow for faster magazine changes.[100]

Throughout the campaign, GIs made improvements to their ability to launch projectiles in a variety of applications. To prevent losses of the M7 rifle grenade launcher, ordnancemen of the 36th Division modified seventy-five M-1 rifles, attaching the grenade launcher permanently.[101] Lieutenant Harry Pender of the 28th Infantry reported the construction of a grenade grapnel to clear trip wires in minefields, with the 1109th Engineer Combat Group and 121st Cavalry Reconnaissance Squadron building a similar antimine grappling hook.[102] The 105th Engineer Combat Battalion attached six- and twelve-strand Primacord "ropes" to bazooka rounds, firing the device into minefields with varying degrees of success.[103] Signal company soldiers used rifle grenade and bazooka rounds to project signal wire or cable distances of 100 to 225 yards, while soldiers of the 39th Infantry did the same using a specially modified mortar round and improvised cable-holding plate.[104]

Officers, in particular, modified vehicles to enhance their overall functionality. Colonel William S. Triplet of the 2nd Armored Division's Combat Command A ordered changes to an M5 Stuart he christened *Tiger Bait.* Inspired by Col. Francis P. Tompkins's modified command car, Triplet ordered ordnancemen to replace the 37 mm main gun in his tank with a section of Belgian pipe. He also stripped ammunition racks and the gunner's seat from his tank, outfitting his turreted "office" with map table and seat, radio, and fifteen-watt red interior lights. Believing it was his job to "tell the other tankers where to go and what to shoot," Triplet described his tank as "sheer luxury," as he found the map table "placed and angled just right for an occasional nap during quiet moments."[105]

Triplet's *Tiger Bait* was only the beginning of tank modifications by GIs. Tankers of the 32nd Armored Regiment up-gunned one of their Mediums, replacing the 75 mm gun standard to most M4A3E2 tanks with a higher-velocity 76 mm gun salvaged from another tank that yielded "excellent results," particularly against enemy armor.[106] Tankers of the 20th Armored and 5th Armored, as well as the 106th, added supplemental armor plate to their M5 and M24 light tanks, while others made similar additions to the M8 armored car.[107] Another tanker reported welding a cut-down .30-caliber machine-gun tripod to their tank turret, firing tracer rounds to indicate targets.[108] Soldiers of the 556th Anti-Aircraft Artillery Battalion secured an M45 multiple .50-caliber machine-gun mount and installed it in an amphibious DUKW; after tests, they found it possessing "definite possibilities for both air and ground action."[109] In addition to up-armoring their M8 armored cars with either additional plate armor or sandbags, the 117th Cavalry Reconnaissance Squadron mounted a variety of machine guns in the turrets of their M8s, leaving the final configuration up to the vehicle commander.[110]

Captain Nicholas Hayden of the 2nd Tank Battalion designated an M3 half-track as his battalion command post, christening it "The Monster." His modified M3 had an armored top, internal radios, and a map table, with seats fashioned from mortar ammunition boxes with internal storage for paper and other supplies. A separate generator charged radio batteries, motor-driven blowers provided fresh air, and internal lighting with blackout security allowed for work at all hours. Hayden ordered installation of racks on the vehicle's exterior to carry crew gear, adding bumper-mounted storage bins for chains and other tools.[111] Elements of the 47th Infantry Regiment, Ninth Infantry Division, traded a quarter-ton truck for a three-quarter-ton 4 × 4 that was converted into the signal group's maintenance vehicle, with a radio added to the right running board of the three-quarter-ton, allowing it to be operated from the front seat. Then they enclosed the truck's rear, transforming it into a maintenance shop.[112] Elements of the 697th Field Artillery Battalion, 194th Field Artillery Group, mounted an SCR-284, SCR-193, and two SCR-608 radio sets into their three-quarter-ton radio truck, preferring it to a lighter command car.[113]

After arriving in Europe in September, the 12th Armored Division's 134th Ordnance and Maintenance Battalion never strayed too far from its mechanical roots. The unit was raised in 1942 from employees of the International Harvester Corporation, and by virtue of the recruits' association with the company, they were skilled in the operation, maintenance, and performance of the latest farm machinery.[114] With company employees forming the battalion's initial cadre, the GIs of the aptly named "Harvester Battalion" were known for constantly modifying, adapting, or creating bits of military technology to aid frontline troops. Drawing on the same ingenuity that produced a prewar "jack and engine stand for servicing tractor clutches," battalion ordnancemen adapted grenade launchers to the M-1 Garand rifle allowing the rifle to be fired with the grenade launcher attached. The "Harvester men" also modified tank suspensions, making elements interchangeable between light and medium tanks. They also tested firebombs by packing artillery shells with flamethrower fuel and aided GIs on the battlefield by manufacturing bipod mounts for the .30-caliber Browning light machine gun.[115] Some soldiers of the 134th made special modifications to the jeep. William Giannopoulos, who served with the battalion throughout the war, added an angle iron "wire catcher" extending upward from the front bumper along with mudflaps and a custom armored windshield.[116] After they witnessed the effectiveness of the recently arrived M4A3E2 "Jumbo" sporting an additional inch and a half of armor plate, elements of C Company of the 134th ventured to Herrlisheim, Germany, to procure armored plate from knocked out tanks to up-armor their Mediums. Conducting tests for their commanding general and his staff, the Harvester men discovered that even at four hundred yards, a single round of 76 mm armor-piercing ammunition passed through the additional armor plate, the tank's normal armor plate, and sandbags.[117]

Virtually every unit improvised to enhance functionality. Well in advance of the Normandy invasion, T.Sgt. Jasper Howard, serving with the medical detachment attached to the 68th Field Artillery, built a frame of conduit that facilitated transporting two hospital litters on the hood of a jeep.[118] By the summer of 1944, the 76th Armored Medical Battalion, Sixth Armored Division, built jeeps capable of carrying four litters simultaneously.[119] Captain Lawrence Loewinthan of the 125th Cavalry Reconnaissance Squadron reconfigured the litter arrangement in their three half-track ambulances to improve loading and unloading. They also repurposed a fourth half-track into a mobile aid station, moving the litter attachments, adding a work table and storage cabinet, and improvising battery-powered headlights. They also transformed a one-ton trailer into a mobile dispensary, with hinged sides opening "in a manner similar to a 'hot dog' stand." A partition allowed two medical teams to work at once, and four portable chests served as independent treatment stations.[120] Captain Harry E. Barnett of the 16th Evacuation Hospital invented a rotating surgical table, built on a frame that allowed a single orderly to rotate the patient from his stomach to his back.[121] The 11th Evacuation Hospital replaced heavy operating tables and a nearly 800 lb urological table with lighter tables fabricated from one-inch steel tubing. A utility workshop assembled from captured lathe, drill press, circular saw, and grindstone greatly facilitated comparable unit projects.[122] In April 1945, Col. R. B. Evans submitted the 114th Medical Evacuation Hospital's "Improvisations and Ideas," including improvised scrub stands, portable tent dividers, and the replacement of complex Wangensteen suction apparatus with a "simple three bottle gravity suction system made from empty Baxter flasks and plasma set tubing." They also built a vertical X-ray cassette holder, and mounted a spent 105 mm shell on an X-ray tube opening to facilitate pictures of mastoids, sinuses, gall bladders, and specific vertebrae.[123]

For modifications that required attaching metal to metal, soldiers needed to weld, so they improvised field welding units. An ordnance officer of XX Corps improvised a two-man-pack welding set, mounting French automobile acetylene and oxygen tanks with ten feet of hose and a welding tip to packboard.[124] Technical Sergeant Anderson Nunnelley, a Texas oil field welder before the war, fabricated a welding trailer used by the 71st Infantry Regiment, 44th Infantry Division. The "result of past needs and experience," he built it on the frame and running gear of a German ammunition trailer, with salvaged wheels, metal toolbox, and acetylene and oxygen tanks. The "mobile, independent unit" was "ready to go to work anytime, anywhere on a moment's notice."[125]

Other fabrications simply helped keep the US Army rolling along. When shrapnel, nails, and bits of metal savaged vehicle tires, soldiers improvised ways to clear the roads of postbattle debris. Soldiers of the 4th Infantry Division recognized the need for a road magnet in every engineering battalion, though it is unknown whether or not these soldiers were familiar with the one fabricated by the army's Wheeled Vehicle Department at Fort Knox, Kentucky, in 1944.[126] Soldiers of the 104th Infantry Division scavenged large magnets from a German steel mill to fabricate a mobile magnet capable of picking up objects that weighed as much as fifteen pounds, or fragments buried in three inches of soft mud. With an eleven-foot sweep, the first two weeks of the roadsweeper's operation recovered five tons of tire-damaging metal.[127]

By the end of the war, few vehicles had undergone as many changes as the jeep. Observers from III, V, XIII, and XXIII Corps all reported the fabrication of angle iron antidecapitation devices, a common feature added to jeeps throughout the ETO.[128] Reconnaissance and airborne units often up-armored their jeeps, adding metal shields around the driver and passenger compartments, while others placed sandbags on the floors front and back to protect against mines. By war's end, jeeps had been enclosed and heated, enclosed and air-conditioned, used as a power source for table saws, encased in tarpaulins and floated across rivers and waterways, and used to tow threshers in the field. And even before the invasion of Europe, *Popular Science* had held a contest among its readers, who devised more than 1,001 uses for the sturdy workhorse of the US Army.

It was the jeep, or rather its absence in the Soviet Army, that captured the attention of Holbrook Bradley, a *Baltimore Sun* correspondent who had accompanied the 29th Division from Normandy to the Elbe River. Despite its possessing deep penetration capabilities that required a mastery of mechanized warfare and combined arms, Bradley characterized the Red Army as a "great surge of Soviet humanity that literally crawled across the land," describing a "mass of Homo sapiens that walked from Kiev, Minsk, and Novgorod hauling ancient Gatling guns, mortars, and equipment . . . Red soldiers pedaling captured bicycles, trying to start German vehicles, or riding decrepit animals." The Red Army was, in Bradley's view, a stark contrast to the "jeep-led motorization of our army."[129] Having been around machines their entire lives, GIs' familiarity with technology came as no surprise even to the editors of the *Military Review*, who recognized that "few American boys grow up without learning to 'tinker,' whether it be with radios, automobiles, or other type of mechanical equipment."[130] While some commanders condemned unnecessary tinkering as leading to "needless and costly damage to equipment," Lt. Col. James Sams, in reviewing ordnance improvisation in Europe, only cautioned that "the tendency to 'gadgeteer' should not be allowed to run wild." Instead, he suggested that "higher headquarters" should provide a more effective avenue for the "submission of ideas."[131]

Such was exactly what happened as the US Army liberated Europe. Presented with a wealth of logistical support, American GIs used what they had, and when what they had failed to meet expectations or requirements, they took what they had, applied American ingenuity, and found the best solution possible. As Capt. Kenneth Barnaby Jr., commander of B Company, 117th Cavalry Reconnaissance Squadron, wrote after the war, "There seems to exist in the Army an unpublished and recorded SOP which dictates: 'No matter what the piece of equipment is, change it.'" Moreover, such efforts came with support from above. Throughout the European campaign, US Army leadership evaluated Americans' varied technical contributions, endorsing what worked and rejecting what did not. Barnaby was "especially grateful to the commanding generals of the VI Corps and Seventh Army for their objective viewpoints in permitting us a latitude of liberal experimentation."[132]

CHAPTER 8

Inventing on the Islands

The American understands machinery and is adroit in handling it. Speed characterizes his construction of airfields, motor roads, and communications networks, and also his strengthening of positions. His strong air forces execute day and night attacks.

—*Japanese Imperial Army Headquarters Officers Report, 1945*

In the wake of Gen. George Kenney's overwhelming success in the March 1943 Battle of the Bismarck Sea, the Joint Chiefs of Staff endorsed Operation Cartwheel, a two-pronged advance through the Western Pacific. In this offensive, General MacArthur and Admiral Halsey drove through the Solomon Islands in mutually supporting avenues of advance, with New Britain and Bougainville, respectively, as their ultimate objectives. This set the stage for a larger offensive in March 1944, with MacArthur advancing toward the Philippines, while Adm. Chester Nimitz, commander in chief Pacific Fleet (CINCPAC), "island-hopped" through the Central Pacific, securing islands close enough to effect a strategic bombing campaign against Japan.

The ensuing Pacific campaign showcased American ingenuity, albeit in a form different from that demonstrated by GIs in Europe. According to General MacArthur, US troops throughout the war in the Pacific continued to make do with what they had, using their meager resources in a campaign relegated secondary by virtue of the Allies' Germany First strategy.[1] While American troops in the Pacific often had an abundance of indigenous labor available on the Pacific islands, they were initially wanting for logistical support. Unlike the campaign in Europe, launched only after the accumulation of tons of supplies that overflowed vast depots in Great Britain, troops in the Pacific faced limited resources, as everything at the end of their supply line had to make its way across the Pacific Ocean by ship.

The nature of the supply chain shaped the Pacific War in two unique dimensions. On the one hand, the Allied offensive was carefully circumscribed, to avoid an all-out and costly assault against the Japanese that would have generated an unrealistic strain on both the manpower and logistical capabilities of US troops in the Pacific. Consequently, the island-hopping campaign worked to "save both time and lives." As the enemy clung to its Pacific holdings, the American decision to bypass and isolate entire island garrisons was a blow to Japanese morale, as their military philosophy and strategy only allowed for a costly fight to the death to protect both personal honor and the Emperor.[2] On the other hand, until American wartime production reached its peak in late 1943, GIs and marines in the Pacific and East Asia were limited to the resources at their immediate disposal, with the vast majority of this wartime production arriving in the form of better ships and planes.

The vastness of the Pacific theater, together with the combination of units involved in myriad campaigns that stretched across thousands of miles, make it difficult to offer an assessment of American ingenuity in that area of operations. The jungles of the Solomons were vastly different from the coral atolls of the Central Pacific, which themselves bore little resemblance to the Philippines, and possessed fewer similarities still to the China-Burma-India theater. While troops on the front lines or actively engaged in combat were frequently limited to what supplies and ammunition they carried on their person, those in rear areas or preparing for their next advance often had access to literally tons of material support.[3] If there is one truth, it was this: US troops had a distinct advantage over their adversaries, for despite fighting the war at the end of a lengthy supply line, they, as MacArthur said, simply made do with what they had, falling back on the fact of American ingenuity generated by growing up in the United States during the Great Depression.

Even before Guadalcanal was secured, this ingenuity was on full display. Capt. Gerald H. Shea observed that "soldiers are jacks of all trades, and will have everything from hot-water showers to flushing commodes if allowed to bivouac in one place."[4] Few demonstrated these abilities better than the US Naval Construction Battalions, the famed Seabees. As Albin Johnson wrote in January 1944, "When equipment failed to arrive, [Seabees] made the best of what they had," making diving apparatus out of gas masks and using old inner tubes to facilitate the placement of concrete slabs on the ocean floor as a foundation for a seaplane ramp.[5] Others repurposed fifty-gallon fuel drums, a staple of Seabee improvisation, welding them together to use as culverts, flattening them for roofing projects, even using them to build a canoe with Japanese seaplane floats for outrigging.[6] Lacking proper construction equipment, Seabees tasked with the repair and restoration of Henderson Field salvaged steel beams from an island junk heap to fabricate a testing machine to gauge the strength of mixtures of concrete, beach sand, slag, silica, crushed rock, and river gravel. Their testing contraption produced results that "probably were within 5 percent of actual values," ensuring that the runways would remain functional under the stress of almost constant use.[7]

The Seabees were not the only construction units utilizing mechanical aptitude to solve problems. Anticipating a need for airfield construction under austere conditions, Brig. Gen. Stuart C. Godfrey called for the organization of Airborne Aviation Engineer Battalions, units that, once created, would typify "American ingenuity and teamwork."[8] Early aviation engineers relied on heavy construction equipment that could only be moved by land or ship. In contrast, Godfrey theorized the airmobile utility of such units. Recognizing that an adversary would "burn, demolish, and tear up" anything rather than have their airfields fall into enemy hands, the army wanted to utilize captured airfields "at as early an hour as possible." Anticipating that airborne engineers could arrive in C-47 transports and CG-4A gliders, Godfrey sought out lightweight equipment capable of being flown in. Discovering a light tractor developed for the US Forest Service; a hydraulic bulldozer and 1.5-yard carryall scraper manufactured by the LaPlant-Choate Company; and a lightweight, thirty-horsepower tractor built by Case Tractor Company, he found the machines that could translate his vision into reality.[9]

The Airborne Aviation Engineers first found employment in June 1943 at Tsili Tsili Airfield, created behind Japanese lines in the isolated Morobe Province of New Guinea. Elements of the 871st Airborne Engineers arrived at the location secretly, using native labor to clear and grade (by hand) a strip capable of landing C-47s. With a rough landing strip in place, C-47s began flying in additional equipment. In addition to the aforementioned graders and scrapers, the engineers pioneered the air transport of 2.5-ton trucks. Removing components and making minor modifications, they cut each truck in half, placing each half in a single aircraft. Upon their arrival, the engineers welded the two halves together and returned other parts to their original positions, quickly returning the trucks to roadworthiness.[10] Elsewhere in New Guinea, a "sergeant in a Headquarters and Service Company of Engineers" repurposed a bulldozer into a crane, replacing the dozer blade with an A-frame unit and winch capable of lifting more than a ton. Other engineers actively embraced the "If we don't have it, we will make it" motto, improvising water sprinklers, mounting an A-frame hoist on a six-ton truck, building a fan-tailed gravel spreader, welding seven oil drums together end to end to make a 350-gallon filling station, and building the "Thick and Thin Lumber Company," with parts salvaged from "a crashed airplane, two wrecked trucks, a worn-out tractor, and machinery from an abandoned copper mine," parts originally of Japanese, German, Australian, British, or American origin.[11] The continued ingenuity of these GIs allowed for the constant leapfrogging across the Pacific that kept the Japanese on the run, suppressed Japanese airpower on Rabaul, and set the stage for the advance beyond New Guinea.

Even before the Solomons campaign reached a conclusion, Adm. Chester Nimitz tasked Adm. Raymond Spruance with Operation Galvanic: the seizure of the Gilbert and Ellice Islands and the island of Nauru. Naming Maj. Gen. Holland M. Smith to execute the largest amphibious operation yet attempted was a tall order, yet one a pioneer of amphibious warfare was well prepared to undertake. Familiar with Andrew Higgins's landing craft designated by the military as the landing craft, vehicle, personnel (LCVP), Smith had trained Marine Corps units for amphibious operations in southern California.

In addition to the LCVP, preparing for Galvanic, required modifications to the Landing Vehicle, Tracked (LVT-1), the "Alligator," invented by Donald Roebling for use in the Florida swamps and waterways in the 1930s.[12] First used in the invasion of Guadalcanal, many of these vehicles had thrown tracks or stalled on account of waterlogged engines. Anticipating their essentiality in navigating the coral atoll that ringed Tarawa, 1st Lt. John Speed of the 2nd Amphibious Tractor Battalion modified his amphtracs to increase their effectiveness. Speed and fellow officer Lt. Mike Sisul, with encouragement from battalion commander Maj. Henry Drewes, welded metal strips over blowers to prevent flooding, added a screw-tightening device to prevent thrown tracks, and waterproofed ignition wires with latex paint procured in Wellington, New Zealand, where the unit was refit before Galvanic. They eventually found lightweight armor plate to protect the driver's compartment, calling on a local automotive factory to produce enough plates to fully up-armor seventy-five Alligators. The trio also added machine guns and grapnels that would allow the LVT to pull out barbed wire entanglements that could impede a vehicle's advance.[13]

These modified Alligators proved invaluable in the opening phases of Operation Galvanic. The operation plan called for initial landings on Betio, followed by movement to secure the rest of the Tarawa atoll. When landing craft carrying Col. David M. Shoup's 2nd Marine Division got hung up on a coral reef that ringed Betio, some troops had to wade nearly five hundred yards to the landing beaches. For others, the tracked Alligators came to the rescue, grinding over the atoll to shuttle marines from their grounded landing craft to the sea wall. In addition to the LVTs, fourteen tanks from the tank battalion of I Marine Amphibious Corps (IMAC) accompanied the initial landings.

Unfortunately, the performance of the marine tanks bordered on disastrous. Lacking extended exhaust stacks that allowed for deepwater operations, 1st Lt. Edward L. Bale's company of fourteen M4A2 Sherman tanks struggled in water deeper than three feet.[14] Of the battalion's fourteen tanks, four remained operational by midafternoon on 20 November, victims of underwater shell craters or concentrated enemy fire. By the end of the day, only two still functioned, though radio failures hindered their ability to communicate.[15] When the marines reduced the last pocket of Japanese resistance on 23 November, only two tanks remained, though Bale's tankers, eager to salvage any recoverable equipment, dried out another that had been disabled when its electrical system shorted in an underwater shell crater.[16]

Mindful of the challenges the marines faced on Tarawa, the US Army took steps to enhance its own amphibious capabilities and looked to providing future landing forces with greater firepower. To these ends, the army organized several existing tank and armored infantry battalions into the 18th Armored Group, naming Col. William S. Triplet to command the unit and ready it for combat. Triplet, who had written a series of fictional articles in the 1930s about a future war against the "Military Union of Germany and Asia" and later commanded another armored unit from his modified M5 *Tiger Bait*, was a progressive thinker.[17] In addition to wrestling with "theories of organization, training problems, and the tactical uses of amphibians in combat," he wanted to increase firepower beyond the one or two machine guns typically mounted on the Alligator. Envisioning a need for something heavier than a 37 mm gun, Triplet theorized grafting a 75 mm howitzer turret taken from the Howitzer Motor Carriage M8 onto an LVT-1, redesignating it as the LVT-A (Armored). Submitting his proposal, he noted, "Never was one of my ideas acted upon with more dispatch."[18] Tasked with testing his creation, Triplet took a prototype built by the Food Machinery Corporation to sea and fired the 75 mm howitzer to ensure that the vessel would not capsize when the gun fired.[19] Successful in the tests, the 776th employed eleven LVT-As equipped with the 75 mm turret and four LVT-As fitted with a 37 mm turret while capturing Angaur Island. Prior to the operation, the 776th spent considerable time modifying the transmissions, building ammunition racks, and welding them into the fighting compartment, "as the hulls were bare upon arrival."[20]

In addition to the up-armored and turreted LVT-As, marine tankers also improved the effectiveness of the M4 Medium tank. On Guadalcanal, marine tanks only engaged the enemy in three instances, and in the later phases of the campaign served as a divisional reserve.[21] Marine tank battalions employed after Tarawa took these costly lessons to heart and, in one case, built their organization around men uniquely suited to transfer their mechanical aptitude to armor operations. Their ingenuity served as a foundation for future tank modifications used throughout the Pacific.

In June 1943, Capt. Robert M. Neiman assumed command of Company C, 4th Marine Tank Battalion. A former life insurance salesman from Maryland, Neiman joined the Marine Corps after graduating from the first officer candidates class and served in the 1st Scout Company before receiving an assignment to the 1st Marine Tank Battalion in April 1942. In November 1942, Neiman relocated to Camp Elliott, California, home of the Marine Force Tank School, Fleet Marine Force Training Command, where Col. Robert Hogaboom promised Neiman command of the next tank company formed on the West Coast. In forming his new company, Hogaboom authorized Neiman to select officers and men from those he encountered in the training program.[22] He selected friends he knew from the Marine Tank School as his first two platoon leaders, and his third platoon leader was the product of a chance meeting during tank training at Jacque's Farm north of San Diego. As fifteen tanks sped through a training course, one of the tanks "came up fast, spun to a halt, and threw a track." The disabled tank's commander dismounted, instructed his driver to drive slowly forward and backward, and with two crewmen using hand tools, quickly walked the track back on, allowing the crew to resume training in no time at all. Impressed, Neiman approached the tank commander, asked his name and how he replaced the thrown track so quickly. Second Lt. Henry Bellmon, the product of a Billings, Oklahoma, wheat farm and recent graduate from Oklahoma A&M College, replied that his familiarity with machines stretched back to when his father began replacing horses with Allis-Chalmers tractors during the Depression. Recognizing the value of a man who knew his way around machinery, Neiman had found his final platoon leader.[23]

Seeking to gain his commander's confidence, Bellmon advised Neiman to select former members of 4-H or the Future Farmers of America, which would "bring in the farm boys who could probably maintain and operate mechanical equipment with a minimum of problems." According to Bellmon, this became one of the criteria for future manpower additions to the company, a decision that eventually yielded remarkable results.[24] Neiman's Company C, 4th Tank Battalion, would not be the first or the last marine tank battalion raised for service in the Pacific. The manpower choices inspired by Bellmon's comments, coupled with 4th Tank Battalion commander Maj. Richard K. Schmidt's decision to allow company commanders latitude to run their individual companies as they saw fit, produced remarkable results, particularly with respect to field ingenuity.[25]

After the Tarawa debacle, the Marine Corps began developing deep-wading kits to vent their engines in water deeper than three feet. While the army used experimental exhaust stacks in Operations Torch and Husky, these developments were independent of marine operations in the Pacific.[26] By the time of the Marshall Islands campaign, not only had elements of the army's 767th Tank Battalion, 7th Infantry Division (destined for landings at Kwajalein), begun employing exhaust stacks, but Neiman's 4th Tank Battalion also adopted them in advance of landings on Roi and Namur.[27]

In addition to exhaust stacks, Neiman's tankers made a number of unique additions to their tanks in efforts to deter attacks by Japanese infantry. Recognizing the threat posed by the Japanese tactic of sticking Type 99 magnetic mines to the tank's vertical sides, Company C installed two-inch-thick Douglas fir planks to the tank's sides to reduce their relative magnetism.[28] Neiman reportedly took this idea from Lt. Leo Case, formerly of the 1st Tank Battalion on Guadalcanal; when Japanese soldiers swarmed the light tanks and damaged or knocked them out using these weapons, Case realized that the addition of wood planking could thwart future attacks.[29]

Case later became 4th Tank Battalion's operations officer, and working with Gerry DeMoss, a communications NCO, and Neiman facilitated better tank-infantry communications. Recognizing the challenges posed by buttoned-up tankers, they installed a field telephone handset in a satchel on the right rear fender of each tank and wired it through the engine compartment into the tank's intercom system. This made tank-infantry communication possible, as the radio nets normally used by tank and infantry battalions were incompatible.[30] These modifications were in place prior to the landings on the Kwajalein atoll's twin islands of Roi and Namur; meanwhile, other tankers in the Pacific made comparable adaptations to their tanks. On Bougainville, in the Solomon Islands, Lt. Col. Wilbur Strand, coordinating operations between the 37th and Americal Divisions with the 754th Tank Battalion, wired an EE8A telephone inside the tank turret in conjunction with a regulation flashlight. Connected to another EE8A handset outside the tank, the butterfly switch on the handset was modified so that it could complete a circuit and turn on the flashlight, alerting the tank commander to a message over the din of battle and the noise of the tank.[31] These ingenious efforts involving tank-infantry communication took place months before the French hedgerow country prompted their development in Europe. As employed by both 4th Marine Tank Battalion and the US Army's 767th Tank Battalion, salt water tended to short out many of the connections, however, leading some tankers to rip them out for fear they would short-circuit their tank intercoms.[32]

Shortly after the isolation of Rabaul and the seizure of the Gilbert Islands, the Joint Chiefs of Staff recast American operations in the Pacific, seeking interservice cooperation between the two commanders in the theater. Building on his earlier success on Bougainville, General MacArthur proposed landing at Hollandia on the northern coast of New Guinea and driving northward to the Philippines. In a mutually supportive drive, Adm. Chester Nimitz would begin "island-hopping" through the Central Pacific, seizing islands large enough to support air operations while bypassing others, adopting a "starve or bomb" strategy as his naval forces effectively cut off Japanese avenues of retreat or resupply.[33] This decision produced starkly different campaigns: one took place on a series of dry and sandy coral atolls and volcanic islands scattered across the Pacific, while the other was composed of campaigns in thick and humid tropical jungles. For success in each, liberal doses of American ingenuity were called for.

After Kwajalein, the 4th Marine Tank Battalion received new M4A2 Medium tanks to replace those used in the Marshalls campaign. According to Lieutenant Bellmon, these tanks came equipped with the new exhaust stacks that helped the tanks navigate in water as deep as "eight feet for several hundred yards."[34] In addition to the Marine Corps' improvements, Neiman's tankers began modifying their new Mediums, reinstalling the additions they had made before the previous operation. In the post-Saipan combat report, battalion commander Major Schmidt noted that "during the period of training allowed this organization following the Roi-Namur Operation, and prior to the Saipan Operation," an "improvised tank-infantry telephone was placed on each tank," with additional communication provided between infantry and tank commanders through the employment of "SCR 536 and TCS equipped jeeps." These makeshift tank-infantry phones, "installed in the tanks before embarking for Saipan," provided "a very satisfactory method of tank-infantry coordination."[35]

Other tankers soon followed Neiman's lead, equipping their tanks with improvised "French phones"; these consisted of "a radio earphone as the receiver and a microphone as the mouthpiece," bound together with tape and mounted on their tank's left rear fender.[36] These phones enjoyed mixed reviews, no doubt a consequence of how well commanders had familiarized marine infantry with the new additions. The forward-thinking Neiman specifically noted that the added intercom system worked best when an infantry officer, usually a company commander or executive officer, walked directly behind the control tank, communicating with the tank constantly. In contrast, Company A commander 1st Lt. Stephen Horton Jr. noted in his combat report that while his company had phones installed, "much confusion was encountered due to people that did not know how to operate them."[37]

In addition to the improvised telephones, Company C up-armored its new Medium tanks to counter evolving Japanese infantry tactics, layering sandbags over the rear engine compartment to protect against satchel charges hurled onto vulnerable vents and hatches by Japanese troops. They also covered "all possible hull armor" with inch-thick lumber planks, then quickly realized that in leaving an inch of air space between the lumber and the hull, they had created "perfect forms for pouring reinforced concrete" and subsequently poured concrete in the space to further protect the hull.[38] Only the tanks of Neiman's Company C received these additions, though by the end of the campaign, 1st Lt. Roger F. Seasholtz, commanding Company B, realized the value of this protective space above the tank's hull to deter the impact of magnetic antitank mines. Noting that the "magnetic antitank mine was effective when thrown or placed on top of the tank" and that such weapons were capable of blowing a hole in the armor plate, he suggested the addition of "chicken wire, metal strips or wood." He professed that the additional space between the mine and the tank hull would "greatly reduce the shock of a magnetic AT mine explosion," stating the desire to test such arrangements when the time and situation permitted.[39] In the ensuing operation on Tinian, which had "much more suitable tank terrain" compared to Saipan, not only did the tanks of the 4th Tank Battalion encounter "little trouble," but 1st Lt. Stephen Horton, Company A commander, realized that "flat surfaces of the tank covered with wood and pouring sand in between the wood and armor plate should neutralize the magnetic mine, as well as minimize the effect of anti-tank fire," as the Japanese also employed 47 mm antitank weapons against the marine tanks. Furthermore, "special attention should be paid to the hatches in protection against magnetic mines," as the Japanese had come to embrace attacking those potential weak points as an antitank tactic.[40]

Neiman specifically mentioned another improvement made by Company C: the addition of an extended periscope made to improve a tank commander's vision. Lengthening a standard periscope by cutting one in half and inserting a periscope base between the two halves, then "welding the three pieces together" gave the tank commander the ability to see the ground directly in front of the tank, something that was not normally possible. To protect this contrivance, the tankers added an armored cage around the longer periscope.[41] In addition to these crew-developed improvements, each platoon in Neiman's company also received an M4 Medium tank with mounted flamethrower, a weapon developed by a joint US Army, US Navy, and Marine Corps effort.[42]

After seizing Saipan and making a "perfect landing" on Tinian, the marines of the 4th Tank Battalion returned to Hawaii to rest and refit.[43] While engaging in a battalion-wide refit, Neiman's tankers discovered an issue of the *Armored Force Journal* or *Infantry Journal* that described the anti-mine "flail" tanks originally developed by the British and used for mine-clearing operations.[44] Recognizing the potential for such apparatus but knowing of none within the

Marine Corps, Neiman and his officers decided to build one from scratch. Sergeant Sam Johnston, who "had worked as an oil field roughneck and driller" in Oklahoma prior to joining the Marine Corps, took the lead in the project, aided by fellow sergeant Ray Shaw. Salvaging a dozer tank, the pair replaced its blade with a homemade flail. Using "the drive shaft and differential of an abandoned truck" with heavy chain attached to a rotating drum, they transferred power from the tank driveshaft via a transmission stripped from a jeep. Following a successful test, Neiman assigned the tank to Bellmon's 2nd Platoon for the Iwo Jima invasion.[45]

The 4th Tank Battalion received new tanks in advance of the Iwo Jima landings, turning in the M4A2 Mediums, powered by twin diesel engines, for the recently developed M4A3 model with a single Ford gasoline engine.[46] Neiman noted that his marine tankers "applied all of our usual modifications to the new tanks before embarking."[47] The result represented the pinnacle in marine field-expedient ingenuity in the Pacific, with Company C in the vanguard. To support their accompanying infantry, Neiman located spare gasoline tanks designed for light tanks, cleaned them, and bolted them to the rear deck of twenty-one of the company's medium tanks. With bungs and spigots on each end, the gas tanks served as supplemental water tanks for marines on foot, an essential addition in the conditions they faced on Iwo Jima.[48] Company C also improvised fire direction methods for marine infantry, painting a clock face on the side of the wading stack closest to the telephone with the simple statement "Target Clock" above it. This allowed any marine to approach the tank, pick up the phone, and ask for suppressing fire at the appropriate direction by simply stating the appropriate time.[49] It should be noted, however, that while Neiman described these additions, he did specifically state that the tank-infantry telephone, which other companies eventually picked up on, was the only additional modification embraced by other companies of 4th Tank Battalion.[50]

The after-action report of the 4th Tank Battalion following the Iwo Jima campaign offers a complete list of modifications made by the tankers of Neiman's company. His marines started by welding spare track blocks to the turrets and front slope plates as added protection against fire from both 47 mm guns and shaped charges. Fifty-four tanks had 1.5-inch wire mesh welded over the tops of all hatches, creating what the marines had come to call "birdcages" that provided space to dissipate the blast of a satchel charge. In forty-five tanks, the crews replaced the 75 mm ammunition ready box on the floor of the turret with a 75 mm ready rack that allowed each tank to carry twenty-five additional rounds of 75 mm ammunition. Ten tanks had their vision cupolas rotated forty-five degrees clockwise, allowing the hatch to open to the rear rather than the right side, to keep "branches, wire, etc., from hitting the hatch," a modification they recommended "should be incorporated in all tanks." Thirty-four others had several pieces of one-inch rod welded perpendicularly to the front slope plate to store the tow cable in a more accessible place. Sixteen tanks lengthened the commander's periscope to provide better vision, and eighteen tanks had their deck escape hatch modified by cutting it in half, hinging it to the deck armor, and securing it from the inside. Two otherwise open-topped M32B3 tank recovery vehicles also received a cover and hatch to protect their crews from small arms fire.[51]

While the innovations in the 4th Tank Battalion apparently were applied to all the tanks in the unit prior to the Iwo Jima landings, other battalions were not as systematic in their retrofitting. Tankers of the 5th Tank Battalion covered tank sponsons with a "small amount of sheet metal," with other tanks mounting wooden planking and track blocks on the hull and turrets in a manner not unlike that of 4th. In lieu of the battalion's birdcages, 5th Tank Battalion used sixteen-penny nails welded point up in a two-inch-square pattern in conjunction with heavy wire netting over hatch and periscope covers. Collectively, these provided a four-inch blast space as well as complicated the enemy's ability to pry open hatches. The marines also affixed wire mesh atop the exhaust stack to prevent grenades from being dropped into the exhaust system, layered sandbags over the engine compartments, and mounted spare bogies on the tank bustles in an effort to thwart magnetic mines and satchel charges.[52] The efforts of the 3rd Tank Battalion were less systematic, though their commander wrote in his after-action report that in future operations "it will be necessary to immediately devise increased armor protection for the M4A2 Medium tank (i.e., additional spaced armor, welded track blocks)," even going so far as to recommend applying white asbestos in the fighting compartment to reduce the fire hazard.[53]

The 4th Tank Battalion performed admirably on Iwo Jima, with Lieutenant Bellmon earning a Silver Star for "conspicuous gallantry and intrepidity" during the campaign. Shortly after landing, a Japanese mine damaged his tank, but he remained with the stricken vehicle, maintaining fire control and further directing his company. Leading his platoon through a heavily mined area the next day, his tank was immobilized "far beyond friendly lines," and he abandoned it, but returned to take command later. Mounting a new tank the next day, he led his platoon in continued attacks until his new tank was hit by an antitank projectile that killed a number of his crew. Undeterred, he commandeered another tank and continued the attack to reduce the enemy position.[54] Bellmon remained in action throughout the battle for Iwo, joining elements of the 3rd, 4th, and 5th Tank Battalions as part of a single armored phalanx led by

Lt. Col. William R. Collins of the 5th Tank Battalion, with 4th Tank Battalion's Major Neiman serving as executive officer.[55]

The battle was costly for the 4th Tank Battalion, as only nine tanks remained operational by the time the marines secured the island.[56] Although Neiman originally believed that the battalion's fabricated flail tank had bogged down and failed to perform, that was not the case. According to tank commander Sgt. Robert Haddix, the tank made it off the beach and as far as the first airfield, where it encountered a series of flags. Initially believing that the flags marked the edges of a minefield, the tankers soon discovered they were in fact range-finding flags for Japanese heavy mortars. When heavy enemy fire damaged the flail mechanism, Haddix and his crew abandoned their tank. Consequently, they never had the opportunity to test its functionality in combat.[57]

Neiman's tankers were not the only marines to modify their equipment for Iwo Jima. Some fabrications had roots well before the volcanic island's invasion. While on Bougainville, Sgt. Mel J. Grevich of the 3rd Marine Parachute Battalion, working in cooperation with his platoon leader, Lt. Phillip Gray, envisioned the need for a light, high-powered automatic weapon. Realizing that the Browning M1919 AN/M2 .30-caliber aircraft machine gun fit the bill, they secured one from a damaged Douglas SBD Dauntless torpedo bomber and went to work. Adding a Browning automatic rifle stock and front sight from an M-1 Garand, they fitted it with a BAR bipod, handle, and improvised trigger. Although the "Stinger," as they christened it, worked as intended, it failed to receive approval from higher authority.[58]

When the 3rd Parachute Battalion was disbanded, Sergeant Grevich was reassigned to G Company, 28th Regiment, 5th Marine Division, as a machine-gun sergeant. "Dissatisfied" with the weight, performance, and three-man crew requirements of the M1919A4 light machine gun, he revisited the Stinger concept prior to Iwo Jima. Engaging with his commanding officer, Capt. R. B. Carney, Grevich secured six AN/M4 machine guns and worked round the clock to convert them. Adding a bipod, BAR stock, and handle, and an aluminum ammunition box carrying one hundred rounds, his new weapon weighed twenty-five pounds with ammunition. He gave one Stinger to each rifle company, one to the demolition company, and kept one for himself; he supplied the final Stinger to Cpl. Tony Stein of A Company. After coming ashore on Iwo, marines found the weapon "very satisfactory" and "very good for patrol work." Grevich used his Stinger to reduce Japanese pillboxes, working in tandem with demolition teams to take out several Japanese strongpoints. Stein wiped out several enemy positions at the base of Mount Suribachi, though the Stinger's high rate of fire forced him to return for ammunition numerous times. As he moved back and forth, he brought several wounded marines back to the aid station.[59] After the battle, marines of the 5th Division recommended replacing the BAR organic to a normal rifle platoon with the battle-tested improvisation.[60]

The Stinger was not the only weapon improvised by marines on Iwo Jima. Throughout the battle, marines relied on flamethrowers, hand grenades, and satchel charges to drive the Japanese defenders from their bunkers and tunnels that honeycombed the island. In the latter stages of the fighting, Capt. A. F. Shaw called on his men to fabricate a satchel charge launcher to hurl satchel charges a considerable distance. Shaw's men built a compressive launch platform that could be ratcheted down against two spring-powered inverters. Releasing the trigger, the launcher hurled the charge into the air toward the enemy. It is not known, however, to what degree Shaw and his men employed their fabrication in the latter stage of the campaign.[61]

While Admiral Nimitz and his marines island-hopped across the Central Pacific, General MacArthur and his GIs mounted a parallel campaign from Australia to the Philippines. The preparation for this advance represented a triumph of American ingenuity of an altogether different sort. While GIs in Europe, as well as the marines advancing through the Central Pacific, relied on the US Navy to deliver their ammunition, vehicles, provisions, and other supplies once they went ashore, the US Army in the Pacific lacked a comparable logistical system. To accumulate the requisite supplies to facilitate each advance, they required deepwater ports capable of accommodating Liberty ships and larger landing craft, facilities that simply did not exist on the jungle islands of the Southwest Pacific. Consequently, the US Army relied on the "resourcefulness, initiative and drive of the American Engineer" to expand wharf capacity at Port Moresby, New Guinea. Capitalizing on the presence of islands with a suitable deep anchorage capable of accommodating multiple ships, engineers connected the mainland to the island with an earthen causeway, building nearly three miles of roads to dramatically increase the discharge capacity of the port.[62] Elsewhere in the SWPA, navy Seabees innovated to increase port capacity, using earth-filled coconut-log bulkheads and salvaged steel cable to expand the number of berthing spaces, and using pontoons to serve as bases for floating cranes, icebreakers, tugs, fuel and water barges, wharves, floating drydocks, and dredges.[63] Each allowed the gradual buildup of supplies needed to support the next advance.

While a wheeled or tracked vehicle provided the foundation for field modification in the European theater of operations, for the GIs of the Southwest Pacific most field modifications were added to things that floated, as the nature of their campaign precluded the widespread use of motor vehicles in other than support roles, though the jeep and "Deuce and a Half" (2.5- ton truck) did perform yeoman service on the rugged and muddy jungle roads of the Southwest

Pacific islands. When it came to adapting their boats, few were as ingenious as the men of the 2nd Engineer Special Brigade. When originally organized, the Engineer Amphibian Command (EAC) sought officers for a "fleet of troop-and-tank-carrying barges and landing boats," men who possessed the "ingenuity and ability to adapt familiar practices to unfamiliar circumstances."[64] While the US Marines as a force had been designed with an amphibious mission, the US Army lacked such capabilities, as the US Navy wished to maintain control over all *ships*. The navy did, however, grant the army the prerogative to operate small boats, specifically thirty-six-foot landing craft, vehicle, personnel (LCVP), and fifty-foot landing craft, mechanized (LCM), as it prepared for potential amphibious operations in World War II. Advertising in *Motor Boating* magazine, among other media outlets, in the summer of 1942, the EAC sought out civilian boat operators, ultimately recruiting four hundred officers directly into what would be designated Engineer Special Brigades (ESBs). All the recruits were "specialists on boats," and "what they lacked in military background was far outweighed by their technical value in their specialties."[65] Shortly after their organization, the Joint Chiefs of Staff ordered the 1st ESB to Europe, where it served with the Center Task Force in Operation Torch, though due to in-theater needs, the brigade's units spent most of their time with shore party, dock operations, and stevedore duties.[66] In contrast, when General MacArthur requested Engineer Amphibian troops for his Southwest Pacific offensive, the 2nd ESB assumed a primary role, moving both men and material from ships to shore, and manning the boats used by the US Army in the Philippines campaign.[67]

When the 2nd ESB arrived in Cairns, Australia, its engineers quickly put their boating expertise to work, assembling landing craft used in the New Guinea campaign, though no production facilities were ready when they arrived. By mid-April 1943, the brigade, working with the 411th Base Shop Battalion, built assembly facilities capable of producing seven LCVPs a day, production that made landings in the Salamaua-Lae campaign and on New Britain possible.[68] By the time of landings at Arawe, on the southern coast of New Britain in December 1943, the 2nd ESB had demonstrated its improvisational capabilities, having mounted 4.5-inch barrage rockets on DUKWs, using that firepower to secure the flanks of the landing beaches while the landing craft came ashore.[69] Landing at Cape Gloucester, the 2nd ESB demonstrated mechanical ingenuity by repairing boats damaged in the landings. Having already built log berthing racks "on the spot," to "park" boats at high tide, leaving them high and dry when the tide receded, the brigade continued such improvisations in a similar manner, performing repairs underwater, applying mechanical expertise to ensure boats' availability for subsequent operations.[70]

The men of the 2nd ESB continued mounting 4.5 -inch rockets on DUKWs, adding a 37 mm antiaircraft gun and 4.5-inch rockets to LVT-2 "Buffaloes" that already sported a pair of .50-caliber machine guns.[71] Recognizing the continued need for antiaircraft support in future landing operations, they built "General Heavey's Battleships," which eventually mounted "the heaviest armament per pound of any ship in the world." Major Elmer Volgenau designed the LCM (Flak), calling on men of the 2nd ESB's 162nd Ordnance Maintenance Company to deck over an LCM and install four Martin A-20 turrets mounting twin .50-caliber machine guns, two 20 mm antiaircraft guns, a 37 mm antiaircraft gun, and multiple 4.5-inch rocket launchers.[72] After initial trials of what became the *Susfu Maru*, the 2nd ESB constructed multiple boats. The men of the 3rd Engineer Special Brigade followed the lead of their sister unit in building their own version of the *Susfu Maru*, as T.Sgt. Oliver R. Smith of the 543rd Engineer Boat and Shore Regiment, 3rd ESB, detailed construction of *Borden's Battleship*, commanded by Newton Borden, which mounted firepower comparable to the flak LCMs of the 2nd ESB.[73] These boats, along with the armored "Buffaloes," found employment throughout the remainder of the Philippines campaign.[74]

Taking the positions that guarded Manila Bay required boat modifications of a different sort. As MacArthur's forces fought to clear the capital city, stubborn Japanese defenders occupying the caves on Caballo Island and tunnels of Fort Drum, the concrete "battleship" constructed on El Fraile island to guard the entrance to Manila Bay stymied the efforts of the 38th Infantry Division, the "Avengers of Bataan."[75] After initial landings on 27 March 1945, it took six days of heavy fighting for the Americans to secure most of Caballo, as a handful of Japanese soldiers clung tenaciously to an underground mortar complex. Lt. Col. William E. Lobit, commander of the 151st Infantry Regiment, proposed pouring diesel oil into air vents and igniting it, though the difficulty of manhandling an adequate number of oil drums up the rocky hill produced an improvised solution. Securing an LCM from the 592nd Engineer Boat and Shore Regiment of the 2nd ESB, two navy fuel cubes, a 110-horsepower aviation gas pump, and pipe fittings along with enough pipe to reach from the water's edge to the entrance of the underground mortar pit, divisional engineers rigged these elements together into what they christened the *Rube Goldberg*. After an initial successful test of the contraption using seawater, the engineers began pumping nearly 2,600 gallons of a three-quarters diesel oil and one-quarter gasoline mix into the subterranean complex occupied by the Japanese defenders. After emptying the fuel cubes, infantrymen dropped a number of white phosphorous mortar rounds into the mortar pit, causing tremendous explosions that rocked the island.[76] After a few more days employing the *Rube*

Goldberg against other island strongpoints, the 151st reported the island secure, having killed 279 enemy and taking 3 prisoners.[77]

Later that month, the division reemployed the *Rube Goldberg* to reduce Fort Drum. A two-story-tall concrete fortification built between 1909 and 1914 at the entrance to Manila Bay, Fort Drum could be accessed only through a sally port on the southeast side of the fortification. An initial attack produced significant casualties. Fresh off success on Caballo, Lieutenant Colonel Lobit opted to attack Fort Drum from the top, using the *Rube Goldberg* to pump its volatile mixture into unprotected ventilation shafts. Reaching the fortification's roof required field modifications to a Landing Ship Medium (LSM), manned by naval personnel. Retreating to Subic Bay, engineers constructed a drawbridge capable of reaching the top of Fort Drum atop an LSM dubbed the *Trojan Horse*. On 13 April, the *Trojan Horse* pulled up to Fort Drum, with four Army LCVPs holding it in position. Once in place, an assault team crossed the drawbridge and snaked the pipe from the *Rube Goldberg* into the first ventilation shaft, pumping 3,000 gallons of the diesel-gas mixture. They concluded the attack with a 500 lb TNT charge with a thirty-minute time-delay fuse. The first explosion, presumably from the TNT, was, according to one observer, "disappointing," though a second that followed a few moments later, according to the 38th Division's official historical report, "sent steel plates hundreds of feet in the air and caused smoke to issue from every vent, gun muzzle and opening," resulting in a towering mushroom cloud a thousand feet into the air.[78]

The Manila Bay conflagrations produced by the aptly named *Rube Goldberg* paled in comparison to the firebombing of Tokyo prosecuted by the Twentieth Air Force operating from India, China, the Marianas, and eventually Iwo Jima. The concentration of these aircrews and their maintainers in isolated locations at the end of a lengthy supply line prompted further demonstrations of American ingenuity as the men balanced their operations with the struggle to maintain morale. Not only did they fabricate the same sorts of ersatz tools comparable to those found among airmen of the Eighth Air Force, but they looked to their airfield boneyards to provide them with the materials for their next project, building go-carts, motorbikes, washing machines, sailboats, barber chairs, refrigerators, and a host of other contraptions to make life more comfortable and to help pass the time, not to mention figuring out how to manufacture ice cream using a repurposed drop tank and .50-caliber ammo can while flying at 33,000 feet.[79]

These tendencies continued in the most remote locations where American soldiers and airmen served during World War II. Beginning in early 1942, C. R. Smith and other American pilots lured into military service by General Arnold began employing expertise gained from employment by American

Airlines in "organizing, maintaining and equipping an air transport component" to support American allies in East Asia.[80] Capitalizing on the almost identical technology required for civil and military air cargo transportation, former civilians possessing the "collective know-how" and accustomed to "flying regular routes" for American Airlines soon found themselves with the "abnormal wartime task of flying incredible routes on schedule."[81] By 1943, crews directed by the former vice president of Trans World Airlines Col. Thomas Hunter ferried a monthly average of 10,000 tons of supplies from India's Assam Province over "The Hump" in the China-Burma-India (CBI) theater.[82]

GIs in the CBI employed American ingenuity while flying missions and maintaining aircraft hundreds of miles from the nearest supply line. When operational requirements of the construction of the Ledo Road dictated that a 32,000 lb one-half-cubic-yard power shovel be sent to Myitkyina, Burma, itself 210 miles from the nearest railhead, a team dismantled the shovel, packed it into six C-47 transports, and flew it to the destination, where they reassembled and put it to use. They repeated the process a few days later, delivering a 33,900 lb Quick-Way crane packed into another six planes.[83] Such efforts quickly garnered the attention of the *CBI Roundup*, the in-theater newspaper founded by Capt. Fred Eldridge, a former *Los Angeles Times* writer and public relations officer serving on Gen. Joseph Stilwell's staff.[84] General Stilwell used the newspaper, first published on 17 September 1942, to "keep the command informed of what is going on at home and in the other theaters of war."[85] By December 1944, the paper maintained a "Yank Ingenuity" editor, who chronicled "countless Goldbergian devices whipped up by imaginative woodswallahs using only twine, paste, matchsticks, and some old jeep parts." The *Roundup* recognized this "native American trait," speculating that when US forces returned home, "a collection of peculiar gadgets will incalculably enhance the American legend." It reported on fabrication of an HVBK (high voltage bug killer) made with charged wires across a wooden frame; lamps made from parachute cord soaked in a C ration can of insect repellent; and the "Hukawng hotplate," a stove made from pouring gasoline into a can and setting it alight.[86] Claiming that "there's nothing (practically) a Yank soldier can't invent," the *Roundup* issued reports of GIs building reading lamps, portable cook stoves, and fans made by "replacing the cutting head of an electric razor with a paper fan blade."[87] Others fabricated barber chairs from the actuating strut of a P-40, contrived a mechanical washing machine christened the "Dhobi Wallah," modified a jeep to patrol the rails between Bengal and Assam like the 94th Infantry Division's "Short Cut" employed in France, or enhanced a cot to accommodate a 332 lb soldier.[88] As Ray Howard wrote in an end-of-war issue on September 1945, "Necessity mothered a lot of inventions," producing boats, monster jeeps capable of transporting eighteen men, a pipe bender, gasket adjuster, fuel drum decanter, water supply system, and ice maker.[89]

Such creations would not have surprised troops who fought in the last battle of the Pacific War. In the invasion of Okinawa, the 1st and 6th Marine Divisions formed part of Lt. Gen. Simon B. Buckner Jr.'s Tenth Army, with the 2nd Marine Division serving as a floating reserve. As part of the 1st Marine Division, tankers of the 1st Tank Battalion demonstrated their ingenuity in making several "special preparations" before the operation, additions similar to those developed by the 4th Tank Battalion during its Pacific campaign. Specifically, 1st Tank Battalion tanks had sections of track block "spot-welded around the turret and front slope plate," beach matting welded onto tank sponsons "as protection against magnetic mines and AT grenades," and plate added to cover spoke-type bogie wheels and rear idlers.[90] The 1st Tank Battalion also improvised tank-infantry phone boxes, welding them onto the left rear sponson of all tanks.[91] The 6th Tank Battalion followed suit, adding tank-infantry radios and sections of steel track blocks to tank turrets with additional plate covering portions of the sponsons and track. Unable to procure enough plating to cover the entire sponson, they welded extra armor protection spaced "about one inch" from areas opposite the driver, assistant driver, and gasoline tanks.[92] Army tankers also tested the "backscratcher," attaching antipersonnel mines on the sides of tank turrets and detonating them when threatened by Japanese soldiers wielding satchel charges, though such efforts were eventually disapproved by General Stilwell.[93] Even with these additions, the 1st Tank Battalion listed seventy-nine tanks damaged, with twenty-seven as "totally lost," while the Japanese knocked out fifty-one of the 6th Tank Battalion's Sherman tanks in the fight for Okinawa. The number of tanks actually damaged in combat was much higher, as marine maintenance crews returned many to battle before the island was considered secure.[94] Elsewhere on the island, marines rigged log bundles to the front of their tanks, equipped with explosive charges that would allow them to drop the bundles into holes or trenches they encountered in front of them, providing a solid base to allow them to continue their advance without having to exit their vehicles.[95] The combined efforts and practical ingenuity of marine and army tankers in the Okinawa campaign were indispensable in winning the bloody battle, as they worked in conjunction with infantry to secure the last island in preparation for the anticipated invasion of Japan.[96]

The dropping of the atomic bombs on Japan obviated the need for Operation Olympic, as Emperor Hirohito announced Japan's surrender on 15 August 1945, only six days after the second atomic bomb had been dropped on Nagasaki. Lasting three years, eight months, three weeks, and five days, the war in the

Pacific was one of unspeakable brutality, a savage contest between an enemy willing to fight to the bitter end and an adversary challenged by the horrific conditions of combat.[97] The two armies could not have been more different, with one rooted in its feudal past, tied to tradition and maintaining productive practices unchanged for generations, while the other actively utilized the latest technology and innovated throughout the conflict, ultimately producing a superweapon capable of destroying entire cities in an instant.[98]

Reflecting on the war in 1946, American-educated Japanese newspaper columnist Masuo Kato recognized Japan's "tragic paradox." Observing that "modern war begins in the mine and in the factory" and that the conflict demanded "steel and oil," these were the real Japanese weaknesses, for they had relied on the United States for such resources in the decade preceding the war. As a result, Japan had strength in neither, and as a result, the country's "relative war potential was pitifully insignificant."[99]

Such was certainly not the case with the United States. Not only did the United States possess the resources, but as William Manchester opined in his memoir of the Pacific War, "To fight World War II, you had to have been tempered and strengthened in the 1930s Depression by a struggle for survival." While all nations of the world faced the economic challenges of the Great Depression, few had done so with the mechanical acumen found in the United States, whose citizens believed that "ingenuity could solve anything by inventing something."[100] While claims of his receipt of the Navy Cross, Silver Star, and two Purple Hearts for combat on Okinawa were later discredited as "fake history" bordering on "stolen valor," Manchester was nonetheless correct in his assessment of American society during World War II.[101] Throughout the war in the Pacific, American GIs and marines repeatedly proved to be more familiar than their foe with modern technology, a product of their experiences in the decades prior to the attack on Pearl Harbor. Throughout the war, they simply *thought* about technology differently, not regarding modern technology as a problem, but rather as something that could and should be improved. Such was the nature of American ingenuity.

CONCLUSION

> The trained American possesses qualities that are unique. Because of his initiative and resourcefulness, his adaptability to change and his readiness to resort to expedient, he becomes, when he has attained a proficiency in all the normal techniques of battle, a most formidable soldier.
>
> —*Gen. Dwight D. Eisenhower*

Dwight David Eisenhower grew up humbly in rural Abilene, Kansas. While the "dreams of a barefoot boy" in the American heartland may border on hyperbole, when the supreme commander of the Allied Expeditionary Forces returned to his hometown to speak shortly after V-E Day on 22 June 1945, he extolled the virtues of an indomitable spirit produced by growing up in the United States. Standing before those who knew him prior to his departure for West Point in 1911, the general fondly remembered the "independent farm and the horse and buggy, where each family was almost self-sustaining." Above all, he recognized the uniqueness of growing up American during the 1920s and 1930s, exposed to the "most modern type of machinery," and acknowledging that with the disappearance of the horse, "we have become mechanized."[1]

As a boy, Eisenhower learned that "most anyone could succeed in the American environment." Raising a family in the rolling hills and farm fields around Abilene, Eisenhower's father, David Jacob, and mother, Ida, instilled in young "Ike" and his five brothers a belief that America was full of opportunity for those in a position to seize it. With this as a foundation, Eisenhower came to recognize the value of ingenuity at a young age. As the United States mechanized, this transformation only elevated his growing sense of initiative and resourcefulness, particularly when applied to mechanical things, something that he later witnessed firsthand as supreme allied commander during World War II.

In his foreword to *Six Armies in Normandy*, John Keegan opined that "armies are universal institutions which, in the dimension of purpose and authority, closely resemble each other." Keegan also recognized that "each is also a mirror of its own society and values."[2] Throughout the course of World War II, both Allied and Axis armies made widespread use of motorized transportation and mechanized vehicles in their efforts to achieve victory. This, however, is where the comparison ends. As the first generation to grow up with the internal combustion engine, Americans of the 1920s and 30s possessed greater access to machines than all the soldiers of the other armies combined. Their starting point, in a Depression-era environment that demanded resourcefulness, gave the average American citizen-soldier a familiarity with machines and machine technology that was well beyond that of other nations that fielded armies during World War II. American planning, as developed by President Roosevelt and General Marshall before the attack on Pearl Harbor, called for the creation of a highly mechanized and mobilized US Army, Air Corps, US Navy, and Marine Corps, with a preponderance of motor vehicles accessible to soldiers, airmen, sailors, and marines at every level of command. As seen throughout World War II, when American soldiers found their tools of war lacking, they had the wherewithal, the capability, the means, and perhaps most importantly, the supporting flexibility of command to allow them to find solutions using the technology at hand, creating solutions from "the bottom up," as opposed to only making use of technology delivered to them from higher up the chain of command.

It is impossible to record every example of field improvisation or ingenuity conceived by American GIs in World War II. The preceding pages offer what I believe to be the tip of a veritable iceberg of other examples of Rube Goldberg–type devices crafted by US servicemen during World War II. For the "Grandpa Willy's" and "Uncle Joe's" who talked about their time in World War II, they probably included stories about how they built something from nothing or improved on what they had in the fight against Hitler or Tojo. Numerous museums hold treasured items fabricated by individual GIs. There are hundreds of Signal Corps photos that show changes made to individual vehicles and airplanes. There are myriad mentions of comparable fabrications in after-action reports, unit histories, memoirs, and oral histories. This book does not profess to include mention of every item related in all these artifacts, official accounts and personal stories. As children of the Depression, those members of the so-called Greatest Generation who became GIs in World War II embraced the "Use it up, wear it out, make it do, or do without" mentality, to solve the problems they encountered, whether enhancing combat effectiveness, protecting themselves more effectively, improving the supply situation, or enriching their personal welfare while in the field. That was GI ingenuity in World War II.

NOTES

Preface

Epigraph: *Saving Private Ryan*, dir. Steven Spielberg (1998).

1. War Department, *Field Service Regulations—Operations*, 161; The regulations repeat suggestions regarding "mines, gasoline, bottles, and grenades, either issue or improvised" that were offered in a 23 September 1940 training circular quoted by G. H. Franke, "Antitank Delusions?" *Field Artillery Journal* 32 (January 1942): 38–40.
2. "The Sticky Grenade in Action," *Infantry Journal* 33 (January 1943): 41–42; "Tank Busters," *Popular Mechanics* 80 (August 1943): 18–27; Donald G. Merritt, "Tank Destruction from Mounted Ambush," *Cavalry Journal* 53 (January–February 1944): 69–72.
3. Eisenhower, *Crusade in Europe*, 269.
4. Murray Illson, "Eisenhower Hails G.I. for Tank Idea," *New York Times*, 6 June 1964, 6; "D-Day Plus 20 Years—Eisenhower Returns to Normandy," hosted by Walter Cronkite, *CBS Reports*, on CBS, 6 June 1964, http://www.youtube.com/watch?v=vNaxTXfjfXk.
5. John O'Reilly, "Ingenuity Is Their Middle Name," *Popular Science* 144 (June 1944): 66–69, 218, 222.
6. Hanson, *Second World Wars*, 224.
7. O'Reilly, "Ingenuity Is Their Middle Name," 66–69, 218, 222.
8. These include Murray and Millett, *Military Innovation*, 329–68, 369–416; Doubler, *Closing with the Enemy*; Mansoor, *G.I. Offensive in Europe*; and Moy, *War Machines*.
9. Kennett, *G.I.*, regards the army as "an authentic slice of American society with all its many layers," recognizing the GI as "something of a tinkerer and improviser by nature" (23, 108–9). Kindsvatter, in *American Soldiers*, recognized the natural tendency of GIs to be both tinkerers and improvisers, explaining that such tendencies led to welded sandbag racks on Sherman tanks and the rhino tank, but his analysis stopped there; see Kennett, *G.I.*; 258–59. Lindermann, *World within War*, offers a similarly terse assessment, arguing that American individualism and inventive genius produced the rhino tank, at the same time noting that such traits were seldom displayed by soldiers of other nations. Schrijvers, *Crash of Ruin*, cites the unique technical ability and mechanical aptitude of the GI, particularly when

compared to soldiers of Germany, France, and Italy, noting the "frontier resourcefulness" of American troops, with American ingenuity going hand-in-hand with mass industrialization; see 89, 123, 130, 227–33. Carafano offers an analysis of "ingenuity" in *G.I. Ingenuity*, though comes up short. He recognized that the World War II generation was "a generation well prepared to improvise, innovate and adapt technology on the battlefield" and emphasized the "transition of the American genius in battle from an industrial-age army to a postmodern military"; see xiii, xvii, xix. In his introduction, Carafano states that "nothing explains 'G.I. Ingenuity' better than battling invaders from space," but begins his analysis of GI ingenuity with the invasion of Normandy and continues through to the end of the war. He largely ignores the impact of the Great Depression and the influence of American machine culture in the 1920s and 1930s. In Carafano's defense, he does mention young men reading *Buck Rogers in the 25th Century* comic books; however, he embraced a futuristic emphasis and science fiction, rather than observing the practical ingenuity demonstrated by, for example, the Hardy Boys and Tom Swift and extolled in publications like *Popular Science* and *Popular Mechanics* (xvii).

Chapter 1

Epigraph: "Emergency Supplemental Appropriation Bill for 1940, Hearings before the Subcommittee of the Committee on Appropriations," House of Representatives, 26th Cong., 3rd Sess. (Washington, DC: GPO, 1939), 6–8.

1. "Emergency Supplemental Appropriation Bill for 1940, Hearings," 1–6.
2. "Emergency Supplemental Appropriation Bill for 1940, Hearings," 6–8.
3. Stockbridge, *Yankee Ingenuity*, 2–4, 14–36.
4. For Stockbridge's career, see Startt, *Woodrow Wilson and the Press*, 117–18; and Marzio, *Rube Goldberg*, 77.
5. Stockbridge, *Yankee Ingenuity*, 370–72.
6. Stockbridge, "Main Street Wants to Know," 547–48; Stockbridge, "Popular Books," 441–44.
7. Stockbridge, "Popular Books," 445–49.
8. "Prizes for Labor Saving Automobile Improvements," *Popular Science Monthly* 92 (April 1918): 550–51; "Who Won the Motor Contest," *Popular Science Monthly* 92 (June 1918): 849. First-prize winner C. A. Butterworth "had no academic mechanical training and . . . had not even had a lesson in mechanical drawing," yet he designed an electrically controlled hydraulic gearshifter with an automatic clutch throw-out. The second-prize winner, P. C. Haas, invented an electrically operated steering gear that reduces the effort required to steer a car (a forerunner of power steering). The schematics for Butterworth's innovation appeared the next month in "Running Your Car with Push Buttons," *Popular Science Monthly* 93 (July 1918): 56; Haas's invention appeared in a subsequent issue.
9. "How *Popular Science Monthly* Is Used in Schools," *Popular Science Monthly* 102 (April 1923): 2; "Practical Suggestions for the Auto Owner," *Popular Science Monthly* 103 (July 1924): 68. The one-page column on automobile "kinks" appeared on a monthly basis until the beginning of World War II, under such titles as "Simple Jobs Any Motorist Can Tackle" (August 1925) and "Kinks for Car Owners" (January 1937); see "The History of Popular Science," http://www.popsci.com/scitech/article/2002-07/history-popular-science.

10. Frank Parker Stockbridge, "Training Boys for Real Life," *Popular Mechanics* (October 1914): 489–94; Frank Parker Stockbridge, "From Catapult to Howitzer," *Popular Mechanics* (November 1914): 675–80.
11. Mary Seelhorst, "Zero to 100," *Popular Mechanics* (March 2002): 117.
12. Charles F. Kettering, "How to Win the Soap Box Derby," *Popular Mechanics* (April 1936): 540–43, quote 541.
13. Francis J. Molson, "American Technological Fiction for Youth: 1900–1940," in Sullivan, *Young Adult Science Fiction*, 9–10.
14. Clarence Young, *The Motor Boys; or, Chums through Thick and Thin* (New York: Cupples and Leon, 1906). Other volumes included *The Motor Boys Overland* (1906), *The Motor Boys in Mexico* (1906), *The Motor Boys Afloat; or, The Stirring Cruise of the Dartaway* (1908), *The Motor Boys under the Sea; or, From Airship to Submarine* (1914), *Ned, Bob and Jerry on the Firing Line; or, The Motor Boys Fighting for Uncle Sam* (1919), concluding with *The Motor Boys on Thunder Mountain; or, The Treasure Chest of Blue Rock* (1924).
15. Victor Appleton, *Tom Swift and His Motor-Cycle* (New York: Grosset and Dunlap, 1910); Prager, "Bless My Collar Button," 64–75; Robert von der Osten, "Four Generations of Tom Swift: Ideology in Juvenile Science Fiction," in *The Lion and the Unicorn* 28 (April 2004): 268–84. Early novels in the Appleton series include *Tom Swift and His Motor Boat; or, The Rivals of Lake Carlopa* (New York: Grosset and Dunlap, 1910); *Tom Swift and His Airship; or, The Stirring Cruise of the Red Cloud* (New York: Grosset and Dunlap, 1910); *Tom Swift and His Electric Runabout; or, The Speediest Car on the Road* (New York: Grosset and Dunlap, 1910), quote 3; and *Tom Swift and His Air Scout; or, Uncle Sam's Mastery of the Sky* (New York: Grosset and Dunlap, 1910), quote 3. Appleton went on to pen novels that included the boy inventor's exploits with electric rifles, giant searchlights and cannons, and the photo telephone.
16. Prager, "Bless My Collar Button," 68.
17. Dixon, *Tower Treasure*, 1–17.
18. Dixon, *Mystery of Cabin Island*, 20; Billman, *Secret of the Stratemeyer Syndicate*; Nye, *Unembarrassed Muse*, 84–85. In his preface to *The Automobile Boys of Lakeport*, Stratemeyer wrote, "Automobiling is to-day one of the best of our sports. This writer is himself the fortunate possessor of a touring-car, and during the times this story was being written enjoyed numerous trips around his home and beyond" (vi).
19. The American fascination with the airplane prior to World War II is ably explored in Corn, *Winged Gospel*.
20. Arnold's Bruce series, consists of six titles, entitled *Bill Bruce and the Pioneer Aviators, Bill Bruce Flying Cadet, Bill Bruce Becomes an Ace, Bill Bruce on Border Patrol, Bill Bruce in the Transcontinental Race*, and *Bill Bruce on Forest Patrol*. Published by A. L. Burt of New York, the series describes the fictional career of Bill Bruce, Air Service aviator, tracing his exploits prior to and during World War I and beyond into the postwar period. Vaughan, "Hap Arnold's Bill Bruce Books," 43–49.
21. Dixon, *Great Airport Mystery*; Appleton, *Tom Swift and His Airline*; Molson, "American Technological Fiction," 15–16; Goulart, *Cheap Thrills*, 90–91. The website An International Catalogue of Superheroes provides a complete record

of all the titles in the G-8 series; see http://www.internationalhero.co.uk/g/g8.htm. Reprints of select issues of the original G-8 magazines published by Popular Publications are available at The Vintage Library, http://www.vintagelibrary.com/pulpfiction/characters/G-8-and-his-Battle-Aces.php.

22. "Build Model Airplanes—and Fly Them," *American Boy* (September 1927): 58. The entire run of *American Boy* aircraft articles was assembled by Frank Zaic in 1982 in *Model Airplanes and the American Boy.*
23. Molson, "American Technological Fiction," 11–12.
24. Molson, "American Technological Fiction," 19.
25. Steinbeck, *Grapes of Wrath*, 111, 257, 252.
26. Wik, *Henry Ford.*
27. Drowne and Huber, *1920s*, 244–45.
28. Rogers, *Wit and Philosophy*, 33.
29. Raff, "Making Cars and Money," 721–53.
30. Bernstein, *Lean Years*, 65.
31. American motor vehicle production (including cars, lorries, omnibuses, and all wheeled transportation excluding tractors) far outstripped vehicular production of the other major powers: Great Britain—445,000, Germany—342,000; France—223,000; USSR—215,000; Italy—69,000; Japan—30,000. League of Nations Economic Intelligence Service, *Statistical Year-Book, 1938/39*, 197.
32. Kennedy, *Freedom from Fear*, 617.
33. Wayne Whittaker, "Chrysler Family Debut," *Popular Mechanics* 91 (April 1949): 122.
34. Wik, *Henry Ford*, 2.
35. Allen, *Only Yesterday*, 5–6.
36. Allen, *Only Yesterday*, 76.
37. Wik, "Henry Ford's Tractors," 79–86.
38. Pettet, *Census 1940: Agriculture*, 3:452–54. In 1930, there were 146 tractors for every 1,000 farms. A decade later, the number increased to 257 tractors for every 1,000 farms.
39. "Mechanizing the Small Farm," *Popular Mechanics* (April 1940), 536–39, 140–43; Morrow May, "The Man on the Tractor," *Harpers* 177 (November 1938): 624, quoted in Worster, *Dust Bowl*, 91.
40. Ford, *My Life and Work*, 73.
41. Pogue, *George C. Marshall*, 126–27.
42. Pogue, *George C. Marshall*, 275–308, quote 308.
43. George C. Marshall, "Comments for the C.C.C. District *Review* on Camp Inspections," July 1937, in Bland, *Papers of George Marshall*, 1:542–44.
44. Yeager and Janos, *Yeager*, 8, 12.
45. Bellmon, *Life and Times*, 30–31, 44–45.
46. Haney, *Caged Dragons*, 5–6.
47. Scott, *Combat Engineer*, 2–15.
48. Kinney, *Wake Island Pilot*, 5–17.
49. LeMay, *Mission with LeMay*, 239–40.
50. Greening, *Not As Briefed*, 3–4.
51. Brulle, *Angels Zero*, 16. Brulle and his comrades would have benefited from reading the "Kinks" section of the July 1930 *Popular Science Monthly*, which offered "Shellaq as Cure for Leaky Gas Tank." *Popular Science* 117 (July 1930): 84.

52. Bendiner, *Fall of Fortresses*, 39.
53. Kinney, *Wake Island Pilot*, 5, 7.
54. Arnold, *Global Mission*, 16–17.
55. Dryden, *A-Train*, 9; Olds, *Fighter Pilot*, 6; Rutter, *Wreaking Havoc*, 6–7; Hynes, *Flights of Passage*, 13; Gamble, *Black Sheep*, 233.
56. Although this quote is often attributed to General Marshall, the statement is perhaps apocryphal, as this author has been unable to locate a definitive citation noting when and where he made the statement. It was first attributed to Marshall in Wells, *Hail to the Jeep*, although that source, in its attempt to offer what was perhaps the earliest complete history of the development, adoption, and employment of the vehicle, continues to perpetuate a number of the popular jeep myths, the least of which being the Willys-Overland Company's primary role in developing the vehicle. Although he does not include the Marshall quote, William Spear attempted to set the record straight on this oft-repeated tale in his rambling *Warbaby*. The Marshall quote also appeared in John Reichley, "50th Anniversary of the Jeep," *Military Review* 71 (July 1981): 78–79, and was repeated in "The Jeep: An American Icon," https://armyhistory.org/the-jeep-an-american-icon/. In his account of World War II, *Crusade in Europe*, General Dwight D. Eisenhower opined that the "four . . . pieces of equipment that most senior officers came to regard as among the most vital to our success in Africa and Europe were the bulldozer, the jeep, the 2-ton truck, and the C-47 airplane" (163–64).
57. Thomson and Mayo, *Ordnance Department*, 271. The 4 x 4 designation meant that the vehicle had four wheels, all of which were powered. Had it been designated 4 x 2, only two wheels received power, with the others rotating freely.
58. Wendell G. Johnson, "The Howie Machine-Gun Carrier," *Infantry Journal* 44 (November–December 1937): 529–31, quote 529.
59. Spear, *Warbaby*, 50–63; John W. Chapman, "The Story behind the Army Jeep," *Illustrated Gazette* (Ottumwa, IA), 1–2, 6.
60. Spear, *Warbaby*, 64–75; Chapman, "Army Jeep"; Lieutenant Colonel Ingomar M. Oseth to General George A. Lynch, "Chronology of ¼ ton Liaison Car Development," 2 January 1941, in Major General George A. Lynch Papers, U.S. Army Heritage and Education Center, Carlisle, PA (hereafter cited as Lynch Papers); Duddy, "Jeep at 70," 366.
61. Chapman, "Army Jeep," 1–2, 6; Lieutenant Colonel Ingomar M. Oseth to General George A. Lynch, "Chronology of ¼ ton Liaison Car Development," 2 January 1941, in Lynch Papers; Wells, *Hail to the Jeep*, 19; Duddy, "Jeep at 70: 364.
62. Spear, *Warbaby*, 99–125; George A. Lynch, "The Genesis of the Jeep," in Lynch Papers.
63. E. P. Hogan, The Army 'Bug': New Quarter-Ton Reconnaissance Car," in *Quartermaster Review* 20 (March–April 1941): 29; George Ruhlen, "The Versatile Jeep," *Field Artillery Journal* 31 (June 1941): 413–16; E. P. Hogan, "The Story of the Quarter-Ton 'Jeep,'" *Quartermaster Journal* 21 (September–October 1941): 53–54, 82–84.
64. Crosswell, *Chief of Staff*, 80–81; George A. Lynch, "Truck, ¼ Ton, Liaison, Characteristics," 17 February 1941, in Lynch Papers, document digitized at Early Jeep Documents Repository, www.willys-overland.com/documents/D-000029.htm. The episode also appears in Spears, *Warbaby*, 38–40.
65. George A. Lynch to Mr. Wade A. Wells, 12 September 1943, and George A. Lynch to Medal for Merit Board, Box 1B, Folder 14, Lynch Papers.

66. Lynch, "Genesis of the Jeep"; Duddy, "Jeep at 70," 366–74; Pyle, *Here Is Your War*, 289. Neither Charles Payne nor Bantam ever received adequate credit for the design of the jeep, a consequence of a vigorous advertising campaign conducted by the Willys-Overland Company. See Rifkind, *The Jeep*, 40–54. The most complete defense of Bantam's role may be found in Spears, *Warbaby*.
67. Franklin D. Roosevelt, "Fireside Chat on National Security," 29 December 1940, in Roosevelt, *Public Papers and Addresses*, 9:633–43.
68. Franklin D. Roosevelt, "Annual Message to Congress," 6 January 1941, Roosevelt, *Public Papers and Addresses*, 10:663–78. President Roosevelt signed the ensuing Lend-Lease Act into law on 11 March 1941.
69. General Henry H. Arnold, "First report of the Commanding General of the Army Air Forces to the Secretary of War," 4 January 1944, in Millis, *War Reports*, 329.
70. Kennedy, *Freedom from Fear*, 478–79; Baime, *Arsenal of Democracy*, 71; Thomas D. Morgan, "The Industrial Mobilization of World War II: America Goes to War," *Army History* 30 (Spring 1994), 31–35.
71. Sorensen, *My Forty Years*, 280.
72. Franklin D. Roosevelt, "Message to the Congress Asking for Additional Appropriations for National Defense, 16 May 1940," in Roosevelt, *Public Papers and Addresses*, 9:202. Almost 300,000 planes would be produced between 1940 and 1945, as noted in Craven and Cate, *Army Air Forces*, 6: 264.
73. Craven and Cate, *Army Air Forces*, 6:27.
74. Nalty, *Winged Shield, Winged Sword*, 1:172.
75. Craven and Cate, *Army Air Forces*, 6:301–3.
76. Nalty, *Winged Shield, Winged Sword*, 1:172; Craven and Cate, *Army Air Forces*, 6:308–13.
77. Craven and Cate, *Army Air Forces*, 6:310.
78. Sorensen, *My Forty Years*, 276–79.
79. Lilly et al., *Problems of Accelerating Aircraft*, 39–40; Sorensen, *My Forty Years*, 280–81; Baime, *Arsenal of Democracy*, 91–93; Herman, *Freedom's Forge*, 222–27.
80. Sorensen, *My Forty Years*, 281–83; Herman, *Freedom's Forge*, 226–29.
81. Craven and Cate, *Army Air Forces*, 6:315.
82. Craven and Cate, *Army Air Forces*, 6:324.
83. Greenfield, Palmer, and Wiley, *Army Ground Forces*, 203.
84. Nalty, *Winged Shield, Winged Sword*, 176, 378; "U.S. Navy Personnel Strength, 1775 to Present," Naval History and Heritage Command, https://www.history.navy.mil/research/library/online-reading-room/title-list-alphabetically/u/usn-personnel-strength.html; "Brief History of the Corps," Marine Corps University, https://www.usmcu.edu/Research/Marine-Corps-History-Division/Brief-Histories/Brief-History-of-the-United-States-Marine-Corps/.
85. Wheeler-Nicholson, "Yankee Ingenuity vs. Hitler!" 35–39, 142, 144. After graduating from Manlius Military Academy in 1910, Malcolm Wheeler-Nicholson served with the 2nd and 9th US Cavalry along the Mexican border, in the Philippines, in Siberia, and in Koblenz, Germany, with occupation forces after World War I. In 1922, he wrote to President Warren G. Harding complaining of the "Prussianism" and "inefficiency" that was having a negative effect on the US Army officer corps. After a much publicized court-martial, he was convicted of communicating outside the chain of command and resigned from the service. He published *Modern*

Cavalry (New York: Macmillan, 1922), a commentary on the state of the horse soldier at the end of the world war. Over the course of the next decade, he published a wide variety of pulp fiction, much of it having cavalry or western themes. Then came publication of his first comic book, *New Fun Comic Magazine*, in 1935. In the years preceding the United States' entry into World War II, Wheeler-Nicholson penned a series of military commentaries, beginning with *Battle Shield of the Republic* (1940) and followed by "For a Modernized Army," *Harpers* 182 (March 1941), and *America Can Win* (1941).

86. Wheeler-Nicholson, "Yankee Ingenuity vs. Hitler!," 35.
87. Wheeler-Nicholson, "Yankee Ingenuity vs. Hitler!," 37.

Chapter 2

Epigraph: MacArthur, *Annual Report*, 4.

1. MacArthur went on to say that "the magnitude of the effort, both of supply and of combat, was so great that individuals were utilized with the minimum of training." MacArthur, *Annual Report*, 4. See also Perret, *Old Soldiers Never Die*, 112–24.
2. Perret, *Old Soldiers Never Die*, 114–17, 129–35.
3. Perret, *Old Soldiers Never Die*, 195–208, 233–34.
4. See Miller, *War Plan Orange*, 223–32.
5. Linn, *Guardians of Empire*, 250–52.
6. Toll, *Pacific Crucible*, 34–36; Brereton, *Brereton Diaries*, 3–20, quotes 8, 20.
7. Prange, *December 7 1941*, 165, 171.
8. Crocker, *Black Cats and Dumbos*, 8–9, 19.
9. On 14 September 1942, Adm. Chester Nimitz awarded Finn the Medal of Honor for courage and valor beyond the call of duty. Collier, *Medal of Honor*, 83.
10. Urwin, *Facing Fearful Odds*, 183, 241–50.
11. Kinney, *Wake Island Pilot*, 40, 51, 59. During the first Japanese air raid against Wake Island on 8 December 1941, the Japanese destroyed seven of the VMF-211's Wildcats and damaged an eighth. When the four remaining Wildcats on combat air patrol returned after the initial raid, a ninth plane was damaged by running into debris on the runway. Kinney and his crew were able to repair one of the damaged fighters before the next air raid on 9 December. Richard D. Camp, "Wake's Valiant Aviators," *Naval History Magazine* 34 (December 2020), https://www.usni.org/magazines/naval-history-magazine/2020/december/wakes-valiant-aviators.
12. Kinney, *Wake Island Pilot*, 59–62; Urwin, *Facing Fearful Odds*, 268–69.
13. Kinney, *Wake Island Pilot*, 69–71.
14. Maj. Paul A. Putnam, quoted in Hough, Ludwig, and Shaw, *Pearl Harbor to Guadalcanal*, 124–25.
15. Hough, Ludwig, and Shaw, *Pearl Harbor to Guadalcanal*, 52, 71–72; Urwin, *Facing Fearful Odds*, 269.
16. Kinney, *Wake Island Pilot*, 72–74, 78.
17. White, *They Were Expendable*, 102–4.
18. Casey, *Memoirs*, 116–23, 131–42.
19. Morton, *Fall of the Philippines*, 80–89.
20. Edmonds, *They Fought*, 279.
21. Weller, "Luck to the Fighters: Part One," 268–70.
22. Weller, "Luck to the Fighters: Part Two," 33.

23. Weller, "Luck to the Fighters: Part Three," 149–50.
24. Casey, *Memoirs*, 161–62.
25. Casey, *Engineers of the Southwest Pacific*, 1:20–21.
26. Casey, *Engineers of the Southwest Pacific*, 1:20–21; Casey, *Engineers of the Southwest Pacific*, 7:11, 239–40. Instructions accompanying the "Improvised Hand Grenade" issued by US Army Forces Far East, Fort Mills, the Philippines, included the following Safety Precautions:

    A. handle the improvised hand grenade with *utmost care.*
    B. Do *not light* the fuse until ready to throw the grenade.
    C. Do *not place* or handle the grenade near an *open light.*
    D. Do *not drop* or *shake* the grenade.
    E. Do *not cut* the fuse short to save time.
    F. Do *not* disturb the cement mortar *seal.*
    G. Do *not* leave the grenade in a *wet* place.
    H. Do not handle or store the grenade near a tent or sleeping place.
    I. *Do not pull the fuse.*
    J. Do *not* carry the grenade *in your pocket.*
    K. Do not throw the grenade where it will hit a tree immediately in your front.

27. Casey, *Memoirs*, 163.
28. Casey, *Memoirs*, 11.
29. Edmonds, *They Fought*, 148.
30. Poncio and Young, *Girocho*, 34.
31. Tenney, *My Hitch in Hell*, 23–24.
32. White, *They Were Expendable*, 88.
33. White, *They Were Expendable*, 4–5, 12–13, 105, 207–9.
34. Chennault, *Way of a Fighter*, 32–60.
35. Chennault, *Way of a Fighter*, 90–91.
36. Pilots received US$600, with $75 more for flight leaders and $150 more for squadron commanders. Ground crewmen received between $150 and $350, depending on experience. For each Japanese plane destroyed, the Chinese paid a $500 bonus to the pilot with the confirmed kill. Whelan, *Flying Tigers*, 35.
37. Smith and Smith, *With Chennault in China*, 2–6; Michael Schaller, "American Air Strategy in China, 1939–1941: The Origins of Clandestine Air Warfare," *American Quarterly* 28 (Spring 1976): 3–19.
38. Chennault, *Way of a Fighter*, 100.
39. Chennault, *Way of a Fighter*, 152.
40. Smith and Smith, *With Chennault in China*, 28–29.
41. Bond and Anderson, *Flying Tiger's Diary*, 43–44, 106–7.
42. George Rodger, "Flying Tigers in Burma," *Life* 12 (30 March 1942): 28–33.
43. Smith and Smith, *With Chennault in China*, 30.
44. Losonsky and Losonsky, *Flying Tiger*, 6, 58–59. Similarly, AVG pilot Gregory H. "Pappy" Boyington, who would go on to command the famed "Black Sheep Squadron," VMF-214, wrote that wrecked planes were the only source of scavenged spare parts, because "there were none to be shipped from the United States," See Boyington, *Baa Baa Black Sheep*, 42.

45. Bond and Anderson, *Flying Tiger's Diary*, 173.
46. Chennault, *Way of a Fighter*, 164–65.
47. Bond and Anderson, *Flying Tiger's Diary*, 214–17.
48. Scott, *Target Tokyo*, 32–37, 42, 47–48, 55–58.
49. Scott, *Target Tokyo*, 58–68.
50. Scott, *Target Tokyo*, 92–93; Greening, *Not As Briefed*, 14.
51. Greening, *Not As Briefed*, 29.
52. Scott, *Target Tokyo*, 112–13.
53. Spector, *Eagle against the Sun*, 149–50.
54. Lundstrom, *First Team*, 12–14, 55–56.
55. Toll, *Pacific Crucible*, 219; Lundstrom, *First Team*, 63; Capt. James S. Gray Jr., "Decision at Midway," The Battle of Midway Roundtable, http://www.midway42.org/Midway_AAR/VF-6-1.aspx; "Action Report—1 February 1942," in *USS Enterprise* CV-6 Action Reports and Logs, http://cv6.org/ship/logs/action19420201.htm.
56. Lundstrom, *First Team*, 139–40, 186.
57. John S. Thach, "Butch O'Hare and the Thach Weave," in Wooldridge, *Carrier Warfare*, 9–13.
58. John S. Thach, "A Beautiful Silver Waterfall," in Wooldridge, *Carrier Warfare*, 56.
59. Thach, "Butch O'Hare," in Wooldridge, *Carrier Warfare*, 9–13.
60. Lundstrom, *First Team*, 310.
61. Lundstrom, *First Team*, 315.
62. Morison, *United States Naval Operations*, 4:55, 63.
63. Bergeron, "Fighting for Survival," 11–12.
64. Morison, *United States Naval Operations*, 4:58.
65. Morison, *United States Naval Operations*, 4:80–81; Toll, *Pacific Crucible*, 383–92.
66. Morison, *United States Naval Operations*, 4:81; Bergeron, "Fighting for Survival," 14–17.
67. Bergeron, "Fighting for Survival," 17–18; Toll, *Pacific Crucible*, 397.
68. Hough, Ludwig, and Shaw, *Pearl Harbor to Guadalcanal*, 1:235–37.
69. Frank, *Guadalcanal*, 15–17, 53; Chief of Naval Operations, *Naval Aviation*, 25.
70. Croizat, *Journey among Warriors*, 10.
71. Croizat, *Journey among Warriors*, 22; Shaw, *First Offensive*, 9.
72. William Gray, "An Experiment on Guadalcanal," *Field Artillery Journal* 33 (April 1943): 294–95; William Gray, "Modifications to the 'Third' Wheel," *Field Artillery Journal* 34 (June 1944): 364.
73. Morison, *United States Naval Operations*, 5:35–64.
74. Miller, *Cactus Air Force*, 26, 30, 52–53; Zimmermann, *Guadalcanal Campaign*, 62–65, 74; Philippart, *Airfield as Center of Gravity*, 7–21; Mrazek, *Dawn Like Thunder*, 356–62; Bergerud, *Fire in the Sky*, 23.
75. Crocker, *Black Cats and Dumbos*, 183–85; Taylor, "Jack Randolph Cram," 1–13; Miller, *Cactus Air Force*, 125–26.

Chapter 3

Epigraph: General George C. Marshall, "Address for Delivery to the Graduates of the First Officer Candidate School," 27 September, 1941," in Bland, *Papers of George Marshall*, 2:620.

1. McNeill, *America, Britain and Russia*, 90–118.
2. See Louis Morton, "'Germany First': The Basic Concept of Allied Strategy in World War II," in Greenfield, *Command Decisions*, 11–48.
3. Calhoun, *McNair*, 250. In addition to McNair's posting, the chief of staff named Lt. Gen. Henry H. Arnold to command the Army Air Forces and Lt. Gen. Brehon B. Somervell to head the Services of Supply.
4. Marshall to General Malin Craig, 19 September 1939, in Bland, *Papers of George Marshall*, 2:59–61; Gabel, *U.S. Army GHQ Maneuvers*, 9–12. The triangular structure was similarly applied to artillery regiments, allowing divisional artillery to be divided into thirds and attached to an infantry regiment, thereby creating a regimental combat team. See also House, *Toward Combined Arms Warfare*, 48, 69–78.
5. Calhoun, *McNair*, 153–70.
6. Kirkpatrick, "Strategic Planning," 17–21.
7. The 2nd Cavalry would be activated in April 1941, then partially disbanded in July 1942 before being fully reactivated in February 1943. Palmer, Wiley, and Keast, *Procurement and Training*, 491, 493.
8. In North Africa, US forces committed included the 1st, 3rd, 9th, and 34th Infantry Divisions, alongside the 1st and 2nd Armored Divisions. In Italy, American forces committed included 1st, 3rd, and 45th Infantry Divisions, with reserves made up of the 9th Infantry, 2nd Armored, and 82nd Airborne Divisions. In Italy, the Fifth Army comprised the 85th and 88th Infantry Divisions in II Corps, the 1st Armored, 3rd, 34th, and 45th as part of VI Corps, and the US-Canadian First Special Service Force, with the 36th Infantry Division in reserve. See Howe, *Northwest Africa*, 675; Garland and Smyth, *Sicily and Italy*, 555; Atkinson, *Day of Battle*, xvi, xvii. Collectively, these were among the older, more established units in the US Army, and many offered cadres for subsequent units, as outlined in Mansoor, *G.I. Offensive in Europe*, 73.
9. Palmer, Wiley, and Keast, *Procurement and Training*, 433–34, 491; Mansoor, *G.I. Offensive in Europe*, 35; Kennedy, *Freedom from Fear*, 630–31; Maurice Matloff, "The 90-Division Gamble," in Greenfield, *Command Decisions*, 365–82.
10. Watson, *Chief of Staff*, 156–60.
11. Secretary of War, *Annual Report, 1941*, 56.
12. Mansoor, *G.I. Offensive in Europe*, 18–19.
13. Lee, *Employment of Negro Troops*, 415.
14. Dickson, *Rise of the G.I. Army*, 241–48.
15. Walter Lippmann, "Notes on the Carolina Maneuvers," *Washington Post*, 20 November 1941.
16. Christopher Gabel, "Tank Destroyer Force," in Hoffman, *History of Innovation*, 63–64.
17. Gabel, *Seek, Strike and Destroy*, 19–27; "Tank Busters," *Popular Mechanics* 80 (August 1943): 18–25, quote 22. Chapter 10 of War Department, *Tank Destroyer Field Manual*, 123–26, addressed "Dismounted Tank Hunting," instructing tank destroyer crewmen to use antitank grenades, improvised or otherwise, to target exposed crew, periscopes and vision slits, turret rings, ventilation ports, and tank treads and their "wits . . . rather than rules" to immobilize or destroy enemy armor.

18. Lippmann, "Notes on the Carolina Maneuvers."
19. Houston, *Hell on Wheels*, 113; Hunnicutt, *Half-Track*, 39–40.
20. Bradley, *Soldier's Story*, 1–6; Ernie Pyle described Bradley's truck as resembling "a tourist trailer." Pyle, *Brave Men*, 310. When Lt. Col. John B. Medaris succeeded Col. Urban Niblo as chief of ordnance for II Corps, he had a similar arrangement in a trailer, a practice borrowed by the British and "adopted by most American commanders in the field" as "the trailer provided a headquarters office that could be hooked to a truck and quickly moved to a new location." Mayo, *Ordnance Department*, 147. Lt. Arthur Paddock devised plans to prepare the 2.5-ton truck as a mobile kitchen; see Paddock, "How to Prepare the 2½ Ton Cargo Truck as a Kitchen Vehicle," *Cavalry Journal* 52 (September–October 1943): 80–82; and John Snodgrass, "More about the Kitchen Truck," *Cavalry Journal* 52 (November–December 1943): 73.
21. Dwight D. Eisenhower, "Report on Operation Torch," https://cgsc.contentdm.oclc.org/digital/collection/p4013coll8/id/110/rec/6, 3–9, in World War II Operational Documents Collection, Ike Skelton Combined Arms Research Library, Fort Leavenworth, KS (hereafter cited as WWII-Skelton).
22. Pyle, *Here Is Your War*, 288.
23. Wells, *Hail to the Jeep*, 3. The same story also appeared in William C. Farmer, "Recovery of Material in Combat," *Military Review* 23 (February 1944): 39–40.
24. Eisenhower, *Crusade in Europe*, 148–49; Pyle, *Here Is Your War*, 133–35. Such practices became commonplace whenever GIs bivouacked for any extended period of time.
25. Eisenhower, *Crusade in Europe*, 148–49; Mayo, *Ordnance Department*, 132; Howe, *Northwest Africa*, 495–99; Bykofsky and Larson, *Transportation Corps*, 161–77.
26. Mayo, *Ordnance Department*, 134; L. R. Fredendall, "Notes on Recent Operations on the Tunisian Front," 10 March 1943, https://cgsc.contentdm.oclc.org/digital/collection/p4013coll8/id/4/, WWII-Skelton; E. P. Hogan, "The Jeep in Action: Some Adventures of the Army's Ubiquitous Vehicle," *Army Ordnance* 27 (September–October 1944): 271–74, quote 272; Burgess Scott, "Second Hand Jeep Corporation Cooks with Gas," *Yank*, 25 (10 December 1943): 9.
27. Mayo, *Ordnance Department*, 147.
28. Mayo, *Ordnance Department*, 148.
29. Byron F. Rampton, "B.V.D. Machine Gun Mount," *Field Artillery Journal* 33 (September 1943): 666–67; Mayo, *Ordnance Department*, 134–35.
30. Mike W. Folk, "Shell Case Straightener for 105-mm Howitzer," *Field Artillery Journal* 33 (December 1943): 927; R. M. Brewster, "'Undenter,' Shell Case, 105-mm Howitzer," *Field Artillery Journal* 33 (December 1943): 932.
31. Mayo, *Ordnance Department*, 155; Zaloga, *US Armored Funnies*, 49.
32. Mayo, *Ordnance Department*, 155; George S. Patton Diaries, Annotated transcripts, Apr. 8–July 1, 1943, Box 2, Folder 15, https://tile.loc.gov/storage-services/service/gdc/gdccrowd/mss/mss35634/002/15/00215.txt.
33. U.S. Army Ground Forces, Observer Board, European Theater, "Headquarters 9th Infantry Division: Experience and Lessons from the campaign of Tunisia and Sicily," 1: Report C-1, in U.S. Army Ground Forces Observer Board, European Theater, "Reports of Observers, ETO, 1944–45," 6 vols., U.S. Army Heritage and Education Center (hereafter cited as Observers Reports–USAHEC).

34. Howe, *Northwest Africa*, 320–44; Martin Blumenson, "Kasserine Pass, 30 January–22 February 1943," in Heller and Stofft, *America's First Battles*, 226–65.
35. Fredendall, "Notes on Recent Operations," 7, WWII-Skelton; Gabel, *Seek, Strike and Destroy*, 33–34; Yeide, *Tank Killers*, 68–69; Fredendall, "Notes on Recent Operations," 7, WWII-Skelton.
36. United States Army, 776th Tank Destroyer Battalion, *Informal History of the 776th*, 24; James P. Barney, "TD's Approach Maturity," *Field Artillery Journal* 34 (November 1944): 775–76.
37. W. W. Ford, "Grasshoppers," *Field Artillery Journal* 33 (September 1943): 651; Cummings, *Grasshopper Pilot*, 8, 10, 17; Schultz, *Janey*, 58.
38. "A 'Grasshopper's' Biography," *Field Artillery Journal* 34 (February 1944): 132.
39. Cumings, *Grasshopper Pilot*, 28–30.
40. Schultz, *Janey*, 44.
41. Cummings, *Grasshopper Pilot*, 31–34.
42. Cummings, *Grasshopper Pilot*, 35–44; Ferguson, *Last Cavalryman*, 180–82.
43. Garland and Smyth, *Sicily and Italy*, 405–10; Pyle, *Brave Men*, 66–70; Truscott, *Command Missions*, 241–42.
44. Gabel, *Seek, Strike and Destroy*, 39–40; Barney, "TD's Approach Maturity, 776–77.
45. P. C. Meachem, "A New Fighting Team," *Field Artillery Journal* 34 (November 1944): 778–80.
46. "With a Quartermaster Truck Company in the Middle East," *Military Review* 23 (September 1943): 59.
47. Ivan Pogue and George Roesinger, "Instrument Mount for Concealed Observers," *Field Artillery Journal* 33 (October 1943): 787. Pogue and Roesinger's contribution appeared in the "Not in the Book" section, which ran in each monthly issue of *Field Artillery Journal* and featured "ideas sent in by our readers describing methods or devices which, though not specified by official literature, have proved useful in service."
48. "Ingenuity," *Infantry Journal* 56 (April 1945): 58.
49. "Improvised Equipment Facilitates Ordnance Maintenance," *Military Review* 24 (September 1944): 52.
50. George D. Pence, "Lessons from the Italian Campaign," Headquarters, Mediterranean Theater of Operations, 15 March 1945, https://cgsc.contentdm.oclc.org/digital/collection/p4013coll8/id/4676/rec/1, 132, WWII-Skelton.
51. "The Priest Moves In," *Field Artillery Journal* 33 (May 1943): 378.
52. Melvin E. Mason and Joe B. Windlay, "Intra-Battery Communication in an Armored Field Artillery Battalion," *Field Artillery Journal* 33 (December 1943): 33.
53. Lt. Col. Gordon J. Wolf, "Emergency Wire Laying by Liaison Airplane," *Field Artillery Journal* 34 (August 1944): 566–67.
54. Eugene W. DeMoore, "Separator for a Semi-Fixed Shell," *Field Artillery Journal* 33 (May 1943): 342–43; "Shell Separator," *Field Artillery Journal* 33 (August 1943): 629; "Plans for a Shell Separator," *Field Artillery Journal* 34 (May 1944): 299; "Shell Separator, Again," *Field Artillery Journal* 34 (August 1944): 529.
55. "Men at War: Kelly Earns a Medal," *Time*, 20 March 1944, 33; Blumenson, *Salerno to Cassino*, 113–14. Atkinson, *Day of Battle*, 222–23; Brager, *Texas 36th Division*, 135–36; Brady, *Death in San Pietro*, 82–84.
56. Pyle, *Brave Men*, 265. The wire-cutting bar practically became a wartime standard on the jeep.

57. Intelligence Report, "Auxiliary Jeep Frame," 8 November 1944, https://cgsc.contentdm.oclc.org/digital/collection/p4013coll8/id/5110/rec/1, WWII-Skelton.
58. "Reports by Observers on Current Operations in North Africa," 10 May 1943, https://cgsc.contentdm.oclc.org/digital/collection/p4013coll8/id/4641/, WWII-Skelton; Army Pictorial Service, "The Nettunia Quads: Homemade Gadget Steps Up Bazooka Power," https://www.youtube.com/watch?v=Olv_htiOM5E; "Ingenuity Is the Mother of Invention: Bazooka-Armed Jeeps," *Journal of Military Ordnance* 9 (January 1999): 21.
59. Scutts, *Republic P-47 Thunderbolt*, 17–23; 30–35; William W. Hahn, personal communication with the author, 4 March 2004; Hahn, "Stratofighter to Dive Bomber," 18–29.
60. In November 1943, the 353rd Fighter Group, based in Metfield, Suffolk, England, began using the P-47 as a fighter-bomber, mounting 40 lb fragmentation bombs in a 500 lb cluster arrangement. Pilots were unable to drop bombs accurately in a dive from 15,000 to 10,000 feet.
61. Headquarters Army Air Forces, Office of Flying Safety, *Pilot Training Manual*, 201. In an initial test, Wymond had placed four different pilots in a P-47 cockpit on a hardstand and challenged them to release 500 lb bombs in test circumstances. Due to the leverage required to pull the release toggles, all were unsuccessful in dropping their bombs.
62. Hahn, "Stratofighter to Dive Bomber," 19–22; William W. Hahn, *My Perspective of WWII, June 1941 thru September 1945* (privately printed, 2004), author's collection; William Hahn, personal communication with the author, 4 March 2004.
63. Hahn, "Stratofighter to Dive Bomber," 22–23; Hahn, *My Perspective of WWII.*
64. Hahn, "Stratofighter to Dive Bomber," 23–24; Hahn, *My Perspective of WWII.*
65. Images 3A06380-72321AC, 3A06369-69608AC, 3A23058-58966AC, 3A06371-69615AC, 3A06511-51388AC—all in RG 342-FH, Records of U.S. Air Force Commands, Activities, and Organizations, Series: Photographs of Activities, Facilities, and Personnel, National Archives and Records Administration II (hereafter cited as RG 342-FH).
66. Hahn, in "Conversion of the P-47D-15 from a High Altitude to a Ground Support Aircraft, January 12–14, 1944," in *My Perspective of WWII*, 5, explains that while the B-7 bomb shackle with individual lug releases was not as effective as the B-10 shackle, it had a positive release on the forward lug and a swinging fulcrum that released when the forward lug was engaged. Once the B-10 bomb shackle was tested, that "in-field" conversion led to the P-47s of the 57th becoming "the most feared ground support aircraft of the war in Italy." Craven and Cate, *Army Air Forces*, 3:373–76.
67. "Sandbagging Vehicles," in War Department, Combat Analysis Section, *Combat Lessons, Rank and File in Combat: What They Are Doing, How They Do It* (hereafter cited as *Combat Lessons*), 2:33. The Combat Analysis Section of the War Department published seven volumes of *Combat Lessons*, offering "the battle experiences of others" during the war, with each volume bearing the endorsement of Chief of Staff Marshall.
68. "Music for Your Dugout," *Field Artillery Journal* 34 (July 1944): 484.
69. Frederick C. Spann and Stephen Barabas, "Field Expedients in Radio Communications in Italy," *Field Artillery Journal* 35 (May 1945): 301.
70. "Collapsible Shower," in *Combat Lessons*, 6:36.

71. Mayo, *Ordnance Department*, 207.
72. Military Intelligence Service, "Schu-Mine 42" *Intelligence Bulletin* 3 (September 1944): 76–78.
73. "Animated Mine Exploders," in *Combat Lessons*, 4:26. This "solution" is also mentioned in Beck et al., *Corps of Engineers*, 182.
74. Lindberg, "Colonel Harry D. Tyson," 34–35.
75. Mayo, *Ordnance Department*, 210.
76. Ricks, *Generals*, 66.
77. Clark, *Calculated Risk*, 342–43.
78. Clark, *Calculated Risk*, 342–44; Mayo, *Ordnance Department*, 210; Shirley, *I Remember*, 9–24; Pence, "Lessons from the Italian Campaign," 31–32; 751st Tank Battalion, Report of Action against the Enemy for the Month of May [1944], https://cgsc.contentdm.oclc.org/digital/collection/p4013coll8/id/3866/, 75–76, WWII-Skelton.
79. Mayo, *Ordnance Department*, 210.
80. Pence, "Lessons from the Italian Campaign," 31–32.
81. Eisenhower, *Crusade in Europe*, 203.
82. Cummings, *Grasshopper Pilot*, 69.

Chapter 4

Epigraph: Steinbeck, *Bombs Away*, 14.

1. Simmonds, *Steinbeck*, 124–36; French, *Steinbeck's Fiction Revisited*, 91–92; Steinbeck, *Bombs Away*, 32.
2. Steinbeck, *Bombs Away*, 140–47.
3. Peter Armenti, "John Gillespie Magee's 'High Flight,'" *From the Catbird Seat*, https://blogs.loc.gov/catbird/2013/09/john-gillespie-magees-high-flight/.
4. Cox, *Beyond the Battle Line*, 17–18, 21–22; Griffith, *MacArthur's Airman*, 17–46; Herman S. Wolk, "George C. Kenney: The Great Innovator," in Frisbee, *Makers of the Air Force*, 130–33.
5. Kenney, *General Kenney Reports*, 7–11; Griffith, *MacArthur's Airman*, 46–56.
6. Kenney, *General Kenney Reports*, 12–13.
7. Kenney, *General Kenney Reports*, 26–30.
8. Brownstein, *Swoose*, 61–66.
9. Kenney, *General Kenney Reports*, 52–53.
10. Kenney, *General Kenney Reports*, 61.
11. Kenney, *General Kenney Reports*, 56–57.
12. Kenney, *General Kenney Reports*, 59–62.
13. Watson, "Air Action," 139–40.
14. Kenney, *General Kenney Reports*, 77. Although much of Gunn's reputation as a gadgeteer was built on his work with aircraft modification, he also fixed General Kenney's electric razor after he dropped it on the floor. Gunn repaired the case with plastic salvaged from an aircraft gun turret dome, replaced the condenser with another taken from an unknown source, and installed a transformer to allow it to run on Australian 220-volt electric current as opposed to hard-to-obtain American batteries. Kenney claimed that, while the razor was heavier and clumsier, the product of Gunn's inventive genius nonetheless gave the general a closer shave. Kenney, *Saga of Pappy Gunn*, 52–53.

15. Kenney, *Saga of Pappy Gunn*, 3–36.
16. Craven and Cate, *Army Air Forces*, 4:106; Gann, *Fifth Air Force*, 10–11; Kenney, *Saga of Pappy Gunn*, 37–50.
17. Kenney, *Saga of Pappy Gunn*, 27, 49–51.
18. Watson, "Air Action," 45.
19. Office of the Assistant Air Chief of Staff, Intelligence, "Kenney Cocktails," *Impact!* 2 (January 1944): 10–11; Rodman, *War of Their Own*, 45.
20. Kenney, *General Kenney Reports*, 94, 98, 106–7; Rodman, *War of Their Own*, 47–49.
21. Kenney, *General Kenney Reports*, 144, 154–55.
22. Kenney, *General Kenney Reports*, 161, 164–65, 173.
23. Griffith, *MacArthur's Airman*, 25–28; Wolk, "George C. Kenney," 129.
24. Kenney, *General Kenney Reports*, 21–22.
25. Kenney, *General Kenney Reports*, 63–64, 105, 117–18; J. Rickard (20 December 2007), 43rd Bombardment Group, http://www.historyofwar.org/air/units/USAAF/43rd_Bombardment_Group.html.
26. Kenney, *General Kenney Reports*, 64, 105, 117–18; McAulay, *Bismarck Sea*, 27–28; Birdsall, *Flying Buccaneers*, 34–36; Griffith, *MacArthur's Airman*, 82–83, 100–101; Richards, "Fortress on the Deck," 43–47.
27. Griffith, *MacArthur's Airman*, 97–98.
28. Griffith, *MacArthur's Airman*, 102–4.
29. Craven and Cate, *Army Air Forces*, 4:139–41; Kenney, *General Kenney Reports*, 199; McAulay, *Bismarck Sea*, 24–31.
30. Craven and Cate, *Army Air Forces*, 4:142.
31. Craven and Cate, *Army Air Forces*, 4:142–46; Kenney, *General Kenney Reports*, 202–5. McAulay, *Bismarck Sea*, 44–111, offers the most detailed version of the attack.
32. Craven and Cate, *Army Air Forces*, 4:145–46, quote 146.
33. Toll, *Conquering Tide*, 223–24; Kenney, *General Kenney Reports*, 209–13.
34. Kenney, *General Kenney Reports*, 126; Craven and Cate, *Army Air Forces*, 4:154.
35. Kenney, *General Kenney Reports*, 181–82; Craven and Cate, *Army Air Forces*, 4:154; Griffith, *MacArthur's Airman*, 100; Birdsall, *Log of the Liberators*, 50–52. The B-24 H became the first Liberator equipped with a nose turret, a feature that became standard on subsequent production models.
36. Kenney, *General Kenney Reports*, 214–15.
37. Kenney, *Saga of Pappy Gunn*, 60–63.
38. Gamble, *Black Sheep*, 233.
39. Early Pacific War strategy had been centered around a primarily defensive posture, though predicated on an absolute defense of Australia, New Zealand, the Hawaiian Islands, and Midway. See Miller, *Cartwheel*, 1–8.
40. Craven and Cate, *Army Air Forces*, 2:8; Rein, *North African Air Campaign*, 44–45.
41. Rein, *North African Air Campaign*, 48–64; Arnold, *Global Mission*, 379.
42. "They Keep 'em Flying in the Desert," *Stars and Stripes*, 26 November 1942; Wilson, *Earthquakers*, 35. Ernie Pyle joined a group of desert-bound scroungers, later preserving their efforts in "Digging and Grousing," an article republished in Nichols, *Ernie's War*, 97–99.
43. *Thunderbolt*, directed by Lt. Col. William Wyler and Capt. John Sturges (Carl Krueger Productions/US War Department, 1947), http://www.youtube.com/watch?v=Da_gbVd6nzM.

44. The pair went on to amass a distinguished record, with Benedict becoming squadron commander and Leaf his operations officer. By war's end, both earned the Distinguished Flying Cross with cluster, the Air Medal with cluster, the British Distinguished Flying Cross, and the French Croix de Guerre. Richard Thruelsen and Elliott Arnold, "Where's That Bomber? It Was Here Just a Minute Ago," *Saturday Evening Post*, 7 October 1944, 22–23, 106, 108.
45. McCarthy, *Battle for Italy*, 25.
46. Tannehill, *Daddy of Them All*, 11–15.
47. Greening, *Not As Briefed*, 52.
48. Fifty-Seventh Bomb Wing Association, *B-25 over the Mediterranean*, 23; Tannehill, *Daddy of Them All*, 18.
49. Wilson, *Earthquakers*, 95.
50. Images 3A23593-51711AC, 3A23596–51714AC, RG 342-FH.
51. Wilson, *Earthquakers*, 95.
52. Image 3A23596-51714AC, RG 342-FH.
53. Images 3A24292-3A24292, 3A23704-55943AC—both in RG 342-FH.
54. Tannehill, *Daddy of Them All*, 29.
55. Tannehill, *Daddy of Them All*, 29.
56. Muirhead, *Those Who Fall*, 6.
57. George Mahoney, personal correspondence with the author, March 2002.
58. Hahn, *My Perspective of WWII*; Wilson, *Earthquakers*, 29.
59. Muirhead, *Those Who Fall*, 6.
60. Harold Kempffer, "Life at the Venosa Airfield during World War II," *Pierced Steel Planking*, 25 July 2022, http://www.storiedelsud.altervista.org/Venosa%20PSP/PSP%20RED%20ENGLL.htm.
61. Image 3A23597-51716AC, RG 342-FH.
62. Image FH-3A23600-52841AC, RG 342-FH.
63. Images 3A23607-53847AC, 3A26026-55098AC, 3A24296-3A24296—all in RG 342-FH.
64. Images 3A29065-76053AC, 3A23629-76129A—both in RG 342-FH.
65. Wilson, *Earthquakers*, 101.
66. Image 3A27079-26306AC, RG 342-FH.
67. Image 3A24138-58475AC, RG 342-FH.
68. *Thunderbolt* (War Department, 1947).
69. Image 3A24314-52392AC, RG 342-FH; "Boat Built of P-38's Tanks," *Popular Mechanics* 84 (October 1945): 33. Sergeant D. L. Davidson and Cpl. Will Fielding built a similar catamaran while serving with the 23rd Bomb Squadron, 5th Bomb Group, 13th Air Force, on Los Negros, one of the Admiralty Islands, using half-inch pipe to connect two drop tanks, powering their craft with a four-cycle one-cylinder gasoline engine. Image 3A31375–51728AC, RG 342-FH.
70. *Thunderbolt* (War Department, 1947).
71. Parton, *Air Force Spoken Here*, 232–34.
72. Nalty, *Winged Shield, Winged Sword*, 2:187–90.
73. LeMay, *Mission with LeMay*, 213, 215.
74. LeMay, *Mission with LeMay*, 228–31.
75. LeMay, *Mission with LeMay*, 233–34, 239; Parton, *Air Force Spoken Here*, 235–37; Copp, *Forged in Fire*, 313–15.

76. LeMay, *Mission with LeMay*, 237–40.
77. Freeman, *Mighty Eighth War Diary*, 26.
78. LeMay, *Mission with LeMay*, 243. Freeman, in *Mighty Eighth War Diary*, notes that of fifty-eight planes dispatched on 23 November, thirty-six were effective, with four lost across the four B-17 bomb groups engaged.
79. Craven and Cate, *Army Air Forces*, 2:250.
80. LeMay, *Mission with LeMay*, 244–45.
81. LeMay, *Mission with LeMay*, 243.
82. Craven and Cate, *Army Air Forces*, 2:264
83. Parton, *Air Force Spoken Here*, 237; Craven and Cate, *Army Air Forces*, 2:266.
84. Freeman, *Mighty Eighth War Diary*, 19, 22; Bove, *First over Germany*, 6; Havelarr, *Ragged Irregulars*, 13.
85. Bove, *First over Germany*, 16.
86. Bove, *First over Germany*, 15; "From This . . . to This," *306th Echoes* 26 (July 2001): 5, https://www.306bg.us/Echoes%20files/097-01jul.pdf; Strong, *First over Germany*, 53; Copp, *Forged in Fire*, 326.
87. Havelarr, *Ragged Irregulars*, 27, 29–31, 36, 65. A B-17 from the 324th Bomb Squadron, *Connecticut Yankee*, had twin .50-caliber guns protruding through two individual ball mounts, which represented a different configuration from seemingly typical twin guns taken from the tail and mounted in the nose. James Cullen, a pilot in the 323rd Bomb Squadron, 91st Bomb Group, commented in his memoirs that the additional .50 guns mounted in the nose "were a deadly presence but didn't work a damn." Cullen, *By the Numbers*, 55.
88. Harry Gobrecht, "303rd Designs, Installs First B-17 Nose Cone Guns in 8th Air Force," *Hell's Angels Newsletter* 24 (May 2001): 12, http://www.303rdbg.com/hanl/2001-05.pdf. The 303rd's installation date of late April/early May 1942 comes after 305th ground crewmen James Green and Ben Marcilonis received their Legion of Merit awards for "designing and fabricating, during the months of December 1942, a new type of machinegun mount." The inconsistent dating makes the 303rd's claim of being first to offer this innovation somewhat questionable.
89. "Notes from the Air Force," *Stars and Stripes*, 17 May 1944.
90. Smith, *Screaming Eagle*, 153.
91. Freeman, *Mighty Eighth War Diary*, 47, 87.
92. "From This . . . to This," 5.
93. Holley, *Aircraft Gun Turrets*, 225–29.
94. Freeman, *Mighty Eighth War Diary*, 25. By Spring 1943, more than forty different modifications with respect to armor and armament were being made to Liberators arriving from the United States. Astor, *Mighty Eighth*, 59. Similar modifications were made to B-25s operating in North Africa, with armor plate being installed behind the pilot's seat and the instrument panel. Image 3A28580-27851AC, RG 342-FH. See also Office of the Assistant Chief of Staff, Intelligence, "Evolution of a B-25," *Impact!* 3 (March 1944): 34.
95. Astor, *Mighty Eighth*, 184.
96. Smith, *Screaming Eagle*, 123.
97. Astor, *Mighty Eighth*, 59.
98. Truluck, *And So It Was*, 72–73.

99. Ibid., 74. Astor, *Mighty Eighth*, 175–77.
100. Truluck, *And So It Was*, 75; Astor, *Mighty Eighth*, 175–77.
101. Truluck, *And So It Was*, 75.
102. LeMay, *Mission with LeMay*, 218–20.
103. Miller, *Masters of the Air*, 168; Havelaar, *Ragged Irregulars*, 87.
104. Jones, *Some Personal Histories*, 22.
105. Muirhead, *Those Who Fall*, 37.
106. Havelaar, *Ragged Irregulars*, 87–89.
107. Image 3A13362-27719AC, RG 342-FH.
108. Bendiner, *Fall of Fortresses*, 108.
109. Astor, *Mighty Eighth*, 62.
110. Image 342-FH 3A23610–54178AC, RG 342-FH.
111. "Jeep Is Welding Shop on Wheels for Battle Line," *Popular Mechanics* 83 (May 1945): 88.
112. Image 3A13385-50509AC, RG 342-FH; Henry Heuberger, "Home-Made Gadget Keeps 'em Flying," *Stars and Stripes*, 3 May 1943, 3.
113. Astor, *Mighty Eighth*, 62.
114. Images 3A23803-72212AC; 3A23616-54185AC; 3A23805-72211AC; 3A26406-59218AC—all in RG 342-FH. Alton's efforts were also featured in "On the Line," *Air Force: The Official Journal of the U.S. Army Air Forces* 28 (December 1945): 47.
115. Bryce Burke, "They Build Radios from Scrap," *Stars and Stripes*, 19 February 1943.
116. Image 3A23611-54179AC, RG 342-FH.
117. Image 3A23613-54181AC, RG 342-FH.
118. Image 3A23614-54183AC, RG 342-FH.
119. Images 3A13526-81277AC; 342-FH 3A27903-25828AC—both in RG 342-FH.
120. Burke, "They Build Radios."
121. "GI's Invention Ends Shortage," *Stars and Stripes*, 28 December 1944, 4.
122. Image 3A15890-73184AC, RG 342-FH.
123. Image 3A15889-73183AC, RG 342-FH.
124. Images 3A13489-A57574AC; 3A13488-5757AC—both in RG 342-FH.
125. Image 3A13521-60169AC, RG 342-FH.
126. Image 3A17544-56227AC, RG 342-FH.
127. Images 3A23622-59455AC; 3A 23802-72210AC—both in RG 342-FH.
128. Image 3A28947-52071AC, RG 342-FH.
129. Images 3A23577-72213AC; 3A15888-73182AC; 3A23623-72207AC; 3A23602-522885AC; 3A23604-B52885AC; 3A23506-C52885AC—all in RG 342-FH.
130. "Notes from the Air Force," *Stars and Stripes*, 20 September 1944.
131. Image 3A23612-54180AC, RG 342-FH.
132. Image 3A12854-66125AC, RG 342-FH.
133. Images 3A35897-81247AC; 3A02007-3A02007; 3A235583-3A23583—all in RG 342-FH. See also "Clever, These Yankees," *Popular Mechanics* 84 (March 1945): 57.
134. LeMay, *Mission with LeMay*, 213–14.
135. LeMay, *Mission with LeMay*, 321–26; 347–55.
136. Steinbeck, *Bombs Away*, 19.
137. General Henry H. Arnold, "First Report of the Commanding General of the Army Air Forces to the Secretary of War," 4 January 1944, in Millis, *War Reports*, 306.
138. Millis, *War Reports*, 305.

Chapter 5

Epigraph: Eisenhower, *Crusade in Europe*, 314.

1. Robert Miller, quoted in Ambrose, *D-Day*, 125. John McManus related the same episode a bit differently in *The Americans at D-Day*. According to McManus, Pvt. Joseph Bria of H Company recalled Goode holding up the phonebook-size invasion order, telling his men, 'Study it; learn it," before dropping it on the floor and telling them, "All the complicated facts amount to one thing: Get off the boat; keep moving, no matter what. Get off the beach no matter how confused the situation," 101.
2. Robinson and Hamilton, *Move Out, Verify*, 19.
3. Mansoor, *G.I. Offensive in Europe*, 133–40.
4. "D-Day statement to soldiers, sailors, and airmen of the Allied Expeditionary Force, 6/44," Collection DDE-EPRE: Eisenhower, Dwight D.: Papers, Pre-Presidential, 1916–1952; Dwight D. Eisenhower Presidential Library, Abilene, KS (hereafter cited as DDEPL); Eisenhower, *Crusade in Europe*, 453.
5. Ambrose, *Citizen Soldiers*, 19, 21.
6. Harrison, *Cross-Channel Attack*, 158.
7. Eisenhower, *Crusade in Europe*, 203.
8. First U.S. Army Operations Plan Neptune, 25 February 1944, https://cgsc.contentdm.oclc.org/digital/collection/p4013coll8/id/3027, 6.
9. Bradley, *Soldier's Story*, 236.
10. Bradley, *Soldier's Story*, 236; Harrison, *Cross-Channel Attack*, 162–63.
11. Gavin, *On to Berlin*, 3, 100. The division also included the 325th Glider Infantry Regiment, which had fought in Italy but had not come in by glider, but by landing craft.
12. Eisenhower, *Crusade in Europe*, 227.
13. "Annex No. 1, Organization of the Assault and Follow Up," First U.S. Army Operations Plan Neptune, 25 February 1944, https://cgsc.contentdm.oclc.org/digital/collection/p4013coll8/id/3027, i, WWII-Skelton.
14. Roy E. Creek, "Invasion," *Infantry School Quarterly* 44 (January 1955): 8; McManus, *Americans at D-Day*, 62.
15. C. B. McCoid, quoted in Astor, *June 6, 1944*, 143.
16. Compton, *Call of Duty*, 12. Guth repeated this modification during the Battle of the Bulge, using company armorer's tools to field-modify a second M-1 carbine, with metal scavenged from a crashed English bomber in the area. De Trez, *Way We Were*, 64. Maj. Richard "Dick" Winters of Easy Company, 506th Parachute Infantry, eventually acquired one of Forrest Guth's modified M-1 carbines that he carried in both World War II and the Korean War. See Ambrose, *Band of Brothers*, 286.
17. Gavin, *On to Berlin*, 102.
18. Compton, *Call of Duty*, 12.
19. Although most paratrooper uniforms were turned in after the Normandy campaign upon issue of the M1943 jacket and trousers, some paratroopers retained their originally issued items, some of which have found their way to museums. One such example is the uniform worn by Stanley Medaj of Headquarters Company, 502nd Parachute Infantry Regiment, 101st Airborne Division. Wounded in the invasion, he was evacuated and sent back to England. His M1942 uniform, which has these

modifications, is part of the collection of the Gettysburg Museum of History. See "Blood-Stained M-42 Reinforced Paratrooper Uniform Worn on D-Day by Stanley Medaj, 502 PIR, 101st Airborne," https://www.gettysburgmuseumofhistory.com/portfolio/8470/; Although John Craig Andrews, "U.S. Airborne Troops, Normandy," *Military Collector and Historian* 23 (Fall 1971): 84–86, does not mention the use of rigger-modified uniforms, they receive mention in a subsequent article: John Craig Andrews, "Pathfinders, 82d and 101st Airborne Divisions, Normandy, 1944," *Military Collector and Historian* 61 (Summer 2009): 122–23.

20. De Trez, *Way We Were*, 32–33; Forrest Guth, personal communication with the author, 26 July 2003. Uniform modifications continued throughout the course of the European campaign. To eliminate the need to carry a map case that would identify him as an officer, Maj. Richard Winters added a zippered map pocket to the tail of his M1943 jacket during the Battle of the Bulge. This jacket is currently held by the December 44 Historical Museum, La Gleize, Belgium, http://www.december44.com/en/history_battle_of_the_bulgela_gleize.htm.
21. "Annex No. 13: Ordnance Section," in United States Army, *First United States Army Report, October 1943–August 1944*, 6:91; Mayo, *Ordnance Department*, 228; Zaloga, *Armored Attack, 1944*, 103.
22. *Combat Lessons*, 2:33; "Annex No. 13," United States Army, *First United States Army Report*, 6:91; Mayo, *Ordnance Department*, 228.
23. Cooper, *Death Traps*, 25.
24. Armored School, *Tank Destroyer Battalions*, 38.
25. Zaloga, *Armored Attack, 1944*, 40.
26. Balkoski, *Utah Beach*, 142–44; Astor, *June 6, 1944*, 158–61; Ambrose, *D-Day*, 219–20; War Department, Historical Division, *Utah Beach to Cherbourg*, 15.
27. O'Donnell, *Dog Company*, 43; Martin K. A. Morgan, "The Men and Guns of Pointe Du Hoc," *American Rifleman*, 17 May 2019, https://americanrifleman.org/content/the-men-and-guns-of-pointe-du-hoc/; "DUKW Extension Ladder," Nevington War Museum, https://nevingtonwarmuseum.com/dukw-extension-ladder.html.
28. War Department, Historical Division, *Omaha Beachhead*, 88; O'Donnell, *Dog Company*, 64, 66; Ambrose, *D-Day*, 407.
29. Historical Section, European Theater of Operations, "506th Parachute Infantry Regiment in Normandy Drop," Regimental Study No. 3, https://cgsc.contentdm.oclc.org/digital/collection/p4013coll8/id/4722/rec/1, 4, WWII-Skelton; Atkinson, *Guns at Last Light*, 47.
30. Ambrose, *D-Day*, 278–79; McManus, *Americans at D-Day*, 272–74.
31. War Department, *Omaha Beach*, 39–40; Harrison, *Cross-Channel Attack*, 309–17.
32. Balkoski, *Omaha Beach*, 191–213.
33. Harrison, *Cross-Channel Attack*, 336.
34. Harrison, *Cross-Channel Attack*, 351.
35. Ruppenthal, *Logistical Support*, 2:46.
36. Harrison, *Cross-Channel Attack*, 422–23; John J. Manning, "Normandy's 'Artificial Harbors,'" *Military Engineer* 36 (December 1944): 389–94.
37. Hartcup, *Code Name Mulberry*, 15–27, 73.
38. Hartcup, *Code Name Mulberry*, 77.
39. Hartcup, *Code Name Mulberry*, 64–66.
40. Hartcup, *Code Name Mulberry*, 15–27.

41. Symonds, *Neptune*, 322.
42. Hartcup, *Code Name Mulberry*, 119; Symonds, *Neptune*, 322–23.
43. Symonds, *Neptune*, 323.
44. Hartcup, *Code Name Mulberry*, 125–29; Blumenson, *Breakout and Pursuit*, 6; Eisenhower, *Crusade in Europe*, 261.
45. Eisenhower, *Crusade in Europe*, 261.
46. Waddell, *United States Army Logistics*, 53–58.
47. Harrison, *Cross-Channel Attack*, 422–26.
48. Ruppenthal, *Logistical Support*, 2:51.
49. Thomson and Mayo, *Ordnance Department*, 448–49.
50. "Annex 8 to Operations Plan Neptune: Ordnance Plan," in Headquarters, U.S. First Army, *Operations Plan Neptune*, 25 February 1944, https://cgsc.contentdm.oclc.org/digital/collection/p4013coll8/id/3026/, 9, WWII-Skelton.
51. "Annex No. 13," United States Army, *First United States Army Report*, 6:61.
52. Pyle, *Brave Men*, 418, 422, 424–25, 429.
53. Cooper, *Death Traps*, 33, 38.
54. Robinson and Hamilton, *Move Out, Verify*, 36; 743rd Tank Battalion, "S-3 Journal, History, Company A, June 1944," *Action against enemy, reports after/after action, 1 Oct [19]44*, https://cgsc.contentdm.oclc.org/digital/collection/p4013coll8/id/3509, WWII-Skelton. The 752nd Tank Battalion had a similar vehicle, which they christened "Big Weldon"; see Zaloga, *US Armored Funnies*, 14.
55. "Annex No. 13," United States Army, *First United States Army Report*, 6:63.
56. `"Memorandum No. 1: Armored Notes," 19 June 1944, 2: C-110, in Observers Reports–USAHEC; Doubler, *Closing with the Enemy*, 44–46.
57. Wilson, *If You Survive*, 12–13; Cawthorn, *Other Clay*, 75–76.
58. Headquarters, European Theater of Operations, US Army (HQETOUSA), Combat Lessons Branch, G-3, "Battle Experiences No. 1, 12 August 1944," in Battle Experiences July 12, 1944–May 5, 1945, https://cgsc.contentdm.oclc.org/digital/collection/p4013coll8/id/4050/rec/1, WWII-Skelton (hereafter cited as Battle Experiences).
59. "Memorandum No. 1: Armored Notes," 19 June 1944, Observers Reports–USAHEC, 1:1.
60. Cawthorn, *Other Clay*, 76.
61. "Memorandum No. 1: Armored Notes," 19 June 1944, Observers Reports–USAHEC, 1:1; HQETOUSA, Combat Lessons Branch, G-3, "Battle Experiences No. 3, 13 July 1944," Battle Experiences.
62. HQETOUSA, Combat Lessons Branch, G-3, "Battle Experiences No. 8, 27 July 1944," Battle Experiences; Robinson and Hamilton, *Move Out, Verify*, 56, 58.
63. HQETOUSA, Combat Lessons Branch, G-3, "Immediate Report No. 27, 10 August 1944," Immediate Reports of Combat Operations, Reports 130 to 1, https://cgsc.contentdm.oclc.org/digital/collection/p4013coll8/id/4651/rec/1, WWII-Skelton (hereafter cited as Immediate Reports).
64. HQETOUSA, Combat Lessons Branch, G-3, "Battle Experiences No. 1, 12 July 1944," Battle Experiences; Doubler, *Closing with the Enemy*, 40–45.
65. "Annex No. 13," United States Army, *First United States Army Report*, 6:91; HQETOUSA, Combat Lessons Branch, G-3, "Battle Experiences No. 16, 10 August 1944," Battle Experiences; "Notes on Interviews with Various Infantry Commanders in Normandy, France, 6 June to 8 July 1944," Observers Reports–USAHEC, 2:

C-157; HQETOUSA, Combat Lessons Branch, G-3, "Immediate Report No. 19," 1, Immediate Reports.

66. "Use of Dozer Tanks and Landing of Tanks in Amphibious Operations," Observers Reports–USAHEC, 2: C-201. By July, First Army had requested an additional 278 dozer blades.
67. 709th Tank Battalion, *After Action Report, 26 August 1944*, https://cgsc.contentdm.oclc.org/digital/collection/p4013coll8/id/3601/, WWII-Skelton.
68. HQETOUSA, Combat Lessons Branch, G-3, "Battle Experiences No. 1, 12 July 1944," Battle Experiences; James D. Sams, "Ordnance Improvisation in the Combat Zone," *Military Review* 28 (May 1948): 33. The "Armored Special Equipment" report of the General Board, United States Forces European Theater, specified that in First Army, "an attempt was made to provide dozer blades on the basis of six per tank battalion (separate or with armored division), plus four additional per armored division. The four D-Day Tank Battalions landed on the Continent with four tank dozers each." See The General Board, United States Forces, European Theater, "Armored Special Equipment," Study No. 52, November 1945, 14, https://carlcgsc.libguides.com/ld.php?content_id=52568406.
69. HQETOUSA, Combat Lessons Branch, G-3, "Battle Experiences No. 9, 28 July 1944," Battle Experiences.
70. "Employment of Tanks and Infantry," Observers Reports–USAHEC, 2: C-129.
71. "Employment of Tanks and Infantry," Observers Reports–USAHEC, 2: C-129.
72. HQETOUSA, Combat Lessons Branch, G-3, "Battle Experiences No. 18, 12 August 1944," Battle Experiences.
73. HQETOUSA, Combat Lessons Branch, G-3, "Immediate Report No. 34, 25 August 1944," Immediate Reports.
74. Charles H. Coates, "Army Ground Forces Observer Report No. 191: Notes on Interviews of Various Commanders in Normandy, 5–10 August, 1944," https://cgsc.contentdm.oclc.org/digital/collection/p4013coll8/id/4453/rec/1, WWII-Skelton.
75. HQETOUSA, Combat Lessons Branch, G-3, "Immediate Report No. 30, 15 August 1944," Immediate Reports; Committee 9, Officers Advanced Course, *Super Sixth in Exploitation (6th Armored Division, Normandy to Brest) Operation Cobra* (Fort Knox, KY: The Armored School, 1949).
76. HQETOUSA, Combat Lessons Branch, G-3, "Immediate Report No. 30, 15 August 1944," 1, Immediate Reports.
77. HQETOUSA, Combat Lessons Branch, G-3, "Immediate Report No. 37, 25 August 1944," Immediate Reports; Committee 13, Officers Advanced Course, *Armor in the Exploitation: The Fourth Armored Division across France to the Moselle River* (Fort Knox, KY: The Armored School, 1949), xii, xiii; After Action Report, 735th Tank Battalion, 1 August 1944, https://cgsc.contentdm.oclc.org/digital/collection/p4013coll8/id/3596, WWII-Skelton; After Action Report, 741st Tank Battalion, 7 August 1944, https://cgsc.contentdm.oclc.org/digital/collection/p4013coll8/id/3512/rec/2, WWII-Skelton; Unit History, 746th Tank Battalion, July 1945, https://cgsc.contentdm.oclc.org/digital/collection/p4013coll8/id/3498/rec/2, WWII-Skelton; Zaloga, *Armored Thunderbolt*, 156–61.
78. Greenwood, *Normandy to Victory*, 50–51; Mayo, *Ordnance Department*, 253–55; Blumenson, *Breakout and Pursuit*, 205–7; Training Branch, G-3, Twelfth Army Group, *Battle Experiences*, No. 34, 31 August 1944, 1, https://cgsc.contentdm.oclc

.org/digital/collection/p4013coll8/id/5681/rec/2, WWII-Skelton; "Annex No. 13," United States Army, *First United States Army Report*, 6:91–92. Accounts of this test are legion, though there is some disagreement as to who was actually there. General Bradley mentions General Gerow, though not Hodges, as present at the test in *Soldier's Story*, 341–42; while Hodges's aides, quoted in Greenwood, *Normandy to Victory* (50–51), specifically mention Hodges, Bradley, and Medaris. Lt. Belton Cooper of the 3rd Armored Division claimed to have seen Patton at the test in *Death Traps* (44–47), though that is doubtful, for whereas Patton claims 3rd Armored invented the "hedge spade," the often self-aggrandizing general makes no mention of a test of the device in his *War as I Knew It* (cf. 96). Mark J. Reardon similarly makes no mention of Patton's presence in "Conquering the Hedgerows," in Hoffman, *History of Innovation*, 95–101.

79. Unit History, 746th Tank Battalion, July 1944, https://cgsc.contentdm.oclc.org/digital/collection/p4013coll8/id/3788/, 20–21, WWII-Skelton; "Annex No. 13," United States Army, *First United States Army Report*, 6:91–92; Mayo, *Ordnance Department*, 254–55; Bradley, *Soldier's Story*, 342–43.
80. Cooper, *Death Traps*, 46–47.
81. Second Armored Division, "Extracts from Operational History: Phase 1 Operation 'Cobra,' 26 July–31 July 1944," https://cgsc.contentdm.oclc.org/digital/collection/p4013coll8/id/4807/rec/2, pt. I, 1–7, WWII-Skelton; Bradley, *Soldier's Story*, 346–49; John J. Sullivan, "The Botched Air Support of Operation Cobra," *Parameters* 18 (March 1988): 103–5; Craven and Cate, *Army Air Forces*, 3:235–35.
82. Second Armored Division, "Extracts from Operational History," pt. III, 1, WWII Skelton; Bradley, *Soldier's Story*, 345–46; Eisenhower, *Crusade in Europe*, 272–74; Blumenson, *Breakout and Pursuit*, 255; Carafano, *After D-Day*, 263.
83. The General Board, United States Forces, European Theater, "Armored Special Equipment."
84. Bradley, *Soldier's Story*, 342.
85. Weigley, *Eisenhower's Lieutenants*, 149, 166. Richard Overy, in *Why the Allies Won*, noted that the rhinoceros "transformed the mobility of American armoured formations" (171). Russell A. Hart, in *Clash of Arms*, professed that the employment of the rhinoceros hedgecutter in late July "helped restore armored mobility" (281). Victor Davis Hanson offers a similar assessment when he lauds the "rhinos that ploughed through the hedgerows," in *Second World Wars*, 375.
86. Doubler, *Closing with the Enemy*, 50.
87. Mansoor, *G.I. Offensive in Europe*, 164–67.
88. Carafano, *After D-Day*, 3, 213, 222.
89. Carafano, *G.I. Ingenuity*, 125–26, 137–38.
90. This is comparable to the assessment offered in Zaloga, *Armored Thunderbolt*, 161.
91. Eisenhower, *Crusade in Europe*, 269.
92. "Annex No. 9: Armored Section," in United States Army, *First United States Army Report, October 1943–August 1944*, 7 August 1944, 5:199–201; 741st Tank Battalion, After Action Report," https://cgsc.contentdm.oclc.org/digital/collection/p4013coll8/id/3512/, 3–4, WWII-Skelton; Unit History, 746th Tank Battalion, July 1944, https://cgsc.contentdm.oclc.org/digital/collection/p4013coll8/id/3496/rec/431, 35, WWII-Skelton. The 747th Tank Battalion mentioned both the "salad forks" and the "greendozer," in its After Action Report, 4 August 1944, https://cgsc

.contentdm.oclc.org/digital/collection/p4013coll8/id/3838/rec/4, WWII-Skelton; 759th Light Tank Battalion, After Action Report, 20 September 1944, https://cgsc.contentdm.oclc.org/digital/collection/p4013coll8/id/3930/rec/1, WWII-Skelton.

93. Blumenson, *Breakout and Pursuit*, 332.
94. 1st Lt. John D. Allbright, "Action against the Enemy Report," in After Action Report, 709th Tank Battalion, July [19]44 thru April [19]45, https://cgsc.contentdm.oclc.org/digital/collection/p4013coll8/id/3601/, 47, WWII-Skelton.
95. Elwood R. Quesada, interview by Dr. Maclyn Burg, 17 October 1973, interview OH #476, DDEPL.
96. Since their arrival in-theater in December 1943, the additional external fuel tanks for the P-51s extended their range considerably, such that by March, they could escort bombers to an unprecedented range of 850 miles. Craven and Cate, *Army Air Forces*, 3:49. General Quesada further elaborated on this division of air assets in a 1983 interview contained in Kohn, *Air*, 57; as the general noted, "The P-51s were assigned to the Eighth Air Force's newly arriving groups and more P-47s to us" (48). See also Army Air Forces Evaluation Board, *Third Phase Tactical Air Operations*, 307, 309.
97. George, *Ninth Air Force*, 53.
98. Quesada interview, Burg, 138, DDEPL; George, *Ninth Air Force*, 60, 98.
99. Turner, *Big Friend, Little Friend*, 108–9.
100. Commanding General, U.S. Army Air Forces, *Technical Order, No. 01-60JD-1*, 10, 51, 53.
101. Turner, *Big Friend, Little Friend*, 119.
102. Quesada interview, Burg, 142, DDEPL.
103. Eisenhower, *Crusade in Europe*, 269.
104. In a 1975 interview, Quesada admitted that although Eisenhower "enjoyed the hell out of it (the flight)," if enemy fire damaged his aircraft to the point where his passenger had to bail out, the tight fit in the improvised rear seat would require that Quesada invert the aircraft and "dump [Eisenhower] out." Quesada interview, Burg, 143–47, DDEPL; Turner, *Big Friend, Little Friend*, 123.
105. Bradley, *Soldier's Story*, 325. Thomas A. Hughes, in *Overlord*, 173–74, recounted this episode, but like Bradley and Eisenhower, he made no mention of the field-modified P-51 as a unique platform. See also photographs FRE 401 and FRE 425, Roger Freeman Collection, Imperial War Museums, https://iwm.org.uk/collections/item/object/205360467 and https://iwm.org.uk/collections/item/object/205360491; and UPL 52078, J Cook Archives and Photo Collection, Imperial War Museums, https://www.americanairmuseum.com/archive/media/media-52078jpeg. The plane initially named "Short-Snorter" was renamed "The Stars Look Down," after Quesada and Eisenhower made their flight.
106. Quesada interview, Burg, 178–79, DDEPL.
107. Bradley, *Soldier's Story*, 337–38; Bechtold, "Unbeatable Combination," 15; Hughes, *Overlord*, 183–84. In a 1976 interview, Quesada misidentifies the unit as the 9th Armored Division, which did not arrive in France until September 1944. Quesada interview, Burg, 180–83, DDEPL.
108. George, *Ninth Air Force*, 129–30.
109. Zimmerman's exploits were reported in numerous locations. They are contained in Twelfth Army Group, *Battle Experiences*, No. 38 "Air Support of Armored

Columns," 3 September 1944, https://cgsc.contentdm.oclc.org/digital/collection/p4013coll8/id/5681/rec/2, WWII-Skelton, with a more extensive version contained in *Combat Lessons*, 5:27–29.

110. Army Air Forces Evaluation Board, *Third Phase Tactical Air Operations*, 309; "Rocket Installations under Wing of a Republic P-47 of the 353rd Fighter Group, England, May 1944," Image 3A0639-69608AC, RG 342-FH.
111. Isaac D. White, "A Report on United States vs. German Equipment," Headquarters, Second Armored Division, 27 March 1945, Box 1, Isaac D. White Papers, 115, DDEPL.
112. "Ground-Air Teamwork in France," *Military Review* 25 (May 1945): 43–46; Blumenson, *Breakout and Pursuit*, 345.
113. HQETOUSA, Combat Lessons Branch, G-3, "Immediate Report No. 38, Air Ground Support of Ground Force Operations, 25 August 1945," Immediate Reports.
114. Blumenson, *Breakout and Pursuit*, 700.
115. Blumenson, *Breakout and Pursuit*, 689.
116. Caddick-Adams, *Snow and Steel*, 83–84.
117. Eisenhower, *Crusade in Europe*, 294.

Chapter 6

Epigraph: Kinney, *Wake Island Pilot*, 97.
Volta Torrey, "Yankee Ingenuity Licks Prison-Camp Hardships," *Popular Science* 147 (July 1945), 65.

1. Dr. Charles Stenger, a former POW in the European theater, produced a series of annual reports and updates for the Veterans Administration, published between 1977 and 2003. See U.S. Department of Veterans Affairs, Office of the Assistant Secretary for Policy and Planning, *American Prisoners of War (POWs) and Missing in Action (MIAs)*, April 2006, https://www.va.gov/vetdata/docs/specialreports/powcy054-12-06jsmwrfinal2.doc (download).
2. International Committee of the Red Cross, "Convention Relative to the Treatment of Prisoners of War, Geneva, 27 July 1929," https://ihl-databases.icrc.org/en/ihl-treaties/gc-pow-1929; Springer, *America's Captives*, 145–46; American National Red Cross, "Rights of Prisoners of War" *Prisoners of War Bulletin* 1 (June 1943): 2.
3. American National Red Cross, "Rights of Prisoners of War," 2–3.
4. POWs used the slang term "kriegie" as a short form of the German word *Kriegsgefangenen*, meaning "prisoner of war." A standard POW parcel prepared by the Red Cross in July 1943 included the following: 8 oz biscuits, 8 oz cheese, two 4 oz chocolate bars, four packs of cigarettes (20 per pack), 4 oz coffee concentrate, 12 oz corned beef, 15 oz dried fruit, 6 oz liver paste, 1 lb. powdered milk, 1 lb. oleomargarine, 4 oz orange concentrate, 12 oz pork luncheon meat, 8 oz salmon, two 2 oz bars of soap, 8 oz sugar. American National Red Cross, "Rights of Prisoners of War," 8–9.
5. Waterford, *Prisoners of the Japanese*, 41–42.
6. American National Red Cross, "Rights of Prisoners of War," *Prisoners of War Bulletin* 1 (June 1943): 8–9.
7. American National Red Cross, "Letters from Prisoners of War and Civilian Internees," *Prisoners of War Bulletin* 1 (July 1943): 10.
8. Sage, *Sage*, 90; Halmos, *Wrong Side*, 143.

9. Halmos, *Wrong Side*, 24, 143.
10. Torrey, "Yankee Ingenuity," 65.
11. Greening and Spinelli, *Yankee Kriegies*, 8.
12. Greening and Spinelli, *Yankee Kriegies*, 5.
13. Sage, *Sage*, 131–33. Sage served as at least part of the inspiration for Steve McQueen's character "Cooler King" Capt. Virgil Hilts in the 1963 film *The Great Escape*. Albert P. Clark, the senior ranking officer in Stalag Luft III and future superintendent of the United States Air Force Academy, recalled Sage as a blithe spirit; see Clark, *33 Months*, 75–76. Harold Spire's performance as Paul Revere was apparently so popular that he reprised the role the following year, joined by Lt. Ellis Porter and Capt. Alexander Kisselburgh, who played the part of Revere's horse, as reported in American National Red Cross, "Extracts from Letters," *Prisoners of War Bulletin* 2 (February 1945): 8.
14. Beattie, *Diary of a Kriegie*, 248–49.
15. Sage, *Sage*, 284–85.
16. Beattie, *Diary of a Kriegie*; 248–49; Greening and Spinelli, *Yankee Kriegies*, 7; Clark, *33 Months*, 163.
17. "Radio Made Out of a Razor Blade," *Popular Mechanics* 82 (October 1944): 11.
18. Sage, *Sage*, 211.
19. Lichtenfeld, *Kriegie 312330*, 24, 29.
20. Clark, *33 Months*, 110; Greening, *Not As Briefed*, 223. The wide variety of camp projects, hobbies, and activities are recounted in Greening and Spinelli, *Yankee Kriegies*, a YMCA publication that accompanied a US Army Air Forces POW exposition emphasizing Yankee ingenuity that first opened in New York on 1 October 1945.
21. In *Yankee Kriegies*, Greening recounted that in his camp alone, prisoners attempted to dig more than a hundred tunnels before they were discovered by the Germans, destroyed, and their locations marked with wooden crosses to ensure that the site would not be reused (13). Wright Lee, who was shot down in March 1944 and sent to Stalag I, reported that at least one-third of the men in his camp attempted to tunnel out. Lee, *Not As Briefed*, 157. See also Joseph Fulling Fishman, "Yankee Ingenuity in Prison Camps," *American Mercury* 62 (March 1946): 300–305.
22. "Harry" was the last of a trio of tunnels (the British called the other two "Tom" and "Dick") initiated as part of a large-scale, coordinated attempt in which British prisoners, led by Roger Bushell, hoped to break two hundred men out at once. Clark, *33 Months*, 72–73.
23. Brickhill, *Great Escape*. For other accounts of escape efforts in Stalag Luft III, see Williams, *Wooden Horse*, Durand, *Stalag Luft II*, Burgess, *Longest Tunnel*, and Carroll, *Great Escape*.
24. Clark, *33 Months*, 1, 17–37, 70.
25. Clark, *33 Months*, 60, 62–64.
26. Sage, *Sage*, 209–10.
27. Clark, *33 Months*, 64.
28. Burgess, *Longest Tunnel*, 36–37.
29. Sage, *Sage*, 210.
30. Fishman, "Yankee Ingenuity," 301–2; Greening and Spinelli, *Yankee Kriegies*, 14.
31. Lee, *Not As Briefed*, 146.
32. Kerr, *Surrender and Survival*, 30; Spector, *Eagle against the Sun*, 398.

33. Spector, *Eagle against the Sun*, 399; Hillenbrand, *Unbroken*, 267.
34. Kinney, *Wake Island Pilot*, 120.
35. Americans in the Philippines adopted the word when they "*quanned* up some coffee," or "*quanned* a papaya off a tree." The word remained dear to the defenders of Bataan and Corregidor: "The Quan" is the newsletter of the American Defenders of Bataan and Corregidor Memorial society, https://www.adbcmemorialsociety.org/Quan. For additional examples, see LaForte, Marcello, and Himmel, *Will to Live*, 150–67; and Caraccilo, *Surviving Bataan and Beyond*, 158.
36. Kinney, *Wake Island Pilot*, 121.
37. Nordin, *Next to Nothing*, 109.
38. Kinney, *Wake Island Pilot*, 124.
39. Louis Read, quoted in LaForte, Marcello, and Himmel, *Will to Live*, 155.
40. Kinney, *Wake Island Pilot*, 123–24.
41. Braly, *Long Way Home*, 38.
42. Braly, *Long Way Home*, 51.
43. Braly, *Long Way Home*, 51.
44. Kinney, *Wake Island Pilot*, 124–26.
45. Boyle, *Yanks Don't Cry*, 115.
46. Holmes, *Unjust Enrichment*, 27.
47. Boyle, *Yanks Don't Cry*, 115.
48. Poncio and Young, *Girocho*, 70–72.
49. Tenney, *My Hitch in Hell*, 94–95, 100, 110.
50. Braly, *Long Way Home*, 187.
51. Iannarelli and Iannarelli, *Eighty Thieves*, 39.
52. Nordin, *Next to Nothing*, 174.
53. Nordin, *Next to Nothing*, 174.
54. Tenney, *My Hitch in Hell*.
55. Alton C. Holbrook, quoted in LaForte, Marcello, and Himmel, *Will to Live*, 74.
56. William A. Visage, quoted in LaForte, Marcello, and Himmel, *Will to Live*, 77.
57. Caraccilo, *Surviving Bataan and Beyond*, 155, 162.
58. Kinney, *Wake Island Pilot*, 129–31.
59. Kirk kept the photographs secret for nearly forty years, until publishing them in *The Secret Camera*, 194–202, 258.
60. Greening, *Not As Briefed*, 229–30.

Chapter 7

Epigraph: Patton, *War as I Knew It*, 366.

1. Twelfth Army Group Training Branch, G-3, "Twelfth Army Group Battle Experiences," in https://cgsc.contentdm.oclc.org/digital/collection/p4013coll8/id/5681/rec/2, WWII-Skelton (hereafter cited as Twelfth Army Battle Experiences).
2. See Observer Reports, U.S. Forces, European Theater, Office of the Assistant Chief of Staff, Battle Lessons Branch, G-3, "Army Ground Forces Observer Reports," 1944–1945, Boxes 1–14, RG 498, Records of Headquarters, European Theater of Operations, U.S. Army, 1942–1947, National Archives and Records Administration (hereafter cited as Battle Lessons–NARA). HQETOUSA distributed these reports in several forms: *(a)* Combat Lessons Branch, G-3, "Battle Experiences, July 12, 1944–May 5, 1945," Battle Experiences; *(b)* Twelfth Army Battle Experiences; *(c)* HQETOUSA, Combat Lessons Branch, G-3, Immediate Reports; and

(d) Observers Reports–USAHEC. In April 1945, the extracts were consolidated and published in a single booklet: HQETOUSA, "Battle Experiences, July 1944 to April 1945," in https://cgsc.contentdm.oclc.org/digital/collection/p4013coll8/id/4046/rec/5, WWII-Skelton. See also Mansoor, *G.I. Offensive in Europe*, 200.

3. Caddick-Adams, *Snow and Steel*, 84.
4. Eisenhower, *Crusade in Europe*, 308; Medford and Frazier, "Keep 'em Rolling," 57–61; Ruppenthal, *Logistical Support*, 2:137; Benjamin King, Richard C. Biggs, and Criner, *Spearhead of Logistics*, 233–36.
5. McGuire, "Judge Hastie," 157–67; Lee, *Employment of Negro Troops*, 241–48; Colley, *Road to Victory*, 87, 67–68, 101–2.
6. David Colley likened the 2.5-ton American-produced GMC "Jimmy" to the M4 Medium tank with respect to its simplicity of construction, ease of manufacture, and ability to be mass-produced. The ready availability of truck transportation, a staple since General Marshall made the decision to motorize the US Army in 1940, placed it in stark contrast to the German army. In his magisterial work on military logistics, Martin Van Crevald noted that when the Wehrmacht launched Operation Barbarossa, it used more than 2,000 different vehicle types, thousands of wagons, and tens of thousands of horses, in essence fielding two forces: "one fast and mobile and one slow and plodding." Colley, *Road to Victory*, 143; Van Crevald, *Supplying War*, 145.
7. Atkinson, *Guns at Last Light*, 241; Colley, *Road to Victory*, 133, 161–62; Waddell, *United States Army Logistics*, 151–57.
8. Cooley, *Road to Victory*, 163–64; McDonald, *Siegfried Line Campaign*, 12–13.
9. "Gasoline Filter," *Infantry Journal* 55 (September 1944): 62.
10. HQETOUSA, Combat Lessons Branch, G-3, "Battle Experiences, No. 99, 5 May 1945," Battle Experiences.
11. Shaffer F. Jarrell, Combat Observer, ETO, VII Corps, "No. 49, 14 September 1944," Box 5, File List J–K, Battle Lessons–NARA. In other cases, open-circuit telephone wire was used to repair damaged antennae on SCR 300 and SCR 536 radios. Combat Lessons Branch, G-3, Twelfth Army Group, No. 66, 17 October 1944, Twelfth Army Battle Experiences.
12. Twelfth Army Group Training Branch, No. 78, 27 October 1944, Twelfth Army Battle Experiences. These solutions were similar to those developed by Capt. Frederick C. Spann and T4 Stephen Barabas, "Field Expedients in Radio Communications in Italy," *Field Artillery Journal* 35 (May 1945): 301.
13. Combat Lessons Branch, G-3, "Battle Experiences No. 1, 18 November 1944," Battle Experiences.
14. "Cavalry and Armored Report, 27 November 1944," 3: C-385, Observers Reports–USAHEC; After Action Report, 712th Tank Battalion, October 1944, 50, https://cgsc.contentdm.oclc.org/digital/collection/p4013coll8/id/3793, WWII-Skelton. The 329th Engineer Battalion, 104th Infantry Division, constructed a similar device for use with both the M32 and the M36 tank recovery vehicle; see Shaffer F. Jarrell, Combat Observer, VII Corps, "Report No. 199, Laying Steel Treadway with M32 Tank Recovery Vehicle," Battle Lessons–NARA.
15. William J. Gallagher, After Action Report, 628th Tank Destroyer Battalion, 1 October 1944, https://cgsc.contentdm.oclc.org/digital/collection/p4013coll8/id/3618/rec/3, WWII-Skelton.

16. Twelfth Army Group Training Branch, "No. 89, 31 August 1944," Twelfth Army Battle Experiences; U.S. Army Ground Forces Observer Board, European Theater, "Report No. 163, Tank Destroyers Employed in Field Artillery, 13 August 1944," vol. 1, Observers Reports–USAHEC.
17. Twelfth Army Group Training Branch, "No. 89, 10 November 1944," Twelfth Army Battle Experiences.
18. Twelfth Army Group Training Branch, "No. 45, 16 September 1944," Twelfth Army Battle Experiences.
19. Twelfth Army Group Training Branch, "No. 84, 6 November 1944," Twelfth Army Battle Experiences.
20. Doug Stewart, "The Little War Wagon That Could," *Smithsonian* 23 (November 1992): 66, additional photo in author's collection.
21. HQETOUSA, Combat Lessons Branch, G-3, "Immediate Report No. 78, 14 October 1944," Immediate Reports; U.S. Army Ground Forces Observer Board, European Theater, "Report No. 261, 2.36-inch Rocket Ammunition and Sights, 5 October 1944," vol. 1, Observers Reports–USAHEC.
22. Training Branch, G-3, "No. 10, 29 July 1944" and "No. 76, 25 October 1944," Twelfth Army Battle Experiences. Curtis Whiteway of the 99th Infantry Division made a similar modification to a 60 mm mortar shell while overlooking Elsenborn Ridge during the Battle of the Bulge. Curtis Whiteway, personal communication with the author, 25 March 2002. Troops from the G Company, 271st Infantry Regiment, offered a similar recommendation in HQETOUSA, Combat Lessons Branch, G-3, "Battle Experiences No. 86, 29 March 1945," Battle Experiences; "Infantrymen Discuss GO Equipment," *Yank* 3 (March 1945): 5.
23. *Combat Lessons*, 6:84.
24. Combat Lessons Branch, G-3, "Battle Experiences No. 11, 13 December 1944," Battle Experiences.
25. Images SC-199504, SC-199505, SC-199506—all in RG 111-SC, Records of the Office of the Chief Signal Officer, NARA (hereafter cited as RG 111-SC).
26. Image 3A17220-54524AC, RG 342-FH.
27. Bradley, *Soldier's Story*, 40–41; Johnson, *Fast Tanks*, 194–95; Caddick-Adams, *Snow and Steel*, 430.
28. William R. Burton, "After Action Report, 46th Armored Infantry Battalion," Action against the Enemy: August 1944, WWII- Skelton, https://cgsc.contentdm.oclc.org/digital/collection/p4013coll8/id/3685/, WWII-Skelton.
29. D'Este, *Decision in Normandy*, 178–92; Atkinson, *Army at Dawn*, 339; Cook and Naisawald, *Allied Tank Casualties*, 81–82.
30. Cook and Naisawald, *Allied Tank Casualties*, 81–82.
31. Cooper, *Death Traps*, 90.
32. "Twelfth Army Group Training Branch, No. 35, 31 August 1944," Twelfth Army Battle Experiences.
33. HQETOUSA, Combat Lessons Branch, G-3, "Notes on Separate Tank Battalions, No. 27, 10 August 1944," 2, Immediate Reports.
34. "Twelfth Army Group Training Branch, No. 51, 31 August 1944," Twelfth Army Battle Experiences, 1.
35. "Twelfth Army Group Training Branch, No. 51, 31 August 1944," Twelfth Army Battle Experiences, 1–2; "Report of Action, 1 September 44 to 30 September, 749th

Tank Battalion," https://cgsc.contentdm.oclc.org/digital/collection/p4013coll8/id/3840/rec/4, WWII-Skelton.

36. George W. Coolidge, "Account of Operations of the 24th Cavalry Reconnaissance Squadron," Observers Reports–USAHEC, 3: C-491.
37. "After Action Report, 48th Tank battalion, 14th Armored Division, Nov. [19]44 thru April [19]45," https://cgsc.contentdm.oclc.org/digital/collection/p4013coll8/id/3766/rec/1, 36, WWII-Skelton.
38. George W. Coolidge, "Defense against Anti-Tank Weapons," Observers Reports–USAHEC, 4: C-694.
39. White, "Report," Exhibit 2, 28, DDEPL.
40. White, "Report," Exhibit 3, 31, DDEPL.
41. White, "Report," Exhibit 3, 40, DDEPL.
42. Albin F. Irzyk, "Galloping Juggernaut," *Military Review* 25 (April 1945): 38.
43. "Bazooka Charlie Goes After Nazis," 8; Combat Command A, Fourth Armored Division, *The Nancy Bridgehead* (War Department, 1945), 27, 28, https://cgsc.contentdm.oclc.org/digital/collection/p4013coll8/id/4610/, WWII-Skelton; see also Busha and Apacki, *Bazooka Charlie*.
44. Cole, *Lorraine Campaign*, 126–28.
45. Doubler, *Closing with the Enemy*, 141–45; Committee 23, Armored Officers Advanced Course, *Armor in the Attack of Fortified Positions* (Fort Knox, KY: The Armored School, 1950).
46. Committee 23, *Armor in the Attack*, 83–89; After Action Report, 735th Tank Battalion, 1 November 1944, 1–2, https://cgsc.contentdm.oclc.org/digital/collection/p4013coll8/id/3596, WWII-Skelton.
47. After Action Report, 735th Tank Battalion, 1 November 1944, 1–2; Committee 23, *Armor in the Attack*, 93–94, 103–5.
48. Zaloga, *Armored Attack*, 115.
49. United States Army, *First United States Army Report, August 1944–February 1945*, 3:42; 602nd Engineer Camouflage Battalion, "Monthly Operational Report, November 1944," Box 633, U.S. Army Unit Records, DDEPL; Kurt Joachim Sommerfeld, "Construction of Roads or Runways," U.S. Patent 2,338,785, filed 23 October 1941 and issued 11 January 1944, patents.google.com/patent/US2338785.pdf; "Magic Carpets Help Keep Our Forces Moving," *War Illustrated* 8 (September 1944): 276.
50. 602nd Engineer Camouflage Battalion, "Monthly Operational Reports," DDEPL. Albin Irzyk of the 4th Armored Division's 8th Tank Battalion reported the addition of Sommerfeld tracking on his tank undertaken by crews from the 126th Armored Ordnance Maintenance Battalion in February 1945, in Irzyk, *He Rode Up Front*, 304.
51. 37th Tank Battalion, "Battalion Diary," WWII-Skelton, https://cgsc.contentdm.oclc.org/digital/collection/p4013coll8/id/3718/rec/5, 34–38, WWII-Skelton; Hartman, *Tank Driver*, 49; Hunnicutt, *Sherman*, 540–45; Zaloga, *Armored Thunderbolt*, 222–23.
52. Mayo, *Ordnance Department*, 281; Province, *Patton's Third Army*, 73.
53. Mayo, *Ordnance Department*, 323; United States Army, *First United States Army Report, August 1944–February 1945*, 3:48; Committee 15, Armored Officers Advanced Course, *The Tenth Armored Division in the Saar-Moselle Triangle* (Fort

Knox, KY: The Armored School, 1949), 14, https://cgsc.contentdm.oclc.org/digital/collection/p4013coll8/id/5990/rec/1, WWII-Skelton; J. Ted Hartman spent twelve hours on Christmas Day 1944 installing connectors on his tank. Hartman, *Tank Driver*, 49.

54. 743rd Tank Battalion, S-3 Journal, 1 January, 1944, 1, 5–11, 14, 15, https://cgsc.contentdm.oclc.org/digital/collection/p4013coll8/id/3553/, WWII-Skelton; Micheal Eastes, "The 251 Calliope: The Facts behind an Unusual Vehicle," *Journal of Military Ordnance* 8 (May 1988): 17; Zaloga, *Armored Attack*, 376–77; Robinson and Hamilton, *Move Out, Verify*, 116. The efforts of the 743rd notwithstanding, later in February 1945, the 48th Tank Battalion claimed "the distinction of being the only unit to have in their possession a multi-barreled rocket launcher mounted on a medium tank." 48th Tank Battalion, Monthly Report, February 1945, 29, https://cgsc.contentdm.oclc.org/digital/collection/p4013coll8/id/3766, WWII-Skelton.
55. 48th Tank Battalion, After Action Report, February 1945, 29, https://cgsc.contentdm.oclc.org/digital/collection/p4013coll8/id/3766/rec/2, WWII-Skelton; H. A. Miller, "Observer's Report No. 8, 22 November 1944," Box 6, Battle Lessons–NARA; 70th Tank Battalion, "After Action Report, Appendix No. 1—Narrative Report of the Engagements of the 70th Tank Battalion during the Period 1 September to 30 September 1944," 38, 39, https://cgsc.contentdm.oclc.org/digital/collection/p4013coll8/id/3653/rec/7, WWII-Skelton; Zaloga, *Armored Attack*, 271–72.
56. Cole, *Ardennes*, 20–27.
57. Caddick-Adams, *Snow and Steel*, 257–61; Kays, *Weather Effects*, 19.
58. Cole, *Ardennes*, 649.
59. Robert E. Kearney to Commanding General, First United States Army, "Snow Camouflage Capes," 11 November 1944, in "Battalion History," Box 633, U.S. Army Unit Records, DDEPL.
60. Combat Lessons Branch, G-3, "Battle Experiences No. 7, 7 December 1944," Battle Experiences. The 48th Armored Infantry Battalion adopted a similar practice, and while frozen ground often prevented a block of TNT from detonating, they discovered the "addition of another [blasting] cap" solved the problem. 48th Armored Infantry Battalion, "After Action Report, 1 February 1945," 5, https://cgsc.contentdm.oclc.org/digital/collection/p4013coll8/id/3740, WWII-Skelton.
61. Colonel Albert F. Peyton, "Observer's Report No. 148, 21 February 1945," vol. 4, Box 8: Records of Headquarters, ETOUSA, Battle Lessons–NARA. The Signal Corps also photographed these booties; see image SC-199353, RG 111-SC.
62. Combat Lessons Branch, G-3, "Battle Experiences No. 66, 22 February 1945," Battle Experiences.
63. Peyton, "Observer's Report No. 148," Battle Lessons–NARA.
64. Combat Lessons Branch, G-3, "Battle Experiences No. 85, 22 March 1945," Battle Experiences; Edwin M. Burnett, "Observer's Report No. 55, 25 December 1945," Box 1, Battle Lessons–NARA; Hervey A. Tribolet, "Army Ground Forces Report No. 677, Regimental Supply Comments and Recommendations," vol. 4, Observers Reports–USAHEC.
65. United States Army, *First United States Army Report, August 1944–February 1945*, 3:42; 737th Tank Battalion, After Action Report, 2 February 1945, 52, https://cgsc.contentdm.oclc.org/digital/collection/p4013coll8/id/3598/rec/1, WWII-Skelton. The 751st Tank Battalion used "white camouflage mantles thrown over tanks."

751st Tank Battalion, Report of Action against the Enemy for the Month of December 1944, https://cgsc.contentdm.oclc.org/digital/collection/p4013coll8/id/3866/, WWII-Skelton. See also Robinson and Hamilton, *Move Out, Verify*, 133.

66. Atkinson, *Guns at Last Light*, 420–31. Caddick-Adams makes the same point repeatedly in *Snow and Steel* (209, 229, 244).
67. Sams, "Ordnance Improvisation," 36; Cole, *Ardennes*, 43.
68. Hunnicutt, *Sherman*, 241; 751st Tank Battalion, Report of Action against the Enemy for December 1944, 169; 737th Tank Battalion, After Action Report for January 1945, 2 February, 52, https://cgsc.contentdm.oclc.org/digital/collection/p4013coll8/id/3866/, WWII-Skelton.
69. Sams, "Ordnance Improvisation," 36.
70. H. A. Miller, "Observer's Report No. 77, 7 February 1945" and "Tank Destroyer Information, 5 February 1945"—both in Box 6, File List L–M, Battle Lessons–NARA.
71. Colonel Edwin M. Burnett, "Observer's Report No. 50, 9 January 1945," Box 6, File List A–B, Battle Lessons–NARA.
72. Combat Lessons Branch, G-3, "Battle Experiences No. 45, 25 March 1945," Battle Experiences; United States Army, *First United States Army Report, August 1944–February 1945*, 3:46–48; Robinson and Hamilton, *Move Out, Verify*, 133.
73. Images SC-199187, SC-199098, RG 111-SC, ROCSO.
74. Cooper, *Death Traps*, 210.
75. Image SC-333019, RG 111-SC, ROCSO. The image caption identifies the tanks as being part of 8th Division, First US Army, lining the streets of Bergerhausen, Germany, after it fell to the Americans. The after-action report of the 740th Tank Battalion places the unit, then attached to 8th Infantry Division, at the same location. See "Annex No. 1—Battle Report for Month of March 1945," in 740th Tank Battalion, After Action Report, January–April 1945, https://cgsc.contentdm.oclc.org/digital/collection/p4013coll8/id/3602/, WWII-Skelton.
76. Images SC-203168, SC-325575, SC-325576—all in RG 111-SC, ROCSO; Cooper, *Death Traps*, 145.
77. Cooper, *Death Traps*, 210.
78. 753rd Tank Battalion, C Company Narrative for the Month of March 1945, https://cgsc.contentdm.oclc.org/digital/collection/p4013coll8/id/3510/, WWII Skelton.
79. Committee 15, *The Tenth Armored Division in the Saar-Moselle Triangle*, 14, https://cgsc.contentdm.oclc.org/digital/collection/p4013coll8/id/3196/rec/2, WWII-Skelton.
80. R. B. Lovett, "Battle Experiences No. 28, 3 January 1945," Battle Experiences.
81. George W. Coolidge, "Army Ground Forces Report No. 685, Organization of Cavalry Reconnaissance Squadrons," 26 February 1945, War Department Observers Board, Headquarters, ETOUSA, 4, https://cgsc.contentdm.oclc.org/digital/collection/p4013coll8/id/4892/rec/1, WWII-Skelton. Coolidge reinforced this opinion in "Army Ground Forces Report No. 693, Armored Notes," 26 February 1945, Observers Reports–USAHEC, 4: C-693, and subsequently in "Defense against Anti-Tank Weapons," Observers Reports–USAHEC, 4: C-694.
82. Richard J. Hunt, "Report on the Light Tank M24," Headquarters, 744th Light Tank Battalion, 1945, https://cgsc.contentdm.oclc.org/digital/collection/p4013coll8/id/3513/rec/1, WWII-Skelton.

83. R. B. Lord, "Immediate Report of Combat Observations No. 75, 11 March 1945," Immediate Reports; R. B. Lord, "Immediate Report of Combat Observations No. 83, 20 March 1945," Immediate Reports.
84. R. B. Evans, Combat Observer, European Theater of Operations, XVI Corps, "No. 7, Tank Destroyer Comments," Box 3, File List E–H, Battle Lessons–NARA.
85. Hervey A. Tribolet, Combat Observer, European Theater of Operations (ETO), XXV Corps, "No. 41, Tank Destroyer Experiences," Box 10, File List S–T, Battle Lessons–NARA; R. B. Lovett, "Battle Experiences No. 91, 11 April 1945," Battle Experiences.
86. Colonel Albert F. Peyton, Combat Observer, ETO, XVI Corps, "No. 77, Tank Destroyer Comments," Box 7, File List P, Battle Lessons–NARA.
87. Patton, *War as I Knew It*, 318. On 29 April 1945, Col. Burton C. Andrus, serving as a member of the HQETOUSA Combat Observers Branch for III Corps, reported in Observers Report No. 112 that tankers of C Company, 48th Tank Battalion, 14th Armored Division, made use of specially prepared sandbag racks on their M4 Mediums, reporting that no tanks of the division equipped with sandbags had been knocked out, "unless hit in the rear, in the engine compartment, or on a track." He also noted that the addition of the sandbags "slowed the tank some, but not over ten miles per hour." However, a subsequent directive issued 9 May 1945 ordered that "Observers Report No. 112 be withheld as this headquarters does not approve of sand bagging tanks." See Andrus, "Observers Report No. 112," 29 April 1945, Box 1, File List A–B, Battle Lessons–NARA; and R. W. Hartman to Commanding General, ETO, U.S. Army Attention Chief, Combat Lessons Branch, G-3, "Memo: Observer's Report No. 112 (Sand Bagging Tanks)," 3 May 1945, Box 1, File List A–B, Battle Lessons–NARA.
88. John Lemp and Ernest C. Hatfield, "Tank Destroyers as Assault Guns," *Field Artillery Journal* 35 (April 19445): 245.
89. Shaffer F. Jarrell, Combat Observer, ETO, VII Corps, "No. 89, Tank Destroyer Comments," Box 5, File List J–K, Battle Lessons–NARA.
90. Armored School, *Four Tank Destroyer Battalions*, 38, 131.
91. Lovett, "Battle Experiences No. 91," Battle Experiences; Colonel Edwin M. Burnett, Combat Observer, ETO, V Corps, "No. 136, M-36 Tank Destroyer," Box 2, File List B–D, Battle Lessons–NARA.
92. 628th Tank Battalion, After Action Report, 1 January 1945, 7, https://cgsc.contentdm.oclc.org/digital/collection/p4013coll8/id/3618, WWII-Skelton.
93. 628th Tank Destroyer Battalion, *Victory, TD: History of the 628th Tank Destroyer Battalion, 1941–1945* (privately printed, 1945), 75–76, https://cgsc.contentdm.oclc.org/digital/collection/p4013coll8/id/3524/rec/1, WWII-Skelton.
94. HQETOUSA, Combat Lessons Branch, G-3, "Immediate Report No. 73, Combat Observations," Immediate Reports.
95. R. B. Evans, Combat Observer, ETO, XVI Corps, "No. 7, Tank Destroyer Comments," Box 3, File List E–H, Battle Lessons–NARA.
96. "Field Mods Dominate M-10 Roof Armor," *Journal of Military Ordnance* 9 (March 1999): 23.
97. Shaffer F. Jarrell, Combat Observer, ETO, VII Corps, "No. 209, Miscellaneous Subjects," Box 5, File List J–K, Battle Lessons–NARA.

98. Shaffer F. Jarrell, Combat Observer, ETO, VII Corps, "No. 207, Tank Destroyer Operations," Box 5, File List J–K, Battle Lessons–NARA.
99. Combat Lessons Branch, G-3, "Immediate Report No. 9, 12 December 1944," Immediate Reports; Edwin M. Burnett, Combat Observer, ETO, V Corps, "No. 102, Use of Flame Thrower Fluid in a Rifle Grenade," Box 2, File List B–D, Battle Lessons–NARA; Twelfth Army Group Training Branch, "No. 72, 23 October 1944," Twelfth Army Battle Experiences.
100. James O'Brien, "Weapons, 6 April 1945" Observers Reports–USAHEC, 4: C-794; George Coolidge, "Army Ground Forces Report No. 677, Notes on Miscellaneous Munitions and Equipment, 22 February 1945," Observers Reports–USAHEC, vol. 4; Pete Heffner, Combat Observer, ETO, VI Corps, "No. 106, Submachinegun Cal. 45, M-3," Box 4, File List H, Battle Lessons–NARA; HQETOUSA, Combat Lessons Branch, G-3, "Immediate Report No. 57, 22 February 1945," Immediate Reports; Pete Heffner, Combat Observer, ETO, VI Corps, "No. 90, Bipod Adaptor for BMG ca1.30 M1919A4," Box 4, File List H, Battle Lessons–NARA; Shaffer F. Jarrell, Combat Observer, ETO, VII Corps, "No. 211, Carbine Cal. 45, M-1," Box 5, File List J–K, Battle Lessons–NARA.
101. Pete Heffner, Combat Observer, ETO, VI Corps, "No. 94, Modification of Grenade Launcher M-7," Box 4, File List H, Battle Lessons–NARA.
102. Harry Pender, "Grenade Grapnel," Observers Reports–USAHEC, vol. 1. Hervey Tribolet, Combat Observer, ETO, XV Corps, "No. 59, Anti-Mine and Booby Trap Grappling Hook," Box 10, File List T, Battle Lessons–NARA.
103. HQETOUSA, Combat Lessons Branch, G-3, "Immediate Report No. 73, 10 March 1945," Immediate Reports.
104. *Combat Lessons No. 6*, 46–47; *Combat Lessons No. 7*, 16–17; H. A. Miller, Combat Observer, ETO, XII Corps, "No. 46, Propelling Wire across Stream," Box 6, File List L–M, Battle Lessons–NARA.
105. Triplet, *Colonel in the Armored Divisions*, 213–14, 223–24.
106. Shaffer F. Jarrell, Combat Observer, ETO, VII Corps, "No. 159, Tank Maintenance," Box 5, File List J–K, Battle Lessons–NARA.
107. Christian Hildebrand, Combat Observer, VI Corps, "No. 115, 26 February," Box 3, File List E–H; Hervey Tribolet, Combat Observer, ETO, XV Corps, "No. 148, Light Tank M-24," Box 10, File List T; B. C. Andrus, Combat Observer, III Corps, "No. 75, Modification of Armor," Box 1, File List A; C. P. Chapman, Combat Observer, XIII Corps, "No. 68, 22 March 1945," Box 2, File List B–D; Lester Webb, Combat Observer, XX Corps, "No. 71, Miscellaneous Matters," Box 11, File List W; Pete Heffner, Combat Observer, VI Corps, "No. 84, Light Tank Modifications," Box 4, File List H—all in Battle Lessons-NARA.
108. Combat Lessons Branch, G-3, "Battle Experiences No. 32, 11 January 1945," Battle Experiences.
109. C. P. Chapman, Combat Observer, XIII Corps, "No. 54, Miscellaneous," Box 2, File List B–D, Battle Lessons–NARA.
110. Kenneth Barnaby, "Face-Lifting a Cavalry Squadron," *Armored Cavalry Journal* 55 (July–August 1946): 8–9.
111. Charles Gillett, "Armored Command Post," *Cavalry Journal* 54 (September–October 1945): 65.

112. HQETOUSA, Combat Lessons Branch, G-3, "Immediate Report No. 82, Combat Observations: Regimental Communications," 1, Immediate Reports.
113. HQETOUSA, Combat Lessons Branch, G-3, "Immediate Report No. 129, Combat Observations," Immediate Reports.
114. T. B. Hale to M. F. Peckels, "Harvester Battalion for Service with the U.S. Army," 30 June 1942, "Harvester Called to the Colors" (privately printed, 1942), "News for Immediate Release—International Harvester Company," "Affiliation Answers Need for Ordnance Men," and "Application for Enlistment"—all in RG 407, E427, Box 16240, World War II Operations Reports, 1940–1948, 12th Armored Division, NARA. See also Ferguson, *Hellcats*.
115. "Jack and Engine Stand for Servicing Tractor Clutches," *Harvester World* 33 (October 1842): 12–13; "Report of the 134th Ordnance and Maintenance Battalion, March 1945," RG 407, E427, Box 16240, World War II Operations Reports, 1940–1948, 12th Armored Division, NARA.
116. William Giannopoulos Collection, 12th Armored Division Memorial Museum, Abilene, TX.
117. Baily, *Faint Praise*, 120–21; Hunnicutt, *Sherman*, 318; "Report of the 134th Ordnance and Maintenance Battalion," RG 407, NARA.
118. War Department, "Auxiliary Jeep Frame" (Washington, DC: War Department, 1944), https://cgsc.contentdm.oclc.org/digital/collection/p4013coll8/id/5110/rec/1, WWII-Skelton.
119. Image SC-339039RG, RG 111-SC.
120. Lawrence Loewinthan, "Medical Evacuation with a Reconnaissance Squadron," *Cavalry Journal* 54 (March–April 1945): 35.
121. Image SC-199176, RG 111-SC.
122. Headquarters, ETOUSA, Combat Lessons Branch, G-3, "Immediate Report No. 118, 25 April 1945," Immediate Reports.
123. R. B. Evans, Combat Observer, European Theater of Operations, XVI Corps, "No. 46, Evac Hospital Improvisations, 22 April 1945," Box 3, File List E–F, Battle Lessons–NARA.
124. Combat Lessons Branch, G-3, "Battle Experiences No. 32, 11 January 1945," Battle Experiences.
125. Hervey A. Tribolet, Combat Observer, ETO, XV Corps, "No. 130, Improvised Field Welding Unit," Box 10, File List T, Battle Lessons–NARA.
126. Combat Lessons Branch, G-3, "Battle Experiences No. 32, 11 January 1945," Battle Experiences; HQETOUSA, Combat Lessons Branch, G-3, "Immediate Report No. 119, 27 April 1945," Immediate Reports; "The Armored School's Road Magnet," *Cavalry Journal* 53 (January–February 1944): 86–87.
127. Shaffer F. Jarrell, Combat Observer, ETO, VII Corps, "No. 187, Ordnance Operations," Box 4, File List H, Battle Lessons–NARA.
128. Felix Gomez, personal communication with the author, 25 May 2002; B. C. Andrus, Combat Observer, ETO, III Corps, "No. 89, 30 March 1945," Box 1, File List A–B, Battle Lessons–NARA; Edwin M. Burnett, Combat Observer, ETO, V Corps, "No. 133, Miscellaneous," and "No. 129, Wire Guard for Jeeps," Box 2, File List B–D, Battle Lessons–NARA; C. P. Chapman, Combat Observer, ETO, XIII Corps, "No. 66, MISCELLANEOUS," Box 2, File List B–D, Battle Lessons–NARA;

M. C. Shattuck, Combat Observer, ETO, XXIII Corps, "No. 89, Wire Cutter on Jeep," Box 9, File List R–S, Battle Lessons–NARA; "Face Lifting Changes Jeep into Limousine," *Popular Science* 145 (July 1944): 22; E. P. Hogan, "The Jeep in Action," *Army Ordnance* 17 (September–October 1944): 273–74; Doug Stewart, "Hail to the Jeep! Could We Have Won without It?" *Smithsonian* 23 (November 1992): 60–72; images SC-251502, RG 111-SC, SC-329452—both in RG 111-SC, ROCSO; Barnaby, "Face Lifting a Cavalry Squadron," 10; John K. Lester, "Memories of Huertgen Forest—World War II," https://members.tripod.com/~msg_fisher/lester-3.html; "1001 Postwar Jobs for the Jeep," *Popular Science* 144 (February 1944): 80–85.

129. Bradley, *War Correspondent*, 157.
130. "Small Arms Care," *Military Review* 25 (April 1945): 35.
131. Sams, "Ordnance Improvisation," 36.
132. Barnaby, "Face-Lifting a Cavalry Squadron," 8.

Chapter 8

Epigraph: "This Is Your Enemy . . . It's Your Life or His," *Air Force Magazine* 28 (February 1945): 13. An excerpt appeared as "Portrait by the Enemy," in *Military Review* 25 (June 1945): 7.

1. Dwight F. Johns, "'We Are Doing What We Can with What We Have,'" *Military Review* 25 (April 1945): 10; MacArthur himself said as much in a February 1944 letter to Dr. A. L. Miller, telling the freshman member of the US House of Representatives, "We are doing what we can with what we have." See Hunt, *Untold Story*, 320–24.
2. Toll, *Conquering Tide*, 235, 239–42.
3. After consolidating their position on Bougainville in mid-1944, troops of XIV Corps in the "city" that was the American garrison benefited from the arrival of 100,000 tons of supplies on a monthly basis; see McManus, *Island Infernos*, 125–28.
4. Gerald H. Shea, "Lessons of Guadalcanal," *Infantry Journal* 53 (July 1943): 13.
5. Albin E. Johnson, "The Seabees Can Do It," *Popular Science* 144 (January 1944): 56.
6. Huie, *Can Do*, 189.
7. Walter D. Hessert, "Seabees Improvise Test Equipment on Guadalcanal," *Military Engineer* 36 (June 1944): 186–87.
8. Brig. Gen. Stuart C. Godfrey, "Airfields and Air Transport in Northern Burma," *Military Review* 25 (June 1945): 66; quote in D. G. Hammond, "The Winged Bulldozer," *Military Review* 24 (May 1944): 9.
9. Hammond, "Winged Bulldozer," 10.
10. Hammond, "Winged Bulldozer," 12–13; "Airborne Two-and-a-Half Ton Trucks," *Military Review* 23 (March 1944): 29; Birdsall, *Flying Buccaneers*, 76; Kenney, *General Kenney Reports*, 270.
11. William B. Allen, "Improvised Crane Built by Engineers in New Guinea," *Military Engineer* 35 (July 1943): 343; Harmon C. Broyles, "Engineers Must Improvise," *Military Engineer* 36 (May 1944): 158–59, 160, 161; Henry H. Arnold, "First Report of the Commanding General of the Army Air Forces, January 4, 1944," in Millis, *War Reports*, 322.
12. Caldwell, "Tracked Amphibian," 70–71.
13. Alexander, *Utmost Savagery*, 83–84; Robert J. Seese, "The Roebling Alligator," *Naval Institute Proceedings* 109 (April 1990): 27; John A. Speed, personal communication

with the author, 1 February 2002. These sorts of field modifications continued for the remainder of the war, as suggested by the archaeological study of LVT(A) 4s that are still in waters off the shore of Saipan from the 1944 invasion. W. Shawn Arnold, "Whatever Works: Amphibious Tractors and Field Expedient Armor Modifications," in McKinnon and Carrell, *Underwater Archaeology*, 63–71.

14. Joseph H. Alexander, "Baptism by Fire: Sherman Tanks at Tarawa," *Leatherneck* 76 (November 1993), 34–37; Gilbert and Cansière, *Tanks in Hell*, 107–10.
15. Gilbert and Cansière, *Tanks in Hell*, 125–86.
16. Gilbert and Cansière, *Tanks in Hell*, 187–91, 195.
17. Mark J. Reardon, "Upgunning the Amphibian Tank," in Coffman, *History of Innovation*, 85–86.
18. Triplet, *Colonel in the Armored Divisions*, 78–79.
19. Ibid., 82–85. Reardon, "Upgunning the Amphibian Tank," 88.
20. Company D, 776th Amphibian Tank Battalion, "Operational Report, Stalemate II, Palau Islands," 1944, 3, https://cgsc.contentdm.oclc.org/digital/collection/p4013coll8/id/3870/rec/1, WWII-Skelton.
21. In August, a five-tank platoon successfully supported infantry in the final stages of fighting along the Tenaru River, attacking enemy machine-gun and mortar positions by crushing the dug-in enemy under their treads. The next day, tanks provided a "morale factor" for marines mopping up the Japanese that had escaped from the previous day's fighting. In September, six tanks supported elements of 3rd Battalion, 1st Marine Division, in "quite disastrous" fighting along Edson's Ridge with enemy fire knocking out three tanks in a short engagement. In the aftermath, Maj. Francis Cooper, commanding B Company, 1st Marine Tank Battalion identified numerous "costly" lessons, notably the tank commanders' minimal visibility, their preoccupation with directing drivers in the jungle environment, and poor reconnaissance in advance of movement over difficult terrain. Thus, the prospect of continued employment of tanks in tropical areas appeared "very limited." Maj. F. H. Cooper, "Notes on the Operations of Tanks (Light) in the Solomons," in Col. B. Q. Jones, "Interviews and Statements by Officers of the First Marine Division on the Guadalcanal Operations," 5 December 1942–19 January 1943, https://cgsc.contentdm.oclc.org/digital/collection/p4013coll8/id/4338/rec/1, WWII-Skelton; See also Zimmermann, *Guadalcanal Campaign*, 69, 89–90.
22. Neiman and Estes, *Tanks on the Beaches*, 16–17, 32–33, 51–52. In his memoir, Neiman recalled seeing General Patton while the latter was commanding the 2nd Armored Division in the GHQ Maneuvers in 1941, as the young lieutenant had been assigned as an observer to an army mechanized cavalry regiment and saw the general while his regiment prepared to ambush elements of Patton's unit when it attacked a trestle bridge.
23. Neiman and Estes, *Tanks on the Beaches*, 51–67, 62; Bellmon, *Life and Times*, 30 39, 45.
24. Bellmon, *Life and Times*, 45.
25. Neiman regarded the failure to "coordinate the efforts of all the companies," particularly with respect to procedures and techniques, as "a big mistake." Neiman and Estes, *Tanks on the Beaches*, 65.
26. Zaloga, *U.S. Amphibious Tanks*, 8–10, 30–36.

27. 767th Tank Battalion, After Action Report, 1 January through 31 December 1944, 2–6, https://cgsc.contentdm.oclc.org/digital/collection/p4013coll8/id/3463/rec/2, WWII-Skelton.
28. War Department, *Japanese Tank and Anti-Tank Warfare*, 169, 178–95.
29. Neiman and Estes, *Tanks on the Beaches*, 85; A Seabee machinist, observing the potential for Japanese soldiers to immobilize a tank by jamming a crowbar through the open drive sprocket, reportedly cut the top of a fuel drum with a torch and welded it to cover the sprocket spokes, though it is unknown the degree to which Neiman used this adaptation, as extant photos do not seem to offer evidence of this modification. Huie, *Can Do*, 180.
30. Gilbert elaborates on these challenges extensively in *Tanks in Hell*, 65–72, noting the absence of any practical communication between tanks and infantry on Tarawa. It is not known whether the lack of communication on Tarawa contributed to Neiman's decision to install phones on Company C's tanks. It can be inferred that this was a result of dealing with the 23rd Marine Regiment at Camp Pendleton in advance of the Kwajalein operation.
31. Wilbur C. Strand, "The Infantry-Tank Team in Jungle Operations," *Cavalry Journal* 55 (March–April 1946): 3. Comparable methods pairing an EE8 handset and lights were also offered in HQETOUSA, *Battle Experiences against the Japanese*, https://cgsc.contentdm.oclc.org/digital/collection/p4013coll8/id/4051/rec/1, 62, WWII-Skelton. Not all tankers in the Pacific made the modifications at the same time. Robert C. Dick, of the US Army's 763rd Tank Battalion, recalled in his memoir that his crew did not install radios in their tanks until the end of the Leyte campaign as they prepared for the landings on Okinawa. Dick, *Cutthroats*, 148.
32. McManus, *Island Infernos*, 52–53.
33. McManus, *Island Infernos*, 130–34.
34. Bellmon, *Life and Times*, 53.
35. Maj R. K. Schmidt, Headquarters report, in "Fourth Marine Division Operations Report—Saipan, Annex K, Report of the 4th Tank Battalion," 20 August 1944, 2; and Maj Robert N. Neiman, Company C report, in "Fourth Marine Division Operations Report—Saipan, Annex K, Report of the Tank 4th Tank Battalion," 20 August 1944, 32—both in *Fourth Marine Division Operations Report, 15 June to 9 July 1944*, in https://cgsc.contentdm.oclc.org/digital/collection/p4013coll8/id/293/, WWII-Skelton.
36. Schmidt, Headquarters report, 6.
37. Neiman, Company C report, 32; and 1st Lt. Stephen Horton Jr., Company A report, in "Fourth Marine Division Operations Report—Saipan, Annex K, Report of the 4th Tank Battalion," 20 August 1944, 16, *Fourth Marine Division Operations Report, 15 June to 9 July 1944*, https://cgsc.contentdm.oclc.org/digital/collection/p4013coll8/id/292, WWII-Skelton. In his report, Company B commander 1st Lt. Roger Seasholtz made an intermediate assessment, as he reported that "phones installed on the right grouser box were of great value in co-ordination to both infantry personal [*sic*] and tank reconnassance [*sic*] personel [*sic*]. Roger Seasholtz, Company B report, in "Fourth Marine Division Operations Report—Saipan, Annex K, Report of the 4th Tank Battalion," 20 August 1944, *Fourth Marine Division Operations Report, 15 June to 9 July 1944*, 28, https://cgsc.contentdm.oclc.org/digital/collection/p4013coll8/id/292, WWII-Skelton.

38. Schmidt, Headquarters report, 6; Neiman and Estes, *Tanks on the Beaches*, 93–94.
39. Seasholtz, Company B report, 29.
40. Maj R. K. Schmidt, Headquarters report, in "Fourth Marine Division Operations Report—Tinian, Annex K, Report of the 4th Tank Battalion," 22 August 1944, 5; 1st Lt. Horton Jr., Company A report, in "Fourth Marine Division Operations Report—Tinian, Annex K, Report of the 4th Tank Battalion," 22 August 1944, 11—both in *Fourth Marine Division Operations Report Tinian, 24 July to 1 August 1944*, https://cgsc.contentdm.oclc.org/digital/collection/p4013coll8/id/299/rec/6, WWII-Skelton.
41. Neiman, Company C report, 34.
42. Zaloga, *U.S. Marine Corps Tanks*, 18–20; McKinney, *Portable Flame Thrower*.
43. Neiman and Estes, *Tanks on the Beaches*, 112.
44. A brief article that could have been the inspiration for the fabrication appeared as "Flail Tanks" in *Military Review* 24 (October 1944): 82.
45. Neiman and Estes, *Tanks on the Beaches*, 113–17, 119; Bellmon, *Life and Times*, 60–61. Bellmon was somewhat critical of his commander in the creation of the ersatz flail, as he noted that "Captain Bob was much taken by this device and bragged about it at every opportunity. Finally, word reached the commanding general who insisted on seeing the machine so he could decide whether or not it might be applicable for use in other war theaters. On the day of the general's inspection, Captain Bob took the general in tow, took full credit for the idea and construction, and received the general's congratulations. The captain never once mentioned Sam's name or even bothered to introduce Sam to the general or his party." Orders note the presence of the 127th Naval Construction Battalion on Maui during the same period as the 4th Tank Battalion. Naval History and Heritage Command, *127th Naval Construction Battalion: Historical Information*, https://www.history.navy.mil/content/dam/museums/Seabee/UnitListPages/NCB/127%20NCB.pdf. The concluding pages of the historical information section includes a photograph of the same Sherman flail tank reportedly built by Neiman's marines, making it altogether unclear as to which unit played the greatest role in its construction, though R. P. Hunnicutt offers the same illustration and notes that the flail was "constructed by the Seabees for the U.S. Marines." Hunnicutt, *Sherman*, 463.
46. Neiman and Estes, *Tanks on the Beaches*, 119; Bellmon gave up his tank Jezebel for a new one that he christened Cairo; see Henry Bellmon to Parents, 18 November 1944, file 7, box 1, Correspondence, September 1943 to 23 November 1944, Henry Bellmon Papers, Special Collections, Edmon Low Library, Oklahoma State University, Stillwater.
47. Neiman and Estes, *Tanks on the Beaches*, 119.
48. Neiman and Estes, *Tanks on the Beaches*, 119.
49. These additions prior to landings on Roi and Namur are described by Neiman and Estes, *Tanks on the Beaches*, 85–86.
50. Neiman and Estes, *Tanks on the Beaches*, 85.
51. "Annex Jig to Fourth Marine Division Operations Report, Iwo Jima, Fourth Tank Battalion Report," 15–17, https://cgsc.contentdm.oclc.org/digital/collection/p4013coll8/id/660/rec/1, WWII-Skelton.
52. "Annex Love, Fifth Tank Battalion, Action Report," in *Fifth Marine Division (Reinforced), Iwo Jima Action Report, 19 February to 26 March 1945*, pt. 5, 2–3, https://cgsc.contentdm.oclc.org/digital/collection/p4013coll8/id/4059, WWII-Skelton.

53. "Enclosure H, Third Tank Battalion, Action Report," in *Third Marine Division, Iwo Jima Action Report, 31 October to 16 March 1945*, pt. 17, 31, https://cgsc.contentdm.oclc.org/digital/collection/p4013coll8/id/1109/rec/31, WWII-Skelton.
54. First Lieutenant Henry L. Bellmon, Silver Star Citation, USMC WW II Silver Star Citations, "USMC WWII Silver Star Citations (B)," 125, https://www.hqmc.marines.mil/Agencies/USMC-FOIA/WWIISSCitations/. Surprisingly, in his memoir Neiman makes no mention of Bellmon's Silver Star.
55. Neiman and Estes, *Tanks on the Beaches*, 133.
56. Neiman and Estes, *Tanks on the Beaches*, 138.
57. Neiman and Estes, *Tanks on the Beaches*, 126.
58. Spalding, "Presenting the Stinger," 55–56; Morgan, "Men and Guns," 59–60.
59. Morgan, "Men and Guns," 59–60; Spalding, "Presenting the Stinger," 56; *Fifth Marine Division, Iwo Jima Action Report*, pt. 11, 3–4, https://cgsc.contentdm.oclc.org/digital/collection/p4013coll8/id/4065, WWII-Skelton.
60. *Fifth Marine Division, Iwo Jima Action Report*, pt. 11, 3–4, https://cgsc.contentdm.oclc.org/digital/collection/p4013coll8/id/4065, WWII-Skelton.
61. Images 127-GW-352-142507, 127-GW-352-142508—both in Record Group 127-PX, Records of the United States Marine Corps, Marine Corps and Noted Civilian Personalities, NARA (hereafter cited as RG 127-PX).
62. Johns, "We Are Doing What We Can," 14–15.
63. Louis Hewitt, "Wharf Construction," *Military Engineer* 36 (November 1944): 364–65; Lewis Combs, "Innovation of Amphibious Warfare," *Military Engineer* 36 (February 1944): 46.
64. Engineer Amphibian Command, "Engineer Amphibian Troops: General Training Guide No. 1," 1943, 1, https://cgsc.contentdm.oclc.org/digital/collection/p4013coll8/id/2742/, WWII-Skelton.
65. "New Army Unit Calling for Experienced Boat Men," *Motor Boating* 70 (August 1942): 89; Heavey, *Down Ramp*, 4–6. General Heavey published *Down Ramp* previously in serial form in *Military Engineer.*
66. Heavey, *Down Ramp*, 16–21.
67. MacArthur, *Reports*, 1:105.
68. Heavey, *Down Ramp*, 49.
69. Heavey, *Down Ramp*, 106.
70. Second Engineer Special Brigade, *History*, 33; Heavey, *Down Ramp*, 107.
71. Second Engineer Special Brigade, *History*, 64.
72. Second Engineer Special Brigade, *History*, 67.
73. "Biography of Oliver R. Smith," Justin Museum of Military History, http://www.justinmuseum.com/famjustin/OSmithbio.html.
74. Heavey, *Down Ramp*, 115, 124, 137–39.
75. John K. Kingman, "The Genesis of Fort Drum, Manila Bay," *Military Engineer* 37 (April 1945): 128–30; William F. Heavey, "Amphibian Engineers in Action, Part III—Corregidor to Tokyo," *Military Engineer* 38 (February 1946): 60–61.
76. Heavey, "Amphibian Engineers in Action," 61; 38th Infantry Division, "Report on the M-7 Operation, 38th Infantry Division, the Avengers of Bataan," 52, https://cgsc.contentdm.oclc.org/digital/collection/p4013coll8/id/2530, WWII-Skelton.
77. 38th Infantry Division, "Report on M-7 Operation," 54.

78. Heavey, "Amphibian Engineers in Action," 61; 38th Infantry Division, "Report on M-7 Operation," 55, 57–59; C. R. Bathurst, "Report on Engineer Operations in the Recapture of Fort Drum," *Military Review* 25 (December 1945): 17–20.
79. For examples of these sorts of contraptions, see images 3A42679-6511AC, 3A42504-650023AC, 3A41776-63531AC, 3A31375-5128AC, 3A45164-67829AC—all in RG 342-FH; "Jap Engine Powers Motorcycle Built by Coastguardsman," *Popular Mechanics* 84 (November 1945): 23; images SC-182505, SC-190528, SC-191968—all in RG 111, SC, ROCSO; "Belly Tank Outriggers Sailed by Flyers," *Popular Mechanics* 84 (August 1945): 88; "Boats from Rope," *Popular Mechanics* 84 (July 1945): 72; Blake Stilwell, "This Is How WW2 Marines Made Ice Cream at 30,000 Feet," https //www.wearethemighty.com/popular/ww2-marines-made-ice-cream/; image 3A44922-52400AC, RG 342-FH; "Manila Railroad," *Yank* 14 (10 August 1945): 22.
80. Plating, *The Hump*, 9–10.
81. American Airlines, *Education of an Airline*, 2.
82. Plating, *The Hump*, 143, 164.
83. William R. Zeigler, "Air Transport Operations in Burma," *Military Engineer* 37 (March 1945): 105.
84. Amy L. Johnson, "What Was the CBI Roundup?," Letters Lost Then Found, letterslostthenfound.com/what-was-the-cbi-roundup/. Carl Warren Weiidenburner maintains an impressive archive of *CBI Roundup* at https://cbi-theater.com /roundup/roundup.html.
85. "Greetings from General Stilwell," *CBI Roundup*, 24 September 1942, https://cbi -theater.com/roundup/roundup0992442.html.
86. Karl Peterson, "Yankee Ingenuity: To Leave Its Imprint in Far East," *CBI Roundup*, 7 December 1944, https://cbi-theater.com/roundup/roundup120744.html.
87. "Ah, G.I. Ingenuity: There's Nothing (Practically) a Yank Soldier Can't Invent," *CBI Roundup*, 5 October 1944, https://cbi-theater.com/roundup/roundup100544 .html.
88. Earl Langenbahn, "Something New in Barber Chairs," "Three G.I.s Improvise Mechanical Dhobi Wallah," and "Paging Casey Jones," *CBI Roundup*, 18 May 1944, https://cbi-theater.com/roundup/roundup051844.html; "A Problem Solved," *CBI Roundup*, 23 November 1944, https://cbi-theater.com/roundup/roundup112344 .html.
89. Ray Howard, "Necessity Mothered a Lot of Inventions," *India-Burma Theater Roundup* 3 (September 1945), https://www.cbi-theater.com/roundup/roundup0 90645.html.
90. As noted previously, comparable efforts had been undertaken since Guadalcanal.
91. "Tank Support Annex: Special Action Report Nansei Shoto, Phase III," *First Marine Division (Reinforced), Special Action Report, Nansei-Shoto Operation, 1 April–30 June 1945*, pt. 3, 198, https://cgsc.contentdm.oclc.org/digital/collection /p4013coll8/id/2233/, WWII-Skelton.
92. "Annex E—Sixth Tank Battalion Report," *Sixth Marine Division, Special Action Report on Okinawa Operations*, 2 vols., 719, box 8, folder 2, World War Two/ Okinawa, Collection 3720, Archives Branch, United States Marine Corps History Division, Quantico, VA.
93. Image 122356, RG 127-PX; Sarantakes, *Seven Stars*, 97–98.

94. "Tank Support Annex: Special Action Report Nansei Shoto," *First Marine Division (Reinforced), Special Action Report, Nansei-Shoto Operation, 1 April–30 June 1945*, pt. 3, 240, https://cgsc.contentdm.oclc.org/digital/collection/p4013coll8/id/2233/, WWII-Skelton; "Annex E—Sixth Tank Battalion Report," *Sixth Marine Division, Special Action Report.*
95. Images 128656, 128657—both in RG 127-PX.
96. McManus, *End of the Earth*, 247–51.
97. For one example, see Sledge, *With the Old Breed*, 121, 152–53, 260. The notion is explored more fully in Dower, *War without Mercy.*
98. Overy, *Why the Allies Won*, 221.
99. Kato, *Lost War*, 157.
100. Manchester, *Goodbye Darkness*, 451–52.
101. R. Emmett Tyrrell Jr. and Daniel J. Flynn, "Stolen Valor: The Fake History from a Real Historian That Fooled Presidents and Publishers," *American Spectator*, 25 May 2017, https://spectator.org/stolen-valor-william-manchester-how-fake-news-became-fake-history/.

Conclusion

Epigraph: Eisenhower, *Crusade in Europe*, 453.

1. Dwight D. Eisenhower, "Homecoming Speech," Abilene, KS, 22 June 1945, Dwight D. Eisenhower Memorial Commission, http://www.eisenhowermemorial.org/pages.php?pid=93.
2. Keegan, *Six Armies in Normandy*, xi.

Selected Bibliography

Archives and Manuscript Collections

Branch History Office. US Army Chemical, Biological, Radiological, and Nuclear School. Fort Leonard Wood, MO.
Clark Special Collections. McDermott Library. United States Air Force Academy. Colorado Springs, CO.
Dwight D. Eisenhower Presidential Library. Abilene, KS.
Edmon Low Library Special Collections. Oklahoma State University. Stillwater, OK.
Ike Skelton Combined Arms Research Library. Fort Leavenworth, KS.
National Archives and Records Administration II. College Park, MD.
12th Armored Division Memorial Museum. Abilene, TX.
United States Army Heritage and Education Center. Carlisle, PA.

Newspapers, Military Journals, and Other Periodicals

Air Force Magazine
American Boy
American Mercury
Armored Cavalry Journal
Army Ordnance
Cavalry Journal
CBI Roundup
Field Artillery Journal
Harvester World
Hell's Angels Newsletter
Impact!
India-Burma Theater Roundup
Infantry Journal
Infantry School Quarterly
Intelligence Bulletin
Journal of Military Ordnance
Leatherneck
Life
Military Collector and Historian
Military Engineer

Military Review
Naval Institute Proceedings
New York Times
Parameters
Prisoners of War Bulletin
Popular Mechanics
Popular Science Monthly, Popular Science
Quartermaster Journal
Quartermaster Review
Ragged Irregulars
Saturday Evening Post
Stars and Stripes
Washington Post
Yank

US Government Publications

Armored School. *Employment of Four Tank Destroyer Battalions in the ETO*. Fort Knox, KY: The Armored School, 1949.

Army Air Forces Evaluation Board. *The Effectiveness of Third Phase Tactical Air Operations in the European Theater, 5 May 1944–8 May 1945*. Orlando, FL: Army Air Forces Evaluation Board, 1945.

Chief of Naval Operations. *U.S. Naval Aviation in the Pacific*. Washington, DC: U.S. Navy, 1947.

Commanding General, U.S. Army Air Forces. *Technical Order, No. 01-60JD-1, Pilot's Flight Operating Instructions: P-51B-1 Airplane*. Evansville, IN: Keller-Crescent, 1943.

Headquarters Army Air Forces. Office of Flying Safety. *Pilot Training Manual for the P-47 Thunderbolt, AAF Manual No. 50-5*. Washington, DC: Headquarters Army Air Forces, Office of Flying Safety, 1944.

Secretary of War. *Annual Report of the Secretary of War to the President, 1941*. Washington, DC: GPO, 1941.

United States Army. *First United States Army Report of Operations, 1 August 1944–22 February 1945*. 4 vols. Washington, DC: GPO, n.d.

———. *First United States Army Report of Operations, 20 October 1943–1 August 1944*. 6 vols. Washington, DC: GPO, n.d.

———. Second Engineer Special Brigade. *History of the Second Engineer Special Brigade, United States Army, World War II*. Harrisburg, PA: Telegraph Press, 1946.

———. 776th Tank Destroyer Battalion. *An Informal History of the 776th Tank Destroyer Battalion*. Privately printed, 1945.

War Department. *Field Service Regulations—Operations*. Washington, DC: GPO, 1941.

———. *Japanese Tank and Anti-Tank Warfare*. Special Series No. 34. Washington, DC: War Department, Military Intelligence Division, 1945.

———. *Tank Destroyer Field Manual—Organization and Tactics of Tank Destroyer Units, 16 June 1942*. Washington, DC: GPO, 1942.

———. *Utah Beach to Cherbourg*. Washington, DC: GPO, 1948.

———. Combat Analysis Section. *Combat Lessons, Rank and File in Combat: What They Are Doing, How They Do It*. 7 vols. Washington, DC: War Department, n.d.

———. Historical Division. *Omaha Beachhead*. Washington, DC: GPO, 1948.

Books and Articles

Alexander, Joseph. *Utmost Savagery: The Three Days of Tarawa*. Annapolis, MD: Naval Institute Press, 1995.

Allen, Frederick Lewis. *Only Yesterday: An Informal History of the Nineteen Twenties*. New York: Harper and Row, 1931. Reprint, John Wiley and Sons, 1997.

Ambrose, Stephen E. *Band of Brothers: E Company 506th Regiment, 101st Airborne Division from Normandy to Hitler's Eagle's Nest*. New York: Simon and Schuster, 1992.

———. *Citizen Soldiers: The U.S. Army from the Normandy Beaches to the Bulge to the Surrender of Germany, June 7, 1944–May 7, 1945*. New York: Simon and Schuster, 1997.

———. *D-Day June 6, 1944: The Climactic Battle of World War II*. New York: Simon and Schuster, 1994.

American Airlines. *The Education of an Airline: Here, There, Anywhere; How an Airline Became a Lifeline around the World*. Privately printed, 1944.

Appleton, Victor. *Tom Swift and His Air Scout; or, Uncle Sam's Mastery of the Sky*. New York: Grosset and Dunlap, 1910.

———. *Tom Swift and His Airline Express; or, From Ocean to Ocean by Daylight*. New York: Grosset and Dunlap, 1926.

———. *Tom Swift and His Airship; or, The Stirring Cruise of the Red Cloud*. New York: Grosset and Dunlap, 1910.

———. *Tom Swift and His Electric Runabout; or, The Speediest Car on the Road*. New York: Grosset and Dunlap, 1910.

———. *Tom Swift and His Motor Boat; or, The Rivals of Lake Carlopa*. New York: Grosset and Dunlap, 1910.

———. *Tom Swift and His Motor-Cycle*. New York: Grosset and Dunlap, 1910.

Arnold, Henry H. *Global Mission*. New York: Harper and Brothers, 1949.

Astor, Gerald. *June 6, 1944: Voices of D-Day*. New York: St. Martin's Press, 1994.

———. *The Mighty Eighth: The Air War in Europe as Told by the Men Who Fought It*. New York: Penguin, 2015.

Atkinson, Rick. *An Army at Dawn: The War in North Africa, 1942–43*. New York: Henry Holt, 2002.

———. *Day of Battle: The War in Sicily and Italy, 1943–44*. New York: Henry Holt, 2007.

———. *The Guns at Last Light: The War in Western Europe, 1944–1945*. New York: Henry Holt, 2013.

Baily, Charles M. *Faint Praise: American Tanks and Tank Destroyers during World War II*. Hamden, CT: Archon Books, 1983.

Baime, A. J. *The Arsenal of Democracy: FDR, Detroit, and an Epic Quest to Arm an America at War*. Boston: Mariner, 2014.

Balkoski, Joseph. *Omaha Beach: D-Day, June 6, 1944* (Mechanicsburg, PA: Stackpole Books, 2004.

———. *Utah Beach: The American Landing and Airborne Operations on D-Day*. Mechanicsburg, PA: Stackpole Books, 2005.

"Bazooka Charlie Goes After Nazis: Former History Teacher Now Makes It with Patton's Force." *Daily Journal-World*, Lawrence, KS, 3 October 1944, 8.

Beattie, Edward W., Jr. *Diary of a Kriegie*. New York: Thomas Y. Crowell, 1946.

Bechtold, Michael. "'The Development of an Unbeatable Combination': U.S. Army Close Air Support in Normandy." *Canadian Military History* 8, no. 1 (1999): 7–20.

Beck, Alfred M., Abe Bortz, Charles W. Lynch, Lida Mayo, and Ralph F. Weld. *The Corps of Engineers: The War against Germany.* Washington, DC: Center of Military History, 1985.

Bellmon, Henry, with Pat Bellmon. *The Life and Times of Henry Bellmon.* Tulsa, OK: Council Oak Books, 1992.

Bendiner, Elmer. *The Fall of Fortresses.* New York: G. P. Putnam's Sons, 1980.

Bergeron, David L. "Fighting for Survival: USS Yorktown (CV5) Damage Control Experiences in 1942." Master's thesis, University of New Orleans, 2016.

Bergerud, Eric M. *Fire in the Sky: The Air War in the South Pacific.* Boulder, CO: Westview, 2000.

Bernstein, Irving. *The Lean Years: A History of the American Worker, 1920–1933.* Boston: Houghton Mifflin, 1960.

Billman, Carol. *The Secret of the Stratemeyer Syndicate: Nancy Drew, the Hardy Boys, and the Million Dollar Factory.* New York: Ungar, 1986.

Birdsall, Steve. *The Flying Buccaneers: The Illustrated Story of Kenney's Fifth Air Force.* Garden City, NY: Doubleday, 1977.

———. *Log of the Liberators.* Garden City, NY: Doubleday, 1973.

Bland, Larry I., general ed. *The Papers of George Catlett Marshall.* 7 vols. Baltimore: Johns Hopkins University Press, 1981–2016.

Blumenson, Martin. *Breakout and Pursuit.* 1961. Reprint, Washington, DC: Center of Military History, 2005.

———. *Salerno to Cassino.* 1969. Reprint, Washington, DC: Center of Military History, 1993.

Bond, Charles R., Jr., and Terry Anderson. *A Flying Tiger's Diary.* College Station: Texas A&M University Press, 1984.

Bove, Arthur P. *First over Germany: A Story of the 306th Bomb Group.* San Angelo, TX: Newsfoto, 1946.

Boyington, Gregory H. *Baa Baa Black Sheep.* New York: G. P. Putnam's Sons, 1958.

Boyle, Martin. *Yanks Don't Cry.* New York: Random House, 1963.

Bradley, Holbrook. *War Correspondent: From D-Day to the Elbe.* New York: iUniverse, 2007.

Bradley, Omar N. *A Soldier's Story.* New York: Holt, Rinehart and Winston, 1951.

Brady, Tim. *A Death in San Pietro: The Untold Story of Ernie Pyle, John Huston, and the Fight for Purple Heart Valley.* Boston: Da Capo, 2013.

Brager, Bruce L. *The Texas 36th Division: A History.* Austin, TX: Eakin Press, 2002.

Braly, William C. *The Long Way Home.* Washington, DC: Infantry Journal Press, 1947.

Brereton, Lewis H. *The Brereton Diaries: The Air War in the Pacific, Middle East, and Europe, 3 October 1941–8 May 1945.* New York: William Morrow, 1946.

Brickhill, Paul. *The Great Escape.* New York: W. W. Norton, 1950.

Brownstein, Herbert S. *The Swoose: Odyssey of a B-17.* Washington, DC: Smithsonian Institution Press, 1993.

Brulle, Robert V. *Angels Zero: P-47 Close Air Support in Europe.* Washington, DC: Smithsonian Institution Press, 2000.

Burgess, Alan. *The Longest Tunnel: The True Story of World War II's Greatest Escape Tunnel.* 1990. Reprint, Annapolis, MD: Naval Institute Press, 2004.

Busha, James P., and Carol (Carpenter) Apacki. *Bazooka Charlie: The Unbelievable Story of Major Charles Carpenter and Rosie the Rocketer.* Atglen, PA: Schiffer Military, 2023.

Bykofsky, Joseph, and Harold Larson. *The Transportation Corps: Operations Overseas.* Washington, DC: Center of Military History, 1957.

Caddick-Adams, Peter. *Sand and Steel: The D-Day Invasion and the Liberation of France.* New York: Oxford University Press, 2019.

———. *Snow and Steel: The Battle of the Bulge, 1944–45.* New York: Oxford University Press, 2015.

Caldwell, Robert C. "The Role of the Tracked Amphibian in Modern Warfare." *Naval War College Review* 22 (January 1970): 68–99.

Calhoun, Mark T. *General Lesley J. McNair: Unsung Architect of the U.S. Army.* Lawrence: University Press of Kansas, 2015.

Caraccilo, Dominic J. *Surviving Bataan and Beyond: Colonel Irvin Alexander's Odyssey as a Japanese Prisoner of War.* Mechanicsburg, PA: Stackpole Books, 1999.

Carafano, James Jay. *After D-Day: Operation Cobra and the Normandy Breakout.* Boulder, CO: Lynne Rienner, 2000.

———. *G.I. Ingenuity: Improvisation, Technology, and Winning World War II.* Westport, CT: Praeger Security International, 2006.

Carroll, Tim. *The Great Escape from Stalag Luft III: The Full Story of How 76 Allied Officers Carried Out World War II's Most Remarkable Escape.* New York: Pocket Books, 2005.

Casey, Hugh J. *Engineers of the Southwest Pacific, 1941–1945.* 8 vols. Washington, DC: GPO, 1947–50.

———. *Memoirs.* Office of History. Washington, DC: U.S. Army Corps of Engineers, 1993.

Cawthorn, Charles R. *Other Clay: A Remembrance of the World War II Infantry.* Boulder: University of Colorado Press, 1990. Reprint, Lincoln: University of Nebraska Press, 2004.

Chennault, Claire Lee. *The Way of a Fighter: The Memoirs of Clair Lee Chennault.* New York: G. P. Putnam's Sons, 1949.

Clark, Albert P. *33 Months as a POW in Stalag Luft III.* Golden, CO: Fulcrum, 2004.

Clark, Mark W. *Calculated Risk.* New York: Harper and Brothers, 1950.

Cole, Hugh M. *The Ardennes: Battle of the Bulge.* Washington, DC: GPO, 1965.

———. *The Lorraine Campaign.* Washington, DC: GPO, 1950.

Colley, David P. *Road to Victory: The Untold Story of World War II's Red Ball Express.* Washington, DC: Brassey's, 2000.

Collier, Peter. *Medal of Honor: Portraits of Valor beyond the Call of Duty.* New York: Workman, 2006.

Compton, Lynn "Buck," with Marcus Brotherton. *Call of Duty: My Life before, during, and after the Band of Brothers.* New York: Berkley Caliber, 2008.

Cook, Alvin D., and L. VanLoan Naisawald. *Survey of Allied Tank Casualties in World War II.* Baltimore: Johns Hopkins University Operations Research Office, 1951.

Cooper, Belton Y. *Death Traps: The Survival of an American Armored Division in World War II.* Novato, CA: Presidio, 1998.

Copp, DeWitt S. *Forged in Fire: Strategy and Decisions in the Air War over Europe, 1940–1945.* Garden City, NY: Doubleday, 1982.

Corn, Joseph J. *The Winged Gospel: America's Romance with Aviation, 1900–1950.* New York: Oxford University Press, 1983.

Cox, Gary C. *Beyond the Battle Line.* Maxwell Air Force Base, AL: Air University Press, 1996.

Craven, Wesley Frank, and James Lea Cate. *The Army Air Forces in World War II.* 7 vols. Chicago: University of Chicago Press, 1948–58. Reprint, Washington, DC: GPO, 1983.

Criner, Eric R. *Spearhead of Logistics: A History of the United States Army Transportation Corps.* Washington, DC: Center of Military History, 2011.

Crocker, Mel. *Black Cats and Dumbos: WWII's Fighting PBYs.* Blue Ridge Summit, PA: Tab Books, 1987.

Croizat, Victor J. *Journey among Warriors: The Memoirs of a Marine.* Shippensburg, PA: Beidel Printing House, 1997.

Crosswell, D. K. R. *The Chief of Staff: The Military Career of Walter Bedell Smith.* New York: Greenwood, 1991.

Cullen, James. *By the Numbers: A World War II Memoir.* Lincoln, NE: iUniverse, 2001.

Cummings, Julian William, with Gwendolyn Kay Cummings. *Grasshopper Pilot: A Memoir.* Kent, OH: Kent State University Press, 2005.

D'Este, Carlo. *Decision in Normandy.* 1983. Reprint, New York: Konecky and Konecky, 1994.

De Trez, Michel. *The Way We Were: Cpl. Forrest Guth, "E" Company, 506th PIR, 101st Airborne Division.* Wezembeek-Oppem, Belgium: D-Day Publishing, 2002.

Dick, Robert C. *Cutthroats: The Adventures of a Sherman Tank Driver in the Pacific.* New York: Ballantine Books, 2006.

Dickson, Paul. *The Rise of the G.I. Army, 1940–41: The Forgotten Story of How America Forged a Powerful Army before Pearl Harbor.* New York: Atlantic Monthly Press, 2020.

Dixon, Franklin W. *The Great Airport Mystery.* New York: Grosset and Dunlap, 1920.

———. *The Mystery of Cabin Island.* New York: Grosset and Dunlap, 1929.

———. *The Tower Treasure.* New York: Grosset and Dunlap, 1927.

Doubler, Michael D. *Closing with the Enemy: How G.I.s Fought the War in Europe, 1944–45.* Lawrence: University of Kansas Press, 1994.

Dower, John W. *War without Mercy: Race and Power in the Pacific War.* New York: Pantheon Books, 1986.

Drowne, Kathleen Morgan, and Patrick Huber. *The 1920s.* Westport, CT: Greenwood, 2004.

Dryden, Charles W. *A-Train: Memoirs of a Tuskegee Airman.* Tuscaloosa: University of Alabama Press, 1997.

Duddy, Brian J. "The Jeep at 70: A Defense Acquisition Success Story." *Defense Acquisitions Research Journal* 64 (October 2021): 360–75.

Durand, Arthur A. *Stalag Luft II: The Secret Story.* Baton Rouge: Louisiana State University Press, 1988.

Edmonds, Walter D. *They Fought with What They Had: The Story of the Army Air Forces in the Southwest Pacific, 1941–1942.* Boston: Little, Brown, 1951. Reprint, Washington, DC: Center for Air Force History, 1992.

Eisenhower, Dwight D. *Crusade in Europe.* Garden City, NY: Doubleday, 1948.

Ferguson, Harvey. *The Last Cavalryman: The Life of Lucian K. Truscott, Jr.* Norman: University of Oklahoma Press, 2015.

Ferguson, John C. *Hellcats: The 12th Armored Division in World War II.* Abilene, TX: State House Press, 2004.

Fifty-Seventh Bomb Wing Association. *The B-25 over the Mediterranean.* Jackson, MI: Creative Graphics, 1992.

Ford, Henry. *My Life and Work.* Garden City, NY: Garden City Publishing, 1922.

Frank, Richard B. *Guadalcanal: The Definitive Account of the Landmark Battle.* New York: Penguin Books, 1990.

Freeman, Roger A. *Mighty Eighth War Diary.* London: Jane's, 1981.

French, Warren. *John Steinbeck's Fiction Revisited.* New York: Twayne, 1994.

Frisbee, John L., ed. *Makers of the United States Air Force.* Washington, DC: Office of Air Force History, 1987.

Gabel, Christopher R. *Seek, Strike, and Destroy: U.S. Army Tank Destroyer Doctrine in World War II.* Fort Leavenworth, KS: Combat Studies Institute, 1985.

———. *The U.S. Army GHQ Maneuvers of 1941.* Washington, DC: Center of Military History, 1991.

Gamble, Bruce. *The Black Sheep: The Definitive Account of Marine Fighting Squadron 214 in World War II.* Novato, CA: Presidio, 2000.

Gann, Timothy D. *Fifth Air Force Light and Medium Bomber Operations during 1942 and 1943: Building Doctrine and Forces That Triumphed in the Battle of the Bismarck Sea and the Wewak Raid.* Maxwell Air Force Base, AL: Air University Press, 1992.

Garland, Albert N., and Howard McGaw Smyth, assisted by Martin Blumenson. *Sicily and the Surrender of Italy.* Washington, DC: GPO, 1993.

Gavin, James A. *On to Berlin: Battles of an Airborne Commander, 1943–1946.* New York: Viking, 1978.

George, Robert H. *Ninth Air Force: April to November 1944.* USAF Historical Study No. 36. Maxwell Air Force Base, AL: Air University, Historical Division, 1945.

Gilbert, Oscar E., and Romain Cansière. *Tanks in Hell: A Marine Corps Tank Company on Tarawa.* Philadelphia: Casemate, 2015.

Goulart, Ron. *Cheap Thrills: An Informal History of the Pulp Magazines.* New Rochelle, NY: Arlington House, 1972.

Greenfield, Kent Roberts, ed. *Command Decisions.* 1960. Reprint, Washington, DC: Center of Military History, 1990.

Greenfield, Kent Roberts, Robert R. Palmer, and Bell I. Wiley. *The Army Ground Forces: The Organization of Ground Combat Troops.* Washington, DC: Center of Military History, 1947.

Greening, Ross C. *Not As Briefed: From the Doolittle Raid to a German Stalag.* Pullman: Washington State University Press, 2001.

———, and Angelo M. Spinelli. *The Yankee Kriegies.* New York: Guide Printing, 1946.

Greenwood, John T., ed. *Normandy to Victory: The War Diary of General Courtney Hodges and the First U.S. Army.* Lexington: University Press of Kentucky, 2008.

Griffith, Thomas E., Jr. *MacArthur's Airman: General George C. Kenney and the War in the Southwest Pacific.* Lawrence: University Press of Kansas, 1998.

Hahn, William W. "From Stratofighter to Dive Bomber." *Air Classics* 38 (February): 18-29.

Halmos, Eugene E., Jr. *The Wrong Side of the Fence: A United States Army Air Corps Pilot in World War II.* Shippensburg, PA: White Mane Publishing, 1996.

Haney, Robert E. *Caged Dragons: An American P.O.W. in WWII Japan.* Ann Arbor, MI: Sabre, 1991.

Hanson, Victor Davis. *The Second World Wars: How the First Global Conflict Was Fought and Won*. New York: Basic Books, 2017.

Harrison, Gordon A. *Cross-Channel Attack*. Washington, DC: GPO, 1951.

Hart, Russell A. *Clash of Arms: How the Allies Won in Normandy*. Norman: University of Oklahoma Press, 2001.

Hartcup, Guy. *Code Name Mulberry: The Planning, Building, and Operation of the Normandy Harbors*. New York: Hippocrene Books, 1977.

Hartman, J. Ted. *Tank Driver: With the 11th Armored from the Battle of the Bulge to VE Day*. Bloomington: Indiana University Press, 2003.

Havelarr, Marion H. *The Ragged Irregulars of Bassingbourn*. Atglen, PA: Schiffer Military/Aviation History, 1995.

Heavey, William F. *Down Ramp: The Story of the Army Amphibian Engineers*. Washington, DC: Infantry Journal Press, 1947.

Heller, Charles E., and William A. Stofft, eds. *America's First Battles, 1776–1965*. Lawrence: University Press of Kansas, 1986.

Herman, Arthur. *Freedom's Forge: How American Business Produced Victory in World War II*. New York: Random House, 2013.

Hillenbrand, Laura. *Unbroken: A World War II Story of Survival, Resilience, and Redemption*. New York: Random House, 2010.

Hoffman, Jon T., ed. *A History of Innovation: U.S. Army Adaptation in War and Peace*. Washington, DC: Center of Military History, 2009.

Holley, I. B. *Development of Aircraft Gun Turrets in the AAF, 1917–1944*. USAF Historical Study No. 54. Maxwell Air Force Base, AL: Air University, Historical Division, 1947.

Holmes, Linda Goetz. *Unjust Enrichment: How Japan's Companies Built Postwar Fortunes Using American POWs*. Mechanicsburg, PA: Stackpole Books, 2001.

Hough, Frank O., Verle E. Ludwig, and Henry I. Shaw Jr. *Pearl Harbor to Guadalcanal: History of U.S. Marine Corps Operations in World War II*. Washington, DC: GPO, 1958.

House, Jonathan M. *Toward Combined Arms Warfare: A Survey of 20th-Century Tactics, Doctrine and Organization*. Washington, DC: GPO, 1984.

Houston, Donald E. *Hell on Wheels; The Second Armored Division*. Novato, CA: Presidio, 1995.

Howe, George F. *Northwest Africa: Seizing the Initiative in the West*. Washington, DC: GPO, 1993.

Hughes, Thomas A. *Overlord: General Pete Quesada and the Triumph of Tactical Air Power in World War II*. New York: Free Press, 1995.

Huie, William Bradford. *Can Do: The Story of the Seabees*. New York: E. P. Dutton, 1944.

Hunnicutt, R. P. *Half-Track: A History of American Semi-Tracked Vehicles*. Novato, CA: Presidio, 2015.

———. *Sherman: A History of the American Medium Tank*. Novato, CA: Presidio, 1978.

Hunt, Frazier. *The Untold Story of Douglas MacArthur*. New York: Devin-Adair, 1954.

Hynes, Samuel. *Flights of Passage: Reflections of a World War II Aviator*. Annapolis, MD: Naval Institute Press, 1988.

Iannarelli, Anthony N., Sr., and John G. Iannarelli. *The Eighty Thieves: American P.O.W.s in World War II Japan*. San Diego: Patriot, 1991.

Irzyk, Albin F. *He Rode Up Front for Patton*. Raleigh, NC: Pentland, 1996.

Johnson, David E. *Fast Tanks and Heavy Bombers: Innovation in the U.S. Army, 1917–1945*. Ithaca, NY: Cornell University Press, 1998.

Jones, Winson. *Some Personal Histories of Surviving Members of the 451st Bomb Group, Fifteenth Air Force, World War II*. Privately printed, 2007.

Kato, Masuo. *The Lost War: A Japanese Reporter's Inside Story*. New York: Alfred A. Knopf, 1946.

Kays, Marvin D. *Weather Effects during the Battle of the Bulge and the Normandy Invasion*. White Sands Missile Range, NM: U.S. Army Electronics Research and Developmental Command Atmospheric Sciences Library, 1982.

Keegan, John. *Six Armies in Normandy: From D-Day to the Liberation of Paris*. New York: Penguin, 1994.

Kennedy, David. *Freedom from Fear: The American People in Depression and War, 1929–1945*. New York: Oxford University Press, 1999.

Kennett, Lee. *G.I.: The American Soldier in World War II*. New York: Charles Scribner's Sons, 1987.

Kenney, George C. *General Kenney Reports*. New York: Duell, Sloan and Pearce, 1949. Reprint, Washington, DC: Office of Air Force History, 1987.

———. *The Saga of Pappy Gunn*. New York: Duell, Sloan and Pearce, 1959.

Kerr, E. Bartlett. *Surrender and Survival: The Experience of American POWs in the Pacific, 1941–45*. New York: William Morrow, 1985.

Kindsvatter, Peter S. *American Soldiers: Ground Combat in the World Wars, Korea, and Vietnam*. Lawrence: University Press of Kansas, 2003.

Kinney, John F. *Wake Island Pilot: A World War II Memoir*. With James M. McCaffrey. Washington, DC: Brassey's, 1995.

Kirk, Terence S. *The Secret Camera: A Marine's Story; Four Years as a WWII POW*. 1982. Reprint, Guilford, CT: Lyons, 2005.

Kirkpatrick, Charles E. "Strategic Planning for World War II: The Victory Plan in Context." *Army History* 16 (Fall 1990): 17–21.

Kohn, Richard H., ed. *Air Superiority in World War II and Korea*. Washington, DC: Office of Air Force History, 1983.

Kroener, Bernhard R., Rolf-Deiter Müller, and Hans Umbreit. *Organisation und Mobilisierung des Deutschen Machtbereichs*. 2 vols. Stuttgart: Deutsche Verlags-Anstalt, 1988.

LaForte, Robert S., Ronald E. Marcello, and Richard L. Himmel. *With Only the Will to Live: Accounts of Americans in Japanese Prison Camps, 1941–45*. Wilmington, DE: Rowman and Littlefield, 1994.

League of Nations Economic Intelligence Service. *Statistical Year-Book of the League of Nations, 1938/39*. Geneva: League of Nations Publications, 1939.

Lee, Ulysses. *The Employment of Negro Troops*. Washington, DC: Center of Military History, 2001.

Lee, Wright. *Not As Briefed: Memoirs of a B-24 Navigator/Prisoner of War, 1943–45*. Spartanburg, SC: Honoribus, 1995.

LeMay, Curtis E. *Mission with LeMay: My Story*. With MacKinley Kantor. Garden City, NY: Doubleday, 1965.

Lichtenfeld, Seymour L. *Kriegie 312330*. Privately printed, 2001.

Lilly, Tom, Pearson Hunt, J. Keith Butters, Frank F. Gilmore, and Paul F. Lawler. *Problems of Accelerating Aircraft Production during World War II*. Boston: Harvard University, Graduate School of Business Administration, Division of Research, 1946.

Lindberg, Kip. "Colonel Harry D. Tyson and the Development of the Mine-Clearing Line Charge." *Army Chemical Review* (March 22, 2021), 34–35.

Lindermann, Gerald. *The World within War: America's Combat Experience in World War II*. New York: Free Press, 1997.

Linn, Brian McAllister. *Guardians of Empire: The U.S. Army and the Pacific, 1902–1940*. Chapel Hill: University of North Carolina Press, 1997.

Losonsky, Frank S., and Terry M. Losonsky. *Flying Tiger: A Crew Chief's Story: The War Diary of a Flying Tiger American Volunteer Group Crew Chief with the 3rd Pursuit Squadron*. Atglen, PA: Schiffer Military/Aviation History, 1996.

Lundstrom, John E. *The First Team: Pacific Air Combat from Pearl Harbor to Midway*. Annapolis, MD: Naval Institute Press, 1984.

MacArthur, Douglas. *Annual Report of the Superintendent, United States Military Academy, 1920*. West Point, NY: United States Military Academy Press, 1920.

———. *Reports of General MacArthur: The Campaigns of MacArthur in the Pacific*. 2 vols. Washington, DC: GPO, 1966.

Manchester, William. *Goodbye Darkness: A Memoir of the Pacific War*. New York: Dell, 1980.

Mansoor, Peter R. *The G.I. Offensive in Europe: The Triumph of American Infantry Divisions, 1941–1945*. Lawrence: University of Kansas Press, 1999.

Marzio, Peter C. *Rube Goldberg: His Life and Work*. New York: Harper and Row, 1973.

Mayo, Lida. *The Ordnance Department: On Beachhead and Battlefront*. Washington, DC: Center of Military History, 1991.

McAulay, Lex. *Battle of the Bismarck Sea*. New York: St. Martin's Press, 1991.

McCarthy, Michael C. *Air-to-Ground Battle for Italy*. Maxwell Air Force Base, AL: Air University Press, 2004.

McDonald, Charles B. *The Siegfried Line Campaign*. Washington, DC: GPO, 1963.

McGuire, Phillip. "Judge Hastie, World War II, and the Army Air Corps." *Phylon* 42 (1981): 157–67.

McKinney, Leonard. *Portable Flame Thrower Operations in World War II*. Washington, DC: Office of the Chief of the Chemical Corps, 1949.

McKinnon, Jennifer F., and Toni E. Carrell, eds. *Underwater Archaeology of a Pacific Battlefield: The WWII Battle of Saipan*. New York: Springer, 2015.

McManus, John C. *The Americans at D-Day: The American Experience at the Normandy Invasion*. New York: Tom Doherty Associates, 2004.

———. *The Deadly Brotherhood: The American Combat Soldier in World War II*. Novato, CA: Presidio, 1998.

———. *Fire and Fortitude: The U.S. Army in the Pacific War, 1941–43*. New York: Dutton Caliber, 2019.

———. *Island Infernos: The U.S. Army's Pacific War Odyssey, 1944*. New York: Dutton Caliber, 2021.

———. *To The End of the Earth: The U.S. Army and the Downfall of Japan, 1945*. New York: Dutton Caliber, 2023.

McNeill, William Hardy. *America, Britain and Russia: Their Cooperation and Conflict, 1941–1946*. New York: Oxford University Press, 1953.

Medford, Edna Greene, and Michael Frazier. "'Keep 'em Rolling': African American Participation in the Red Ball Express." *Negro History Bulletin* 51/57 (December 1993): 57–61.

Miller, Donald L. *Masters of the Air: America's Bomber Boys Who Fought Against Nazi Germany*. New York: Simon and Schuster, 2006.

Miller, Edward S. *War Plan Orange: The U.S. Strategy to Defeat Japan, 1897–1945*. Annapolis, MD: Naval Institute Press, 1991.

Miller, John, Jr. *Cartwheel: The Reduction of Rabaul*. Washington, DC: GPO, 1959.

Miller, Thomas G., Jr. *The Cactus Air Force*. New York: Harper and Row, 1969.

Millis, Walter, ed. *The War Reports of General of the Army George C. Marshall, General of the Army H. H. Arnold, and Fleet Admiral Ernest J. King*. Philadelphia: J. B. Lippincott, 1947.

Morgan, Martin K. A. "The Men and Guns of Iwo Jima." *American Rifleman* 168 (May 2020): 59–60.

———. "The Men and Guns of Pointe Du Hoc." *American Rifleman*, 17 May 2019, https://americanrifleman.org/content/the-men-and-guns-of-pointe-du-hoc/.

Morgan, Thomas D. "The Industrial Mobilization of World War II: America Goes to War." *Army History* 30 (Spring 1994): 31–35.

Morison, Samuel Eliot. *History of United States Naval Operations in World War II*. 15 vols. Boston: Little, Brown, 1947–62.

Morton, Louis. *Fall of the Philippines*. Washington, DC: GPO, 1953.

Moy, Timothy. *War Machines: Transforming Technologies in the U.S. Military, 1920–1940*. College Station: Texas A&M University Press, 2001.

Mrazek, Robert J. *A Dawn Like Thunder: The True Story of Torpedo Squadron Eight*. Boston: Back Bay Books, 2009.

Muirhead, John. *Those Who Fall*. New York: Random House, 1986.

Murray, Williamson, and Allan R. Millett. *Military Innovation in the Interwar Period*. Cambridge: Cambridge University Press, 1996.

Nalty, Barnard C. *Winged Shield, Winged Sword: A History of the United States Air Force*. 2 vols. Washington, DC: Air Force History and Museums Program, 1997.

Neiman, Robert M., and Kenneth W. Estes. *Tanks on the Beaches: A Marine Tanker in the Pacific War*. College Station: Texas A&M University Press, 2003.

Nichols, David, ed. *Ernie's War: The Best of Ernie Pyle's World War Dispatches*. New York: Simon and Schuster, 1986.

Nordin, Carl S. *We Were Next to Nothing: An American POW's Account of Japanese Prison Camps and Deliverance in World War II*. Jefferson, NC: McFarland & Company, 1997.

Nye, Russell. *The Unembarrassed Muse: The Popular Arts in America*. New York: Dial, 1970.

O'Donnell, Patrick K. *Dog Company: The Boys of Pointe du Hoc—the Rangers Who Accomplished D-Day's Toughest Mission and Led the Way across Europe*. Philadelphia: Da Capo, 2012.

Olds, Robin. *Fighter Pilot: The Memoirs of Legendary Ace Robin Olds*. With Christina Olds and Ed Rasimus. New York: St. Martin's Griffin, 2010.

Overy, Richard. *Why the Allies Won*. New York: W. W. Norton, 1985.

Palmer, Robert R., Bell I. Wiley, and William R. Keast. *The Procurement and Training of Ground Combat Troops*. 1948. Reprint, Washington, DC: GPO, 1991.

Parton, James. *Air Force Spoken Here: Ira Eaker and the Command of the Air*. Bethesda, MD: Adler and Adler, 1986. Reprint, Maxwell Air Force Base: Air University Press, 2000.

Patton, George S., Jr. *War as I Knew It*. Boston: Houghton Mifflin, 1947.

Perret, Geoffrey. *Old Soldiers Never Die: The Life of Douglas MacArthur.* New York: Random House, 1996.

Pettet, Zellmer R. *Sixteenth Census of the United States: 1940; Agriculture.* 6 vols. Washington, DC: GPO, 1941–44.

Philippart, Jeff D. *The Airfield as a Center of Gravity: Henderson Field during the Guadalcanal Campaign (August 1942–February 1943).* Maxwell Air Force Base, AL: Air University Press, 2004.

Plating, John D. *The Hump: America's Strategy for Keeping China in World War II.* College Station: Texas A&M University Press, 2011.

Pogue, Forrest. *George C. Marshall: Education of a General, 1880–1939.* New York: Viking,1963.

Poncio, John Henry, and Marlin Young. *Girocho: A GI's Story of Bataan and Beyond.* Baton Rouge: Louisiana State University Press, 2003.

Prager, Arthur. "Bless My Collar Button, If It Isn't TOM SWIFT." *American Heritage* 28 (December 1976): 64–75.

Prange, Gordon W. *December 7, 1941: The Day the Japanese Attacked Pearl Harbor.* With Donald M. Goldstein and Katherine V. Dillon. New York: McGraw Hill, 1988.

Province, Charles M. *Patton's Third Army: A Chronology of the Third Army Advance, August, 1944 to May, 1945.* New York: Hippocrene Books, 1992.

Pyle, Ernie. *Brave Men.* New York: Henry Holt, 1944.

———. *Here Is Your War.* New York: Henry Holt, 1943.

Raff, Daniel M. G. "Making Cars and Making Money in the Interwar Automobile Industry: Economies of Scale and Scope and the Manufacturing behind the Marketing." *Business History Review* 65 (Winter 1991): 721–53.

Rein, Christopher M. *The North African Air Campaign: U.S. Army Air Forces from El Alamein to Salerno.* Lawrence: University Press of Kansas, 2012.

Richards, David L. "Fortress on the Deck: The B-17 as a Low-Level Anti-Shipping Bomber in the Southwest Pacific." *Air Power History* 67 (Summer 2020): 43–47.

Ricks, Thomas. *The Generals: American Military Command from World War II to Today.* New York: Penguin, 2021.

Rifkind, Herbert R. *The Jeep—Its Development and Procurement under the Quartermaster Corps, 1940–42.* Washington, DC: Office of the Quartermaster General, Historical Section, 1943.

Robinson, Wayne, and Norman E. Hamilton. *Move Out, Verify: The Combat Story of the 743rd Tank Battalion.* Frankfurt am Main, Germany: Privately printed, 1945.

Rodman, Matthew K. *A War of Their Own: Bombers over the Southwest Pacific.* Maxwell Air Force Base, AL: Air University Press, 2005.

Rogers, Will. *Wit and Philosophy from Radio Talks of Will Rogers.* New York: ER Squibb and Sons, 1930.

Roosevelt, Franklin Delano. *The Public Papers and Addresses of Franklin D. Roosevelt.* New York: Macmillan, 1938–45.

Ruppenthal, Roland G. *Logistical Support of the* Armies. 2 vols. 1959. Reprint, Washington, DC: Center of Military History, 1995.

Rutter, Joseph W. *Wreaking Havoc: A Year in an A-20.* College Station: Texas A&M University Press, 2004.

Sage, Jerry. *Sage: The Man the Nazis Couldn't Hold.* Wayne, PA: Tobey, 1985.

Sarantakes, Nicholas Evan, ed. *Seven Stars: The Okinawa Battle Diaries of Simon Bolivar Buckner, Jr., and Joseph Stillwell.* College Station: Texas A&M University Press, 2004.

Schaller, Michael. "American Air Strategy in China, 1939–1941: The Origins of Clandestine Air Warfare." *American Quarterly* 28 (Spring 1976): 3–19.

Schrijvers, Peter. *The Crash of Ruin: American Combat Soldiers in Europe during World War II.* Washington Square, NY: New York University Press, 1998.

Schultz, Alfred W. *Janey: A Little Plane in a Big War.* With Kirk Neff. Middletown, CT: Southfarm, 1998.

Scott, Jack L. *Combat Engineer.* Baltimore: American Literary Press, 1999.

Scott, James M. *Target Tokyo: Jimmy Doolittle and the Raid That Avenged Pearl Harbor.* New York: W. W. Norton, 2015.

Scutts, Jerry. *Republic P-47 Thunderbolt: The Operational Record.* Osceola, WI: Motorbooks International, 1998.

Shaw, Henry I. *First Offensive: The Marine Campaign for Guadalcanal.* Washington, DC: Marine Corps Historical Center, 1992.

Shirley, John B. *I Remember: Stories of a Combat Infantrymen in Italy, France, and Germany in World War II.* Privately printed, 1993.

Simmonds, Roy. *John Steinbeck: The War Years, 1939–1945.* Lewisburg, PA: Bucknell University Press, 1997.

Sledge, E. B. *With the Old Breed: At Peleliu and Okinawa.* New York: Oxford University Press, 1990.

Smith, Dale O. *Screaming Eagle: Memoirs of a B-17 Group Commander.* Chapel Hill, NC: Algonquin Books, 1990.

Smith, R. Elberton. *The Army and Economic Mobilization.* Washington, DC: Center of Military History, 1991.

Smith, Robert Moody, and Philip D. Smith. *With Chennault in China: A Flying Tiger's Diary.* Blue Ridge Summit, PA: TAB Books, 1984.

Sorensen, Charles E. *My Forty Years with Ford.* With Samuel T. Williamson. New York: W. W. Norton, 1956.

Spalding, V. G. "Presenting the Stinger." *Marine Corps Gazette* 30 (February 1946): 55–56.

Spear, William. *Warbaby: The True Story of the Original Jeep.* Juneau, AK: Points North Press, a division of Wm Spear Design, 2016.

Spector, Ronald H. *Eagle Against the Sun: The American War with Japan.* New York: Macmillan, 1985.

Springer, Paul J. *America's Captives: Treatment of POWs from the Revolutionary War to the War on Terror.* Lawrence: University Press of Kansas, 2010.

Startt, James D. *Woodrow Wilson and the Press: Prelude to the Presidency.* New York: Palgrave Macmillan, 2001.

Steinbeck, John. *Bombs Away: The Story of a Bomber Team.* New York: Viking, 1942.

———. *The Grapes of Wrath.* Commemorative ed. New York: Viking, 1989.

Stockbridge, Frank Parker. "Main Street Wants to Know." *Bookman* 66 (January 1928): 546–51.

———. "What Are the 'Popular Books'—and Why?" *English Journal* 20 (June 1931): 441–49.

———. *Yankee Ingenuity in the War.* New York: Harper and Brothers, 1920.

Stratemeyer, Edward. *The Automobile Boys of Lakeport.* Boston: Lothrop, Lee and Shephard, 1910.

Strong, Russell A. *First over Germany: A History of the 306th Bomb Group.* Winston-Salem, NC: Hunter Printing, 1990.

Sullivan, C. W., III, ed. *Young Adult Science Fiction*. Westport, CT: Greenwood, 1999.

Symonds, Craig. *Neptune: The Allied Invasion of Europe and the D-Day Landings*. New York: Oxford University Press, 2014.

Tannehill, Victor C. *Daddy of Them All: Story of the 17th Bombardment Group in World War II*. Arvada, CO: Boomerang, 1990.

Taylor, Cal. "Jack Randolph Cram: Airport Manager to USMC General." *American Aviation Historical Society Journal* 58 (Fall 2013): 1–13.

Tenney, Lester I. *My Hitch in Hell: The Bataan Death March*. Washington, DC: Brassey's, 1995.

Thomson, Harry C., and Lida Mayo. *The Ordnance Department: Procurement and Supply*. Washington, DC: Center of Military History, 1960.

Toll, Ian W. *The Conquering Tide: War in the Pacific Islands, 1942–1944*. New York: W. W. Norton, 2015.

———. *Pacific Crucible: War at Sea in the Pacific, 1941–42*. New York: W. W. Norton, 2012.

———. *The Twilight of the Gods: War in the Western Pacific, 1944–1945*. New York: W. W. Norton, 2020.

Triplet, William S. *A Colonel in the Armored Divisions: A Memoir, 1941–1945*. Edited by Robert H. Ferrell. Columbia: University of Missouri Press, 2001.

Truluck, John H., Jr. *And So It Was: Memories of a World War II Fighter Pilot*. Walterboro, SC: The Press and Standard, 1988.

Truscott, Lucian. *Command Missions: A Personal Story*. New York: E. P. Dutton, 1954.

Turner, Richard E. *Big Friend, Little Friend: Memoirs of a World War II Fighter Pilot*. Garden City, New York: Doubleday, 1969.

Urwin, Gregory J. W. *Facing Fearful Odds: The Siege of Wake Island*. Lincoln: University of Nebraska Press, 1997.

Van Crevald, Martin. *Supplying War: Logistics from Wallenstein to Patton*. Cambridge: Cambridge University Press, 1977.

Vaughan, David K. "Hap Arnold's Bill Bruce Books." *Air Power History* 40 (Winter 1993): 43–49.

Waddell, Steve R. *United States Army Logistics: The Normandy Campaign, 1944*. Westport, CT: Praeger, 1994.

Waterford, Van. *Prisoners of the Japanese in World War II: Statistical History, Personal Narratives and Memorials Concerning POWs in Camps and on Hellships, Civilian Internees, Asian Slave Laborers and Others Captured in the Pacific Theater*. Jefferson, NC: McFarland & Company, 1994.

Watson, Mark Skinner. *Chief of Staff: Prewar Plans and Preparations*. 1950. Reprint, Washington, DC: GPO, 1991.

Watson, Richard L. "Air Action in the Papuan Campaign, 21 July 1942 to 23 January 1943." Army Air Forces Historical Study No. 17. Maxwell Air Force Base, AL: USAF Historical Research Agency, 1944.

Weigley, Russell. *Eisenhower's Lieutenants: The Campaigns of France and Germany, 1944–45*. Bloomington: Indiana University Press, 1981.

Weller, George. "Luck to the Fighters: Part One." *Military Affairs* 8 (Winter 1944): 259–96.

———. "Luck to the Fighters: Part Two, The Battle for Java." *Military Affairs* 9 (Spring 1945): 33–62.

———. "Luck to the Fighters: Part Three, Conclusion." *Military Affairs* 9 (Summer 1945): 124–50.

Wells, Albert Wade. *Hail to the Jeep: A Factual and Pictorial History of the Jeep.* New York: Harper and Brothers, 1946.
Wheeler-Nicholson, Malcolm. *America Can Win.* New York: Macmillan, 1941.
———. *Battle Shield of the Republic.* New York: Macmillan, 1940.
———. *Modern Cavalry.* New York: Macmillan, 1922.
———. "Yankee Ingenuity vs. Hitler!" *Mechanix Illustrated* 26 (August 1941), 35–39, 142, 144.
Whelan, Russell. *The Flying Tigers: The Story of the American Volunteer Group.* New York: Viking, 1942.
White, W. L. *They Were Expendable.* New York: Harcourt, Brace, 1942.
Wik, Reynold M. *Henry Ford and Grass-Roots America: A Fascinating Account of the Model T Era.* Ann Arbor: University of Michigan Press, 1972.
———. "Henry Ford's Tractors and American Agriculture." *Agricultural History* 38 (April 1964): 79–86.
Williams, Eric. *The Wooden Horse.* New York: Harper, 1950.
Wilson, George. *If You Survive: From Normandy to the Battle of the Bulge to the End of World War II—One American Officer's Riveting True Story.* New York: Ivy Books, 1987.
Wilson, R. E. *The Earthquakers: Overseas History of the 12th Bomb Group.* Tacoma, WA: Dammeier Printing, 1947.
Wooldridge, E. T., ed. *Carrier Warfare in the Pacific: An Oral History Collection.* Washington, DC: Smithsonian Institution Press, 1993.
Worster, Donald. *The Dust Bowl: The Southern Plains in the 1930s.* New York: Oxford University Press, 1979.
Yeager, Chuck, and Lee Janos. *Yeager: An Autobiography.* New York: Bantam Books, 1985.
Yeide, Harry. *The Tank Killers: A History of America's World War II Tank Destroyer Force.* Philadelphia: Casemate, 2007.
Zaic, Frank. *Model Airplanes and the American Boy, 1927–1934.* Northridge, CA: Model Aeronautics Publications, 1982.
Zaloga, Steven J. *Armored Attack, 1944: U.S. Army Tank Combat in the European Theater from D-Day to the Battle of the Bulge.* Mechanicsburg, PA: Stackpole Books, 2011.
———. *Armored Thunderbolt: The U.S. Army Sherman in World War II.* Mechanicsburg, PA: Stackpole Books, 2008.
———. *U.S. Amphibious Tanks of World War II.* Oxford: Osprey, 2021.
———. *US Armored Funnies: U.S. Specialized Armored Vehicles in the ETO in World War II.* Hong Kong: Concord Publications, 2004.
———. *U.S. Marine Corps Tanks of World War II.* Long Island City, NY: Osprey, 2012.
Zimmermann, John L. *The Guadalcanal Campaign.* Washington, DC: Headquarters U.S. Marine Corps, Historical Division, 1949.

Index

Locators in italics indicate illustrations.

www.ingramcontent.com/pod-product-compliance
Lightning Source LLC
Chambersburg PA
CBHW030848050625
27758CB00001B/1/J

* 9 7 8 0 8 0 6 1 9 5 3 9 1 *